Redefining Urban and Suburban America

BROOKINGS METRO SERIES

The Center on Urban and Metropolitan Policy at the Brookings Institution is integrating research and practical experience into a policy agenda for cities and metropolitan areas. By bringing fresh analyses and policy ideas to the public debate, the center hopes to inform key decisionmakers and civic leaders in ways that will spur meaningful change in our nation's communities.

As part of this effort, the Center on Urban and Metropolitan Policy has established the Brookings Metro Series to introduce new perspectives and policy thinking on current issues and attempt to lay the foundation for longer-term policy reforms. The series will examine traditional urban issues, such as neighborhood assets and central city competitiveness, as well as larger metropolitan concerns, such as regional growth, development, and employment patterns. The Metro Series will consist of concise studies and collections of essays designed to appeal to a broad audience. While these studies are formally reviewed, some will not be verified like other research publications. As with all publications, the judgments, conclusions, and recommendations presented in the studies are solely those of the authors and should not be attributed to the trustees, officers, or other staff members of the Institution.

The Brookings Metro Series

Edgeless Cities: Exploring the Elusive Metropolis
Robert E. Lang

Evaluating Gun Policy: Effects on Crime and Violence
Jens Ludwig and Philip J. Cook, editors

Growth and Convergence in Metropolitan America
Janet Rothenberg Pack

Laws of the Landscape:
How Policies Shape Cities in Europe and America
Pietro S. Nivola

Low-Income Homeownership: Examining the Unexamined Goal
Nicolas P. Retsinas and Eric S. Belsky, editors

Reflections on Regionalism
Bruce J. Katz, editor

Savings for the Poor:
The Hidden Benefits of Electronic Banking
Michael A. Stegman

Redefining Urban and Suburban America

EVIDENCE FROM CENSUS 2000

VOLUME ONE

Bruce Katz and Robert E. Lang
Editors

BROOKINGS INSTITUTION PRESS
Washington, D.C.

THE BROOKINGS INSTITUTION
1775 Massachusetts Avenue, N.W.
Washington, D.C. 20036

www.brookings.edu

Library of Congress Cataloging-in-Publication data

Redefining urban and suburban America : evidence from Census 2000 /
Bruce Katz and Robert E. Lang, eds.
p. cm.
Includes bibliographical references and index.
ISBN 0-8157-4860-4 (cloth : alk. paper) –
ISBN 0-8157-4859-0 (pbk. : alk. paper)
1. Metropolitan areas—United States. 2. Suburbs—United States. 3.
City and town life—United States. 4. United States—Population. 5.
Sociology, Urban—United States. I. Katz, Bruce. II. Lang, Robert E.,
1959-

HT334.U5 R43 2003
307.76'4'0973—dc21 2002151690

9 8 7 6 5 4 3 2 1

The paper used in this publication meets minimum requirements of the American National Standard for Information Sciences—Permanence of Paper for Printed Library Materials: ANSI Z39.48-1992.

Typeset in Minion and Univers Condensed

Text design and composition by Circle Graphics
Columbia, Maryland

Printed by R. R. Donnelley
Harrisonburg, Virginia

Contents

Foreword

Since 1790 the United States has conducted a national census every ten years. While in the past not everyone was counted equally, today, the census constitutes a routine expression in democracy—every individual literally counts, irrespective of race, ethnicity, religion, or social status. The census represents a remarkable logistical undertaking given the sheer size and diversity of this country.

Census 2000 is perhaps the most important census in living memory. Conducted at a time of dynamic change in the United States, it is comparable in scale and complexity to a census taken in the latter part of the nineteenth century. Our population is growing older, which is affecting settlement patterns, life-style choices, and consumption trends. We are becoming a more diverse nation; the past decade witnessed the most significant wave of immigration in one hundred years. And for the first time, responders could designate more than one racial group of origin. Our economy is in a state of continuous transition, fueled by global, technological, and social factors. The demographic, social, and market forces are shaping dramatically the places where we live, work, and play and are writing a new chapter in the development of America's communities.

This census, therefore, gives us a snapshot of a nation in rapid change. It captures a moment in time of a country and people in perpetual motion. The release of results from Census 2000 represents the beginning, not the end, of national self-examination.

For the next several years, scholars across the country will examine the census to inform us about the changing nature of our society. Government at all levels will use the census results to alter the allocation of public resources, redraw legislative districts, and design and implement policy. The private sector will use census data to drive market behavior and activity.

This book is the first of a series aimed at uncovering what Census 2000 tells us about American cities and suburbs and the economic, social, and political changes that are occurring. It contains a collection of analyses that were performed during the past two years by leading demographers, economists, and urban experts. Topics examined include population growth, racial and ethnic diversity, and household change.

The title of the book, *Redefining Urban and Suburban America: Evidence from Census 2000*, reflects its central premise: the changes in our population are fundamentally redefining America's notion of cities and suburbs. Cities, after decades of real and perceived decline, may be finding a new life and purpose given the changes. Suburbs—in their increasing diversity and newfound status as major employment centers—are playing roles historically associated with our central cities. Results from Census 2000 are blurring the traditional distinctions between cities and suburbs and may signal a new wave of regional consciousness in the country.

This book and this series represent a partnership among Living Cities (formerly the National Community Development Initiative), the Fannie Mae Foundation, and the Brookings Institution Center on Urban and Metropolitan Policy. These analyses inform us of the profound changes that are occurring in metropolitan America and provoke our thinking about what these changes mean for places, policy, and politics. This series gives context and definition to a changing nation at the beginning of a new century.

FRANKLIN D. RAINES
Chairman, Fannie Mae Foundation

Redefining Urban and Suburban America

Introduction

BRUCE KATZ
ROBERT E. LANG

The U.S. Census provides researchers, policymakers, planners, business leaders, journalists, and other interested parties with a valuable once-in-a-decade snapshot of the social, demographic, and economic makeup of America. This was not the original purpose of the census; the framers of the U.S. Constitution designed the population count to regulate democratic representation through population size and distribution. However, the census's value for understanding and tracking change among the American populace has become of paramount interest. The nearly $200 billion in federal funds that are distributed annually to states based on the decennial census attest to its importance.[1]

Americans have long been fascinated with numbers—especially when they reveal who we are as a nation. Francis Walker, director of the 1870 and 1880 censuses, capitalized on an American "passion for statistics" to greatly expand the census beyond its original purpose.[2] Under his leadership, the census invented such concepts as the center of population statistic in 1870 that tracked America's westward movement back to 1790. This measure helped the public to visualize national settlement, which the census found shifting westward an average of about seventy feet a day. Walker also added dozens of new questions to the census. The so-called jumbo census of 1880 was so stuffed with questions that it took the better part of a decade to analyze. Problems with data tabulation in the 1880 census led to the

1. Kent and others (2001).
2. Quoted in Schlereth (1991, p. 3).

invention of a keypunch counter in 1890, whose commercial application led to the formation of IBM.

The 2000 census remains a treasure trove of information. It confirms that our nation is undergoing a period of dynamic, volatile change; and cities and suburbs are the places where these trends play out most vividly. The residents of our metropolitan areas are growing older, while the proportion of young workers is starting to shrink. Cities and suburbs are more diverse, as a surge of new immigrants into the country locates first in our metro areas and increasingly in the suburbs. Singles and older Americans living alone have now surpassed married couples with children as the prevailing household type in suburbs. And despite the rebirth of many U.S. cities, the census confirms that suburban growth still dominates.

The evidence from Census 2000 explodes many long-held stereotypes about cities and suburbs. Government, businesses, and nonprofits must now change their policies and practices to reflect the new metropolitan reality. This series, sponsored by the Brookings Institution Center on Urban and Metropolitan Policy and the Fannie Mae Foundation, brings together analyses of Census 2000 data to depict the latest picture of urban and suburban America. The series outlines what this new reality means for the vast array of policies, politics, and programs shaping these places. This first volume is based on the first release of "short-form" data from the census on population, race and ethnicity, and household types in this country. Future volumes will reveal deeper spatial trends provided by "long-form" data and Public Use Micro Sample data, as they are released by the Census Bureau.

PEOPLING THE UNITED STATES FROM THE NINETEENTH CENTURY TO TODAY

During the nineteenth century, Americans created a vast, coast-to-coast network of cities so that by 1900 the core of every major U.S. region, except for Las Vegas, was established. During the twentieth century, and especially in the years following World War II, growth spread from these urban cores, giving us today's vast metropolis. During the past two centuries, settlement swept into every corner of the nation, the census-defined "frontier" opened and closed (in 1890), waves of immigrants came from all parts of the globe (and keep coming), and the United States shifted from being majority rural to majority urban (1920) and is now half suburban (2000). Thus we have shifted from settling the original frontier of Daniel Boone's Kentucky to the crabgrass frontier at the metropolitan fringe.

CENSUS 2000: DATA RELEASE AND NEW PROCEDURES ON RACE

Census 2000 is the first decennial U.S. census to be released via the Internet. This creates opportunities for a wide range of users to have firsthand access to the data. The data are being released over a two-year period, with basic demographic information released first, followed by more detailed data.

What Do Researchers Mean by Short- and Long-Form Data?
In March 2001, the Census Bureau released the first data from Census 2000, the Redistricting Data Summary File, which provided population counts for race and Hispanic categories. Other files with data from the census short form followed. These data, referred to as 100 percent items because they derive from questions asked of all U.S. households and residents, include household relationship, sex, race, age, and Hispanic or Latino origin, and housing data related to tenure and occupancy status. All of the chapters in this volume contain analyses derived from short-form data.

The long-form questionnaire asked all of the same questions as the short form, as well as detailed questions relating to the social, economic, and housing characteristics of each individual and household. Information derived from the long form is referred to as sample data, because approximately one in six households receives the long-form questionnaire.

Data files are tabulated from the long form for a range of geographic entities, including states, metropolitan areas, census tracts, and block groups. The Census Bureau began releasing sample data files from Census 2000 in July 2002. Future editions in this series will include analyses of long-form data.

How Did the Census Bureau Collect Race Data This Time?
One of the most important changes in Census 2000 was the way data were collected on race and Hispanic origin. The federal government considers race and Hispanic origin distinct concepts and therefore captures information on them in two separate questions. These two questions appeared on the census short form and were thus asked of every individual residing in the United States. Respondents were first asked to identify whether they were of "Spanish, Hispanic or Latino" origin. That question was then followed by another question that asked people to identify whether they were white, black, Asian, American Indian, Native Hawaiian, or "some other race." For the first time, respondents could check off more than one race to describe themselves. While race in the 1990 census was limited to six response categories, the ability to choose one or more race categories in 2000 raised the number of potential responses to 63. Adding the Hispanic or Latino dimension raises the possible identity combinations to 126. Because of these changes, racial and ethnic data from Census 2000 are not directly comparable to those from 1990.

Birth and death rates have also shifted dramatically during the past two centuries. In 1800 the United States had a demographic profile not unlike some current third world nations with high birth and death rates. Because of improvements in the late nineteenth and early twentieth centuries (especially in sanitation), death rates began to fall dramatically as life expectancy climbed. The nation's natural increase in population surged as birth rates remained high. The slow fall-off in birth rates was partly because of recent immigrants who maintained a higher fertility pattern reflecting their country of origin. By the 1930s, however, more restrictive immigration laws and the Great Depression began to significantly bring down birth rates. Increasingly assimilated immigrants and their children began to have lower fertility rates in line with native-born Americans. And as the nation shifted from rural to urban and mandatory elementary education laws became common, the demand for children as farm laborers diminished, and family size dropped.

By World War II, the nation was on the path of much slower growth than the previous century and a half, but a postwar baby boom and renewed immigration reversed this trend. The generation born during the 1920s and 1930s, for reasons often debated by social scientists, defied the downward trend in birth rates and instead parented the baby boom. This boom began in 1946 and gathered speed during the 1950s. By the late 1950s, births exceeded 4 million a year and the fertility rate climbed to more than 3.7 births a woman in child-bearing years (the rate is now below 2.1). The baby boom ended by the mid-1960s, and fertility rates began a steady fall, yet during these same years, the United States reformed immigration laws and set in place the next wave of renewed population growth.

While population growth dipped in the 1970s, it gained momentum in the 1980s and accelerated in the 1990s. By 2000, America's population had reached a high of more than 281 million. The nation grew by nearly 33 million during the 1990s, or a number equivalent to the total population at the start of the Civil War. This was the largest U.S. numerical increase ever seen. The decade's 13.2 percent increase was the fastest growth since the 1960s.

Metropolitan areas were clearly at the vanguard of the nation's latest growth trends. By 2000, more than eight out of every ten persons in the United States resided in metropolitan areas, up from less than two-thirds in 1960.[3] Nearly one-third of all Americans lived in large metro areas of 5 million persons or more.

3. Nucci and Long (1995).

METROPOLITAN AMERICA IN 2000

The dawn of a new century presents an opportune moment to take stock of the health and function of America's metropolitan areas. This is particularly true given the immense pace and scope of change under way in the United States. Cities and their suburbs do not exist in a vacuum. Rather, they reflect the "fashions and feasibilities" of American society.[4] Yet discussions about cities and metropolitan areas often rely more on rhetoric than reality. There are knowledgeable urban observers who use the emergence of "living downtowns" as evidence of a broader back-to-the-city movement in the United States. But the renewed activities in a refurbished downtown may not capture the larger trends occurring in the remainder of the city or the metropolitan area as a whole.

The chapters in this volume turn to the first round of Census 2000 data on population, race and ethnicity, and household composition to begin to sort out the debate about the health of cities and suburbs. This volume attempts to answer these simple questions:

—Are cities coming back?

—Are all suburbs growing?

—Are cities and suburbs becoming more alike?

What emerges is a story of immense change and heterogeneity. Some of the distinctions relate to which region a city or suburb is located in, the South or the Northeast, the West or the Midwest. These regional variations are further distinguished by differences in economic function (for example, hi-tech economies rather than older manufacturing places) and in historic racial and ethnic composition (for example, immigration centers rather than primarily white-black metro areas).

Are Cities Coming Back?

Several factors define the health of a central city, but population growth is often used as a common barometer of city vitality. Population change is one of the first measures provided by the decennial census that gives urban observers, experts, and leaders a sense of the state of America's cities.

Without a doubt, central cities performed better in the 1990s than they did in the 1980s when it came to population growth. In chapter 1, Edward L. Glaeser and Jesse M. Shapiro show us that U.S. cities of 100,000 persons or more grew at twice the rate in the 1990s than they did in the 1980s. But despite this good news, there were some large variations in city population

4. Warner (1972).

growth—from as high as 85 percent growth in Las Vegas to as low as a 15 percent decline in Hartford. Western cities grew the fastest, at an average pace of 19.5 percent, while the cities in the Northeast, on average, lost population. The authors offer several explanations for the different patterns of city growth. Cities were more likely to grow if they had high percentages of educated residents and thus strong human capital, if they had a service sector—rather than a manufacturing—economy, and if they began the decade with a large immigrant population base. Ironically, the most important factor affecting the population growth of cities may be the one factor that leaders simply cannot control: the weather. Glaeser and Shapiro state it plainly, "these regional patterns can be understood as the result of the tyranny of the weather. Warm, dry places grew. Cold, wet places declined."

Alan Berube's analysis in chapter 2 reinforces Glaeser and Shapiro's cautionary note that not all cities did well in the 1990s, especially if one compares their population growth rates to those of their suburbs. On the whole, the top 100 cities gained population in the 1990s; however, 28 of these cities lost residents or did not grow at all. As Glaeser and Shapiro reveal, most of these cities were located in the Northeast or Midwest. Furthermore, only five central cities experienced a true comeback in that they had converted their 1980s population loss into a net gain in the 1990s. These "renaissance cities" were Denver, Memphis, Atlanta, Chicago, and Yonkers. Berube finds that no matter how strongly or weakly cities grew in population in the 1990s, their suburbs fared better. Although the top 100 cities grew by 9 percent as a whole, their suburbs grew twice as fast—by 18 percent. Suburban growth outpaced city growth in four out of every five cities.

It is evident that despite the strength of the 1990s economy, Rust Belt cities in the Midwest and Northeast still struggled to attract new residents and hold on to existing ones. But, no matter whether they gained residents or lost them, Patrick A. Simmons and Robert E. Lang find that the 1990s were still the best decade for older, industrial cities since the 1940s. In chapter 3, they examine population growth trends for thirty-six older, industrial cities during the past five decades—from the 1950s to today—and then rank the decades by how well the cities fared during that period. The authors find that, as a group, the older cities performed best during the 1990s when they together added approximately 580,000 people. The worst decade was the 1970s, when suburban expansion took off and twenty-nine cities suffered their worst postwar population declines. Many of these cities have not yet regained the population levels of their heyday; however, several, including Chicago and New York, have grown again since the 1970s.

The 1990s were clearly a positive decade for many cities. As Rebecca R. Sohmer and Robert E. Lang confirm in chapter 4, the 1990s were also a good decade for the nation's downtowns. Out of a selection of twenty-four cities, the authors find that eighteen actually saw their downtown populations grow in the past decade. For half of the cities, like Seattle and Denver, the explosive growth in downtown residents mirrored the overall population growth in the city. The real high performers were six cities in the Midwest and Northeast that were able to increase their downtown populations despite their citywide loss in residents—Cleveland, Norfolk, Baltimore, Philadelphia, Detroit, and Milwaukee. Although it is unclear whether this trend is due to changing demographics at the heart of central cities, or residential choices that people are making, the proximity of downtowns to work and transit offer hope of a continued steady growth into the next decade.

These chapters show that most cities and downtowns grew in the 1990s, but Alan Berube and Benjamin Forman argue that these trends mask a larger unevenness of population growth inside our central cities. In chapter 5, the authors note that while about two-thirds of downtown census tracts in the 100 largest cities added population, this growth was dwarfed by the larger population loss in surrounding neighborhoods or by the expansive population growth at the cities' edge. In fact, more than 60 percent of the overall population growth in these largest cities occurred in the outer ring of neighborhoods bordering the suburbs, while only 11 percent took place in inner-core neighborhoods. As such, most cities actually decentralized within their own borders in the 1990s. These trends were accentuated in the South and West, where growth at the periphery overwhelmed growth in the core, and in the Midwest, where outer-ring neighborhoods grew despite residential declines surrounding downtowns. These patterns serve as a reminder that not all neighborhoods shared in the benefits of city population growth in the 1990s.

Are All Suburbs Growing?

The American suburb continued to show its strength—and dominance—by the year 2000. As mentioned earlier, suburban growth outpaced city growth irrespective of whether a city's population was falling like Baltimore's, staying stable like Kansas City's, or rising rapidly like Denver's. Even Sun Belt cities like Phoenix, Dallas, and Houston grew more slowly than their suburbs. But as with cities, there are growth variations among suburbs. Chapters 6 and 7 show us a contrasting picture of the new, rapidly growing suburbs in the Southwest and the declining ones in the colder regions of the country.

In chapter 6, Lang and Simmons describe a new suburban phenomenon dubbed the "boomburb," which may indicate the direction of many suburban cities in the Sun Belt. These cities are products of newer master-planned community-oriented growth in metropolitan areas largely in the Southwest. While all of these cities had more than 100,000 people living in them in 2000, they are most notable for their explosive growth during the past few decades. Suburban cities such as Irving, Arlington, and Plano near Dallas-Fort Worth, Chandler near Phoenix, and Henderson outside Las Vegas grew by more than forty times their size, from just a few thousand people in the 1950s, to populations of several hundred thousand by 2000. Such rapid growth raises many questions about the pressures of service delivery, the quality of new construction, and the capacity of transportation and road systems in these places.

Meanwhile, some of the suburbs of the Midwest and Northeast struggled with the same population declines that pervaded their central cities, and some of the loss was fairly rapid. In the 2,600 suburbs analyzed by William H. Lucy and David L. Phillips in chapter 7, there were 700 that lost population at an average rate of 6.1 percent of residents per suburb. Sometimes population decline occurred in the inner-ring suburbs, but often declining suburbs were scattered across metropolitan areas. While most of America's shrinking suburbs were in the older regions of the country, suburbs in the South and West were not immune to population loss. For instance, while Pittsburgh had the largest number of declining suburbs (108), Denver's suburbs had the highest average population loss (at 35.7 percent).

Are Cities and Suburbs Becoming More Alike?

Beyond the continued growth and dispersal of the American population, the 1990s ushered in a period of greater diversity. First, the U.S. population became even more racially and ethnically diverse, with four out of every five new additions to the population being a person of color. Notably, Hispanics passed African Americans as the nation's largest racial/ethnic group, while the Asian American population strengthened its presence by more than 50 percent. Second, the nation also became more diverse in household formation. The traditional nuclear family is a shrinking phenomenon as changes in social norms regarding marriage, divorce, cohabitation, and childbearing are becoming more acceptable, and as the baby boomer generation enters its empty-nester years. Together, these larger demographic trends are redefining cities and suburbs.

One of the most dramatic changes in cities in the 1990s is that the majority of central cities became majority "minority" for the first time in American history. Berube's analysis in chapter 8 describes the transformation of the nation's 100 largest cities into truly multiracial, multicultural centers. First, the share of non-Hispanic whites in these cities decreased from 52 percent in 1990 to 44 percent by 2000. Cities like Anaheim, Philadelphia, and Albuquerque now have more persons of color than non-Hispanic whites. While the white population shrank in the 100 largest cities by more than 2 million, their Hispanic population ballooned by 3.8 million. Nearly every city (97 out of 100) experienced a growth in Hispanics—at a typical rate of 64.5 percent. If not for the growth in Hispanic population, 19 out of 74 growing cities would have lost population in the 1990s. Just as widespread as the growth in Hispanics was the increase in Asians; 95 out of 100 cities added Asian residents, though at a slower pace. Meanwhile, the share of African Americans in the largest cities shrank slightly, from 24.7 percent in 1990 to 24.1 percent in 2000. The cities that lost black residents were mostly found in California and in cities in the Rust Belt region. The combination of deep declines of white residents, modest changes in the black population, and explosive growth in Hispanics and Asians explains the tipping of America's cities into primarily communities of color.

As central cities solidify their place as the nation's centers of racial and ethnic diversity, the nation's suburbs are also becoming more heterogeneous. Nationwide, 95 percent of the foreign-born population in 2000 lived in metropolitan areas, with slightly more than half residing outside of central cities. In chapter 9, William H. Frey tracks the dramatic shift of the minority population into suburban areas across the country. Overall, the share of racial and ethnic minorities living in the suburbs increased substantially in the 1990s, moving from less than one-fifth to more than one-quarter of all suburbanites. This trend is most evident in metro areas that already had a strong immigrant base. The suburbs in these melting pot metro areas had sizable portions of their population that were Hispanic, Asian, and African American. In contrast, Hispanics were the largest community of color in the suburbs of largely white metro areas in the South and West, while African Americans were the largest suburban minority population in other metro areas. Frey also finds that, just as in cities, the growth of racial and ethnic groups fueled the bulk of the population growth in suburbs in the 1990s.

The rapid rise of Hispanics in the United States not only transformed cities and suburbs but also affected many new parts of the country, particularly many smaller metro areas that had experienced little immigrant settlement in the past. In chapter 10, Roberto Suro and Audrey Singer describe how the explosive growth of the Latino population has created many new

Latino destination areas in the United States while cementing the dominance of traditional immigration gateways as immigration centers. The authors find that places like Minneapolis-St. Paul, MN, Portland, OR, and Raleigh-Durham, NC, which had relatively few Latinos two decades ago, saw their Latino populations triple in size between 1980 and 2000. Meanwhile, long-established Latino metros such as New York, Los Angeles, and Miami experienced the largest absolute gains in Latinos and remain home to more than half of the nation's Hispanics. The chapter also echoes Frey's conclusions about the rise of multicultural suburbia: more than half of all Latinos in the United States now live in the suburbs; they increased their presence in the suburbs by 71 percent in the decade.

As the wave of new Hispanics, Asians, and the foreign-born sweeps over U.S. cities and suburbs, it is important to consider how these changes are affecting the pattern of opportunities in our country. Two chapters, one by Glaeser and Jacob L. Vigdor and the other by John R. Logan, provide different—but not opposing—views about what the latest census data tell us about the state of racial segregation in America.

In chapter 11, Glaeser and Vigdor present the promising news from the 1990s; the level of black to nonblack segregation in the country reached its lowest point since 1920. Although African American segregation remains very high in general, it continued a three-decade decline in the 1990s. In fact, segregation levels in the 300 metro areas studied dropped in all but nineteen places. The authors find that the decline in segregation occurred primarily because of the black integration of white neighborhoods and not the nonblack movement into African American areas, which on the whole have remained isolated. The authors also find that most of the promising trends occurred in rapidly growing metro areas, and metro areas in the West and South. However, segregation remained severe in highly populous metro areas, particularly those located in the Midwest and Northeast.

John Logan similarly acknowledges in chapter 12 that black-white segregation in the country has been dropping. But he also urges us to not lose sight of its severity and to look beyond the black-white color line as this country's diversity accelerates, especially in the suburbs. First, Logan asserts that while black-white segregation dropped in both the 1980s and 1990s, the progress remains glacial, considering how high segregation remains. Meanwhile, in the past two decades, segregation levels of Hispanics and Asians from whites have remained largely unchanged, despite the swift rise of these two groups in the country. In general, whites still live in primarily all-white neighborhoods, while blacks, Hispanics, and Asians live in more integrated places, often with other communities of color. This chapter also details that as suburbs have grown more diverse, minority segregation there has increased. As they increasingly take on urban characteristics, the suburbs may also be replicating the cities' pattern of neighborhood segregation and thus the growing inequality of life chances among communities of color that live in them.

Finally, chapter 13 completes the early picture of the dynamic change taking place in our cities and suburbs. Frey and Berube examine the shifting household composition in metropolitan America and find that certain cities are looking more stereotypically suburban while some suburbs are attracting households that have traditionally been associated with cities. For instance, the authors document that the rapidly growing cities in the Sun Belt saw significant increases in married couples with children, while their Rust Belt counterparts continued their loss of such families. Nearly all suburbs, however, saw faster growth in all types of households compared with their cities. Most noteworthy is that by 2000, the largest household type in the suburbs was nonfamilies (29 percent)—young singles and elderly persons living alone— followed by married couples with children (27 percent).

The findings presented in this volume are unequivocal. Cities and suburbs are undergoing a dynamic metamorphosis. Cities are growing, bolstered by a strong economy and the growth of new immigrants, but their suburbs are growing faster. As suburban expansion continues, the demographic differences between cities and suburbs are narrowing. Many immigrants today are bypassing cities and heading straight for the suburbs, joining other persons of color who are increasingly locating there. And as these and other changes unfold, it appears that the metro areas in the South and West are moving in opposite trajectories to their neighbors in the Midwest and Northeast. In the end, there are clear regional differences in the country, and even stark differences among individual metro areas. Government, business, and nonprofit leaders must know the demographic context of the communities in which they work. These demographic shifts are signaling changes in demand for housing and services such as schools and childcare, healthcare, and eldercare, as well as changing consumer preferences for private sector goods. They also signal the shifting nature of politics in our cities and suburbs, redefining the coalitions for change and the voting behaviors that may play out at the state and national levels.

REFERENCES

Kent, Mary M., Kelvin M. Pollard, John Haaga, and Mark Mather. 2001. "First Glimpses from the 2000 Census." *Population Bulletin* 56 (2). Washington: Population Reference Bureau.

Nucci, Alfred, and Larry Long. 1995. "Spatial and Demographic Dynamics of Metropolitan and Nonmetropolitan Territory in the United States." *International Journal of Population Geography* (1): 165–81.
Schlereth, Thomas J. 1991. *Victorian America: Transformation in Everyday Life, 1876–1915.* Harper Collins.
Warner, Sam Bass, Jr. 1972. *The Urban Wilderness: A History of the American City.* Harper and Row.

1

City Growth

Which Places Grew and Why

EDWARD L. GLAESER
JESSE M. SHAPIRO

Urban growth rates in the 1990s reveal the heterogeneity of American cities. The nation is filled with cities that grew by 20 percent or more during the decade and also with cities experiencing serious population declines. But population growth and decline are not random. Clear patterns describe which cities grew and which ones did not. A variety of attributes that a particular city might have had in 1990 can explain whether it grew or shrank over the ensuing decade. Some of these attributes are susceptible to policy fixes, but others are not. This study documents and explains the patterns of population growth and decline among American cities having populations of more than 100,000 in 1990.[1]

METHODS

Tables 1-1 through 1-4 show the basic data set among 195 U.S. cities that had populations of more than 100,000 in 1990. We included the following in each of these tables:

- Population in 2000;
- Population in 1990;

1. Our comparison data set for the 1980s also consists only of cities with a population greater than 100,000 in 1980. We are focusing on cities, not on metropolitan areas. This is in part to make our work more compatible with previous literature, but we also think that the somewhat smaller size of cities makes them better than metropolitan areas for some forms of urban analysis.

TABLE 1-1. High Fliers—Cities That Grew by More than 10 Percent

			Brookings city growth model		
City	Population, 1990	Population, 2000	Growth rate, 1990–2000 (percent)	Predicted growth rate, 1990–2000 (percent)	Growth rate, 1980–90 (percent)
Las Vegas, NV	258,295	478,434	85.2	33.1	56.9
Plano, TX	128,713	222,030	72.5	30.7	78.0
Scottsdale, AZ	130,069	202,705	55.9	38.1	46.8
Boise City, ID	125,738	185,787	47.8	22.0	23.0
Glendale, AZ	148,134	218,812	47.7	33.7	52.5
Laredo, TX	122,899	176,576	43.7	22.2	34.4
Bakersfield, CA	174,820	247,057	41.3	30.0	65.5
Austin, TX	465,622	656,562	41.0	20.8	34.6
Salinas, CA	108,777	151,060	38.9	11.3	35.2
Mesa, AZ	288,091	396,375	37.6	31.2	89.0
Durham, NC	136,611	187,035	36.9	10.3	35.1
Charlotte, NC	395,934	540,828	36.6	13.1	25.5
Santa Clarita, CA	110,642	151,088	36.6	25.6	n.a.
Reno, NV	133,850	180,480	34.9	17.3	32.9
Phoenix, AZ	983,403	1,321,045	34.4	32.4	24.5
Overland Park, KS	111,790	149,080	33.4	23.2	36.7
Raleigh, NC	207,951	276,093	32.8	15.4	38.4
Chesapeake, VA	151,976	199,184	31.1	12.6	32.8
Santa Rosa, CA	113,313	147,595	30.3	10.3	37.1
Irvine, CA	110,330	143,072	29.7	28.9	77.6
Winston-Salem, NC	143,485	185,776	29.5	8.1	8.8
Chula Vista, CA	135,163	173,556	28.4	14.3	61.1
Colorado Springs, CO	281,140	360,890	28.4	16.0	30.7
Arlington, TX	261,721	332,969	27.2	23.0	63.5
Salem, OR	107,786	136,924	27.1	3.8	21.0
Rancho Cucamonga, CA	101,409	127,743	26.0	27.1	83.6
Hayward, CA	111,498	140,030	25.6	12.6	19.1
Oceanside, CA	128,398	161,029	25.4	13.6	67.4
Aurora, CO	222,103	276,393	24.4	19.9	40.1
Irving, TX	155,037	191,615	23.6	20.9	41.0
Anaheim, CA	266,406	328,014	23.1	17.7	21.4
Sioux Falls, SD	100,814	123,975	23.0	18.0	23.9
Escondido, CA	108,635	133,559	22.9	14.8	68.8
Mesquite, TX	101,484	124,523	22.7	23.1	51.4
Eugene, OR	112,669	137,893	22.4	4.2	6.6
San Antonio, TX	935,933	1,144,646	22.3	18.3	19.1
Greensboro, NC	183,521	223,891	22.0	10.3	17.9
Portland, OR	437,319	529,121	21.0	2.5	18.8
Fresno, CA	354,202	427,652	20.7	22.4	62.9
Tallahassee, FL	124,773	150,624	20.7	13.7	53.0
Hialeah, FL	188,004	226,419	20.4	2.5	29.4
Tucson, AZ	405,390	486,699	20.1	25.7	22.7
Moreno Valley, CA	118,779	142,381	19.9	24.5	n.a.
Houston, TX	1,630,553	1,953,631	19.8	12.0	2.2
Oxnard, CA	142,216	170,358	19.8	14.9	31.4
Fort Worth, TX	447,619	534,694	19.5	16.6	16.2

(*continued*)

TABLE 1-1. High Fliers—Cities That Grew by More than 10 Percent (*continued*)

			Brookings city growth model		
City	*Population, 1990*	*Population, 2000*	*Growth rate, 1990–2000 (percent)*	*Predicted growth rate, 1990–2000 (percent)*	*Growth rate, 1980–90 (percent)*
Garland, TX	180,650	215,768	19.4	22.5	30.1
Fort Wayne, IN	173,072	205,727	18.9	6.7	0.4
Pasadena, TX	119,363	141,674	18.7	10.2	6.0
Ontario, CA	133,179	158,007	18.6	16.4	49.9
Denver, CO	467,610	554,636	18.6	14.9	–5.1
Dallas, TX	1,006,877	1,188,580	18.1	18.0	11.3
Lincoln, NE	191,972	225,581	17.5	19.0	11.7
Fremont, CA	173,339	203,413	17.4	18.3	31.4
Nashville-Davidson, TN	488,374	569,891	16.7	11.2	7.2
Albuquerque, NM	384,736	448,607	16.6	26.1	15.6
Orange, CA	110,658	128,821	16.4	23.0	21.0
Omaha, NE	335,795	390,007	16.1	14.8	7.0
Jacksonville, FL	635,230	735,617	15.8	11.3	17.4
Lexington-Fayette, KY	225,366	260,512	15.6	11.1	10.4
Stockton, CA	210,943	243,771	15.6	16.4	42.3
Garden Grove, CA	143,050	165,196	15.5	18.6	16.0
Alexandria, VA	111,183	128,283	15.4	17.1	7.7
Santa Ana, CA	293,742	337,977	15.1	12.4	44.0
Anchorage, AK	226,338	260,283	15.0	12.3	29.7
Modesto, CA	164,730	188,856	14.7	20.6	54.0
Hollywood, FL	121,697	139,357	14.5	5.0	0.3
San Jose, CA	782,248	894,943	14.4	16.0	24.3
Lakewood, CO	126,481	144,126	14.0	22.5	11.1
Oklahoma City, OK	444,719	506,132	13.8	17.1	10.1
Salt Lake City, UT	159,936	181,743	13.6	17.7	–1.9
Pomona, CA	131,723	149,473	13.5	14.2	42.0
Wichita, KS	304,011	344,284	13.3	14.2	8.6
San Bernardino, CA	164,164	185,401	12.9	18.5	38.2
Orlando, FL	164,693	185,951	12.9	10.5	28.4
Riverside, CA	226,505	255,166	12.7	23.0	32.8
Columbus, OH	632,910	711,470	12.4	8.2	12.0
Sunnyvale, CA	117,229	131,760	12.4	12.5	10.0
Thousand Oaks, CA	104,352	117,005	12.1	23.4	35.4
Tempe, AZ	141,865	158,625	11.8	35.1	32.7
Simi Valley, CA	100,217	111,351	11.1	21.0	29.3
Cedar Rapids, IA	108,751	120,758	11.0	12.1	–1.4
Spokane, WA	177,196	195,629	10.4	10.9	3.4
Fullerton, CA	114,144	126,003	10.4	20.6	11.6
Sacramento, CA	369,365	407,018	10.2	17.1	34.0
San Diego, CA	1,110,549	1,223,400	10.2	19.2	26.8
Amarillo, TX	157,615	173,627	10.2	19.7	5.6

Source: See details in text for tables 1-1 through 1-5.
Note: See note 2 in text for additional explanation.
n.a. Not available.

TABLE 1-2. Modest Growers—Cities That Grew between 2 and 10 Percent

City	Population, 1990	Population, 2000	Brookings city growth model: Growth rate, 1990–2000 (percent)	Brookings city growth model: Predicted growth rate, 1990–2000 (percent)	Brookings city growth model: Growth rate, 1980–90 (percent)
Waco, TX	103,590	113,726	9.8	18.1	2.3
Elizabeth, NJ	110,002	120,568	9.6	–3.0	3.6
Tacoma, WA	176,664	193,556	9.6	1.0	11.5
Hampton, VA	133,793	146,437	9.5	10.2	9.1
El Paso, TX	515,342	563,662	9.4	23.9	21.2
Concord, CA	111,348	121,780	9.4	24.3	7.3
New York, NY	7,322,564	8,008,278	9.4	–8.5	3.6
El Monte, CA	106,209	115,965	9.2	8.3	33.6
Seattle, WA	516,259	563,374	9.1	3.3	4.5
Madison, WI	191,262	208,054	8.8	13.3	12.1
Abilene, TX	106,654	115,930	8.7	23.8	8.5
Tampa, FL	280,015	303,447	8.4	10.3	3.1
Stamford, CT	108,056	117,083	8.4	6.7	5.5
Glendale, CA	180,038	194,973	8.3	18.6	29.5
Indianapolis, IN	731,327	791,926	8.3	9.1	4.4
Virginia Beach, VA	393,069	425,257	8.2	18.3	49.9
Providence, RI	160,728	173,618	8.0	–4.2	2.5
Springfield, MO	140,494	151,580	7.9	10.4	5.5
Corpus Christi, TX	257,453	277,454	7.8	19.5	10.9
Montgomery, AL	187,106	201,568	7.7	11.7	5.2
Rockford, IL	139,426	150,115	7.7	1.4	–0.2
Long Beach, CA	429,433	461,522	7.5	13.1	18.8
Oakland, CA	372,242	399,484	7.3	1.4	9.7
San Francisco, CA	723,959	776,733	7.3	–0.8	6.6
Lubbock, TX	186,206	199,564	7.2	24.1	6.8
Tulsa, OK	367,302	393,049	7.0	16.2	1.8
Vallejo, CA	109,199	116,760	6.9	9.2	36.0
Memphis, TN	610,337	650,100	6.5	7.2	–5.6
Los Angeles, CA	3,485,398	3,694,820	6.0	13.7	17.4

(continued)

- Growth rate during the 1990s;
- A measure called the Brookings City Growth Model, which predicts the growth rate for a particular city on the basis of certain key factors[2];
- Growth rate during the 1980s (for comparison).

2. The Brookings City Growth Model predicts the growth rate of city *i* using the following formula: Growthi = –63.85 – 0.3023*Raini + 0.7397*Tempi + 18.09*Carsi + 0.2309*Educi – 0.2945*Manufi, where "Growthi" refers to the percent growth rate of city *i* and is calculated as Growthi = 100*(Population in 2000 of city *i* – Population in 1990 of city *i*)/ (Population in 1990 of city *i*), and where "Raini" refers to average annual precipitation in city *i* measured in inches, "Tempi" refers to mean July temperature in city *i* measured in degrees Fahrenheit, "Carsi" refers to average number of vehicles per household in city *i* in 1990, "Educi" refers to the percentage of persons 25 years and older in city *i* in 1990 with a college degree or higher, and "Manufi" refers to the percentage of civilians in city *i* in 1990 employed in manufacturing. This formula was obtained using multiple regression, and all coefficients are statistically significant. This model is able to explain 43.46 percent of the overall variation in growth rates in our sample of 195 cities with populations greater than 100,000 in 1990.

TABLE 1-2. Modest Growers—Cities That Grew between 2 and 10 Percent (*continued*)

			Brookings city growth model		
City	*Population, 1990*	*Population, 2000*	*Growth rate, 1990–2000 (percent)*	*Predicted growth rate, 1990–2000 (percent)*	*Growth rate, 1980–90 (percent)*
Newport News, VA	170,045	180,150	5.9	7.7	17.4
Springfield, IL	105,227	111,454	5.9	13.7	5.2
Paterson, NJ	140,891	149,222	5.9	–8.5	2.1
Atlanta, GA	394,017	416,474	5.7	4.2	–7.3
Sterling Heights, MI	117,810	124,471	5.7	11.3	8.1
St. Paul, MN	272,235	287,151	5.5	6.6	0.7
Knoxville, TN	165,121	173,890	5.3	6.9	–5.7
Jersey City, NJ	228,537	240,055	5.1	–6.8	2.2
Grand Rapids, MI	189,126	197,800	4.6	3.1	4.0
Huntington Beach, CA	181,519	189,594	4.5	20.1	6.5
Columbus, GA	178,681	186,291	4.3	9.0	5.5
Yonkers, NY	188,082	196,086	4.3	0.2	–3.7
Little Rock, AR	175,795	183,133	4.2	12.4	10.5
Ann Arbor, MI	109,592	114,024	4.0	19.1	1.5
Chicago, IL	2,783,726	2,896,016	4.0	–2.5	–7.4
St. Petersburg, FL	238,629	248,232	4.0	8.8	–0.0
Minneapolis, MN	368,383	382,618	3.9	6.6	–0.7
Baton Rouge, LA	219,531	227,818	3.8	9.7	–0.4
Torrance, CA	133,107	137,946	3.6	17.7	2.5
Des Moines, IA	193,187	198,682	2.8	12.3	1.1
Inglewood, CA	109,602	112,580	2.7	9.1	16.4
Boston, MA	574,283	589,141	2.6	–1.7	2.0
South Bend, IN	105,511	107,789	2.2	1.4	–3.8
Topeka, KS	119,883	122,377	2.1	14.6	1.0
Chattanooga, TN	152,466	155,554	2.0	4.2	–10.1
Fort Lauderdale, FL	149,377	152,397	2.0	6.7	–2.6

Note: See note 2 in text for additional explanation.

The tables are ordered by the rate of growth in the 1990s: table 1-1 lists the eighty-seven "high-fliers" (those cities with a growth rate greater than 10 percent); table 1-2 lists the fifty-five modest growers (cities with growth rates between 2 percent and 10 percent); table 1-3 includes the twenty unchanged cities (those with growth between –2 percent and 2 percent); and table 1-4 shows the thirty-three declining cities (those that shrank by more than 2 percent). Table 1-5 gives the mean growth rate for cities in three size categories in the 1980s and 1990s. Then in order to discern elements shared by the faster-growing cities, the studied cities were examined in terms of several factors, including the following: location and climate; residents' educational level and median annual household income; unemployment rate and the prominence of manufacturing in the city's economy; the city's position in regard to the predominant means of transportation and the age of the housing stock; and the city's immigration level.

TABLE 1-3. Unchanged Cities—Cities That Lost or Gained No More than 2 Percent

City	Population, 1990	Population, 2000	Brookings city growth model: Growth rate, 1990–2000 (percent)	Brookings city growth model: Predicted growth rate, 1990–2000 (percent)	Brookings city growth model: Growth rate, 1980–90 (percent)
Pasadena, CA	131,591	133,936	1.8	18.0	11.5
Honolulu CDP, HI	365,272	371,657	1.8	18.0	0.1
Worcester, MA	169,759	172,648	1.7	–3.8	4.9
Lowell, MA	103,439	105,167	1.7	–3.9	11.9
Kansas City, MO	435,146	441,545	1.5	11.0	–2.9
Allentown, PA	105,090	106,632	1.5	–1.7	1.3
Mobile, AL	196,278	198,915	1.3	6.0	–2.1
Miami, FL	358,548	362,470	1.1	–1.0	3.4
Independence, MO	112,301	113,288	0.9	11.6	0.5
Shreveport, LA	198,525	200,145	0.8	11.2	–4.1
Berkeley, CA	102,724	102,743	0.0	9.8	–0.6
Gary, IN	116,646	116,646	0.0	–2.2	–23.2
Livonia, MI	100,850	100,545	–0.3	16.4	–3.8
Beaumont, TX	114,323	113,866	–0.4	7.7	–3.2
Peoria, IL	113,504	112,936	–0.5	8.1	–8.6
Newark, NJ	275,221	273,546	–0.6	–9.2	–16.4
Huntsville, AL	159,789	158,216	–1.0	11.9	12.1
Bridgeport, CT	141,686	139,529	–1.5	–4.9	–0.6
Waterbury, CT	108,961	107,271	–1.6	–4.4	5.5
Kansas City, KS	149,767	146,866	–2.0	7.3	–7.1

Note: See note 2 in text for additional explanation.

FINDINGS

A survey of Census 2000 data reveals the following in regard to U.S. cities with 1990 populations greater than 100,000:

- The median growth rate for cities in the 1990s was 8.7 percent, or more than double the median growth rate of the 1980s, but the average city growth rate was similar during both decades, in part because the 1990s had fewer high-fliers than did the 1980s. An extremely strong correspondence exists between many cities' growth rate in the 1980s and their growth rate in the 1990s.
- Western cities grew the fastest, with an average growth rate of 19 percent. Cities of the Northeast, on average, declined. Cities in the South grew substantially but at about half the rate of cities in the West, and cities of the Midwest grew at 3 percent on average.
- "High-human-capital" cities grew. The levels of residents' education and income are consistent predictors of urban growth.

TABLE 1-4. Declining Cities—Cities That Lost More than 2 Percent

			Brookings city growth model		
City	*Population, 1990*	*Population, 2000*	*Growth rate, 1990–2000 (percent)*	*Predicted growth rate, 1990–2000 (percent)*	*Growth rate, 1980–90 (percent)*
New Orleans, LA	496,938	484,674	−2.5	1.1	−10.9
Richmond, VA	203,056	197,790	−2.6	4.5	−7.4
Akron, OH	223,019	217,074	−2.7	2.7	−6.0
Springfield, MA	156,983	152,082	−3.1	−0.8	3.1
Portsmouth, VA	103,907	100,565	−3.2	3.1	−0.6
Evansville, IN	126,272	121,582	−3.7	5.6	−3.2
Philadelphia, PA	1,585,577	1,517,550	−4.3	−3.9	−6.1
Savannah, GA	137,560	131,510	−4.4	7.6	−2.9
Warren, MI	144,864	138,247	−4.6	7.5	−10.1
Erie, PA	108,718	103,717	−4.6	−5.8	−8.7
Louisville, KY	269,063	256,231	−4.8	2.5	−9.9
Milwaukee, WI	628,088	596,974	−5.0	−0.2	−1.3
Rochester, NY	231,636	219,773	−5.1	−4.6	−4.2
New Haven, CT	130,474	123,626	−5.3	−0.7	3.5
Albany, NY	101,082	95,658	−5.4	3.5	−0.6
Cleveland, OH	505,616	478,403	−5.4	−6.8	−11.9
Washington, DC	606,900	572,059	−5.7	6.4	−5.0
Toledo, OH	332,943	313,619	−5.8	4.1	−6.1
Jackson, MS	196,637	184,256	−6.3	12.0	−3.1
Lansing, MI	127,321	119,128	−6.4	6.4	−2.4
Detroit, MI	1,027,974	951,270	−7.5	−2.6	−14.6
Birmingham, AL	265,968	242,820	−8.7	4.1	−6.5
Dayton, OH	182,044	166,179	−8.7	0.9	−5.9
Macon, GA	106,612	97,255	−8.8	9.3	−8.8
Cincinnati, OH	364,040	331,285	−9.0	2.7	−5.5
Pittsburgh, PA	369,879	334,563	−9.6	−1.4	−12.8
Syracuse, NY	163,860	147,306	−10.1	−2.3	−3.7
Norfolk, VA	261,229	234,403	−10.3	6.7	−2.2
Buffalo, NY	328,123	292,648	−10.8	−5.9	−8.3
Flint, MI	140,761	124,943	−11.2	−3.6	−11.8
Baltimore, MD	736,014	651,154	−11.5	−3.0	−6.5
St. Louis, MO	396,685	348,189	−12.2	1.7	−12.4
Hartford, CT	139,739	121,578	−13.0	−7.6	2.5

Note: See note 2 in text for additional explanation.

- Cities with large manufacturing bases grew much more slowly than cities with strong service industries. Cities with high unemployment rates grew more slowly than those with low unemployment rates.
- Cities built for pedestrians and for mass transit shrank (with a few exceptions), while auto-dependent cities grew. Similarly, older cities declined and younger cities grew.
- Foreign-born residents contributed to strong city growth rates. Cities with more foreign-born residents in 1990 grew more quickly than other cities, up to a point.

TABLE 1-5. City Growth and Initial City Size

Population, 1990	Number of cities, 1990–2000	Growth rate, 1990–2000 (percent)	Number of cities, 1980–90	Growth rate, 1980–90 (percent)
100,000–250,000	131	11.7	114	10.6
250,000–1,000,000	56	10.5	50	6.5
More than 1,000,000	8	7.0	6	–0.8
Total	195	11.2	170	9.0

Median Growth Rates

The median growth rate for cities in the 1990s was 8.7 percent, or more than double the median growth rate of the 1980s, but the average city growth rate was similar during both decades. The average city growth level in the 1990s was mildly positive: 11.2 percent. Despite recent media reports of the growth of the largest cities, this rate is extremely close to the average growth rate of cities in the 1980s (9 percent); the two figures are not statistically different. But the median growth rate in the 1990s was 8.7 percent, almost double the median growth rate in the 1980s. This difference between the mean and the median stems primarily from the fact that the 1980s had more high-fliers (affecting the mean but not the median) than did the 1990s.

Weighting by population in the calculation of the average growth rate tends to put cities' 1990s growth performance in a better light vis-à-vis the 1980s. The average growth rate of cities in the 1990s (calculated weighting by 1990 population) was 9.8 percent, and the analogous growth rate in the 1980s was 6.2 percent. The differential impact of population weighting on 1980s and 1990s data reflects modest differences in the relationship between initial city population and average growth rates in the 1980s compared with the 1990s. In the 1990s, big cities did better (relative to medium-sized cities) than in the 1980s, even though in general, no statistically significant relationship exists between initial city size and later growth.

Nevertheless, interesting differences do exist in that regard between the 1980s and the 1990s. Cities with initial population levels between 100,000 and 250,000 grew only slightly faster in the 1990s than in the 1980s (11.7 percent versus 10.6 percent on average). But cities with more than a million people grew much faster in the 1990s than in the 1980s (7.0 percent versus –0.8 percent). It is tempting for us to see this relative growth of the largest cities as vindication of earlier work arguing that big cities were not dying.[3] But these differences are not statistically significant, because of the stunning

3. See Glaeser (1998); Gaspar and Glaeser (1998).

variety of growth experiences across cities. The data certainly do suggest a continuing resilience of the largest cities, but this suggestion is far from proof of long-run success. We shall all have to wait until later decades to find out if advances in information technology (and other trends) really mean the end of our densest cities.

Indeed, there has been a dizzying array of growth rates across cities. Las Vegas (which has generally been the fastest-growing city in the postwar era) grew by 85 percent, while St. Louis (one of the reliably declining cities) shrank by almost 13 percent. It may be tempting to read much into a 9.3 percent increase in population in New York City or a 4 percent increase in Chicago, but in fact more than 25 percent of cities in our sample grew by 18 percent or more. New York and Chicago are actually among the moderately growing cities—they are not high-fliers.

No cities fell by more than 13 percent, but more than one-third grew by more than 13 percent. One explanation for this fact is that as long as a city has homes, people will live in them, which puts something of a brake on population loss. Because the change in population is tied to a change in housing, there is a natural asymmetry between population increases (which can always be accommodated by more building) and population decreases (which are unlikely to be very large, because then large numbers of houses would be vacant, which does not really happen). Thus St. Louis survives because of the extraordinary permanence of its housing stock. Although economic opportunities in the city may have diminished, the housing stock remains, and people stay in the city to take advantage of that housing stock.

A final basic fact about city growth, true for many decades now, is the extremely strong relationship in a given city's growth rate from one decade to the next.[4] Cities that grew fast in the 1980s grew fast in the 1990s. Despite the few exceptions (Arlington did better in the 1980s than in the 1990s, and Las Vegas did better in the 1990s), this is an extremely strong relationship—indeed, the strongest relationship seen in this present study. This persistence in growth rates suggests that the same factors that explained growth in the 1980s also explain growth in the 1990s. Of course, no one yet really understands why growth rates are so strongly correlated over time. That remains one of the important unsolved puzzles of urban growth.

Variation in Growth Rates

Western cities grew the fastest, followed by southern cities and midwestern cities, while northeastern cities lost population. Almost one-fourth of the

4. See Glaeser, Scheinkman, and Shleifer (1995).

variation in growth rates across cities in the 1990s can be explained by differences in cities' regional locations. The average growth rate across cities in the West was 19.5 percent; this is close to the average growth rate in the West in the 1980s, which was 23.4 percent. The South is the second-fastest-growing region; the average growth rate in the 1990s across cities in the South was 12 percent, while the comparable rate in the 1980s was 9 percent. These two regions have been the big success stories of the postwar era, and their growth is the tale of the rise of the Sun Belt.

The 1990s were much better to midwestern cities than were previous decades. Cities in the Midwest grew by an average of 3.4 percent in the 1990s after shrinking by 2.5 percent in the 1980s. This difference comes in part from the fact that in the 1990s several midwestern cities were high-fliers. Sioux Falls, South Dakota, grew by 22 percent, and Overland Park, Kansas, grew by 33 percent. For comparison, Madison, Wisconsin, had been the Midwest's fastest-growing city in the 1980s, expanding by 12 percent. Weighting by population causes the average 1990s growth rate in the Midwest to fall to 2.3 percent, but it also reduces the growth rate of the 1980s. The rise of some midwestern cities is an interesting feature of urban growth in the 1990s.

In the 1990s cities in the East had the slowest growth—often negative growth. In both the 1980s and the 1990s the average eastern city shrank by around 1 percent. No eastern cities are high-fliers, and most eastern cities' populations declined. The eastern cities' growth performance in the 1990s looks a bit better if their growth rates are averaged weighting by 1990 population. In that case, cities grew by 4 percent on average, which reflects the relative success of New York City and Boston.

Why are these regional patterns so strong? One simple explanation is that the growth of the South and West simply reflects the importance of the weather. To examine this hypothesis we first look at the relationship between city growth and average January temperature in a city between 1960 and 1990. Cities with an average daily January temperature of less than 30 degrees Fahrenheit grew by less than 5 percent on average, while cities with a daily January temperature above 50 degrees grew by more than 15 percent (figure 1-1). We can perform a similar exercise for average annual rainfall. Cities with less than fifteen inches of average annual precipitation grew by more than 20 percent on average, while cities with more than forty-five inches of annual precipitation grew by less than 10 percent.

Why is weather so important a determinant of city growth? There are three schools of thought on this issue. The first view is that the spread to the West and South is the continuation of a nearly 400-year process initiated

FIGURE 1-1. Temperature and City Growth

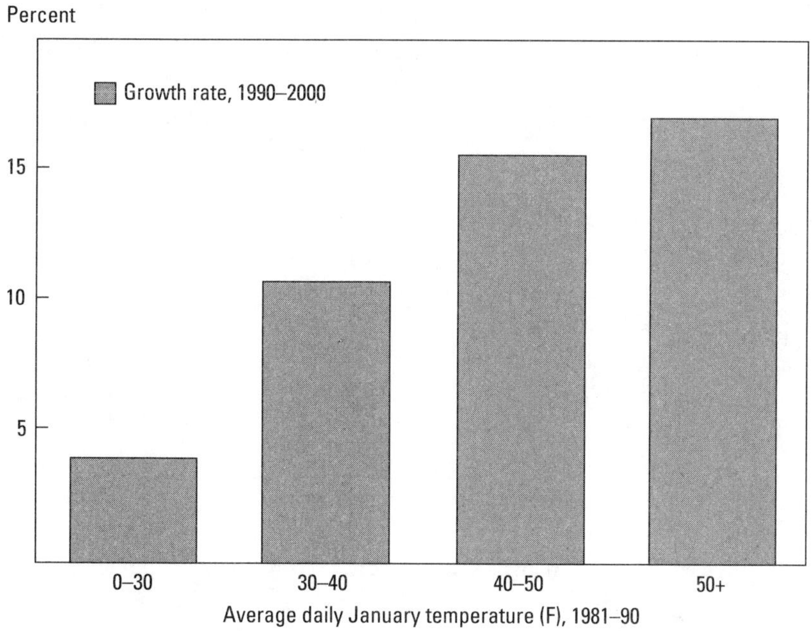

when European settlers originally came to the cold, wet part of the country and continuing as these settlers' descendants and other immigrants steadily spread out southward and westward. Although this view perhaps holds some truth, the South did not experience relative population growth for the eighty years between 1860 and 1940, which does not corroborate the hypothesis of the steady spreading out of the settlers' descendants. A second view is that technological advances made it easier to live and work in hotter climates. The postwar period has seen the rise of the air conditioner and the elimination of malaria in the South. Both of these advances make warmer climates more appealing. A third view is that location decisions in the past were driven primarily by factors driving the productivity of firms. The Midwest was very desirable to companies because of its proximity to the Great Lakes, for example. But as transport costs have fallen, businesses can now locate much more freely, and the residential tastes of consumers have become more dominant.[5] We suspect that all three hypotheses have some truth.

5. See Glaeser, Kolko, and Saiz (forthcoming).

Cities and Human Capital

High-human-capital cities grew in the 1990s, as did cities with wealthier residents. Much of the literature on city growth has focused on cities and human capital.[6] A community's human capital has generally been measured by the median level of schooling in the community or by the percentage of community residents 25 and older with a college education. This literature has repeatedly found that the average skill level in a city is a very good predictor of whether that city's population will rise or fall. Skilled communities rise, and unskilled communities fall. This has been true in every decade going back to the late nineteenth century.[7] The relationship between human capital and growth became even stronger in the 1970s and 1980s than it had been in the 1950s and 1960s,[8] and it appears to have been at least as strong in the 1990s as in earlier decades. From cities with the lowest levels of human capital (less than 15 percent college educated) to cities with the highest levels (more than 25 percent college educated) the average population growth rate increases from 7.5 percent to 16 percent.

Income level is commonly thought to be another measure of human capital. Cities with a median annual household income below $20,000 grew by only 0.3 percent. By comparison, as figure 1-2 shows, cities with median annual household income above $30,000 grew by 18.9 percent. Of course, higher incomes will also be associated with robust labor markets, so the attractiveness of these robust labor markets is another reason that high-income cities are growing. The impact of human capital can also be seen in the effect of the poverty rate on urban growth. A 1 percent increase in the poverty rate is associated with a 1 percent reduction in city population growth during the 1990s. This relationship is about the same as the relationship in the 1980s and corresponds well with results from prior research.[9] Cities with high percentages of poor people tend to lose population.

What causes this relationship between measures of human capital and later growth? One interpretation of the income and poverty numbers is that these figures are just reflecting bad labor market conditions. This is certainly a possibility, but earlier research has strongly suggested that high poverty levels in cities tend to be permanent features of those cities and reflect the city residents' underlying skill distribution more than they do the local labor markets.[10]

6. See Glaeser (1994); Glaeser and others (1995); and Simon and Nardinelli (1996).
7. See Simon and Nardinelli (1996).
8. See Glaeser and others (1995).
9. See Glaeser and others (1995).
10. See Glaeser (1994).

FIGURE 1-2. Income and City Growth

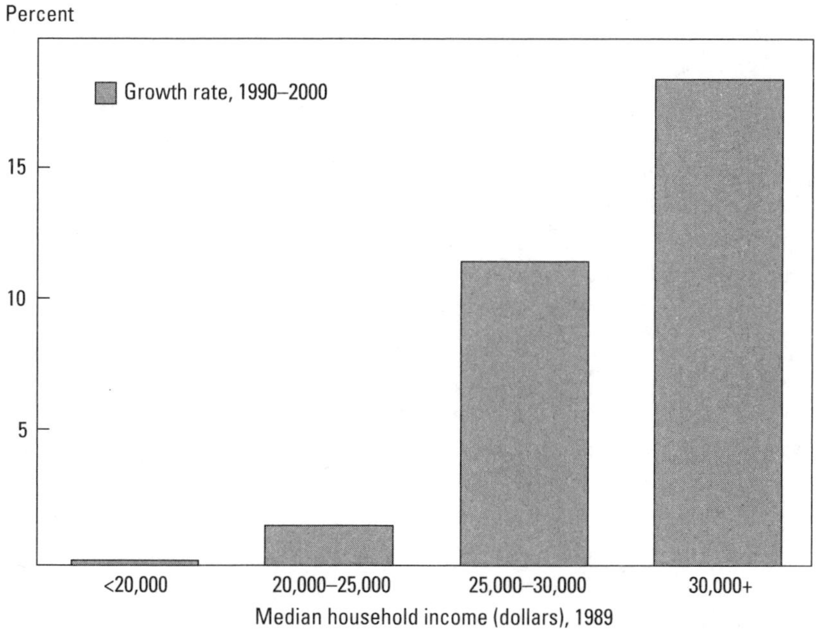

Alternatively, it could be that places with a greater proportion of highly skilled workers have simply gotten more attractive, for various reasons. First, skilled workers may be better at generating new ideas, and these ideas lead to expanding labor market opportunities. Second, people learn from their neighbors, and being around skilled workers may be valuable to prospective residents and may have become even more so as the country enters into a more skill-intensive era. Finally, less-skilled workers may be associated with more social problems, and these social problems may deter prospective residents. Further investigation of this issue is needed.

Industry Mix

Cities with a large manufacturing base grew much more slowly than cities dependent on service industries. Previous research suggests that industry mix is an important determinant of which cities grow and which shrink.[11] In particular, cities that have a large share of their employment in manufacturing will shrink, and cities that are concentrated in services, wholesale and retail trade, or finance, insurance, and real estate will grow. The decline of

11. See Glaeser and others (1995).

manufacturing-based cities in part reflects the general decline of manufacturing in the United States. But this general decline is accompanied by the massive de-urbanization of manufacturing in America.[12] Manufacturing was once centered in American cities. Now it is found in lower-density, less expensive areas. This basic pattern has held up for the 1990s (figure 1-3).

Cities that had more than 20 percent of their labor force in manufacturing grew quite slowly during the 1990s. The average rate of growth for these places was 6.3 percent (5.5 percent if the average is weighted by city population). Cities with moderate levels of manufacturing—between 10 percent and 20 percent of the labor force—grew at an average 12.3 percent rate (10.2 percent if the average is weighted by city population). The growth rate of cities with very little manufacturing, less than 10 percent of the work force, was 13.3 percent (11.9 percent if the average is weighted by city population). The 7 percentage point growth rate gap between cities with significant manufacturing and cities with little manufacturing reflects the consistent movement of people away from the manufacturing centers toward places that specialize in trade and services. This effect is primarily a regional shift representing the move away from the Rust Belt.

Nevertheless, this connection between manufacturing and city growth has gotten much weaker during the postwar period. In the 1980s and 1990s, a city's level of involvement in manufacturing did predict that city's population growth, but the impact was not all that strong and reflected primarily the regional movements in the country. In the 1950s and 1960s, manufacturing's share in a city's economic base strongly predicted urban decline and in fact was one of the most important predictors of decline.[13] In general, industry mix has become somewhat less important as a predictor of city growth.

The one exception to this statement is the odd relationship between population growth during the 1990s and city residents' degree of employment in the health industry (as of 1990). This connection is quite strong—cities with the highest percentage of health services employment grew at least 20 percentage points more slowly than did cities with the least health services employment. This relationship does not come about because cities with bigger health sectors have older residents and therefore have less growth. A slight connection does exist between a city's levels of employment in the health sector and the median age of community residents, but only a very weak connection exists between the median age of community resi-

12. See Glaeser (1998).
13. See Glaeser and others (1995).

FIGURE 1-3. Manufacturing Employment and City Growth

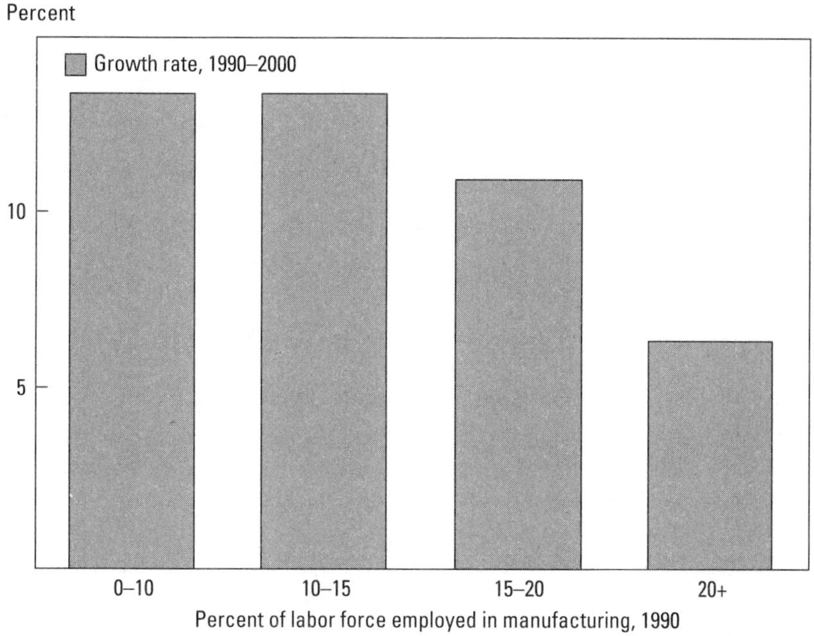

dents and community population growth rates, and in fact the growth rate gap between cities with the oldest and the youngest residents is less than 4 percent. Thus it is really not true that community residents' age drives city growth. Instead, our explanation for this relationship between population growth during the 1990s and city residents' degree of employment in the health industry (as of 1990) is that the health industry is concentrated primarily in poorer places and population has drained away from areas of low human-capital levels.

A final and unsurprising employment fact relates to the connection between city unemployment rates and city growth. The average 1990s population growth rate was less than 3 percent for cities with 1990 unemployment rates greater than 10 percent. The average population growth rate was 21 percent for cities with unemployment rates below 5 percent. Part of this connection stems from the fact that unemployment is related to the human-capital level of the community, and part of the connection stems from the general appeal of communities with robust labor markets.[14]

14. See Blanchard and Katz (1992) for evidence on migration.

Cars and American Cities

Cities built for cars grew, but cities designed for mass transit and for pedestrians tended to shrink As incomes have risen and as automobile technology has improved, cars have become an increasingly important element in American life and in American cities. Within metropolitan areas the flight to the suburbs reflects in part a movement toward auto-dependency and away from mass transit, with people moving first and employment following. A parallel shift can be seen in the movement of people between cities. "Driving cities" have grown, and "public transportation cities" have not (figure 1-4). Population grew by an average of less than 2 percent in cities with less than 65 percent of their commuters driving unaccompanied to their jobs, while other cities grew by an average of more than 12 percent. This phenomenon is not merely another example of regional growth; it survives controlling for regions, as emphasized by a growth comparison between nondriving cities (such as San Francisco) and driving cities (such as Los Angeles) within the same region.

Naturally, this connection can also be seen in the decline of cities oriented toward public transport. Cities with substantial public transportation systems lost population during the 1990s. The average growth rate for those cites in which more than 10 percent of commuters took public transportation to work in 1990 was nearly zero. The average growth rate for those cities in which less than 3 percent of commuters used public transportation in 1990 was almost 17 percent. A huge shift has occurred away from the older walking-oriented and public-transport-oriented cities of the past toward the driving-oriented cities of today. Of course, certain public transport cities such as New York and Chicago were somewhat exceptional during the 1990s in that they actually grew, but they were balanced by shrinking cities like Pittsburgh and Philadelphia.

It may be that the rise of driving cities represents an even broader phenomenon of an urban life cycle. It is possible that in every age, new technologies have come along that have made some of the features of older cities somewhat obsolete. As a result, people have moved to newer cities built around different technologies.

In the case of the American cities in the 1990s, urban age as determined by housing stock is one of the most powerful determinants of city growth. The average growth rate is nearly 20 percent for those cities in which less than 10 percent of the housing stock was constructed before 1939. The average growth rate is only 5.9 percent for cities in which between 10 percent and 40 percent of the building stock existed before 1939. The average growth rate is −1.2 percent for cities in which more than 40 percent of the building stock

FIGURE 1-4. Commuting by Car and City Growth

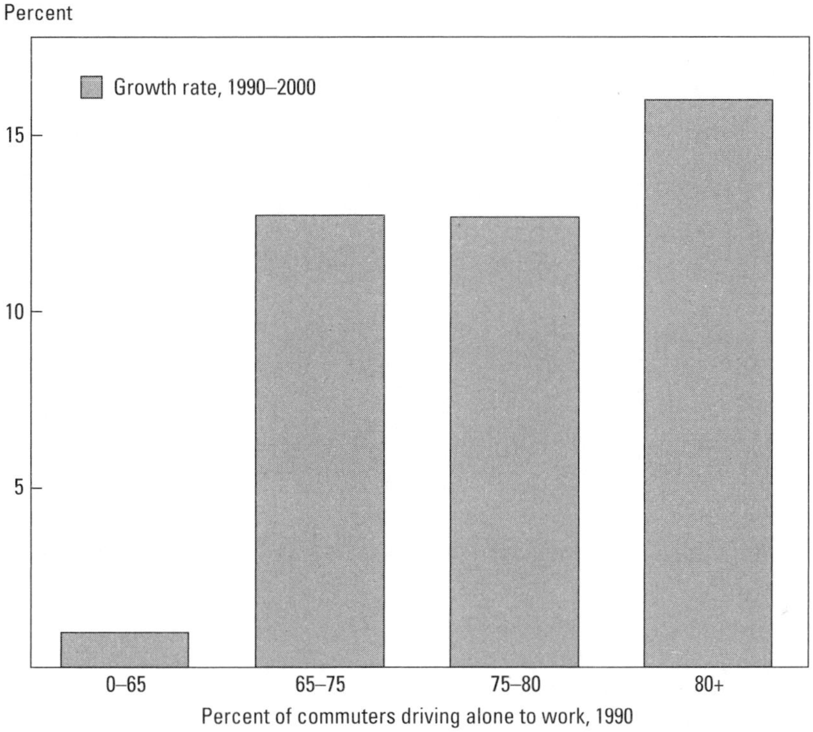

is more than sixty-two years old. Of course, much of the effect of housing stock age comes about because nongrowing cities will tend to have few new houses (almost by definition). As a result, it is useful to check whether this city age result withstands controlling for the previous decade's growth rate. We find that the impact of the age of the building stock gets much weaker but still remains quite significant. It appears to be true that newer cities are replacing older cities—in part because newer cities are oriented toward cars, not toward public transportation or walking.

Immigrants and City Growth

The relationship between city growth and the share of the population that is foreign born has not been examined in the previous literature, but given the large wave of immigrants into the United States during the 1990s, it is important to ask whether cities that attract immigrants have grown faster than those that do not.

Figure 1-5 compares average growth rates for four classes of cities: cities with less than 3 percent foreign-born residents as of 1990, cities with between 3 percent and 8 percent foreign-born residents in 1990, cities with between 8 percent and 15 percent foreign-born residents in 1990, and cities with more than 15 percent foreign-born residents in 1990. The average overall city population growth rates for the four classes are 5.3 percent, 10.9 percent, 17.5 percent, and 12.1 percent respectively. When these averages are found by weighting city population, they are 4.8 percent, 7.5 percent, 19.5 percent, and 9.7 percent respectively. The basic pattern is one in which cities with more foreign-born residents as of 1990 generally grew more quickly than did cities with fewer foreign-born residents, although the cities with the highest percentages of foreign-born residents did not grow the most.

What explains the connection between attracting immigrants and later growth? Perhaps the presence of immigrants appears to increase growth rates only because immigrant communities have been better measured as the census has improved its counting; according to this view the connection between growth and immigrant population is merely an artificial feature of the data. A second hypothesis is that growing cities simply tend to attract more foreign-born people, in much the same way as growing cities tend to attract other domestic migrants. Or the presence of immigrant communities in 1990 may have made the area more attractive to newer immigrants, making the cities that attracted those immigrants grow relatively more quickly than other cities as a result of the large immigration waves of the 1990s. Further investigation of this effect is an important area for future research.

CONCLUSION

Cities have displayed remarkable diversity in their rates of population growth during the 1990s. A full quarter of the group of 195 U.S. cities with more than 100,000 people in 1990 grew by more than 16 percent during the decade. A full quarter of that same group of cities also declined. A massive amount of heterogeneity exists within the growth spectrum between Las Vegas with its 85 percent growth rate and St. Louis with its 13 percent decline. But within this diversity certain patterns seem clear, and these patterns force us to recognize the similarities between the 1990s and earlier decades.

The basic regional patterns remained the same: the West grew most, the South grew significantly, and the Northeast and the Midwest stagnated.

FIGURE 1-5. Immigrants and City Growth

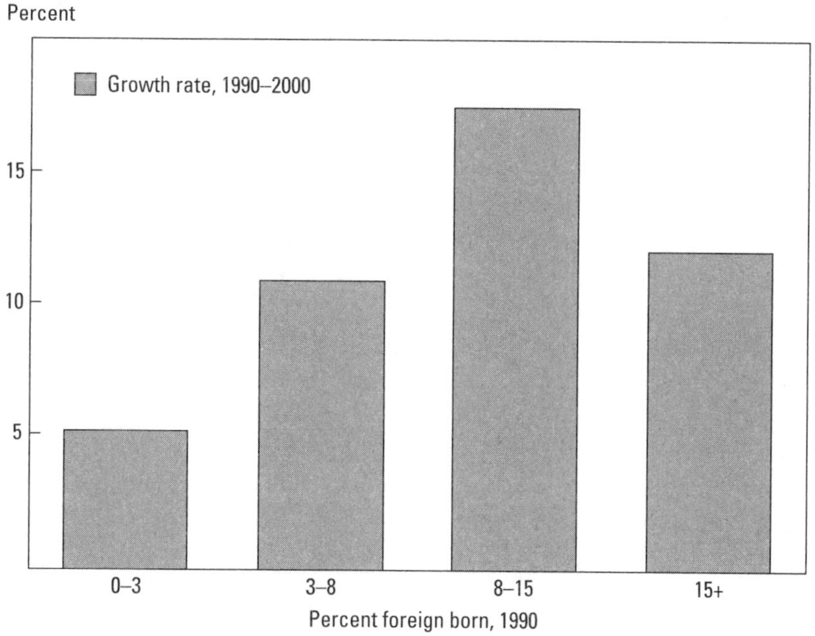

These regional patterns can be understood as the result of the tyranny of the weather. Warm, dry places grew. Cold, wet places declined. This has been true throughout the postwar period.

Beyond cities' regional location and climate, the most important factor driving the population growth of a city is its human-capital base. Cities with skilled workers or high median incomes grew, and cities with high levels of poverty shrank. This finding suggests that leaders who want to encourage growth in their communities need to think about whether their policies are attracting skilled workers to live there.

Industry mix still matters. Manufacturing cities are still doing badly, and although this seems to be less important than it once was, apparently there is still reason for skepticism about the idea that mayors will be able to revitalize their cities by luring big manufacturing plants. Surprisingly, cities with big health industries did particularly badly during the 1990s, a result that is difficult to understand.

Cities built to accommodate lots of cars and lots of driving gained residents; cities built for public transportation generally did not. This finding could reflect a larger trend in which older cities are losing residents and newer cities are gaining them. The age of the city's population does not have an impact on city growth, but the age of the building stock does, and the old cities did quite poorly during the 1990s. This phenomenon generally captures the remarkable transformation of the American city as it moves from the walking-based city of the nineteenth century to the car-based environment of the present and future.

Immigrant cities did relatively well, particularly those cities with moderate-sized immigrant populations. The cities with the very highest immigration levels were actually less successful in terms of their overall population growth than were those cities with foreign-born populations ranging between 5 percent and 15 percent of the total.

Overall, the pattern of city growth in the 1990s shows remarkable continuity with previous decades. Growth among the largest cities has been higher than in previous decades, but the overall patterns look quite similar. The same factors that explained city growth in the 1980s predicted city growth in the 1990s. Although economists may have trouble predicting long-term movements in the gross national product, we can do a little better in predicting changes in city populations.

REFERENCES

Blanchard, O. J., and L. Katz. 1992. "Regional Evolutions." *Brookings Papers on Economic Activity* 1: 1–61.

Gaspar, J., and E. Glaeser. 1997. "Information Technology and the Future of Cities." *Journal of Urban Economics* 43: 136–56.

Glaeser, E. 1998. "Are Cities Dying?" *Journal of Economic Perspectives* 12 (2):139–60.

———. 1994. "Cities, Information, and Economic Growth." *Cityscape* 1:1: 9–47. U.S. Department of Housing and Urban Development, Office of Policy Development and Research.

Glaeser, E., J. Kolko, and A. Saiz. Forthcoming. "Consumer City." *Journal of Economic Geography.*

———, J. A. Scheinkman, and A. Shleifer. 1995. "Economic Growth in a Cross-Section of Cities." *Journal of Monetary Economics* 36: 117–43.

Simon, C. J., and C. Nardinelli. 1996. "The Talk of the Town: Human Capital, Information, and the Growth of English Cities, 1861–1961." *Explorations in Economic History* 33:3: 384–413.

2

Gaining but Losing Ground

Population Change in Large Cities and Their Suburbs

ALAN BERUBE

The results of Census 2000 regarding population change in the 1990s have fueled a great deal of excitement among city policymakers and observers. The terms "comeback" and "urban renaissance" have been used to describe cities' population performance during the decade. The cities that have drawn the most attention are those that had fallen on hard times in the 1980s but posted a population gain in the 1990s—Chicago, Atlanta, and Denver foremost among them.

A closer look at the numbers, however, suggests a more complicated and somewhat more sobering story behind population change in large cities in the 1990s. The present analysis finds that the story of the urban "recovery" during the past decade does not capture the diversity of large-city experience in the 1990s and fails to place cities within their metropolitan context. Although the largest cities grew during the decade, the growth pattern was quite uneven, with more than a quarter of cities stagnating or losing population. More important, although most cities experienced population growth, such growth was far outpaced by the population growth of their suburbs. There also emerged important regional patterns in city and metropolitan growth and decline.

METHODS

The present chapter uses data from the Census 2000 Redistricting Data Summary File to describe 1990s population trends in the 100 largest U.S. cities and in their suburbs. The cities analyzed in this chapter are 1990's

100 largest "places" as defined by the Census Bureau.[1] Suburban population figures represent the population in the entire PMSA (primary metropolitan statistical area) or MSA (metropolitan statistical area) (as defined by the Office of Management and Budget, OMB) minus the population of the central city (or cities, in the case of metros containing more than one city in the largest 100). The definitions of PMSAs and MSAs in effect for Census 2000 are used consistently in 1990 and 2000. In 1990 these largest 100 cities had populations ranging from 171,000 (Newport News) to 7.3 million (New York City). The top 100 cities are measured as of their 1990 population levels (as opposed to their 2000 populations) to avoid biasing the 1990–2000 analysis toward fast-growing cities.[2]

Cities are categorized not only by their size but also by their geographic location within the United States. For this purpose the survey uses the state groupings shown in figure 2-1. With one exception, these groupings are the equivalent of census divisions, which are components of the four census regions.[3] Using census divisions enables a somewhat more nuanced view of change, especially in the U.S. South, which stretches from Virginia to Texas and encompasses three census divisions.

The cities studied are not distributed throughout the United States in exactly the same way as the population at large. Table 2-1 shows how cities of different size among the top 100 are distributed regionally. The Pacific and West South Central regions were home to only 26 percent of the nation's population but to 37 of the largest 100 cities; California (15 cities) and Texas (10 cities) dominate within these two regions. In contrast, states of the Northeast (including Maryland and Delaware) were home to 23 percent of the nation's population but to only 10 of the 100 largest cities. Other areas of the United States, however, contained shares of the nation's population similar to their shares of the country's 100 largest cities.[4]

1. A "place" is a concentration of population either legally bounded as an incorporated place or delineated for statistical purposes as a census designated place (CDP). The 100 cities analyzed in this survey include places defined as cities, consolidated cities (Augusta-Richmond [Georgia], Nashville, and Indianapolis), independent cities (St. Louis and Baltimore), and CDPs (Honolulu).

2. The 100 largest cities as of 2000 are the same as the 100 largest as of 1990, with the exception of the bottom six cities in table 2A-1. The cities that replaced those 6 in the top 100 are Chesapeake (Virginia); Fremont (California); Glendale (Arizona); Irving (Texas); Plano (Texas); and Scottsdale (Arizona).

3. The analysis makes one modification to the census divisions: New England states, Middle Atlantic states, and Maryland and Delaware are labeled as "Northeast" states. This permits Baltimore and Boston to be considered alongside eastern seaboard neighbors like New York and Philadelphia.

4. Some 14 small states contained no cities in the largest 100 in 1990: Connecticut, Delaware, Idaho, Maine, Montana, New Hampshire, North Dakota, Rhode Island, South

FIGURE 2-1. U.S. Regional Classifications

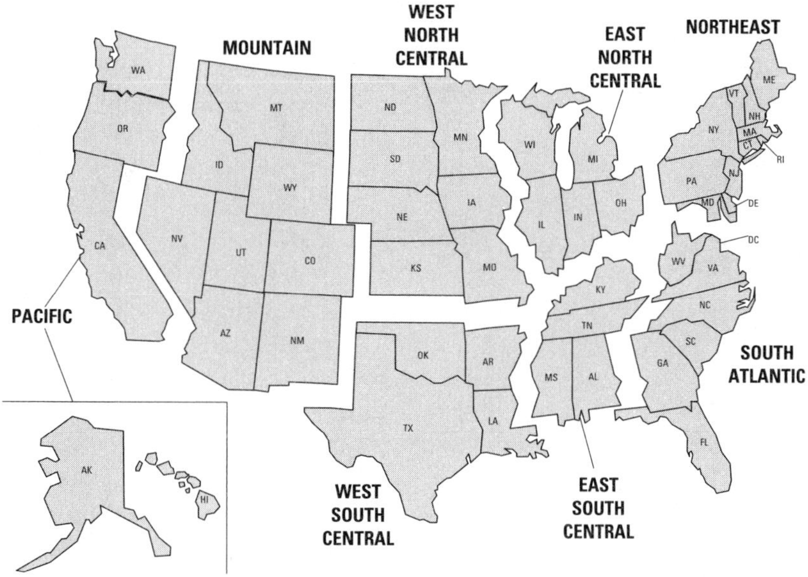

These cities are distributed unevenly throughout the range of population as well. Table 2-1 shows that only 8 were "metropolises" with populations exceeding 1 million in 1990; about half had populations under 300,000 (table 2A-1 ranks all 100 cities by their 2000 populations). Nonetheless, the 100 places studied are of a size that conforms with general notions of what constitutes a city. Most have familiar names, but others are Sun Belt "boomburbs" as described by Robert Lang and Patrick A. Simmons—places like Garland (Texas), Hialeah (Florida), and Mesa (Arizona) that emerged as cities in the late twentieth century and are already the size of older cities like Dayton and Newark.[5] Other analyses have taken different approaches to defining *city* that include a wider variety of states as well as smaller census *places*, some of which may not be familiar to the average observer.[6]

Carolina, South Dakota, Utah, Vermont, West Virginia, and Wyoming. These states represented only 7 percent of the U.S. population in 1990.

5. Lang and Simmons (2001).

6. For instance, HUD's annual *State of the Cities* report focuses on the 100 largest U.S. cities, plus the largest cities in states not containing one of the 100 largest cities. This set includes places like Burlington, Vermont, with fewer than 50,000 people. Other studies focus on places with population greater than 100,000, of which there were 195 in 1990; this set includes less recognizable cities like Moreno Valley (California); Sterling Heights (Michigan);

TABLE 2-1. Regional Distribution of Largest 100 Cities, by City Size

	Number of cities								
City population (1990)	*North-east*	*South Atlantic*	*East North Central*	*East South Central*	*West North Central*	*West South Central*	*Mountain*	*Pacific*	*Total*
Over 1 million	2	—	2	—	—	2	—	2	8
500,000 to 1 million	2	2	4	1	—	2	1	3	15
300,000 to 500,000	2	4	2	1	5	5	3	6	28
200,000 to 300,000	3	5	2	3	1	3	4	5	26
Under 200,000	1	5	3	3	2	4	—	5	23
Total	10	16	13	8	8	16	8	21	100
Share of U.S. population (percent)	23	15	17	6	7	11	7	15	100

Source: Based on U.S. Bureau of the Census (2001).

FINDINGS

The analysis produced several interesting findings as follows.

- Overall the largest 100 cities grew at a faster rate in the 1990s than they did in the 1980s, although not all cities shared in the expansion.
- Only 5 of the top 100 cities—Atlanta, Chicago, Denver, Memphis, and Yonkers—turned a 1980s population loss into a 1990s population gain.
- The 100 largest cities grew only half as fast as their suburbs; growth in 80 of the top 100 cities was outpaced by growth in the suburbs.
- Average population growth in suburbs of the Southeast was three times that of the region's central cities, while cities in the West tended to keep pace with population growth of their suburbs.

Growth and Decline

The total population of the 100 largest cities grew by only 6.3 percent in the 1980s versus 9.1 percent in the 1990s. A greater number of these cities experienced gains in population during the 1990s than during the previous decade: only 63 cities gained population in the 1980s versus 74 cities in the 1990s (figure 2-2).

and Overland Park (Kansas) and is weighted somewhat more toward California and Texas than the top 100 cities. See Glaeser and Shapiro (2001). Still others focus on the largest metropolitan areas and their central cities. The metro areas studied are generally of significant size, but their central cities vary greatly in population, and some of the largest metros (including four in New Jersey) have no central cities at all.

FIGURE 2-2. Population Change Rates in the 100 Largest Cities, 1980s versus 1990s

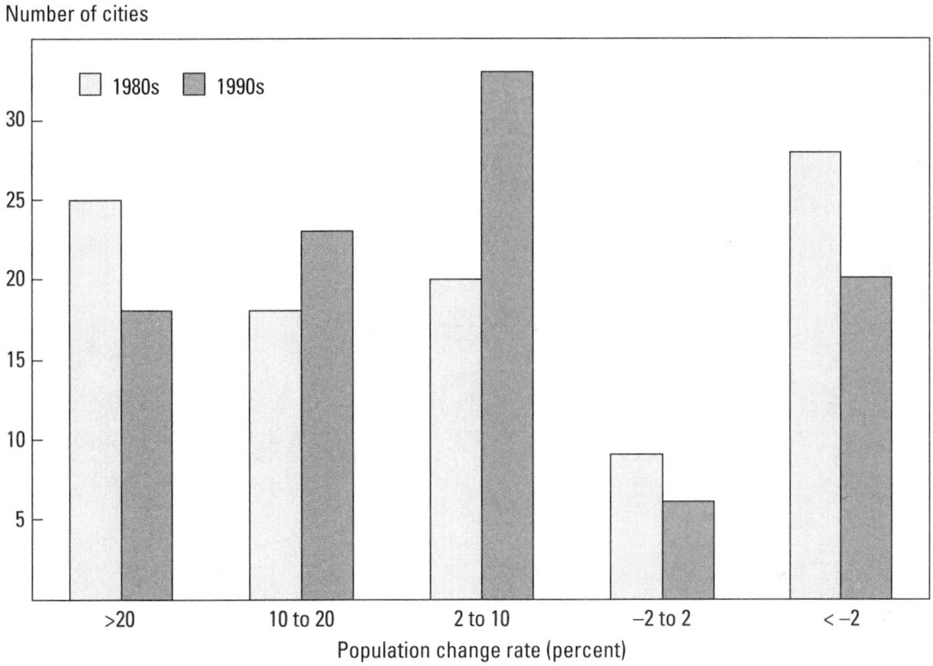

Source: Based on U.S. Bureau of the Census (2001).

But notably, the 1980s saw a greater number of cities make rapid population gains of 20 percent or more. As a result, average population growth in the 1980s among the top 100 cities (11.2 percent) was faster than in the 1990s (9.8 percent). In the 1990s, a larger share of the top 100 cities experienced modest population growth of between 2 percent and 10 percent.

Not all cities shared in the 1990s expansion. Of 1990's largest 100 cities, 20 actually lost population during the 1990s, and 6 did not grow at all. This performance was an improvement vis-à-vis the 37 cities in the 1980s that declined or did not grow, but the fact remains that slightly more than one out of every four large U.S. cities failed to grow during the longest national economic expansion on record.

Regional patterns told much of the story. Figure 2-3 shows average population change for the top 100 cities by region. Many declining cities were found in the Northeast and the eastern states of the Midwest—9 of the 20 cities were in Ohio, Pennsylvania, and upstate New York alone. Nonetheless, nearly every region of the country was home to one or more

FIGURE 2-3. Average Population Change for 100 Largest Cities by U.S. Region, 1990–2000

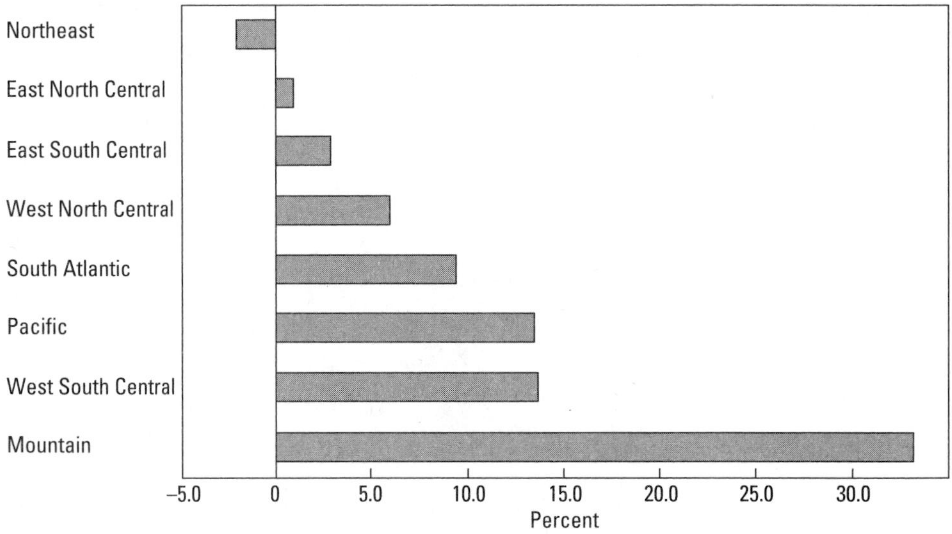

Source: See figure 2-2.

cities that posted a loss or no gain in population during the 1990s. Many of these cities were clustered in one or two states in each region (appendix 2A-2 shows all 100 cities ranked by their population change during the decade).

While it may come as no surprise that the Northeast and Midwest experienced slower (and sometimes negative) population change in their cities, a number of cities in fast-growing regions also experienced population loss. Eight of the 26 declining/stagnating cities were in the U.S. Southeast, including two each in Virginia and Alabama—states with populations that grew by 14 percent and 10 percent respectively in the 1990s. In Louisiana, both New Orleans and Shreveport posted population losses. Missouri, too, was home to two declining cities, although the state itself grew by 9 percent during the 1990s. Only the booming Mountain region had no large cities that stagnated or lost population during the decade.

Cities with the largest population gains in the 1990s were not as geographically widespread. The eighteen cities in which population grew by 20 percent or more were confined to four of eight U.S. regions—the Mountain, South Atlantic, Pacific, and central Southwest states. Six of the eight Mountain cities were in this category; Albuquerque's robust 16.6 percent growth in the 1990s represented the smallest population increase among the eight. All three North Carolina cities (Charlotte, Raleigh, and Greensboro) experienced very strong growth, as did smaller cities in central and southern California—Bakersfield, Anaheim, Glendale, and Fresno.

Population Turnaround or More of the Same?

An extremely strong relationship exists in city growth levels from one decade to the next, as Edward L. Glaeser and Jesse M. Shapiro have noted. This observation clearly held true in the 1980s and 1990s for the largest 100 cities. During the 1990s the large majority of these cities continued on their population growth/loss trajectory from the 1980s.

The urban "comeback," as defined by population loss in the 1980s and population gain in the 1990s, occurred in only 5 of the top 100 cities—Denver, Memphis, Atlanta, Chicago, and Yonkers. To be sure, these cities experienced rather dramatic turnarounds from significant losses to significant gains and therefore merit attention as examples of renewed urban health. Still, these "comeback cities" proved the exception to the rule.

Table 2-2 demonstrates the relationship between the 1980s and the 1990s in terms of large-city growth/decline. Of the top 100 cities, fully 83 followed the same population path in the 1990s (growth, decline, or no change) as in the 1980s. Notably, among these cities the average population changes of the 1990s were not considerably different from those of the 1980s. Among the 20 cities that lost population in both decades, the average population loss in each decade was about the same, 7 percent. Among the 62 cities that gained in both decades, growth in the 1980s was actually faster, 20 percent versus 16 percent.

The difference between the 1980s and 1990s in terms of overall city population change was driven by cities that "tipped" from loss to "no change" or from "no change" to gain. Table 2-2 shows that the five "comeback" cities lost almost 6 percent of their residents in the 1980s on average but added nearly 8 percent in the 1990s. The seven cities that stagnated in the 1980s but grew in the 1990s turned their earlier negligible population gains into increases of nearly 7 percent on average.[7] And four cities that lost more than 6 percent in the 1980s gained back a small amount of population in the 1990s. These cities are among those considered to have "come back" in the 1990s by virtue of their population trend.

In addition, as noted by observers such as Simmons and Lang, cities like Cleveland, Richmond, New Orleans, and Akron lost population at a slower

7. These seven cities were Baton Rouge, Des Moines, Fort Wayne, Minneapolis, St. Paul, St. Petersburg, and Tulsa.

TABLE 2-2. Population Change in the 100 Largest Cities, 1990s versus 1980s

Change in 1990s	*Change in 1980s*	*Number of cities*	*Average change in 1990s (percent)*	*Average change in 1980s (percent)*
+	+	62	16.0	19.7
+	0	7	6.6	0.4
+	–	5	7.8	–5.8
0	+	1	1.1	3.4
0	0	1	1.7	0.1
0	–	4	0.8	–6.4
–	+	none	–	–
–	0	none	–	–
–	–	20	–6.9	–7.3

Source: Based on 1980–2000 census data.
+ more than 2 percent increase.
0 –2 percent to 2 percent change.
– more than 2 percent decrease.

rate in the 1990s than in previous decades, a possible sign of improved city health.[8] Yet for each large city that lost a smaller share of its population in the 1990s than in the 1980s, there was a city in which the 1990s population loss was greater—Baltimore, Buffalo, Cincinnati, and Milwaukee are examples. (Additional evidence related to the "urban comeback" story is discussed later in the chapter.)

Suburban Growth Outpaced City Growth

The top 100 cities grew faster in population in the 1990s than in the 1980s, and a large number of them experienced growth. But decentralization of the population was still the dominant overall trend. Nearly every one of the top 100 cities grew considerably more slowly than its surrounding suburbs. The pattern of faster suburban growth held for different-sized cities as well as for cities with either growing or declining populations. But the interesting relationships that emerged between city and suburban growth suggest a degree of common metropolitan destiny.

The bottom of table 2A-2 shows that the top 100 cities (with the exception of Anchorage, which has no suburbs) grew by an average of almost 10 percent each in the 1990s and as a whole grew by a little more than 9 percent. Their suburbs, however, grew roughly twice as fast—by 21 percent on average and by 18 percent in total.

8. Simmons and Lang (2001).

Faster suburban growth was a widespread phenomenon. Overall, 80 suburbs grew faster than their central cities, six grew at about the same rate, and 13 grew more slowly (table 2A-2). Absolute difference between central city growth and suburban growth was greatest in El Paso, where the suburbs grew by more than half but the city grew by less than 10 percent. The suburbs of the "comeback" cities grew very quickly compared with their central cities; disparities ranged from Denver, where suburbs grew roughly twice as fast as the central city (37 percent versus 18.6 percent) to Atlanta, where suburbs grew almost eight times as fast as the city (44 percent versus 5.7 percent).

Some 20 of the top 100 cities lost population in the 1990s, but none of their suburbs did. Several suburbs, including a number in the Southeast (such as Jackson, Norfolk, Birmingham, and Washington), enjoyed significant growth despite population declines in their central cities. Only three suburban areas, all located in a narrow band of the Rust Belt (namely, the suburbs surrounding Buffalo, Dayton, and Pittsburgh), failed to grow during the decade.

Although nearly every suburban area experienced growth, that growth was not independent of central city growth. Population change in suburbs and city was linked. Rapidly growing central cities were generally located in rapidly growing metro areas, and cities in which population stagnated or fell were in slower-growing metro areas. A fairly strong correlation (R=0.68) exists between population change in central cities and in suburbs during the decade. Figure 2-4 shows this correlation graphically, displaying average city and suburban growth rates for different categories of city growth. It indicates that average population growth in the suburbs of declining cities was about one-third of that in the suburbs of high-flying cities where population grew more than 20 percent. Thus population change in suburbs and city was interrelated, although the suburbs of declining cities still managed to post considerable gains.

Regional Patterns in City-Suburb Growth Differences

A significant difference in population growth between city and suburb can serve as a first-order indicator of metropolitan sprawl, which is often characterized by rapid growth at the fringe of a region coupled with slow growth or decline at the core. Of course, population change at the aggregate suburban level reveals little about whether growth is occurring in existing communities close to the urban core or in previously undeveloped land at the rural edge of the region, but nonetheless, from the analysis of population

FIGURE 2-4. Average Central City and Suburban Population Change by City Growth Category, 1990–2000

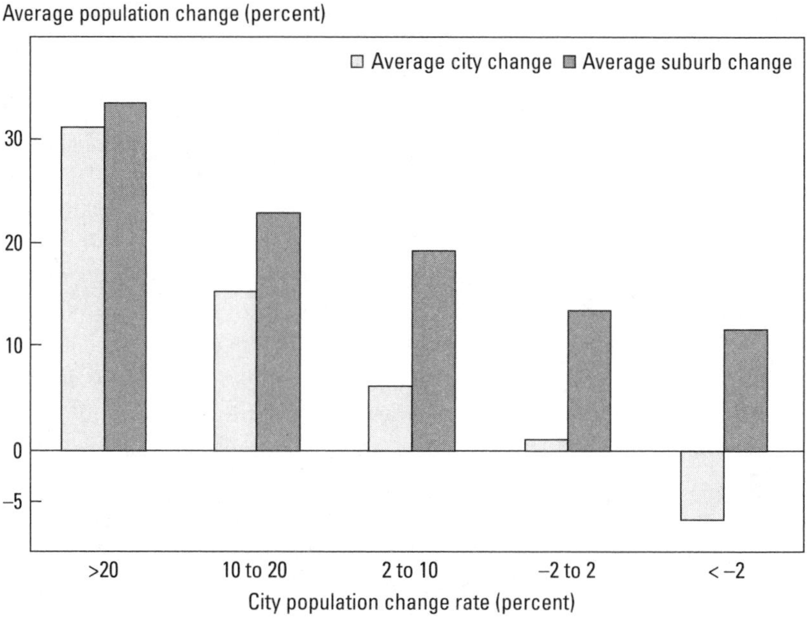

Source: See figure 2-2.

change in the largest 100 cities and their suburbs, interesting patterns emerge that point to differing growth pressures among regions.

Specifically, cities in the Southeast lagged the farthest behind their suburbs in growth. Meanwhile, in the Northeast and eastern Midwest, suburbs experienced population gains at the same time that many of their cities lost residents or stagnated in population. And West Coast cities were more likely to keep pace with population change in their suburbs.

Growth in cities of the Southeast trailed that in the suburbs by the widest margins. As table 2-3 shows, in the South Atlantic states, the average suburb grew 13.5 percentage points faster than its central city. In the East South Central states, suburbs grew by nearly one-fourth on average, while the average city grew by only 3 percent. Overall, average population growth in suburbs of the Southeast was more than three times that in the central cities.

These disparities, as noted earlier, are in part the result of population declines in a number of cities of the Southeast despite significant suburban growth. However, several metros in the Southeast followed the average trend of slow growth in the city and rapid growth in the suburbs. The cities of Mobile and Augusta-Richmond grew by 1.3 percent and 4.4 percent,

TABLE 2-3. Average City and Suburb Population Change by U.S. Region, 1990–2000

Region	Number of cities	Average city change (percent)	Average suburb change (percent)	Suburb advantage over city (percent)
Northeast (NE)	10	–2.1	8.0	10.1
South Atlantic (SA)	16	9.4	22.9	13.5
East North Central (ENC)	13	0.9	12.7	11.8
East South Central (ESC)	8	2.9	23.5	20.6
West North Central (WNC)	8	6.0	15.9	9.9
West South Central (WSC)	16	13.7	25.9	12.2
Mountain (M)	8	33.2	46.8	13.6
Pacific (P)[a]	22	13.5	17.0	3.6
All metros	99	9.8	20.8	11.0

Source: See table 2-1.

a. Anchorage, AK, is excluded because the city encompasses the entire OMB-defined metropolitan area.

respectively, while their suburbs boomed by 22 percent and 24 percent. Even the city of Nashville, which grew by an above average 12 percent rate, was far outpaced by its suburbs, where population surged by 38 percent.[9]

Metro areas in the northern United States were also home to striking growth disparities. The average large-city population of the Northeast states declined in the 1990s and that of the East North Central states stagnated, but the suburbs of the Northeast and East North Central cities grew by 8 percent and 12.7 percent respectively. Forthcoming long-form data from Census 2000 will help to reveal the extent to which growth in these suburbs is the result of families' leaving the cities or of immigrants' settling into the suburbs instead of the cities.[10]

It was in the Pacific states, California in particular, that city and suburban population change were most closely related. Table 2-3 shows that population change in the 22 Pacific cities among the top 100 averaged 13.5 percent. These cities grew only slightly more slowly than their suburbs, where population increased by 17 percent during the decade. Of the six cities that grew at roughly the same rate as their suburbs, three were in California: Los Angeles, San Francisco, and Long Beach (table 2A-2). Another four California cities (San Diego, Santa Ana, Stockton, and Fresno) grew at rates

9. Fulton and others (2001) also found that while the West averaged 3.6 new residents for each new acre of urbanized land between 1982 and 1997, the South averaged only 1.4. Of the ten metropolitan areas with the greatest loss in density (population per acre of urbanized land) during that period, three were located in Alabama.

10. For an overview of immigrant settlement patterns in the suburbs of the Washington, D.C., area, see Singer and others (2001).

within 5 percentage points of their suburbs, and 4 more were among the 13 cities that actually grew faster than their suburbs (Anaheim, San Jose, Glendale, and Bakersfield). During the 1982–97 period, note Fulton and others, metropolitan areas in the West were the most likely to add urbanized land at a rate commensurate with their population growth; the 2000 population figures suggest that population growth in their urban cores is one of the reasons.[11]

CONCLUSION

The evidence presented in this chapter confirms that suburbanization of the nation remained alive and well in the 1990s, with the largest cities growing at only half the rate of their suburbs. Even so, the notion of an urban "turnaround" in comparison with prior decades proliferated through much of the popular press in 2001.[12] The number of large cities that turned a population loss in the 1980s into a population gain in the 1990s was in fact relatively small, but the size of these changes and the size of the cities in which some of those changes occurred (Chicago, Denver, Atlanta) helped to fuel that notion. The results from other large cities that did not experience a true "turnaround"—gainers like New York and Boston and decliners like Philadelphia and Washington—may also have contributed to these perceptions, because census estimates set low expectations for these cities.

Census 1990 Undercounts and Intercensal Underestimates

Each year, the Census Bureau produces population estimates for all local jurisdictions in the United States, including central cities. These intercensal population estimates are used extensively in the public and private sectors for planning, funding allocation, regulatory actions, and the development of data sources used for business marketing and site location. Perhaps most important, these estimates act as indicators of central city health, offering local officials a glimpse at population change on a year-to-year basis in the absence of an actual census enumeration.

An estimate, however, is only as good as the baseline data from which it is derived. Evidence from the 1999 Census Bureau population estimates for

11. Fulton and others (2001).

12. See, for instance, Karen Branch-Brioso, "Stemming the Flight to the Suburbs: Some Cities Begin Rebirth with Young Families," *St. Louis Post-Dispatch* April 29, 2001, p. A1; David Firestone, "The Slowing Growth of Suburbia: Cities Are Denser, Metro Fringes Are More Detached," *Chicago Tribune*, May 5, 2001, p. 23; Gene Marlowe, "City Dwellers Coming Back from the Edge," *Tampa Tribune*, May 30, 2001, p. 11; and Eric Schmitt, "Cities and Their Suburbs Are Seen Growing as Units," *New York Times*, July 10, 2001, p. A10.

large cities suggests that the 1990 decennial census (the basis for intercensal estimates) undercounted city population relative to Census 2000—and by significant amounts in many cities. The 1999 population estimates for the 100 largest cities indicate that in 70 cities, the estimates undercount the census-enumerated 2000 population by more than 2 percent. In only 13 cities did the estimates *overcount* 2000 population by the same degree.[13] Underestimates were not confined to fast-growing cities: cities with large 1990s population gains, such as Dallas, Denver, and Las Vegas, do show up among the places with the largest underestimates, but so do Boston, New York, Philadelphia, and Washington—cities with only modest gains as well as declines. For some of the cities with the largest underestimates, table 2-4 displays projected and actual population in 2000 and the difference between the two. Boston, Chicago, Memphis, Minneapolis, New York, and Oakland were all estimated to have lost population or not to have grown, yet the 2000 count revealed considerable population gains in these cities. Based on the estimates, Philadelphia and Washington experienced double-digit population losses, but their actual losses according to Census 2000 were much less dramatic.

City population turnaround was not particularly widespread, but many cities—especially older, larger ones—did exceed the expectations set by these intercensal estimates. Thus at the time the Census 2000 population counts were released in April 2001, many cities that did not actually "turn around" had reason to perceive that they did. The extensive underestimates call into question the accuracy of the Census 1990 enumeration in large cities and raise uncertainty about the degree to which population gains in the 1990s reflect a better overall count by Census 2000 rather than true population growth in the cities.[14]

The Larger Picture

Whatever the size of the role that the 1990 count played in determining the figures for population change in cities during the 1990s decade, the results from Census 2000 reflect healthy growth in some cities and a continued

13. For each city, the 1999 estimate is projected forward to 2000 using the annualized growth rate implied by the difference between the estimate and the Census 1990 population count.

14. For instance, New York City's Census 2000 population count was bolstered by address list updates submitted to the bureau by the city's planning department; 370,000 households were added as a result. Most of these households were probably there in 1990 but were missed in that year's decennial count. Janny Scott, "Census Figures May Give City a Bonus Prize," *New York Times,* March 5, 2001, p. A1.

TABLE 2-4. Intercensal Population Underestimates in Large Cities, 1990–2000

	Population					Population change	
City	1990 actual	2000 estimate[a]	2000 actual	Difference	As percent of actual	Estimate 1990–2000	Actual 1990–2000
Boston	574,283	553,173	589,141	35,968	6.1	–3.7	2.6
Chicago	2,783,726	2,800,758	2,896,016	95,258	3.3	0.6	4.0
Dallas	1,006,877	1,084,207	1,188,580	104,373	8.8	7.7	18.0
Denver	467,610	503,483	554,636	51,153	9.2	7.7	18.6
Memphis	610,337	605,641	650,100	44,459	6.8	–0.8	6.5
Minneapolis	368,383	351,768	382,618	30,850	8.1	–4.5	3.9
New York	7,322,564	7,439,989	8,008,278	568,289	7.1	1.6	9.4
Oakland	372,242	364,437	399,484	35,047	8.8	–2.1	7.3
Philadelphia	1,585,577	1,400,072	1,517,550	117,478	7.7	–11.7	–4.3
Washington	606,900	510,055	572,059	62,004	10.8	–16.0	–5.7

Source: See table 2-1; 1999 census population estimates.

a. Estimated 1999 population multiplied by annualized 1990–99 growth rate.

decline in others, against the backdrop of a metropolitan America that is increasingly suburban in character. During the 1990s there emerged important regional trends in growth and decline that remind us to distinguish between the Akrons and Anaheims in describing the state of urban America.

City and suburb population change is, of course, a blunt instrument with which to measure urban and suburban health. But these population trends do provide a useful foundation for analyzing more detailed information from Census 2000 on the social and economic status of cities, suburbs, and regions.

TABLE 2A-1. One Hundred Largest Cities in 1990, Ranked by 2000 Population

	City	2000 population		City	2000 population
1	New York, NY	8,008,278	51	Santa Ana, CA	337,977
2	Los Angeles, CA	3,694,820	52	Pittsburgh, PA	334,563
3	Chicago, IL	2,896,016	53	Arlington, TX	332,969
4	Houston, TX	1,953,631	54	Cincinnati, OH	331,285
5	Philadelphia, PA	1,517,550	55	Anaheim, CA	328,014
6	Phoenix, AZ	1,321,045	56	Toledo, OH	313,619
7	San Diego, CA	1,223,400	57	Tampa, FL	303,447
8	Dallas, TX	1,188,580	58	Buffalo, NY	292,648
9	San Antonio, TX	1,144,646	59	St. Paul, MN	287,151
10	Detroit, MI	951,270	60	Corpus Christi, TX	277,454
11	San Jose, CA	894,943	61	Aurora, CO	276,393
12	Indianapolis, IN	781,870	62	Raleigh, NC	276,093
13	San Francisco, CA	776,733	63	Newark, NJ	273,546
14	Jacksonville, FL	735,617	64	Lexington-Fayette, KY	260,512
15	Columbus, OH	711,470	65	Anchorage, AK	260,283
16	Austin, TX	656,562	66	Louisville, KY	256,231
17	Baltimore, MD	651,154	67	Riverside, CA	255,166
18	Memphis, TN	650,100	68	St. Petersburg, FL	248,232
19	Milwaukee, WI	596,974	69	Bakersfield, CA	247,057
20	Boston, MA	589,141	70	Stockton, CA	243,771
21	Washington, DC	572,059	71	Birmingham, AL	242,820
22	El Paso, TX	563,662	72	Jersey City, NJ	240,055
23	Seattle, WA	563,374	73	Norfolk, VA	234,403
24	Denver, CO	554,636	74	Baton Rouge, LA	227,818
25	Nashville-Davidson, TN	545,524	75	Hialeah, FL	226,419
26	Charlotte, NC	540,828	76	Lincoln, NE	225,581
27	Fort Worth, TX	534,694	77	Greensboro, NC	223,891
28	Portland, OR	529,121	78	Rochester, NY	219,773
29	Oklahoma City, OK	506,132	79	Akron, OH	217,074
30	Tucson, AZ	486,699	80	Garland, TX	215,768
31	New Orleans, LA	484,674	81	Madison, WI	208,054
32	Las Vegas, NV	478,434	82	Fort Wayne, IN	205,727
33	Cleveland, OH	478,403	83	Montgomery, AL	201,568
34	Long Beach, CA	461,522	84	Shreveport, LA	200,145
35	Albuquerque, NM	448,607	85	Lubbock, TX	199,564
36	Kansas City, MO	441,545	86	Mobile, AL	198,915
37	Fresno, CA	427,652	87	Des Moines, IA	198,682
38	Virginia Beach, VA	425,257	88	Grand Rapids, MI	197,800
39	Atlanta, GA	416,474	89	Richmond, VA	197,790
40	Sacramento, CA	407,018	90	Yonkers, NY	196,086
41	Oakland, CA	399,484	91	Spokane, WA	195,629
42	Mesa, AZ	396,375	92	Augusta-Richmond, GA	195,182
43	Tulsa, OK	393,049	93	Glendale, CA	194,973
44	Omaha, NE	390,007	94	Tacoma, WA	193,556
45	Minneapolis, MN	382,618	95	Huntington Beach, CA	189,594
46	Honolulu, HI	371,657	96	Columbus, GA	185,781
47	Miami, FL	362,470	97	Jackson, MS	184,256
48	Colorado Springs, CO	360,890	98	Little Rock, AR	183,133
49	St. Louis, MO	348,189	99	Newport News, VA	180,150
50	Wichita, KS	344,284	100	Dayton, OH	166,179

Source: Based on U.S. Bureau of the Census (2001).

TABLE 2A-2. Population Change for 100 Largest Central Cities and Their Suburbs

1990 population rank	City[a]	1980 population	1990 population	2000 population	Percent population change: City - 1990s	Percent population change: Suburbs - 1990s
Cities that grew more than 20 percent (18)						
63	Las Vegas, NV	164,674	258,295	478,434	85.2	82.5
98	Bakersfield, CA	105,611	174,820	247,057	41.3	12.5
27	Austin, TX	345,890	465,622	656,562	41.0	55.9
53	Mesa, AZ	152,404	288,091	396,375	37.6	58.7
35	Charlotte, NC	315,474	395,934	540,828	36.6	25.1
9	Phoenix, AZ	785,940	983,403	1,321,045	34.3	58.7
75	Raleigh, NC	150,255	207,951	276,093	32.8	40.8
54	Colorado Springs, CO	215,105	281,140	360,890	28.4	34.7
61	Arlington, TX	160,113	261,721	332,969	27.2	28.1
72	Aurora, CO	158,588	222,103	276,393	24.4	37.0
59	Anaheim, CA	219,494	266,406	328,014	23.1	19.3
10	San Antonio, TX	789,704	935,933	1,144,646	22.3	15.2
89	Greensboro, NC	155,642	183,521	223,891	22.0	18.6
93	Glendale, CA	139,060	180,038	218,812	21.5	7.9
30	Portland, OR	368,148	437,319	529,121	21.0	28.8
47	Fresno, CA	217,491	354,202	427,652	20.7	23.3
85	Hialeah, FL	145,254	188,004	226,419	20.4	19.7
33	Tucson, AZ	330,537	405,390	486,699	20.1	36.5
Average					31.1	33.5
Cities that grew between 10 percent and 20 percent (23)						
4	Houston, TX	1,595,138	1,630,553	1,953,631	19.8	31.5
28	Fort Worth, TX	385,164	447,619	534,694	19.5	28.1
92	Garland, TX	138,857	180,650	215,768	19.4	42.1
99	Fort Wayne, IN	172,391	173,072	205,727	18.9	4.7
26	Denver, CO	492,686	467,610	554,636	18.6	37.0
8	Dallas, TX	904,599	1,006,877	1,188,580	18.0	42.1
81	Lincoln, NE	171,932	191,972	225,581	17.5	14.0
38	Albuquerque, NM	332,920	384,736	448,607	16.6	29.2
48	Omaha, NE	313,939	335,795	390,007	16.1	7.6
15	Jacksonville, FL	571,003	635,230	735,617	15.8	34.4
70	Lexington-Fayette, KY	204,165	225,366	260,512	15.6	21.1
74	Stockton, CA	148,283	210,943	243,771	15.6	18.6
52	Santa Ana, CA	204,023	293,742	337,977	15.1	19.3
69	Anchorage, AK	174,731	226,338	260,283	15.0	
11	San Jose, CA	629,400	782,248	894,943	14.4	10.1
29	Oklahoma City, OK	404,014	444,719	506,132	13.8	12.3
51	Wichita, KS	279,838	304,011	344,284	13.2	10.9
68	Riverside, CA	170,591	226,505	255,166	12.7	27.0
16	Columbus, OH	565,021	632,910	711,470	12.4	16.3
25	Nashville-Davidson, TN	477,811	488,374	545,524	11.7	38.1
95	Spokane, WA	171,300	177,196	195,629	10.4	20.7
41	Sacramento, CA	275,741	369,365	407,018	10.2	25.8
6	San Diego, CA	875,538	1,110,549	1,223,400	10.2	14.6
Average					15.2	23.0
Cities that grew between 2 percent and 10 percent (33)						
96	Tacoma, WA	158,501	176,664	193,556	9.6	23.9
22	El Paso, TX	425,259	515,342	563,662	9.4	52.0
1	New York, NY	7,071,639	7,322,564	8,008,278	9.4	7.1
21	Seattle, WA	493,846	516,259	563,374	9.1	22.0

TABLE 2A-2. Population Change for 100 Largest Central Cities and Their Suburbs (*continued*)

1990 population rank	*City*[a]	*1980 population*	*1990 population*	*2000 population*	*Percent population change City - 1990s*	*Percent population change Suburbs - 1990s*
82	Madison, WI	170,616	191,262	208,054	8.8	24.3
55	Tampa, FL	271,577	280,015	303,447	8.4	19.0
37	Virginia Beach, VA	262,199	393,069	425,257	8.2	17.9
64	Corpus Christi, TX	232,134	257,453	277,454	7.8	11.8
86	Montgomery, AL	177,857	187,106	201,568	7.7	24.7
32	Long Beach, CA	361,498	429,433	461,522	7.5	7.9
39	Oakland, CA	339,337	372,242	399,484	7.3	16.5
14	San Francisco, CA	678,974	723,959	776,733	7.3	8.5
88	Lubbock, TX	174,361	186,206	199,564	7.2	18.2
43	Tulsa, OK	360,919	367,302	393,049	7.0	20.1
13	Indianapolis, IN	711,539	731,327	781,870	6.9	27.2
18	Memphis, TN	646,174	610,337	650,100	6.5	22.3
2	Los Angeles, CA	2,968,528	3,485,398	3,694,820	6.0	7.9
100	Newport News, VA	144,903	170,045	180,150	5.9	17.9
36	Atlanta, GA	425,022	394,017	416,474	5.7	44.0
57	St. Paul, MN	270,320	272,235	287,151	5.5	21.1
67	Jersey City, NJ	223,532	228,537	240,055	5.0	13.7
83	Grand Rapids, MI	181,843	189,126	197,800	4.6	19.0
91	Huntington Beach, CA	170,505	181,519	189,594	4.4	19.3
87	Augusta-Richmond, GA	179,810	186,953	195,182	4.4	23.7
84	Yonkers, NY	195,351	188,082	196,086	4.3	7.1
97	Little Rock, AR	159,159	175,795	183,133	4.2	18.8
3	Chicago, IL	3,005,072	2,783,726	2,896,016	4.0	16.2
65	St. Petersburg, FL	238,647	238,629	248,232	4.0	19.0
94	Columbus, GA	170,108	178,681	185,781	4.0	8.1
42	Minneapolis, MN	370,951	368,383	382,618	3.9	21.1
73	Baton Rouge, LA	220,394	219,531	227,818	3.8	21.5
80	Des Moines, IA	191,003	193,187	198,682	2.8	28.8
20	Boston, MA	562,994	574,283	589,141	2.6	6.2
Average					6.2	19.3
Cities that neither grew nor declined (6)						
44	Honolulu, HI	365,048	365,272	371,657	1.7	7.1
31	Kansas City, MO	448,028	435,146	441,545	1.5	16.3
79	Mobile, AL	200,452	196,278	198,915	1.3	21.6
46	Miami, FL	346,681	358,548	362,470	1.1	19.7
77	Shreveport, LA	206,989	198,525	200,145	0.8	8.1
56	Newark, NJ	329,248	275,221	273,546	–0.6	7.2
Average					1.0	13.3
Cities that declined (20)						
24	New Orleans, LA	557,927	496,938	484,674	–2.5	8.2
76	Richmond, VA	219,214	203,056	197,790	–2.6	20.5
71	Akron, OH	237,177	223,019	217,074	–2.7	10.0
5	Philadelphia, PA	1,688,210	1,585,577	1,517,550	–4.3	7.4
58	Louisville, KY	298,694	269,063	256,231	–4.8	13.2
17	Milwaukee, WI	636,297	628,088	596,974	–5.0	12.4
66	Rochester, NY	241,741	231,636	219,773	–5.1	14.0
23	Cleveland, OH	573,822	505,616	478,403	–5.4	4.5
19	Washington, DC	638,432	606,900	572,059	–5.7	20.3
49	Toledo, OH	354,635	332,943	313,619	–5.8	8.3
78	Jackson, MS	202,895	196,637	184,256	–6.3	29.1

(*continued*)

TABLE 2A-2. Population Change for 100 Largest Central Cities and Their Suburbs (*continued*)

1990 population rank	City[a]	1980 population	1990 population	2000 population	Percent population change	
					City - 1990s	Suburbs - 1990s
7	Detroit, MI	1,203,368	1,027,974	951,270	–7.5	7.8
60	Birmingham, AL	284,413	265,968	242,820	–8.7	18.1
90	Dayton, OH	193,536	182,044	166,179	–8.7	2.0
45	Cincinnati, OH	385,409	364,040	331,285	–9.0	13.2
40	Pittsburgh, PA	423,959	369,879	334,563	–9.5	0.0
62	Norfolk, VA	266,979	261,229	234,403	–10.3	17.9
50	Buffalo, NY	357,870	328,123	292,648	–10.8	1.9
12	Baltimore, MD	786,741	736,014	651,154	–11.5	15.5
34	St. Louis, MO	452,801	396,685	348,189	–12.2	7.6
Average					–6.9	11.6
Total (100 cities)		48,693,607	51,765,359	56,465,754	9.1	18.3
Average					9.8	20.8

Source: See table 2A-1.

a. City of Anchorage, AK, encompasses entire OMB-defined Anchorage metropolitan area.

b. See table 2-3 for abbreviations.

REFERENCES

Fulton, William, Rolf Pendall, Mai Nguyen, and Alicia Harrison. 2001. "Who Sprawls Most? How Growth Patterns Differ across the United States." Washington: Brookings Institution Center on Urban and Metropolitan Policy (July).

Glaeser, Edward, and Jesse Shapiro. 2001. "City Growth and Census 2000: Which Places Grew and Why." *Census 2000 Series.* Brookings Institution Center on Urban and Metropolitan Policy (May).

Lang, Robert, and Patrick Simmons. 2001. "Boomburbs: The Emergence of Large, Fast-Growing Suburban Cities in the United States." *Census Note* 06. Washington: Fannie Mae Foundation (June).

Simmons, Patrick, and Robert Lang. 2001. "The Urban Turnaround: A Decade-by-Decade Report Card on Postwar Population Change in Older Industrial Cities." *Census Note* 01. Washington: Fannie Mae Foundation (April).

Singer, Audrey, Samantha Friedman, Ivan Cheung, and Marie Price. 2001. "The World in a Zip Code: Greater Washington, D.C., as a New Region of Immigration." Brookings Institution Center on Urban and Metropolitan Policy (April).

U.S. Bureau of the Census. 2001. Census 2000 Redistricting Data (P.L. 94-171). Summary File and 1990 Census. Department of Commerce.

3

The Urban Turnaround

PATRICK A. SIMMONS
ROBERT E. LANG

The postwar years were not kind to America's older industrial cities. Most endured substantial population decline—particularly during the 1970s, when municipalities such as Chicago, Detroit, New York City, and Philadelphia each lost enough residents to populate a good-sized city.

Many older industrial cities have rebounded considerably from the traumatic population losses of the 1970s. During the 1970s, *all* of the thirty-six cities in this study lost population, and twenty-nine experienced their worst decade of the postwar period. By the 1990s, fifteen were growing again, and the remainder were losing population at often greatly reduced rates. Not one of the thirty-six cities experienced its worst postwar decade during the 1990s. For the first time since World War II, the combined population of these cities increased.

This analysis shows that the 1990s were the best postwar decade for the thirty-six cities as a group. A summary index assigning a grade to each decade based on cities' numeric change in population levels gives the 1990s a grade of *B*. By contrast, the 1950s and 1980s received only a *C+*, the 1960s a *C*, and the 1970s an *F*. A grading system based on percentage of population change yields similar results.

The authors thank Frank Popper and Elvin K. Wyly for invaluable comments on a draft of this chapter.

METHODS

The methodology employed in the present study involved selecting the cities to be examined and then determining the most appropriate way of measuring the decade's population changes in each of those cities.

Selecting the Cities

Cities in this analysis were selected by a two-step process. The first step identified the fifty most populous cities in the nation as of 1950.[1] This initial group included all cities with a 1950 population of 200,000 or more.

To better capture the experience of traditionally "declining" cities, the second step screened out those places that did not experience at least two decades of population decline in the postwar period. The excluded cities—Columbus, Dallas, Fort Worth, Houston, Indianapolis, Jacksonville, Long Beach, Los Angeles, Memphis, Miami, Oklahoma City, Omaha, San Antonio, and San Diego—were primarily rapidly growing Sun Belt metropolises.[2]

The final list included thirty-six cities that had 1950 populations ranging from 203,000 (Worcester, Mass.) to 7.9 million (New York City). Together these cities contained 30 million residents in 1950 and accounted for 20 percent of the nation's total population at that time. By 2000 they were home to 5 million fewer residents and just 9 percent of all Americans.

Most of the cities on the final list are located in the Northeast and Midwest, regions together accounting for twenty-three of the thirty-six municipalities studied, or almost two-thirds. The list includes all of the major Rust Belt cities frequently associated with postwar urban decline such as Buffalo, Cleveland, Detroit, Newark, Pittsburgh, and St. Louis. (The complete list of cities is provided and discussed in the section on findings.)

Measuring Population Changes

Population data for each city are from the 1950–2000 decennial censuses.[3] The numeric and percentage changes in populations were calculated for

1. The year 1950 is a significant starting point because it represents the population and economic peak for many of the nation's older industrial cities. The thirty-six cities in the present study grew by almost 2.5 million people during the 1940s, before commencing a long period of population decline.

2. These places also tend to grow by urban annexation. Interdecade expansion of city boundaries can distort the analysis by making additions of existing households appear as actual population growth. Thus the removal of these cities dampens this distortion.

3. Data on population and land area for 1950 through 1990 were obtained from Gibson (1998). Population data for 2000 were obtained from U.S. Bureau of the Census (2001a, 2001b, 2001c).

each city for each of the five postwar decades. These measures were then used to identify the best and worst decade of population change for each city and to rank each of those five decades.[4]

A summary index that works like a college grade point average (GPA) was used to compare or "grade" each decade in terms of the cities' overall population performance. The summary index was created using the following steps. First, every city was assigned a different number for each decade in accordance with that city's relative numeric population growth or decline during that decade, from 0 to 4—with 4 corresponding to the best decade for that city and 0 corresponding to the worst decade for that city.[5] At the end of this first step, each decade comprised thirty-six city ranks ranging from 0 to 4. Next, the thirty-six ranks were averaged for each of the five decades in order to obtain a GPA for each decade. The GPA was then converted into a letter grade.[6]

Each city had the same five rank scores (0, 1, 2, 3, and 4) to assign to each of the five decades covered, with a different number corresponding to each of the different decades in accordance with the individual city's population growth performance during that decade. A city's best decade for growth (or its slowest loss) gets a 4; a city's worst decade, the decade of its biggest loss, gets a 0; and a city's three middle decades also receive a 1, 2, or 3. What varies is the decade in which the different cities register their high, low, and three middle-growth ranks. Most cities had their low point during the 1970s, which is in large part why that decade gets the lowest GPA and a corresponding letter grade of *F*. In contrast, no city during the 1990s had its low point of 0, which helped lift that decade to a high GPA.

The cities themselves *do not* receive a grade. Rather, the decade is assigned a grade in accordance with the cities' *group* performance during that decade as derived from a cumulative ranking of between 0 and 4 for each city. A city's individual population change is not compared with that of other cities but is instead rated against the city's own historical performance during each of the five decades examined.

The grading system distills data from all thirty-six cities into one summary measure while dampening the effects of extreme values of population

4. Note that the "best" postwar decade for some of these cities was a decade in which the city *lost* population. In such cases, the numeric or percentage decrease was less than in any other postwar decade.

5. For a city that lost population in each postwar decade, the highest score was assigned to the decade in which the fewest residents were lost.

6. The cutoffs for each grade are as follows: *A* = 3.85–4.0; *A–* = 3.50–3.85; *B+* = 3.15–3.50; *B* = 2.85–3.15; *B–* = 2.50–2.85; *C+* = 2.15–2.50; *C* = 1.85–2.15; *C–* = 1.50–1.85; *D+* = 1.15–1.50; *D* = 0.50–1.15; *F* = 0.0–0.50.

TABLE 3-1. Grades for Decade-by-Decade Population Change

Decade	Numeric population change		Percent population change	
	Grade	Average score	Grade	Average score
1950s	C+	2.5	B–	2.8
1960s	C	2.0	C	2.1
1970s	F	0.3	F	0.3
1980s	C+	2.2	C	2.1
1990s	B	3.1	B–	2.8

Source: Fannie Mae Foundation, Urban and Metropolitan research division, Washington. Tabulations of decennial census data by Patrick A. Simmons and Robert E. Lang.

change, such as those caused by annexations.[7] That also protects the analysis from potential distortion caused by large numeric population changes for huge metropolises such as Chicago and New York City.

FINDINGS

The performance report for each decade follows.

The 1990s: The Best Decade; the 1970s, the Worst

The 1990s was graded the best decade for cities, while the 1970s was the worst. Grades based on numeric population change reveal that the thirty-six older industrial cities performed better during the 1990s than during any other decade since World War II (table 3-1) As a group, these cities "gave" the 1990s a B (average ranking of 3.1)—a big improvement over the F (average ranking of 0.3) given to the 1970s. Switching to the grading system based on percentage population change produces similar results, although under this system the 1950s and 1990s tie for the best postwar decade, with each receiving a B– (based on a 2.8 GPA).

The 1990s: Highest Number of Growing Cities; the 1970s, No Cities Grew

In general, most of the thirty-six cities lost population between 1950 and 2000. The decade of the 1990s compared favorably with earlier decades based on the number of cities experiencing population growth and decline (figure 3-1). During the 1990s, fifteen cities experienced population growth,

7. Urban annexation was much more common in the 1950s and 1960s according to Rusk (1993), and therefore its effect (which is mostly mitigated by the screening and indexing methods used here) tends to favor earlier decades in the analysis.

FIGURE 3-1. Number of Older Industrial Cities Gaining and Losing Population, by Decade, 1950–2000

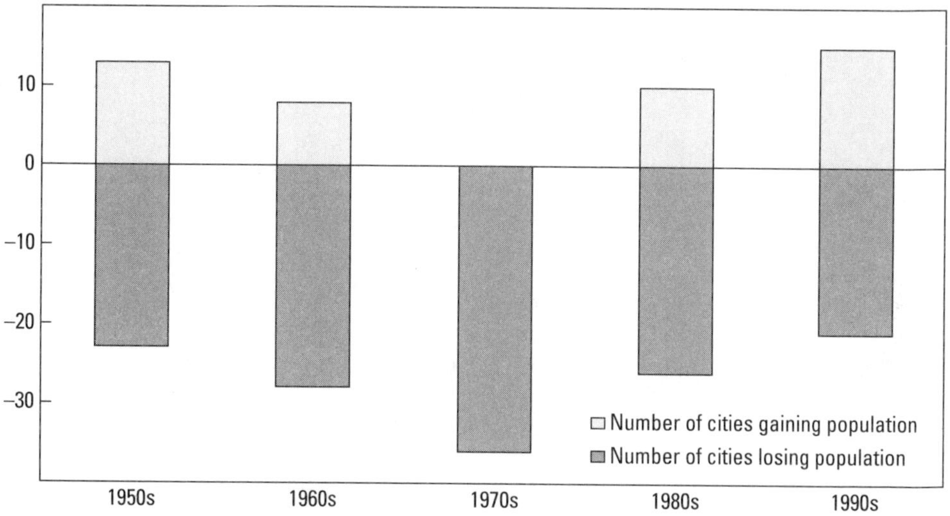

Source: Fannie Mae Foundation, Urban and Metropolitan research division, Washington. Tabulations of decennial census data by Patrick A. Simmons and Robert E. Lang.

a greater number than in any other decade—while twenty-one cities declined. During the 1970s, every city in the study lost population, which illustrates how far these cities have come in recent decades.

Biggest Population Growth and Biggest Loss

Most cities had their biggest population growth in the 1950s and the 1990s. The biggest losses were in the 1970s. Among the thirty-six cities included in the analysis, some twenty-nine cities experienced their worst decade in the 1970s, three cities during the 1950s and 1980s, and one city during the 1960s. Not even one of them experienced its worst postwar decade during the 1990s (figure 3-2); in fact, fifteen cities experienced their best postwar population change during the 1990s. The second-best decade was the 1950s, during which twelve cities had their best population performance.[8]

In the aggregate, cities added population in the 1990s and lost population in the four previous decades. Analysis of raw population data can be

8. Half of these twelve cities increased in land area by at least 25 percent during the 1950s (analysis by the authors using data on city land area from Gibson [1998]). At the time this chapter was prepared, information was not available on changes in city land area between 1990 and 2000.

FIGURE 3-2. Best and Worst Decades for Population Growth in Older Industrial Cities (based on numeric population change)

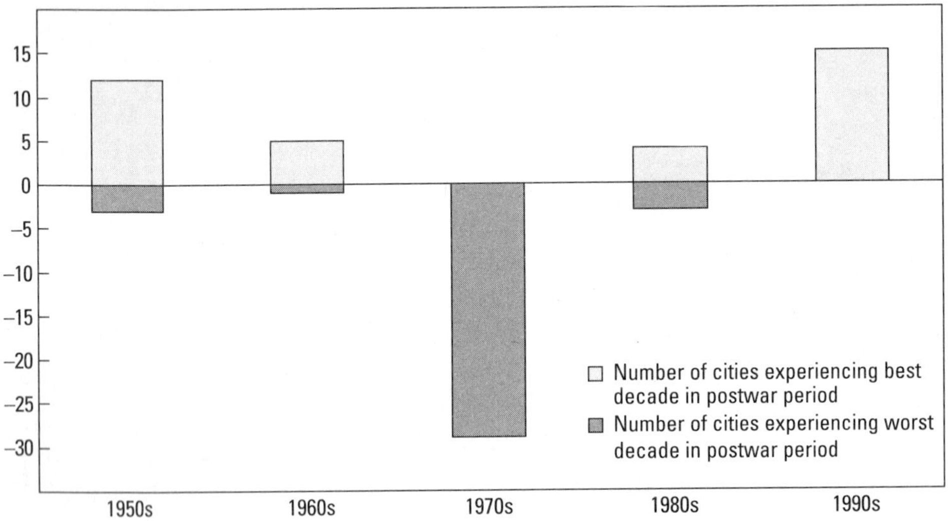

Source: Fannie Mae Foundation, Urban and Metropolitan research division. Tabulations of decennial census data by Simmons and Lang.

distorted by annexations or large population changes for individual cities, as noted earlier. Even so, it is informative to note that such an analysis reinforces the finding that the decade of the 1990s was the best postwar decade for our thirty-six municipalities, registering a total growth of roughly 580,000 persons for the cities as a group.[9] In all other postwar decades, the combined population of the cities decreased, with total population declining most during the 1970s, when the group of municipalities lost 3.6 million persons.

Substantial Population Turnarounds in Recent Decades

Population turnarounds in some individual cities have been remarkable (table 3-2). Fifteen cities converted their population losses in their worst decade into population gains in the 1990s. Chicago went from losing 360,000 residents during the 1970s to gaining more than 100,000 residents in the 1990s. Similarly, New York City lost 800,000 residents in the 1970s but gained almost 700,000 during the 1990s and for the first time now has

9. As shown later, the huge increase in New York City is largely responsible for this aggregate gain.

TABLE 3-2. Comparison of Worst Postwar Decade with the 1990s for Individual Cities

	Worst postwar decade[a]			1990s population change		
		Population change				
City	Decade	Number	Percent	Numeric	Percent	Decade rank[b]
Akron, OH	1970s	–38,248	–13.9	–5,945	–2.7	3
Atlanta, GA	1970s	–71,951	–14.5	22,457	5.7	3
Baltimore, MD	1970s	–118,984	–13.1	–84,860	–11.5	1
Birmingham, AL	1960s	–39,977	–11.7	–23,148	–8.7	1
Boston, MA	1950s	–104,247	–13.0	14,858	2.6	4
Buffalo, NY	1970s	–104,898	–22.7	–35,475	–10.8	3
Chicago, IL	1970s	–361,885	–10.7	112,290	4.0	4
Cincinnati, OH	1970s	–67,067	–14.8	–32,755	–9.0	2
Cleveland, OH	1970s	–177,081	–23.6	–27,213	–5.4	4
Dayton, OH	1970s	–40,230	–16.5	–15,865	–8.7	3
Denver, CO	1980s	–24,755	–5.0	87,026	18.6	4
Detroit, MI	1970s	–308,143	–20.4	–76,704	–7.5	4
Jersey City, NJ	1970s	–37,013	–14.2	11,518	5.0	4
Kansas City, MO	1970s	–58,928	–11.6	6,399	1.5	2
Louisville, KY	1970s	–63,021	–17.4	–12,832	–4.8	3
Milwaukee, WI	1970s	–80,887	–11.3	–31,114	–5.0	1
Minneapolis, MN	1970s	–63,449	–14.6	14,235	3.9	4
New Orleans, LA	1980s	–60,577	–10.9	–12,264	–2.5	3
New York, NY	1970s	–823,223	–10.4	685,714	9.4	4
Newark, NJ	1980s	–54,027	–16.4	–1,675	–0.6	4
Norfolk, VA	1970s	–40,972	–13.3	–26,826	–10.3	1
Oakland, CA	1970s	–22,224	–6.1	27,242	7.3	3
Philadelphia, PA	1970s	–260,399	–13.4	–68,027	–4.3	3
Pittsburgh, PA	1970s	–96,179	–18.5	–35,316	–9.5	4
Portland, OR	1970s	–16,236	–4.2	91,802	21.0	4
Providence, RI	1950s	–41,176	–16.6	12,890	8.0	4
Richmond, VA	1970s	–30,407	–12.2	–5,266	–2.6	3
Rochester, NY	1970s	–54,492	–18.4	–11,863	–5.1	3
San Francisco, CA	1970s	–36,700	–5.1	52,774	7.3	4
Seattle, WA	1970s	–36,985	–7.0	47,115	9.1	3
St. Louis, MO	1970s	–169,151	–27.2	–48,496	–12.2	4
St. Paul, MN	1970s	–39,750	–12.8	14,916	5.5	4
Syracuse, NY	1970s	–27,103	–13.7	–16,554	–10.1	2
Toledo, OH	1970s	–29,183	–7.6	–19,324	–5.8	2
Washington, DC	1970s	–118,177	–15.6	–34,841	–5.7	2
Worcester, MA	1950s	–16,899	–8.3	2,889	1.7	3

Source: Fannie Mae Foundation, Urban and Metropolitan research division. Tabulations of decennial census data by Simmons and Lang.

a. Based on numeric population change. In only one city (Worcester) was there a difference in identification of worst decade depending on whether numeric or percent change was used. The worst decade for Worcester based on percent change was the 1970s, during which it lost 14,773 persons, or 8.4 percent of its population.

b. Based on numeric population change. A rank of 4 indicates that the 1990s were the best postwar decade for the city. No city experienced its worst decade of population change (rank of 0) during the 1990s.

more than 8 million people. However, even among the cities that have not returned to growth, the rate of population loss has slowed dramatically. Cleveland went from losing a quarter of its population during the 1970s to losing only 5 percent in the 1990s. Newark, which dropped roughly 15 percent in both the 1970s and 1980s, remained essentially unchanged in the last decade. Thus even those cities that are still losing residents have made substantial strides toward achieving population stability, suggesting that the wave of population decline associated with postwar urban-industrial restructuring may have run its course.

CONCLUSION

It is beyond the scope of the present analysis to identify the causes of population trends, but several factors probably contributed to the examined cities' improved population performance during the 1990s.

Factors Influencing Population Change

The unusually robust economy of the mid- to late 1990s most likely supported urban population growth—or at least greater population stability. Cities with large economic bases in outperforming sectors such as advanced services were particularly well positioned to take advantage of the strong economy.

Immigration also bolstered the population of many of the analyzed cities. Census 2000 data on the foreign-born population have not yet been released, but several previous studies, such as those by Dowell Myers and by William H. Frey and Elaine L. Fielding, point to the important role of immigration in urban population growth.[10] For instance, were it not for the arrival of more than 800,000 immigrants, New York City would have lost population during the 1980s rather than gained a quarter of a million residents.[11]

In addition, interdecade differences in the censuses' population coverage rates may also have artificially inflated population growth during the 1990s. Preliminary analyses indicate that census coverage improved between the 1990 and 2000 censuses.[12] Because the net undercount rate actually

10. Myers (1999); Frey and Fielding (1995).

11. New York City Department of City Planning. (1996).

12. Ericksen (2001a) found that the biggest numerical improvement in the net undercount between 1990 and 2000 was in Texas and California, which together accounted for almost two-thirds (64 percent) of the improvement of the net undercount. The 2000 net undercount was higher in twelve states in the Northeast and Midwest (Connecticut, Indiana,

increased between 1980 and 1990, changes in census population coverage probably had the greatest effect on comparisons between the 1980s and 1990s.[13]

Implications of Population Change for the Health of Older Industrial Cities

Renewed population growth has several positive implications for the health of older industrial cities. First, it could lead to increased representation and government funding. By supporting stronger housing demand, renewed population growth could also lead to reclamation of deteriorating or abandoned housing stock and to renewal of inner-city neighborhoods. Population gains induce other forms of economic activity as well, such as the formation of new businesses to meet the consumer needs of new residents. Furthermore, population growth increases city tax revenues, although the net fiscal impact hinges not only on the numbers of new residents but also on their socioeconomic characteristics.

Even in this post-1970s period of urban turnaround, however, most of the cities in the study (twenty-one out of thirty-six) are still losing population. This is not surprising, given that the metropolises analyzed were selected because they had experienced at least two decades of population loss during the past five decades and are thus prone to decline. But the rate of loss has indeed slowed dramatically (table 3-2). Some twenty-nine cities had double-digit population declines (four of them at more than 20 percent) during their worst decade, but only five cities in the 1990s experienced double-digit percentage losses. And most city population losses in the 1990s were slight and were accounted for by shifts in household structure rather than by the wholesale abandonment of dwellings.

It is also important to put urban population decline into regional context.[14] Places such as Cleveland, Detroit, and St. Louis are at the center of slow-growing metropolitan areas, and even as they lose people, their relative position in the region may slip very little. In a few instances, the

---

Iowa, Maine, Massachusetts, Nebraska, New Hampshire, New Jersey, Pennsylvania, Rhode Island, Vermont, and Wisconsin). Ericksen (2001b) also compared undercounts in four cities that are included in this analysis: Atlanta, Chicago, New York City, and Philadelphia. He estimated that the biggest improvement occurred in New York City, which missed 3.2 percent of people in 1990 and 2.3 percent in 1990. The rankings for these four cities would not have changed had the census coverage remained the same in 2000 and 1990.

13. Nevertheless, the difference between urban population change in the 1980s and 1990s is much too large to be attributed mostly to an improvement of census coverage in the 1990s.

14. The authors are grateful to Elvin K. Wyly for this point.

population gains made by cities in the 1990s kept pace with or—as in the case of New York City—actually exceeded regional growth rates.

The encouraging findings of the study are also tempered by the limitations of the analysis. Total population change is a single—and admittedly limited—dimension of a city's health. Changes in residents' characteristics are probably as important as changes in total population. For instance, scholars such as John D. Kasarda and Frey and Fielding have pointed to growth in poverty populations in cities and growth in extremely poor neighborhoods as signs of mounting urban distress.[15] Kasarda showed that some of these same cities with improved population trends have also experienced substantial increases during recent decades in the number of residents living in high-poverty neighborhoods. Besides trends related to total population and to resident characteristics, then, long-term changes in social, economic, and fiscal conditions need to be examined in order to draw firmer conclusions about the revitalization of older industrial cities.

Improvements in city population trends occurred during the longest economic expansion in American history. The population turnaround also happened during a period in which changing immigration policies renewed an important urban-population growth source dormant for decades. Interruption of these important forces, or strengthening of countervailing trends such as the settlement of new immigrants directly into suburban communities, will affect future prospects for urban population growth. Thus an additional consideration in interpreting the findings of the present analysis is whether the recent reversal in city population fortunes can be sustained in a less favorable environment.

REFERENCES

Ericksen, Eugene. 2001a. "A Comparison of 1990 and 2000 Net Undercount by State." Analysis provided to *USA Today* on figures derived from Census 2000 Redistricting Data (P.L. 94-171) Summary (March 28).

———. 2001b. "A Comparison of 1990 and 2000 Net Undercount for Five Cities." Analysis provided to *USA Today* on figures derived from Census 2000 Redistricting Data (P.L. 94-171) Summary (March 28).

Frey, William H., and Elaine L. Fielding. 1995. "Changing Urban Populations: Regional Restructuring, Racial Polarization, and Poverty Concentration." *Cityscape* 1 (2):1–66. U.S. Department of Housing and Urban Development, Office of Policy Development and Research.

Gibson, Campbell. 1998. "Population of the 100 Largest Cities and Other Urban Places in the United States: 1790 to 1990." Working Paper 27. Department of Commerce, Bureau of the Census, Population Division (June).

15. Kasarda (1993); Frey and Fielding (1995).

Kasarda, John D. 1993. "Inner-City Concentrated Poverty and Neighborhood Distress: 1970 to 1990." *Housing Policy Debate* 4 (3): 253–302.

Myers, Dowell. 1999. "Immigration: Fundamental Force in the American City." *Housing Facts and Findings* 1 (4):3–5. Washington: Fannie Mae Foundation.

New York City Department of City Planning. 1996. *The Newest New Yorkers: 1990–1994*. New York.

Rusk, David. 1993. *Cities without Suburbs*. Johns Hopkins University Press.

U.S. Bureau of the Census. 2001a. Census 2000 Redistricting Data (P.L. 94-171). *www.census.gov/clo/www/redistricting.html* (March 2001).

———. 2001b. *Report of the Executive Steering Committee for Accuracy and Coverage Evaluation Policy*. Department of Commerce (March 1).

———. 2001c. "Population Change and Distribution." *Census 2000 Brief*. Department of Commerce (April 2).

4

Downtown Rebound

REBECCA R. SOHMER
ROBERT E. LANG

Houston's downtown business area in 1975, as aptly described by Kirkpatrick Sale, serves as a typical example of what was happening to most American downtowns in the 1970s and 1980s: "[It is] made up almost entirely of high-rise office buildings and large department stores, with a few smaller restaurants to refuel the denizens of both, but nobody lives there."[1]

Downtown Houston 2000 is an altogether different story. Houston's downtown population rose 69 percent in the 1990s. "Downtown is back" seemed to be a common observation throughout the 1990s. It turns out that this was more than wishful thinking. Among a sample of twenty-four cities, eighteen saw increases in their downtown populations.

In a lot of ways, the story of downtown is a countertrend to what is happening in the rest of urban America. Most central cities are losing population relative to their surrounding metropolitan statistical area, but most downtowns within these central cities are gaining a larger share of metropolitan statistical area population. (There are, of course, exceptions: while cities such as Charlotte and Phoenix are booming, their downtowns are getting weaker.)

In downtowns, race and immigration are playing a role different from their role in the rest of urban America. Compared with cities' overall population changes, the downtown population gain is less weighted toward

The authors thank Eugenie Birch for her contributions to this analysis.
1. Sale (1975).

blacks and Hispanics. Increases in white residents are leading the resurgence in downtown living—in stark contrast to the general decline in city white population.

The actual numbers of downtown growth are relatively small. The trend toward downtown living is still more a trickle than a rush. Nevertheless, the downtown population gain is important because it may be the harbinger of future central city growth. If people continue to move downtown, neighboring areas may experience spillover effects. The stronger downtown gets, the more likely it is that the surrounding central city neighborhoods will strengthen as well.

METHODS

Because the Bureau of the Census does not officially define "downtown," a standardized definition was unavailable. What constitutes downtown varies from city to city. Depending on the city, a downtown can be several square miles, or it can be several square blocks. But downtowns do have some things in common. They contain the "100 percent corner" (place of maximum rent for commercial office space), and each downtown is the central business district of its respective city. The downtown is often the oldest, most established part of a city.

Building on research conducted by the Fannie Mae Foundation and the Brookings Institution, researchers at the University of Pennsylvania are in the process of trying to define downtown boundaries in cities throughout the country.[2] The researchers determined downtown census tracts by interviewing leaders of city organizations and municipal governments and by examining historic maps of each city's downtown.

The downtowns surveyed vary by region and size. Using 1990 census numbers, the University of Pennsylvania mapped boundaries for more than thirty downtowns.[3] The twenty-four downtowns in the present study are derived from that list. The list was reduced from thirty-four to twenty-four because some cities (such as Dallas, Minneapolis, and Pittsburgh) changed their 2000 census tracts, making it impossible to track population accurately. Other cities were eliminated to round out the regional representation of these downtowns.

2. Sohmer (1999); Sohmer and Lang (1999).
3. Birch (2000).

FINDINGS

We focused on characteristics of downtown such as racial composition and various aspects of population growth.

Downtowns Vary

Like census tracts themselves, downtowns vary widely in population size and geographic area. San Antonio is the geographically largest downtown at 5.5 square miles, while the downtowns in Cincinnati, Lexington, and Norfolk are each just 0.8 square miles. Boston had the largest downtown population in 2000 with almost 80,000, while Norfolk had slightly fewer than 3,000 (table 4-1).

Most downtowns are getting denser, while a few are losing density (table 4-2). The most densely populated downtowns are Baltimore and Philadelphia, but the downtowns that had the highest density percentage gains during the 1990s are Chicago, Houston, and Seattle.

More Winners than Losers in the 1990s

Overall, downtowns are winners in the population game. Three-fourths of the studied downtowns gained population during the 1990s. Only six downtowns had fewer inhabitants in 2000 than ten years earlier. Each downtown falls into one of four scenarios (table 4-3).

Downtown Population Up; City Population Up

Half of the twenty-four downtowns fall into the first scenario: the city as a whole is gaining population, and downtown is growing as well. Most of the downtowns in the category are even outpacing the city's growth rate. The downtowns of Chicago, Denver, Houston, and Seattle are growing from 2.5 times as quickly (Denver) to 12 times as quickly (Chicago) as their cities. The downtowns of only two metropolitan statistical areas (MSAs)—Colorado Springs and Des Moines—are growing at a slower rate than their cities.

Downtown Population Up; City Population Down

Six downtowns are in the second category: while the city is losing people, downtown population is up. This is the most interesting group. These

TABLE 4-1. Selected Downtown Population Change, 1990–2000

	1990			2000			Change between 1990 and 2000		
City[a]	Downtown	City	MSA	Downtown	City	MSA	Downtown	City	MSA
Atlanta	19,763	394,017	2,959,950	24,731	416,474	4,112,198	4,968	22,457	1,152,248
Baltimore	28,597	736,014	2,382,172	30,067	651,154	2,552,994	1,470	(84,860)	170,822
Boston	75,823	574,283	3,227,707	79,251	589,141	3,406,829	3,428	14,858	179,122
Charlotte	6,370	395,934	1,162,093	6,327	540,828	1,499,293	(43)	144,894	337,200
Chicago	27,760	2,783,726	7,410,858	42,039	2,896,016	8,272,768	14,279	112,290	861,910
Cincinnati	3,838	364,040	1,526,092	3,189	331,285	1,646,395	(649)	(32,755)	120,303
Cleveland	7,261	505,616	2,202,069	9,599	478,403	2,250,871	2,338	(27,213)	48,802
Colorado Springs	13,412	281,140	397,014	14,377	360,890	516,929	965	79,750	119,915
Denver	2,794	467,610	1,622,980	4,230	554,636	2,109,282	1,436	87,026	486,302
Des Moines	4,190	193,187	392,928	4,204	198,682	456,022	14	5,495	63,094
Detroit	5,970	1,027,974	4,266,654	6,141	951,270	4,441,551	171	(76,704)	174,897
Houston	7,029	1,630,553	3,322,025	11,882	1,953,631	4,177,646	4,853	323,078	855,621
Lexington, KY	5,212	225,366	405,936	4,894	260,512	479,198	(318)	35,146	73,262
Los Angeles	34,655	3,485,398	8,863,164	36,630	3,694,820	9,519,338	1,975	209,422	656,174
Memphis	7,606	610,337	1,007,306	8,994	650,100	1,135,614	1,388	39,763	128,308
Milwaukee	10,973	628,088	1,432,149	11,243	596,974	1,500,741	270	(31,114)	68,592
Norfolk, VA	2,390	261,229	1,443,244	2,881	234,403	1,569,541	491	(26,826)	126,297
Philadelphia	74,655	1,585,577	4,922,175	78,349	1,517,550	5,100,931	3,694	(68,027)	178,756
Phoenix	6,517	983,403	2,238,480	5,925	1,321,045	3,251,876	(592)	337,642	1,013,396
Portland, OR	9,528	437,319	1,515,452	12,902	529,121	1,918,009	3,374	91,802	402,557
San Antonio	23,588	935,933	1,324,749	22,206	1,144,646	1,592,383	(1,382)	208,713	267,634
San Diego	15,417	1,110,549	2,498,016	17,894	1,223,400	2,813,833	2,477	112,851	315,817
Seattle	9,824	516,259	2,033,156	16,443	563,374	2,414,616	6,619	47,115	381,460
St. Louis	9,109	396,685	2,492,525	7,511	348,189	2,603,607	(1,598)	(48,496)	111,082

Sources: University of Pennsylvania (2001); U.S. Bureau of the Census (1990, 2000).

a. In alphabetical order.

TABLE 4-2. Downtown Density

City	Area (square miles)	1990 density	2000 density	Change
Downtowns increasing density				
Seattle	1.2	8,485	14,202	5,717
Chicago	3.7	7,422	11,240	3,818
Houston	1.8	3,950	6,676	2,727
Portland	1.8	5,425	7,346	1,921
Denver	0.9	3,234	4,895	1,662
Atlanta	3.5	5,710	7,146	1,435
Philadelphia	4.3	17,476	18,341	865
Boston	4.4	17,282	18,063	781
Norfolk	0.8	3,053	3,680	627
San Diego	4.3	3,611	4,191	580
Baltimore	2.5	11,228	11,805	577
Cleveland	4.3	1,707	2,256	550
Los Angeles	4.6	7,550	7,980	430
Memphis	3.9	1,928	2,280	352
Colorado Springs	3.9	3,428	3,675	247
Detroit	1.4	4,264	4,386	122
Milwaukee	2.2	4,911	5,032	121
Des Moines	2.5	1,705	1,710	6
Downtowns decreasing density				
Charlotte	3.0	2,116	2,101	(14)
San Antonio	5.5	4,307	4,055	(252)
Phoenix	1.5	4,295	3,905	(390)
Lexington	0.8	6,452	6,058	(394)
St. Louis	3.4	2,718	2,241	(477)
Cincinnati	0.8	4,893	4,066	(827)

Sources: University of Pennsylvania (2001); U.S. Bureau of the Census (1990, 2000).

downtowns are the surprise heroes of their cities. Even in an environment in which city population is slumping, these downtowns are managing to attract new populations. The city of Cleveland saw a 5 percent population loss in the 1990s, yet its downtown population grew by a third.

Downtown Population Down; City Population Up

Four downtowns are in the third group: downtown population down and city population up. This scenario and the one following were familiar stories to the metropolitan America of the postwar years. It appears that the tide has now turned. The scenario of a downtown losing population despite increases in the city overall is no longer the dominant pattern. Here the surprise in fact is that downtowns in these fast-growing cities are indeed losing population. The city of Phoenix grew by 34 percent, yet its downtown lost

TABLE 4-3. The Four Different Downtown Trends—Downtown Population Change and Its Relationship to City Population Change

	Percent change	
Area	*Downtown*	*City*
Downtown up, city up		
Houston	69.0	19.8
Seattle	67.4	9.1
Chicago	51.4	4.0
Denver	51.4	18.6
Portland, OR	35.4	21.0
Atlanta	25.1	5.7
Memphis	18.2	6.5
San Diego	16.1	10.2
Colorado Springs	7.2	28.4
Los Angeles	5.7	6.0
Boston	4.5	2.6
Des Moines	0.3	2.8
Downtown up, city down		
Cleveland	32.2	–5.4
Norfolk, VA	20.5	–10.3
Baltimore	5.1	–11.5
Philadelphia	4.9	–4.3
Detroit	2.9	–7.5
Milwaukee	2.5	–5.0
Downtown down, city up		
Charlotte	–0.7	36.6
San Antonio	–5.9	22.3
Lexington, KY	–6.1	15.6
Phoenix	–9.1	34.3
Downtown down, city down		
Cincinnati	–16.9	–9.0
St. Louis	–17.5	–12.2

Sources: University of Pennsylvania (2001); U.S. Bureau of the Census (1990, 2000).

9 percent of its residents. Possibly, people are leaving downtown in these cities to be closer to employment centers that are in the areas' burgeoning suburbs.

Downtown Population Down; City Population Down

Generally speaking, in cities losing population, it is not surprising to see the downtowns also losing population. But the downtowns of Cincinnati and St. Louis—the only two downtowns in the fourth category of our analysis—are both outpacing their respective cities in losing people.

Downtowns' Share Grows While Cities' Share Declines

The raw number of people moving into downtown may be relatively small, but many downtowns are gaining a bigger share of their MSAs' population, while their respective cities are losing share. All but three downtowns improved or maintained their standing in the MSA (table 4-4). Seattle's downtown again tops the list—it increased its share of the overall MSA population by 0.3 percent.

Meanwhile, only two cities as a whole increased their share of MSA population: Charlotte and San Antonio (both of which lost downtown population during the 1990s) (table 4-5). The rest of the cities fared poorly. Thus

TABLE 4-4. Downtown's Share of MSA Population[a]

Percent

Area	*1990*	*2000*	*Change*
Downtowns that increased their share of MSA population			
Seattle	0.4	0.7	0.3
Colorado Springs	2.6	2.8	0.2
Portland, OR	0.5	0.7	0.2
Chicago	0.3	0.5	0.2
Memphis	0.7	0.8	0.1
Atlanta	0.5	0.6	0.1
Houston	0.2	0.3	0.1
Cleveland	0.3	0.4	0.1
Boston	2.2	2.3	0.1
San Diego	0.5	0.6	0.1
Philadelphia	1.5	1.5	0.1
Denver	0.1	0.2	0.1
Baltimore	1.1	1.2	0.1
Downtowns that maintained their share of MSA population			
Norfolk, VA	0.2	0.2	0.0
Los Angeles	0.4	0.4	0.0
Milwaukee	0.7	0.7	0.0
Detroit	0.1	0.1	0.0
Des Moines	0.9	0.9	0.0
Charlotte	0.4	0.4	0.0
Phoenix	0.2	0.2	0.0
Cincinnati	0.2	0.2	0.0
Downtowns that decreased their share of MSA population			
St. Louis	0.3	0.3	–0.1
Lexington, KY	1.1	1.0	–0.1
San Antonio	1.5	1.4	–0.1

Source: U.S. Bureau of the Census (1990, 2000).

a. Primary metropolitan statistical area was used when provided.

TABLE 4-5. Cities' Share of MSA Population[a]

Percent

Area	1990	2000	Change
Cities that increased their share of MSA population			
Charlotte	34	36	2.0
San Antonio	71	72	1.2
Cities that decreased their share of MSA population			
Boston	18	17	–0.5
Los Angeles	39	39	–0.5
San Diego	44	43	–1.0
Colorado Springs	71	70	–1.0
Lexington, KY	56	54	–1.2
Portland, OR	29	28	–1.3
Cleveland	23	21	–1.7
Seattle	25	23	–2.1
Houston	49	47	–2.3
Philadelphia	32	30	–2.5
Denver	29	26	–2.5
St. Louis	16	13	–2.5
Chicago	38	35	–2.6
Detroit	24	21	–2.7
Norfolk, VA	18	15	–3.2
Atlanta	13	10	–3.2
Phoenix	44	41	–3.3
Memphis	61	57	–3.3
Cincinnati	24	20	–3.7
Milwaukee	44	40	–4.1
Baltimore	31	26	–5.4
Des Moines	49	44	–5.6

Source: U.S. Bureau of the Census (1990, 2000).

a. Primary metropolitan statistical area was used when provided.

it appears that in terms of population, cities' relative importance is declining vis-à-vis their respective downtowns.

Downtowns' Racial Composition Shifts

Comparing the downtowns of 1990 with those of 2000 is complicated by the fact that the Bureau of the Census adjusted race categories for the 2000 census by breaking out Asians and Hawaiian or Pacific Islanders into their own categories and adding a category of "two or more races."

Grouping the twenty-four downtowns together, there are 7.5 percent more whites living downtown than in 1990, some 4.8 percent more Hispanics, and 6 percent more blacks. This contrasts interestingly with city data. There are 10.5 percent *fewer* whites living in the twenty-four studied cities in 2000 than in 1990, 43 percent more Hispanics, and 2.4 percent more blacks.

In 2000 the group of twenty-four downtowns was 54.9 percent white; 21.2 percent black; 13.4 percent Hispanic; 8 percent Asian; 1.8 percent of more than one race; and 0.6 American Indian, Hawaiian, or other. The 2000 figures show small percentage decreases by the white and black populations and small increases by the Asian and Hispanic populations compared with 1990 figures (57.2 percent white; 22.1 percent black; 14.4 percent Hispanic; 5.4 percent Asians and Pacific Islanders; and 0.6 percent American Indians or other).

In individual downtowns, whites gained more of a percentage share of the population in seven of twenty-four downtowns in 2000. Some eighteen downtowns now have a greater percentage of Hispanics vis-à-vis 1990, and eleven downtowns have a higher percentage of blacks compared with 1990 (table 4-6).

CONCLUSION

Several trends are helping U.S. downtowns' new period of growth. The population of empty nesters will continue to grow as baby boomers age. Without children, empty nesters often change their lifestyles in a way that favors downtown. Besides having more leisure time to dine out and take part in cultural activities (museums, concerts), empty nesters often choose to downsize their housing—trading in the lawn care and upkeep of a large home for the convenience of living in a downtown condominium. If even a modest portion of empty-nester households trades suburban homes for urban ones, downtown populations will continue to grow.

The other emerging population that is probably aiding downtown's comeback consists of young professionals in their twenties and thirties who have yet to start families. This group—often consumers of downtown-friendly services and amenities such as coffeehouses and nightclubs—is frequently in the market for low-maintenance, urban housing convenient to work and amenities.

Downtowns throughout the country are capitalizing on their historic character. Downtowns offer a niche market for those seeking a "sense of place." For instance, downtown San Diego gained residents in part because it offers an alternative to the rapidly expanding (and often monotonous) suburban developments that dominate the region. Perhaps Charlotte and Phoenix lost downtown population in part because their downtowns do not offer enough to distinguish themselves from their suburbs.

TABLE 4-6. Racial Composition in Selected Downtowns, 1990, 2000

City	*Year*	*Total*	*Hispanic*	*White*	*Black*	*American Indian*	*Asian/Pacific Islander*	*Asian*	*Hawaiian*	*Other*	*Two or more races*
Atlanta	1990	19,763	161	2,328	17,077	29	154	n.a.	n.a.	14	n.a.
	2000	24,731	1,002	4,466	18,750	50	n.a.	299	8	45	311
Baltimore	1990	28,597	502	18,793	8,507	83	692	n.a.	n.a.	20	n.a.
	2000	30,067	690	18,263	9,012	80	n.a.	1,490	14	85	433
Boston	1990	75,823	4,368	57,916	3,562	164	9,681	n.a.	n.a.	132	n.a.
	2000	79,251	5,432	57,227	3,486	128	n.a.	11,416	39	244	1,279
Charlotte	1990	6,370	205	2,309	3,811	28	17	n.a.	n.a.	—	n.a.
	2000	6,327	97	2,710	3,332	27	n.a.	62	10	6	83
Chicago	1990	27,760	1,424	20,916	4,170	49	1,185	n.a.	n.a.	16	n.a.
	2000	42,039	2,216	27,623	6,912	62	n.a.	4,388	25	71	742
Cincinnati	1990	3,838	24	2,350	1,391	9	62	n.a.	n.a.	2	n.a.
	2000	3,189	78	1,737	1,241	9	n.a.	61	6	2	55
Cleveland	1990	7,261	228	2,500	4,285	27	213	n.a.	n.a.	8	n.a.
	2000	9,599	311	2,663	6,012	21	n.a.	384	3	20	185
Colorado Springs	1990	13,412	1,379	10,815	903	129	155	n.a.	n.a.	31	n.a.
	2000	14,377	1,681	11,132	842	90	n.a.	195	13	34	390
Denver	1990	2,794	230	2,217	164	14	163	n.a.	n.a.	6	n.a.
	2000	4,230	445	3,147	229	26	n.a.	271	1	19	92
Des Moines	1990	4,190	70	3,310	670	24	111	n.a.	n.a.	5	n.a.
	2000	4,204	271	2,978	674	20	n.a.	100	8	56	97
Detroit	1990	5,970	92	1,687	4,133	25	31	n.a.	n.a.	2	n.a.
	2000	6,141	124	1,290	4,518	13	n.a.	84	—	11	101

Houston	1990	7,029	1,370	2,061	3,449	48	76	n.a.	n.a.	25	n.a.
	2000	11,882	2,688	4,158	4,837	11	n.a.	131	2	2	53
Lexington, KY	1990	5,212	70	3,718	1,360	17	42	n.a.	n.a.	5	n.a.
	2000	4,894	182	3,153	1,368	17	n.a.	88	6	7	73
Los Angeles	1990	34,655	20,648	5,198	5,456	195	3,048	n.a.	n.a.	110	n.a.
	2000	36,630	18,529	4,621	6,481	199	n.a.	6,098	40	46	616
Memphis	1990	7,606	36	1,820	5,706	19	24	n.a.	n.a.	1	n.a.
	2000	8,994	138	4,158	4,369	21	n.a.	208	—	7	93
Milwaukee	1990	10,973	330	8,160	2,238	45	185	n.a.	n.a.	15	n.a.
	2000	11,243	341	8,141	1,998	38	n.a.	513	16	12	184
Norfolk	1990	2,390	36	1,269	1,034	8	43	n.a.	n.a.	—	n.a.
	2000	2,881	46	1,474	1,274	1	n.a.	52	3	3	28
Philadelphia	1990	74,655	2,404	57,707	11,067	147	3,250	n.a.	n.a.	80	n.a.
	2000	78,349	3,172	57,419	9,707	132	n.a.	6,226	35	234	1,424
Phoenix	1990	6,517	1,977	3,163	860	455	60	n.a.	n.a.	2	n.a.
	2000	5,925	1,763	2,931	751	320	n.a.	78	1	3	78
Portland, OR	1990	9,528	429	7,611	516	154	806	n.a.	n.a.	12	n.a.
	2000	12,902	645	9,651	831	213	n.a.	1,032	29	38	463
San Antonio	1990	23,588	18,191	3,131	2,010	51	116	n.a.	n.a.	89	n.a.
	2000	22,206	16,837	3,375	1,640	66	n.a.	104	11	19	154
San Diego	1990	15,417	4,504	8,086	2,139	156	506	n.a.	n.a.	26	n.a.
	2000	17,894	4,354	9,728	2,079	136	n.a.	1,007	29	56	505
Seattle	1990	9,824	573	6,372	1,194	280	1,398	n.a.	n.a.	7	n.a.
	2000	16,443	1,004	9,901	1,830	310	n.a.	2,622	46	57	673
St. Louis	1990	9,109	79	2,399	6,555	30	43	n.a.	n.a.	3	n.a.
	2000	7,511	106	1,614	5,580	28	n.a.	79	2	7	95

Source: U.S. Bureau of the Census (1990, 2000).
n.a. Not available.

Downtown areas' unique history and their central location and proximity to mass transit, work, and amenities offer potential for the growth of the 1990s to continue into the next decade.

REFERENCES

Birch, Eugenie L. 2000. "The Rise in Downtown Living: A Deeper Look (Part II)." Paper presented at the annual conference of the Association of Collegiate Schools of Planning. Atlanta (November).

Sale, Kirkpatrick. 1975. *Power Shift: The Rise of the Southern Rim and Its Challenge to the Eastern Establishment.* Random House.

Sohmer, Rebecca. 1999. "Downtown Housing as an Urban Redevelopment Tool: Hype or Hope?" *Housing Policy Debate* 10 (2): 477–505.

Sohmer, Rebecca, and Robert E. Lang. 1999. "Life at the Center: The Rise of Downtown Housing." *Housing Facts and Findings* 1 (1): 3–5.

U.S. Bureau of the Census. 1990. 2000. Profile of General Demographic Characteristics in the Census 2000. Summary File 1.

———. 2000. 2001. *www.census.gov* (March 2001).

University of Pennsylvania, Department of City and Regional Planning. 2001.

5

Patchwork Cities

Patterns of Urban Population Growth in the 1990s

ALAN BERUBE
BENJAMIN FORMAN

Analysis of population trends in the nation's cities during the 1990s has largely focused on city-level statistics. For instance, in population growth, the 1990s were the best decade during the past fifty years for thirty-six older industrial cities.[1] Among the 100 largest cities in 1990, nearly three out of four grew over the decade, while one in five lost population.[2] A similar trend prevailed in medium-sized cities.[3] Glaeser and Shapiro found strong regional-industrial patterns in city growth—western cities grew faster than cities in other U.S. regions, and cities with large manufacturing bases grew much more slowly than service-oriented cities.[4]

This chapter departs from Census 2000 analysis to date by examining population changes in the 1990s that took place within cities. It uses a new collection of data from the 1990 and 2000 decennial censuses to examine population change in city neighborhoods, as represented by census tracts. This area of inquiry is not novel. For example, studies from as early as the 1940s and 1950s examined census tract population change patterns by their proximity to the city center.[5]

The issue of neighborhood population change has continued relevance today and deserves scrutiny for fiscal, social, economic, and political reasons. Neighborhood population growth can raise local property values,

1. Lang and Simmons (2001).
2. See Alan Berube, chapter 2, in this volume .
3. Vey and Forman (2002).
4. Glaeser and Shapiro (2001).
5. Thompson (1947); Redick (1954).

attract commercial development, and create job growth, all of which can improve citywide fiscal conditions. In particular, there is a growing interest nationwide in bolstering downtown populations, which many city leaders believe could serve as an anchor for strengthening surrounding central city neighborhoods.[6] Neighborhood population decline, however, may reflect increasing incidence of crime, may create greater concentrations of poverty and segregation, and may result in housing abandonment and the attendant negative impacts on neighborhood quality.[7] Many government antipoverty programs at the federal and state levels (for example, Empowerment Zones, the Community Development Block Grant, the New Markets Tax Credit) target submunicipal geographies; how neighborhood population changes in response to these programs should be of interest to researchers and policymakers. More broadly, those concerned about the overall population trajectory of cities should be interested in whether all types of neighborhoods contributed to city growth or shared in city decline.

This chapter finds that population change among large-city neighborhoods in the 1990s generally reflected cities' overall population trends—growing cities tended to have larger proportions of growing census tracts than shrinking cities. However, in some growing cities, neighborhood population loss was more common than population gain. There were also notable trends in the spatial pattern of neighborhood growth and decline across U.S. regions; the bulk of central city population growth occurred at the suburban edge, with many midwestern and southern cities experiencing extensive population decentralization within their own borders. While downtowns grew in most of the 100 largest cities, even in cities that experienced overall population declines, they often represented islands of population growth within a larger sea of population loss in the urban core.

METHODOLOGY

Our analysis focuses on population changes within the 100 largest cities as of 1990. In 1990, these cities had population ranging from 171,000 (Newport News, Va.) to 7.3 million (New York, N.Y.). The top 100 cities are measured as of their 1990 populations (as opposed to their 2000 populations) to avoid biasing the 1990–2000 analysis toward fast-growing cities.[8]

Using these data, we present census tract–level population change data between 1990 and 2000 for tracts located within the city in 2000. Census

6. See Rebecca R. Sohmer and Robert E. Lang, chapter 4, in this volume.
7. Morenoff and Sampson (1997); Quillian (1999); Scafidi and others (1998).
8. See Alan Berube, chapter 2, for further discussion about this selection of cities.

tract boundaries, however, do not necessarily respect city borders; tracts are statistical subdivisions of counties, not cities. For this reason, we first identify the census blocks that are located within each city's borders. Blocks are the smallest geographic entities for which the Census Bureau tabulates decennial census data. Using the consistent block definitions from the software, we tabulate population change in each city block between 1990 and 2000. We then aggregate those population figures up to their corresponding census tracts. Census tracts are often used to represent neighborhoods within cities, and it is for this reason that we present our analysis at the tract level, rather than at the block level. Throughout this chapter, the word "neighborhood" is used interchangeably with "census tract."

Other analyses of 2000 Census data focus on the determinants of city tract population change in the 1990s by examining the tract's demographic and economic characteristics in 1990.[9] This chapter concentrates primarily on neighborhood and downtown population change as they relate to overall city population change. The unique contribution of this analysis is that by using block-level data (aggregated to the tract level for presentation), we are able to capture the exact population change that occurred within a city's borders during the decade and its distribution at the neighborhood level.[10]

One consequence of using a consistent set of tracts between 1990 and 2000 is that city boundaries are fixed. Over the 1990s, however, a number of large cities grew by annexing suburban land. Census Bureau estimates reflect that 15 of the 100 largest cities changed their borders in the 1990s such that their population increased by at least 2 percent. Because we use 2000 city borders to examine census tract population in both 1990 and 2000, population increases that result solely from the addition of new land (and its residents) to a city are not captured in the statistics we present here.[11] However, the population change that occurred over the decade within these new city tracts is captured.

We investigate how population growth and decline played out spatially in different cities and different regions of the United States. Two cities that

9. Kingsley and Pettit (forthcoming).

10. Treating all census tracts that intersect the borders of the 100 largest cities as part of those cities leads to an overstatement of city population of roughly 25 percent. Treating only those census tracts whose centers lie within the 100 largest cities' borders as part of those cities leads to an understatement of city population of roughly 20 percent. Using census blocks is thus essential for accurately representing within-city population change.

11. One specific result of using this methodology is that the city of Memphis, which grew by 6.5 percent according to the official 1990 and 2000 census counts, actually *decreased* in population by a little under 2 percent within its 2000 city boundaries over the decade.

experience similar levels of neighborhood growth and decline may differ greatly on where those trends took place. One city may experience downtown revitalization and growth while losing population in neighborhoods on its struggling suburban fringe; another may undergo a "hollowing out" with population loss in the city center but growth in farther-out neighborhoods. To better understand the spatial patterns of growth and decline within cities, we split each city's census tracts into three "rings," and analyze population change within each ring. We accomplish this by ranking all of a city's census tracts according to the distance between their center and the city's central business district, and splitting the ordered tracts into three groups. These tract groups do not form perfect concentric rings, because cities are not circles, but for ease of description, we refer to the groups as "inner core" (including the CBD), "middle ring," and "outer ring." Even this analysis can disguise important patterns of growth that occur along east-west or north-south lines, so in the following pages we present maps of cities that illustrate common spatial patterns of neighborhood population change.

Finally, we present tabulations of population change for city "downtowns," as represented by central business districts (CBDs). The 1982 Census of Retail Trade defined CBDs as representing areas "of very high land valuation characterized by a high concentration of retail businesses, service businesses, offices, theaters, and hotels, and by a very high traffic flow."[12] The CBDs were designed to follow 1980 census tract boundaries; in the few cities where those boundaries changed over the past two decades, we used 2000 blocks to reconstruct the boundaries. While what constitutes the downtown area in many of these cities is undoubtedly different today from twenty years ago, most CBDs retain the same commercial character that originally resulted in their designation, and all CBDs constitute at least the core of their city's downtown.[13]

12. U.S. Bureau of the Census (2001).

13. Researchers at the University of Pennsylvania, building on efforts of the Fannie Mae Foundation and the Brookings Urban Center, are in the process of defining downtown boundaries in cities throughout the country by conducting interviews with local leaders and analysis of historical maps. While their definitions reflect a more contemporary view of the geography of city downtowns, they are focused on a smaller sample of cities than is analyzed in this report. The lead researcher on the project noted, "there is no single socioeconomic meaning nor geographical boundary for the term [downtown]. While U.S. downtowns share several common characteristics (a central business district at the core, access to substantial transportation networks, a supply of high-density buildings), they differ dramatically in their age, territory, functions, contents and character." Birch (2002).

FINDINGS

An analysis of census tract population changes in the 100 largest cities between 1990 and 2000 indicates that:

- Large cities exhibited uneven growth patterns in the 1990s: though 72 percent of large cities grew in the 1990s, only 55 percent of neighborhoods added population. At the same time, growing neighborhoods grew almost three times as fast (22 percent) as total city population (8 percent).
- While growing cities were primarily made up of growing neighborhoods, nine such cities actually saw a majority of their neighborhoods decline in population. By contrast, all twenty cities that lost population overall had more declining than growing neighborhoods.
- More than 60 percent of central city population growth occurred in outer-ring neighborhoods, compared with just 11 percent in inner-core neighborhoods. Midwestern cities were most likely to exhibit hollowing out, with growth closer to the city edge and decline closer to the center. Southern cities grew rapidly at the suburban fringe, while growth and decline were spread somewhat more evenly throughout cities in the Northeast and West.
- About two-thirds of all downtown census tracts gained population, including many in cities that lost population overall. Growth in CBD populations, however, was quite small compared with overall city population change and was often overshadowed by population loss elsewhere in the urban core.

Growth of Large Cities and Neighborhood Populations

The 1990s were a decade of relatively widespread overall population growth in large U.S. cities. Overall, the top 100 cities increased in population by a little over 8 percent, and the overwhelming majority—72 of 100—gained residents. Among the remaining 28 cities, population was stable in 8, and declined in 20.

Population growth also predominated at the neighborhood level in cities during the 1990s. A majority—56 percent—of the 15,033 census tracts within the 100 largest cities experienced increases in population. As table 5-1 shows, population in these tracts grew at a 22 percent clip overall, much faster than the nation's 13 percent overall increase in population. The average growing central city tract added 739 people.

Neighborhood growth, however, was somewhat less prevalent than citywide growth. Amid the prevailing trend of neighborhood population

TABLE 5-1. Neighborhood Population Change in 100 Largest Cities, 1990–2000

Neighborhood type	*Share of all tracts (percent)*	*Average population, 2000*	*Average population change*	*Average change (percent)*
Increasing (N 8,288)	55.1	4,093	739	22
Decreasing (N 4,899)	32.6	3,145	386	11
Stable (N 1,846)	12.3	3,849	—	—
Total (N 15,033)	100	3,754	282	8.1

growth, about one-third of all central city census tracts lost population from 1990 to 2000. The declining tracts were somewhat larger on average than were the growing tracts in 1990—3,531 residents versus 3,354 residents—but by the decade's end, about 850 fewer people resided there on average than in growing tracts. Notably, though, the average population loss in these neighborhoods—11 percent—was only about half the size of the corresponding gain in growing neighborhoods.

In this fashion, large cities exhibited quite uneven growth patterns in the 1990s that saw fewer census tracts gaining population, and more tracts losing population, than city-level statistics suggest.

Neighborhood Growth and City Population Change

For the most part, city neighborhood growth mirrored citywide growth in the 1990s. The fastest-growing cities contained more gaining tracts than declining and stable ones. In cities that lost population, declining tracts predominated. Figure 5-1 shows this pattern graphically for groups of cities that experienced varying levels of overall growth or decline in the 1990s (table 5A-1 in the appendix to this chapter contains neighborhood population change statistics for each of the 100 largest cities).

Comparing each city's overall population change to change within its neighborhoods highlights three surprising patterns. First, as shown in figure 5-1, modestly growing cities (2 to 10 percent growth) had the same share of growing neighborhoods as rapidly growing cities (10 to 20 percent growth). This was the case in large part because of the presence of New York City in the "modest growers" category. An astounding 81 percent of the city's nearly 2,200 census tracts added residents, placing it thirteenth among the top 100 cities in the share of its neighborhoods that grew. Without the

FIGURE 5-1. Percent of Census Tracts Gaining Population, by City Growth Category, 1990–2000

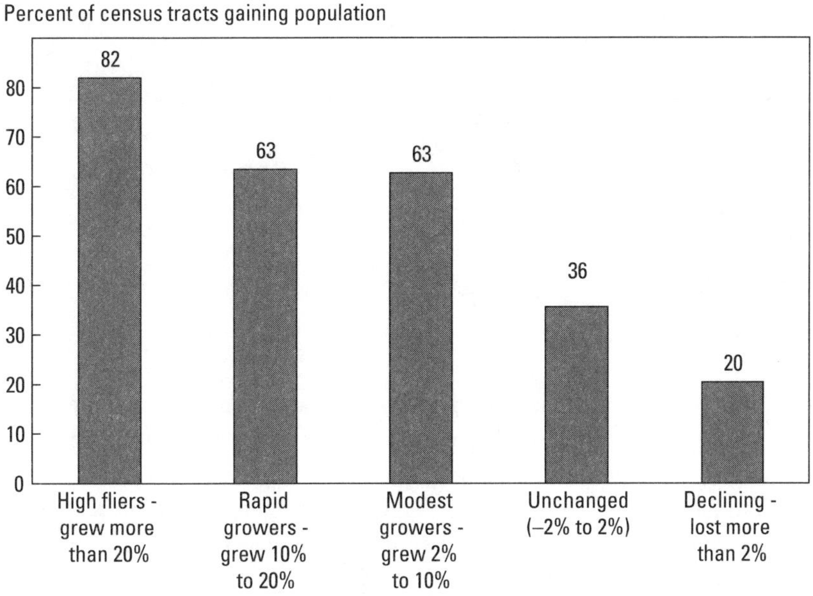

presence of New York in this category, only 54 percent of modest grower census tracts would have gained population in the 1990s.

Second, not every city that experienced an overall population increase saw most of its neighborhoods grow as well. In fact, 9 of the 100 largest cities had more declining than growing census tracts, even though they gained population citywide. Because the losses in their shrinking census tracts were smaller, on average, than the gains in their growing tracts, they were able to grow despite a relatively high incidence of neighborhood population loss (table 5-2).

All nine of these cities were located in either the midwestern or southern regions of the United States. They were led by Columbus, Ohio, which grew overall at a considerable 12 percent rate even as a plurality of its neighborhoods lost residents. In effect, the cities in table 5-2 boosted their population through increased density in some areas, while at the same time they "thinned out" in a larger number of areas. The patterns of neighborhood growth and decline in these cities help to explain why, even as 72 of the top 100 cities gained population in the 1990s, only 55 percent of their census tracts grew.

TABLE 5-2. Growing Cities with Greater Number of Declining than Growing Neighborhoods, 1990–2000

City	*Overall population change (percent)*	*Number of growing tracts*	*Number of declining tracts*	*Number of stable tracts*
Columbus, OH	11.7	85	99	23
El Paso, TX	9.4	32	62	16
Indianapolis, IN	6.9	78	105	21
Montgomery, AL	5.8	19	26	5
Augusta-Richmond, GA	5.3	15	20	5
Omaha, NE	4.6	52	62	18
Columbus, GA	3.9	21	27	8
Little Rock, AR	3.3	16	22	8
Des Moines, IA	2.7	19	22	15

Third, the reverse pattern—a citywide loss with more growing than shrinking tracts—was not present in any of the twenty declining cities. As figure 5-1 shows, across these cities, only 20 percent of all tracts gained population. Still, it is noteworthy that even in a city such as Baltimore, which lost nearly 12 percent of its population over the decade, one in six neighborhoods added residents, at an average rate of 11 percent. Clearly, there are islands of population gain amid seas of population decay in these cities. Often, there were explicit spatial patterns to that growth, which we examine in the next two sections.

Growth in Outer-Ring Neighborhoods Compared with Inner-Core Neighborhoods

Initial analysis from the 2000 Census indicated that, despite a population renaissance of sorts in many formerly struggling U.S. cities, decentralization remained the dominant trend across all metropolitan areas.[14] Suburban population grew at twice the rate of central city population, and no matter how fast cities grew, their suburbs consistently grew faster. In many metropolitan areas, the bulk of employment is located ten miles or more from the traditional city center, and people appear to be following employment out to the suburbs.[15]

Our analysis of population changes within cities reveals that decentralization is occurring even inside city borders. In the 1990s, the population of most large U.S. cities shifted toward the outskirts, with the bulk of growth taking place along the suburban border. Between 1990 and 2000, the inner

14. Katz and Berube (2002).
15. Glaeser, Kahn, and Chu (2001).

FIGURE 5-2. Neighborhood Population Change by Region and Distance from CBD, 100 Largest Central Cities, 1990–2000

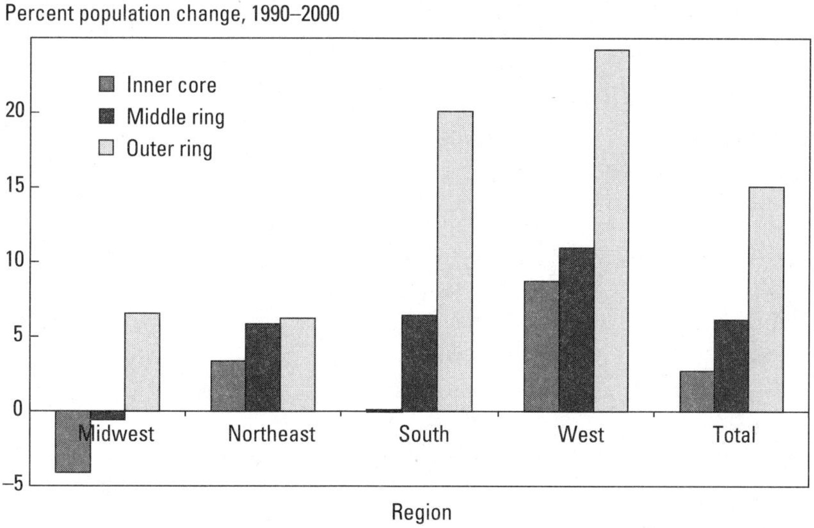

core of central city census tracts—those located in and around the CBD—increased in population by only 2.7 percent overall (figure 5-2). The middle ring grew at a little more than twice that rate (6.2 percent), while the outer ring boomed in population (15.1 percent growth). As a result of this population shift toward city borders, more people across the 100 largest cities now live in outer-ring neighborhoods (19.5 million) than in middle-ring (19.4 million) or inner-core (16.9 million) neighborhoods.

The outer census tracts were the drivers of central city population growth during the 1990s. Fully 62 percent of growth across the cities occurred in these neighborhoods, compared with only 11 percent in the inner core. Notably, this was not the result of astounding growth in a few decentralizing cities. More than three-quarters of all cities analyzed (seventy-six out of ninety-eight) experienced their fastest population growth (or slowest population decline) in census tracts located farthest from the CBD.

In many of these cities with fast growth in the outer neighborhoods, the CBD itself gained population, but change in the downtown area was far outpaced by that in the outer tracts. Oklahoma City, for instance, added 1,100 new residents to its CBD in the 1990s, and its inner-core neighborhoods grew by a little over 5 percent. Over the same period, the city's outer periphery of tracts grew by a staggering 34 percent, adding 50,000 new residents.

The pattern of increasing growth with increasing distance from the city center held across all regions of the country, although there were some very significant differences among regions in the size of the disparity between inner and outer tracts (table 5A-1 shows the population gain and loss in each third of neighborhoods for all 100 central cities). In general, hemmed-in cities in the Northeast experienced relatively even growth across inner, middle, and outer neighborhoods. Larger cities throughout the Midwest, South, and West that had more room to develop, and greater ability to annex land, saw population explode at the edges as it often stagnated or eroded at the core.

Northeast. Amid their lower overall population increases, cities in the Northeast were the most balanced in the spatial distribution of their growth and decline across neighborhoods. Growth in their inner, middle, and outer tracts averaged 3.4 percent, 5.9 percent, and 6.2 percent, respectively. Many northeastern cities are landlocked in the sense that they border other incorporated jurisdictions on all sides and so cannot add land to their outer ring through annexation. Land in these cities is often as expensive—or more expensive—in neighborhoods located near the city borders as it is near downtown areas. Not coincidentally, hemmed-in cities like Boston, Newark, and Yonkers experienced their fastest growth in neighborhoods near the city center, while they grew little in neighborhoods on the city outskirts.

For Boston, this did not mean that all inner-core tracts gained, or that all outer-ring tracts declined (map 5-1). Increases and decreases in neighborhood population could be found throughout the city, while a population resurgence in close-in neighborhoods like the Back Bay, Beacon Hill, and East Boston drove the city's overall growth. Downtown-growing cities like Boston represented one side of the coin in the Northeast in the 1990s; cities including Buffalo, Philadelphia, and Rochester represented the other side. These cities experienced overall population declines, and at the neighborhood level, population loss was greatest in the city center and less dramatic in the outer reaches of the city.

Midwest. The Midwest was the only region in which cities generally hollowed out. Overall, midwestern cities lost population in their inner-core neighborhoods (–3.1 percent), experienced neither a gain nor a loss in their middle third, and saw considerable growth in their outermost neighborhoods (6.9 percent). The growth that occurred in the outer neighborhoods of midwestern cities essentially saved them from overall population decline.

Columbus (Ohio), Fort Wayne, Indianapolis, and Kansas City all exemplified the midwestern hollowing out trend, with significant population loss

MAP 5-1. Boston, MA: Population Change by Census Tract, 1990–2000

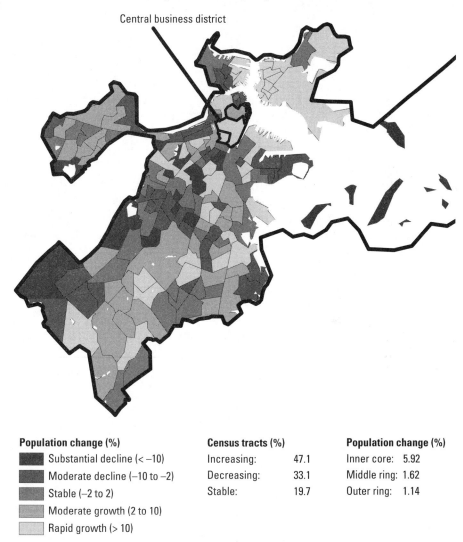

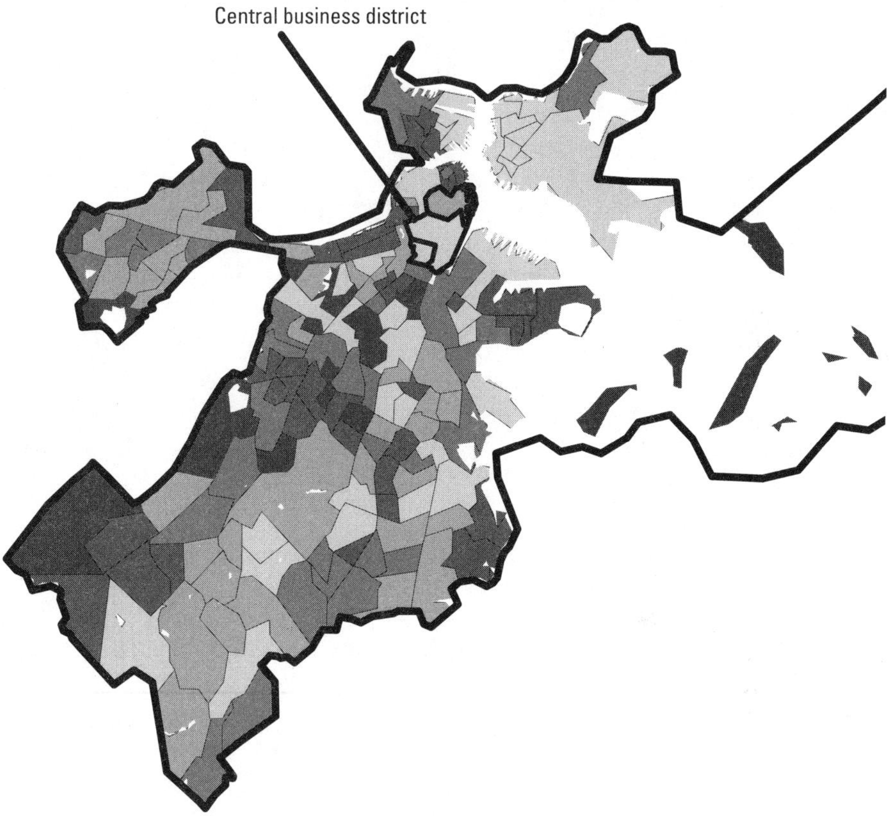

Population change (%)
- Substantial decline (< –10)
- Moderate decline (–10 to –2)
- Stable (–2 to 2)
- Moderate growth (2 to 10)
- Rapid growth (> 10)

Census tracts (%)	
Increasing:	47.1
Decreasing:	33.1
Stable:	19.7

Population change (%)	
Inner core:	5.92
Middle ring:	1.62
Outer ring:	1.14

at the core and significant growth at the periphery. In Columbus and Fort Wayne, annexation freed up land for new development and population growth on the city outskirts.[16] In Indianapolis and Kansas City, sheer city

16. As noted in the Methodology section, however, because we use consistent 2000 boundary definitions for cities, population growth in cities that annexed land in the 1990s reflects actual net population change at the tract level. Additions to population that result

size left more room to develop, and more room for population growth, in the outermost areas. Besides their greater annexation powers and overall size, midwestern cities have fewer physical obstacles to growth—unlike in Denver, Boston, or Phoenix, no mountains, ocean, or desert impedes growth in the Indianapolis hinterlands.

There were a few cities in the Midwest where gains in the core helped to drive population growth—Minneapolis and St. Paul, most notably—but decentralization dominated across the region, in both growing and shrinking cities. In Wichita, the inner-core neighborhoods lost about 3 percent of their population, while the outer ring grew by an astounding 45 percent (map 5-2). Local analysts note that one traditionally black downtown neighborhood lost 65 percent of its population between 1970 and 2000. The deterioration of these neighborhoods has spread to more than twenty blocks on the edge of downtown, where upward of half of all houses and apartments are vacant. In the city's outskirts, by contrast, developers are building new, larger houses on vacant land, and people are buying in droves.[17]

South. In the 1990s, growth in cities in the Southeast trailed that in the suburbs by wide margins. In the Mobile area, for instance, central city population grew by only 1.3 percent, but suburban population expanded by 22 percent. Average population growth in suburbs across the region was three times the central city average.[18]

Cities throughout the South mirrored this dramatic decentralization trend. Overall, cities in the South were largely stagnant in their core areas, had modest gains in their middle thirds, and experienced tremendous population increases—more than 20 percent—in their outermost areas. The rapid growth in the outer ring of southern cities reflects the fact that they are typically larger in size than cities in other regions, and that they have access to more undeveloped land within their own borders and in nearby unincorporated jurisdictions.[19]

Charlotte, Raleigh, and Greensboro together typify the growth patterns in cities throughout the Southeast. Two-thirds of their combined popula-

solely from the acquisition of existing residents in annexed tracts are not included in our calculations.

17. Dan Voorhis, "Fleeing the City's Core: Is Anybody Home?" *Wichita Eagle*, July 1, 2001, p. 1A.

18. Berube (2002).

19. Rusk (1995) referred to "elastic cities" like those in the South that are large and are able to expand their borders through annexation. In 2000, the average size of the southern cities in this study was 239 square miles, compared with 186 in the West, 117 in the Midwest, and 75 in the Northeast.

MAP 5-2. Wichita, KS: Population Change by Census Tract, 1990–2000

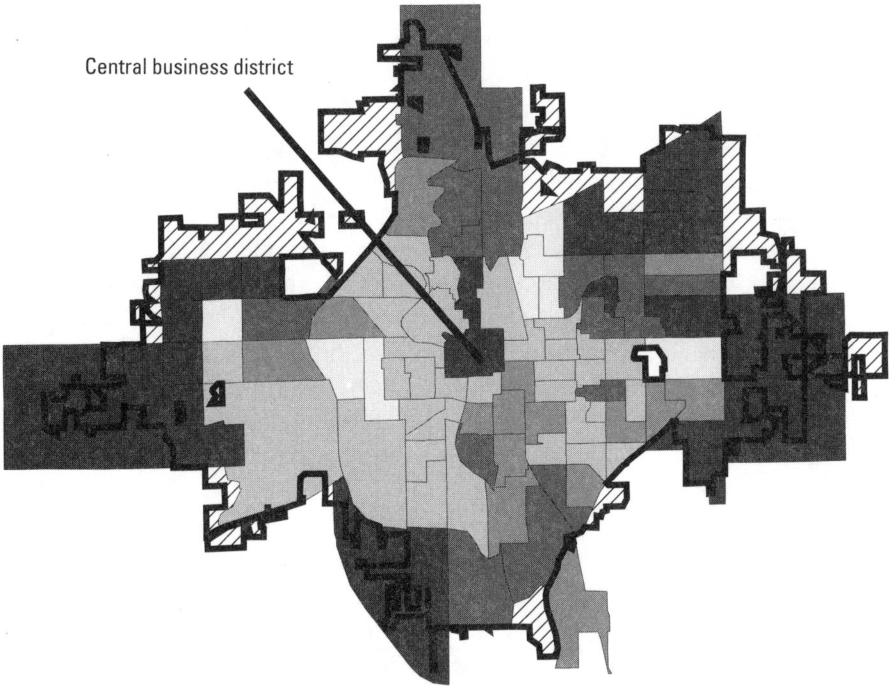

Population change (%)

- Substantial decline (< –10)
- Moderate decline (–10 to –2)
- Stable (–2 to 2)
- Moderate growth (2 to 10)
- Rapid growth (>10)
- No data

Census tracts (%)

Increasing:	20.6
Decreasing:	64.7
Stable:	14.7

Population change (%)

Inner core:	2.7
Middle ring:	0.3
Outer ring:	44.8

tion gain occurred in outer-ring neighborhoods, owing in large part to development in newly annexed land—each city added to its land area by more than one-third during the 1990s. At the same time, very little population growth occurred in and around the downtowns of these cities; only 4 percent of their net new residents resided in inner-core neighborhoods.[20] Nearly all of the action on growth took place in the farthest reaches of these North Carolina cities.

The growth problems in the southern cities varied somewhat, however. A number of cities in the southwestern part of the region, such as Austin, Dallas, Fort Worth, and Houston experienced more substantial population gains in their core areas, though neighborhoods at their suburban edges still boomed. One southwestern city, however, provides an illustration of the predominant growth pattern in the South during the 1990s (map 5-3). In San Antonio, declining tracts were clustered around the city core and often found on one side of the core (in this case, the lower-income southern side). At the same time, tracts throughout the northernmost and southernmost reaches of San Antonio experienced substantial population gains. In the outer third of the city, the average census tract grew by 47 percent.

West. Consistent with their faster overall growth than cities in other regions, western cities experienced the most rapid population increases in each of their neighborhood rings. While growth in these cities was more evenly distributed among the inner, middle, and outer neighborhoods than in the Midwest or South, large disparities still existed between growth at the core and growth at the periphery. Overall, inner-core neighborhoods in western cities averaged 8.4 percent growth, and outer-ring neighborhoods averaged 24.1 percent growth. San Diego (map 5-4) illustrates this disparity; some growth occurred in neighborhoods in the downtown area, but areas farther north and northeast of the core such as Carmel Valley captured the bulk of the city's population increase over the decade. Some growth also occurred in the far southern part of the city along the Mexican border.

In the West, many cities are also notable for having experienced extremely rapid growth in their outer reaches. Many of these places saw the construction of enormous subdivisions in the 1990s that, in older metro-

20. Interestingly, two of the largest cities in this region, Atlanta and Washington, bucked this trend. Atlanta densified in its core, thanks largely to an increase in "downtown living." Washington managed to stabilize population in its downtown area, as poorer neighborhoods in the farther-flung northeastern and southeastern sections of the city experienced substantial population loss.

MAP 5-3. San Antonio, TX: Population Change by Census Tract, 1990–2000

Population change (%)

- Substantial decline (< –10)
- Moderate decline (–10 to –2)
- Stable (–2 to 2)
- Moderate growth (2 to 10)
- Rapid growth (>10)
- No data

Census tracts (%)	
Increasing:	65.6
Decreasing:	23.8
Stable:	10.7

Population change (%)	
Inner core :	0.3
Middle ring :	7.1
Outer ring :	47.1

MAP 5-4. San Diego, CA: Population Change by Census Tract, 1990–2000

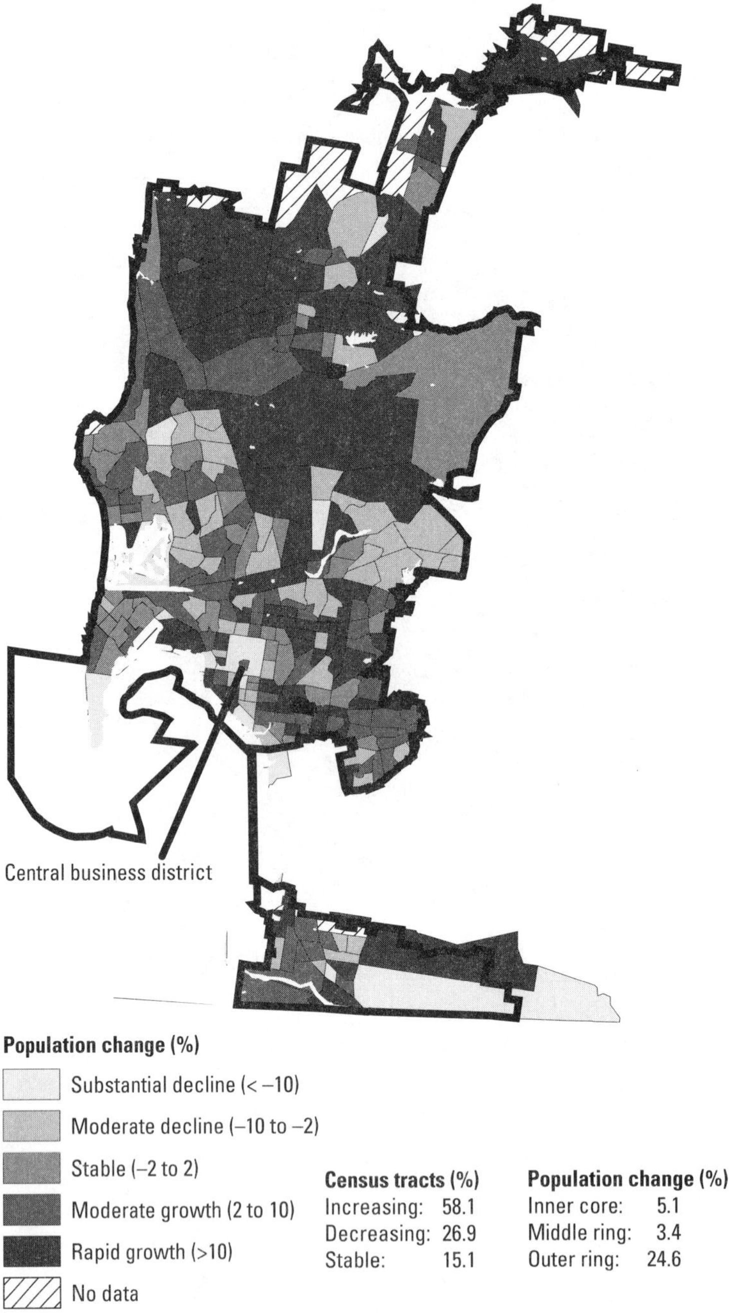

politan areas, would often be relegated to the suburbs. Cities like Colorado Springs (65 percent outer-third growth), Bakersfield (116 percent), Mesa (119 percent), and Las Vegas (528 percent) were able to accommodate this type of population boom within their own expansive borders.

Population Increase in Downtown Census Tracts

Researchers have already noted what has been called a "downtown rebound" in a number of U.S. cities in the 1990s. After decades of population loss, many city downtowns are capturing increasing shares of metro area population. One analysis found that eighteen of twenty-four large-city downtowns gained population in the 1990s, including six that added residents even as the city lost population overall.[21] As Eugenie Birch notes, however, the recent rise in downtown populations has been "small and delicate" when viewed over the longer term. Only 38 percent of the downtowns she analyzed had more people in 2000 than they did in 1970.[22]

This examination of CBD populations in a larger sample of 98 cities largely confirms findings from the earlier Birch analysis, corroborating evidence of a resurgence in city downtown populations.[23] Of the 232 census tracts that make up the CBDs of these cities, 151 (65 percent) experienced population increases over the decade. The overall population of CBDs jumped nearly 13 percent, considerably higher than the 8 percent overall increase across the 100 cities.

Viewed from the city level, downtown growth was similarly widespread. Overall, 68 of the 98 cities we analyzed saw increases in their CBD populations during the decade (figure 5-3). In contrast to neighborhood growth citywide, though, there seemed to be no strong relationship between population change in cities at large and population change in their CBD tracts. In fact, of the 20 cities among the top 100 that declined in population during the 1990s, fully 17 (85 percent) experienced *increases* in their CBD populations. Table 5-3 displays the ten cities with the fastest overall population gains despite population loss in their CBDs, and the ten cities with the largest population decline despite population gain in their CBDs. Cities with overall population losses such as Buffalo, Pittsburgh, and Cleveland all posted considerable percentage gains in their downtown populations, sometimes as a result of concerted municipal strategies to create "living" downtowns.

21. Sohmer and Lang (2002).

22. Birch (2002).

23. The figures presented in this section are for ninety-eight cities; neither Hialeah, FL, nor Virginia Beach, VA, had a census-defined CBD in 1982.

FIGURE 5-3. Number of Growing and Declining Downtowns, by Overall City Population Change, 1990–2000

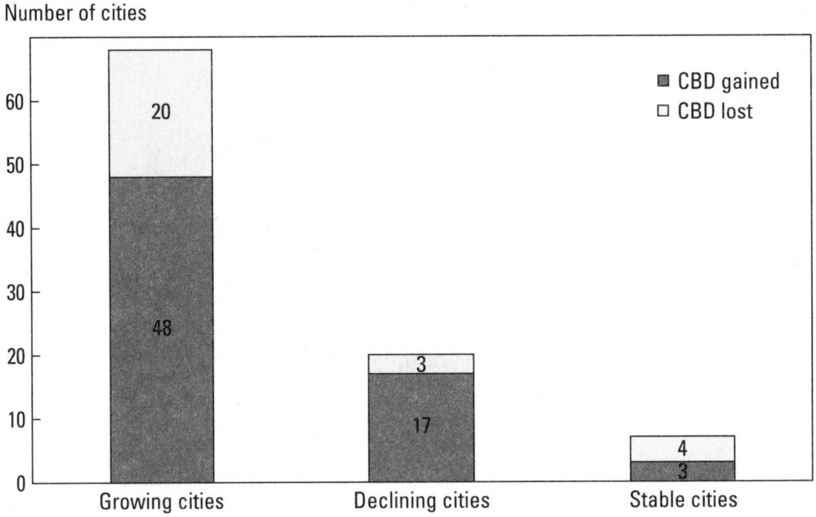

In these cities, however, a growing downtown often represented an isolated instance of population growth in the urban core. In fact, 40 percent of cities with growing CBDs in the 1990s experienced population loss in their inner-core census tracts. For example, Cleveland's strategy to create a "24-hour downtown" paid off in the addition of 2,700 new residents to its CBD, a 51 percent increase from 1990. Yet that growth occurred amid the loss of 8,200 residents elsewhere in Cleveland's inner-core neighborhoods—a 6 percent population decline. Maps of San Antonio and San Diego (Maps 5-3 and 5-4 both show that growing downtown neighborhoods lie alongside core neighborhoods that lost residents over the decade.)

The complicated relationship between city growth and downtown growth was also evident in the growing cities. Of sixty-eight growing cities analyzed, twenty (29 percent) lost CBD population during the 1990s. Many of these twenty cities and their downtowns—such as Bakersfield, El Paso, Mesa, and St. Petersburg—are more suburban in feel than older northeastern and midwestern places. Some have posited that these mostly southern and western downtowns do not offer consumers enough in the way of amenities that help to distinguish them from suburbs or from the rest of the city.[24] They may also lack the job concentrations characteristic of many

24. Sohmer and Lang (2001).

TABLE 5-3. City Population Change versus Central Business District Population Change, 1990–2000

	Total population			CBD population		
City	*1990*	*2000*	*Change (percent)*	*1990*	*2000*	*Change (percent)*
Cities with fastest population growth and declining CBD population[a]						
Mesa, AZ	290,165	396,369	36.6	3,206	2,864	−10.7
Bakersfield, CA	188,069	246,985	31.3	1,521	1,187	−22.0
Dallas, TX	1,005,685	1,188,493	18.2	3,443	2,188	−36.5
Lexington, KY	225,347	260,487	15.6	5,212	4,894	−6.1
Stockton, CA	211,305	243,700	15.3	8,459	7,102	−16.0
Houston, TX	1,696,462	1,953,261	15.1	7,005	6,678	−4.7
Riverside, CA	226,857	255,166	12.5	5,428	4,845	−10.7
Columbus, OH	634,890	709,398	11.7	1,656	1,621	−2.1
El Paso, TX	514,957	563,605	9.4	2,817	1,797	−36.2
Tampa, FL	279,654	303,439	8.5	1,171	709	−39.5
Cities with fastest population decline and growing CBD population[a]						
St. Louis, MO	396,489	348,182	−12.2	3,250	3,385	4.2
Baltimore, MD	736,014	651,154	−11.5	1,683	1,739	3.3
Buffalo, NY	328,045	292,644	−10.8	1,440	1,939	34.7
Norfolk, VA	261,228	234,399	−10.3	2,402	2,881	19.9
Pittsburgh, PA	369,804	334,524	−9.5	3,785	5,222	38.0
Dayton, OH	182,500	166,080	−9.0	1,470	2,044	39.0
Detroit, MI	1,027,671	951,213	−7.4	5,970	6,141	2.9
Washington, DC	606,827	572,044	−5.7	2,708	3,188	17.7
Cleveland, OH	505,291	478,330	−5.3	5,367	8,105	51.0
Milwaukee, WI	628,078	596,938	−5.0	2,750	3,334	21.2

a. CBD population of at least 1,000 in 1990.

older downtowns that appeal to people looking to live and work in the same area.

In general, CBD population gains made only minor contributions to overall population change in cities in the 1990s. In the forty-eight growing cities that also had a growing CBD, the downtown contribution to city population growth was only 2.4 percent on average. Similarly, in the seventeen shrinking cities that had a growing CBD, the average downtown offset of city population loss was 2.4 percent. This should not be surprising, given the small geographic size of CBD areas in comparison to their cities. Still, these statistics serve as a reminder that downtown gains and losses form only a small part of the broader population trends affecting cities and their neighborhoods.

CONCLUSION

Viewed at the city level, demographic shifts such as population and income growth and decline, racial and ethnic change, aging, and migration can indicate important changes in the ability of cities to serve public needs. At the end of the day, the city itself must deliver services to its residents and raise the revenues to fund those services (or seek them from another level of government).

Changes at the neighborhood level, in comparison, may better signal changes in the private markets in which city residents operate. Neighborhood population growth, for instance, can lead to increasing property values and new jobs and retail opportunities for existing residents. In some cases, it may lead to displacement of lower-income residents owing to higher housing costs. As such, exploring population dynamics at the municipal and neighborhood levels is crucial for understanding the changing fortunes of cities and their residents.

This study finds that America's cities underwent complex patterns of neighborhood population change in the 1990s. As with cities themselves, most urban neighborhoods grew over the decade, and not surprisingly, cities that grew had more growing neighborhoods. Yet in many cities that grew overall, neighborhood population loss was pervasive. And most cities, especially those in the Midwest and South, experienced the bulk of their population growth in neighborhoods far from the core—and sometimes at its expense. Central business districts—the core of downtowns—were often buffered from these losses, in part because of concerted municipal strategies to create living downtowns. But in many cases, those strategies seem to have fallen short of creating growth throughout the urban core.

Our findings confirm that citywide indicators hide a more complex story about which neighborhoods benefited from the economic boom of the 1990s, and which were left behind. The design of targeted reinvestment strategies must begin with neighborhood-level analysis. Although population change is only one part of an informed analysis, this chapter's core findings about the pattern of within-central city decentralization raise three interesting implications.

First, it appears that the larger trend of metropolitan decentralization begins inside city borders—that is, sprawl does not start at the city's edge. Central cities are made up of healthy and distressed neighborhoods, and efforts to help slow the tide of decentralization must be focused on reinvigorating areas of slow growth or decline—whether these neighborhoods are located in the inner core (as in many midwestern cities) or in farther-out city neighborhoods (as in Atlanta and Washington).

Second, there is a common perception that the growing cities in the South and West are healthy compared with their midwestern and northeastern counterparts. However, the large geographies of many of these places mask the fact that they, too, often have weaker cores. The inner neighborhoods of cities like Bakersfield and El Paso, if left unattended, may contribute to further hollowing out and help to accelerate larger decentralization patterns.

Third, the fact that growing CBDs were often surrounded by declining inner-core neighborhoods suggests the need for more inclusive downtown strategies. In developing targeted revitalization strategies for downtown areas, city leaders should include efforts to engage or respond to the needs of surrounding neighborhoods. These can range from putting in safeguards to protect the affordability of some housing as property prices increase to involving residents in center city redevelopment plans to ensure that downtown growth redounds to the benefit of surrounding neighborhoods.

As more detailed data become available from the census long form, researchers will gain better insight into the push-and-pull forces that drove population changes in cities in the 1990s.[25] These data will also provide clues as to what those changes mean for the overall social and economic health of city neighborhoods in the next decade.

25. Kingsley and Pettit (forthcoming).

TABLE 5A-1. Neighborhood Population Change Characteristics in 100 Largest Cities, 1990–2000

Percent unless noted otherwise

Region/city	*Region*	*Overall population change*[a]	*Increasing tracts (number)*	*Decreasing tracts (number)*	*Stable tracts (number)*	*CBD population change*	*Inner ring population change*	*Middle ring population change*	*Outer ring population change*	*Average land area (sq mi)*
Midwest (21 cities)		1.2	35	53	12	18.4	–4.1	–0.6	6.6	117.4
Northeast (9 cities)		5.2	65	24	11	6.9	3.4	5.9	6.2	75.1
South (41 cities)		9.0	52	36	12	6.2	0.1	6.4	20.1	238.8
West (29 cities)		14.4	68	18	14	16.9	8.7	11.0	24.2	185.6
Total—Top 100 cities		8.1	55	33	12	12.9	2.7	6.2	15.1	183.1
Midwest										
Akron, OH	MW	–2.7	21	65	15	–21.9	–4.3	–4.9	1.9	62.1
Chicago, IL	MW	4.1	50	41	9	34.4	1.9	4.5	4.7	227.1
Cincinnati, OH	MW	–9.0	10	79	11	–16.9	–15.2	–7.3	–6.6	78.0
Cleveland, OH	MW	–5.3	20	61	19	51.0	–5.9	–5.0	–5.4	77.6
Columbus, OH	MW	11.7	41	48	11	–2.1	–9.1	6.9	40.1	210.3
Dayton, OH	MW	–9.0	15	80	5	39.0	–10.1	–9.3	–6.5	55.8
Des Moines, IA	MW	2.7	34	39	27	0.3	2.4	2.4	3.4	75.8
Detroit, MI	MW	–7.4	21	71	8	2.9	–9.6	–9.1	–4.6	138.8
Fort Wayne, IN	MW	–0.1	32	52	15	1.5	–7.8	–0.3	7.1	79.0
Grand Rapids, MI	MW	4.5	46	27	27	18.2	2.9	4.3	6.4	44.6
Indianapolis, IN	MW	6.9	38	51	10	35.4	–7.5	2.2	22.8	361.5
Kansas City, MO	MW	1.5	30	56	13	–13.1	–6.5	–3.7	14.4	313.5
Lincoln, NE	MW	17.3	65	17	17	12.3	3.4	14.2	41.1	74.6
Madison, WI	MW	8.1	45	36	18	7.1	0.5	–3.9	40.1	68.7
Milwaukee, WI	MW	–5.0	27	62	11	21.2	–9.6	–6.2	–0.8	96.1
Minneapolis, MN	MW	3.9	53	35	12	20.1	7.5	7.7	–1.6	54.9
Omaha, NE	MW	4.6	39	47	14	32.0	2.2	–0.1	13.3	115.7
St. Louis, MO	MW	–12.2	12	77	12	4.2	–19.4	–11.3	–7.8	61.9
St. Paul, MN	MW	5.5	46	33	21	39.1	9.3	8.4	0.4	52.8
Toledo, OH	MW	–5.8	12	80	8	27.7	–9.8	–6.4	–2.3	80.6
Wichita, KS	MW	10.6	44	43	14	–8.4	–2.7	–0.3	44.8	135.8

Northeast										
Boston, MA	NE	2.6	47	33	20	29.7	5.9	1.6	1.0	48.4
Buffalo, NY	NE	−10.8	9	83	8	34.7	−14.7	−13.9	−6.0	40.6
Jersey City, NJ	NE	5.0	61	29	11	5.2	4.3	4.9	5.8	14.9
New York, NY	NE	9.5	81	10	9	−0.6	6.3	10.9	11.4	303.3
Newark, NJ	NE	−0.5	48	43	9	−11.4	3.8	1.4	−4.8	23.8
Philadelphia, PA	NE	−4.0	27	57	16	8.8	−7.2	−4.9	−1.1	135.1
Pittsburgh, PA	NE	−9.5	8	89	3	38.0	−9.0	−8.8	−10.7	55.6
Rochester, NY	NE	−4.9	12	64	23	5.4	−6.8	−5.4	−3.2	35.8
Yonkers, NY	NE	4.3	67	10	24	8.2	6.9	4.1	0.9	18.1
South										
Arlington, TX	S	27.2	85	12	3	17.8	15.1	23.9	45.2	95.8
Atlanta, GA	S	5.7	57	31	12	110.9	13.8	0.9	5.5	131.8
Augusta–Richmond, GA	S	5.3	38	50	13	16.6	−9.2	−4.6	19.1	302.1
Austin, TX	S	31.9	87	6	7	−7.3	17.7	26.5	71.8	251.5
Baltimore, MD	S	−11.5	17	74	10	3.3	−17.3	−12.6	−6.7	80.8
Baton Rouge, LA	S	2.1	47	45	8	17.6	−3.3	5.2	2.7	76.8
Birmingham, AL	S	−8.5	30	61	9	−12.9	−13.4	−6.6	−0.2	149.9
Charlotte, NC	S	26.6	70	22	7	25.9	0.4	16.9	74.0	242.3
Columbus, GA	S	3.9	38	48	14	−10.2	−10.6	−4.9	18.3	216.1
Corpus Christi (part), TX	S	7.4	53	23	25	18.3	−3.9	2.6	28.4	154.6
Dallas, TX	S	18.2	69	23	8	−36.5	11.6	16.5	27.2	342.5
El Paso, TX	S	9.4	29	56	15	−36.2	−8.5	5.0	36.7	249.1
Fort Worth, TX	S	19.5	73	20	7	75.3	7.7	13.6	44.9	292.5
Garland, TX	S	19.3	84	5	11	−3.0	18.8	18.5	20.7	57.1
Greensboro, NC	S	16.8	67	20	14	−31.0	0.9	11.9	40.4	19.2
Hialeah, FL[b]	S	20.5	77	13	10					579.4
Houston, TX	S	15.1	70	23	7	−4.7	6.5	16.9	23.1	579.4
Jackson, MS	S	−6.2	25	60	15	79.5	−19.3	−1.4	−1.0	104.9
Jacksonville, FL	S	15.8	51	34	15	−55.9	−3.2	7.9	41.3	1,964.8
Lexington–Fayette, KY	S	15.6	53	37	10	−6.1	−2.9	3.6	43.4	284.5
Little Rock, AR	S	3.3	35	48	17	17.4	−19.8	−1.4	19.6	116.2
Louisville, KY	S	−4.9	22	65	13	3.1	−2.9	−5.3	−6.7	62.1

(continued)

TABLE 5A-1. Neighborhood Population Change Characteristics in 100 Largest Cities, 1990–2000 (*continued*)

Percent unless noted otherwise

Region/city	*Region*	*Overall population change*[a]	*Increasing tracts (number)*	*Decreasing tracts (number)*	*Stable tracts (number)*	*CBD population change*	*Inner ring population change*	*Middle ring population change*	*Outer ring population change*	*Average land area (sq mi)*
Lubbock, TX	S	6.7	63	20	17	–5.5	–3.5	1.4	23.7	114.8
Memphis, TN	S	–1.8	35	54	11	–4.8	–16.2	–3.6	10.9	279.3
Miami, FL	S	1.0	41	41	18	285.2	1.0	2.5	–1.1	35.7
Mobile, AL	S	0.5	31	57	13	–75.0	–5.4	1.2	4.8	117.9
Montgomery, AL	S	5.8	38	52	10	–38.8	–15.0	1.8	28.7	155.4
Nashville–Davidson, TN	S	11.7	60	29	11	3.4	–1.3	5.3	28.0	473.3
New Orleans, LA	S	–2.5	29	50	20	15.5	–6.1	–3.0	–0.1	180.6
Newport News, VA	S	5.9	46	43	11	11.8	–10.5	18.9	5.9	68.3
Norfolk, VA	S	–10.3	25	55	19	19.9	–7.6	–1.4	–17.1	53.7
Oklahoma City, OK	S	13.8	60	27	13	28.8	5.4	3.1	34.0	607.0
Raleigh, NC	S	25.4	71	16	13	27.3	8.3	24.9	50.3	114.6
Richmond, VA	S	–2.5	28	54	18	15.8	–5.2	–3.9	0.0	60.1
San Antonio, TX	S	14.8	66	24	11	27.1	–0.3	7.1	47.1	407.6
Shreveport, LA	S	0.4	48	38	13	17.5	–6.9	–1.9	6.2	103.1
St Petersburg, FL	S	4.0	47	23	30	–12.9	–6.4	6.1	9.1	59.6
Tampa, FL	S	8.5	53	30	16	–39.5	–1.1	2.5	22.7	112.1
Tulsa, OK	S	7.0	54	33	13	34.2	3.6	2.3	15.4	182.7
Virginia Beach, VA[b]	S	8.2	51	34	15					248.3
Washington, DC	S	–5.7	21	64	15	17.7	–0.2	–6.6	–9.2	61.4

West										
Albuquerque, NM	W	15.6	44	42	14	45.2	2.2	23.2	24.1	180.6
Anaheim, CA	W	23.1	89	7	4	34.0	21.5	18.5	30.7	48.9
Anchorage, AK	W	15.0	89	4	7	78.2	9.2	16.6	17.9	1,697.2
Aurora, CO	W	24.3	83	10	7	75.5	31.1	13.7	31.0	142.5
Bakersfield, CA	W	31.3	77	11	12	–22.0	3.3	20.4	116.3	113.1
Colorado Springs, CO	W	27.5	84	3	12	16.0	10.1	17.1	65.4	185.7
Denver, CO	W	18.7	76	7	16	51.4	14.9	14.3	26.4	153.4
Fresno, CA	W	20.4	70	19	11	21.3	5.7	13.5	55.3	104.4
Glendale, CA	W	8.3	83	6	11	7.7	8.5	8.4	7.9	30.7
Honolulu, HI	W	–1.3	30	54	16	18.6	2.1	–2.5	–3.4	85.7
Huntington Beach, CA	W	4.7	37	37	26	16.2	11.3	1.2	1.5	26.4
Las Vegas, NV	W	84.4	86	6	8	37.4	26.2	54.9	528.2	113.3
Long Beach, CA	W	9.4	66	15	20	15.5	5.1	5.2	11.8	50.4
Los Angeles, CA	W	6.0	59	23	18	–8.5	1.5	5.6	10.8	469.1
Mesa, AZ	W	36.6	84	8	9	–10.7	16.5	21.5	119.0	125.0
Oakland, CA	W	7.3	68	15	17	36.3	5.4	6.6	9.6	56.1
Phoenix, AZ	W	33.9	87	8	5	9.5	24.8	19.5	64.9	474.9
Portland, OR	W	8.8	65	20	15	14.6	5.3	4.2	17.9	134.3
Riverside, CA	W	12.5	64	21	15	–10.7	3.3	12.6	23.8	78.1
Sacramento, CA	W	10.2	59	26	15	8.8	0.3	9.1	20.6	97.2
San Diego, CA	W	10.1	58	27	15	20.1	5.1	3.4	24.5	324.3
San Francisco, CA	W	7.3	69	15	15	21.6	10.1	2.1	10.0	46.7
San Jose, CA	W	14.2	74	14	13	5.0	12.5	15.8	14.2	174.9
Santa Ana, CA	W	15.0	85	5	10	33.2	12.0	16.2	18.2	27.1
Seattle, WA	W	9.1	76	9	15	43.6	14.8	5.2	8.9	83.9
Spokane, WA	W	9.8	79	9	12	2.4	4.1	7.0	27.3	57.8
Stockton, CA	W	15.3	49	30	21	–16.0	6.7	33.2	9.6	54.7
Tacoma, WA	W	9.6	61	22	16	26.2	2.9	13.8	14.6	50.1
Tucson, AZ	W	16.8	74	12	14	17.7	8.0	18.1	27.8	194.7

Source: Authors' analysis of 1990 and 2000 Census data.

a. Population change figures are based on consistent use of 2000 city boundaries in both decades. As a result, additions to population that occurred solely as a result of annexation between 1990 and 2000 are not reflected.

b. Hialeah, FL, and Virginia Beach, VA, have no census-defined central business districts.

REFERENCES

Birch, Eugenie Ladner. 2002. "Having a Longer View on Downtown Living." *Journal of the American Planning Association* 68(1): 5–21.

Glaeser, Edward L. and Jesse Shapiro. 2001. "City Growth and the 2000 Census: Which Places Grew, and Why." Brookings.

Glaeser, Edward L., Matthew Kahn, and Chenghuan Chu. 2001. "Job Sprawl: Employment Location in U.S. Metropolitan Areas." Brookings.

Katz, Bruce, and Alan Berube. 2002. "Cities Rebound—Somewhat." *American Enterprise* 13(4): 47.

Kingsley, G. Thomas, and Kathryn L. S. Pettit. Forthcoming. "Population Growth and Decline in City Neighborhoods." Washington: Urban Institute.

Lang, Robert, and Patrick Simmons. 2001. "The Urban Turnaround: A Decade-by-Decade Report Card on Postwar Population Change in Older Industrial Cities." Washington: Fannie Mae Foundation.

Morenoff, J., and R. J. Sampson. 1997. "Violent Crime and the Spatial Dynamics of Neighborhood Transition: Chicago, 1970–1990." *Social Forces* 76: 31–64.

Quillian, Lincoln. 1999. "Migration Patterns and the Growth of High-Poverty Neighborhoods, 1970–1990." *American Journal of Sociology* 105 (1):1–37.

Redick, Richard W. 1954. "Population Growth and Distribution in Central Cities, 1940–1950." *American Sociological Review* 21(1): 38–43.

Rusk, David. 1995. *Cities without Suburbs*. Washington: Woodrow Wilson Center Press.

Scafidi, Benjamin P., Michael H. Schill, Susan M. Wachter, and Dennis P. Culhane. 1998. "An Economic Analysis of Housing Abandonment." *Journal of Housing Economics* 7(4): 287–303.

Thompson, Warren S. 1947. *Population: The Growth of Metropolitan Districts in the United States, 1900–1940*. Washington: U.S. Bureau of the Census.

U.S. Bureau of the Census. "Central Business Districts: 1982 Census of Retail Trade." *www.census.gov/geo/www/cbd.html* (accessed October 1, 2002).

Vey, Jennifer, and Benjamin Forman. 2002. "Demographic Change in Medium-Size Cities: Evidence from the 2000 Census." Brookings.

6

"*Boomburbs*"

The Emergence of Large, Fast-Growing Suburban Cities

ROBERT E. LANG
PATRICK A. SIMMONS

When late-nineteenth and early-twentieth-century satellite cities reached a large scale, they developed as dense urban cores. But in the latter part of the twentieth century, along with the Sun Belt and the suburban-dominated metropolis there emerged a new type of large, rapidly growing suburban cities (or "boomburbs"), most of which remain essentially suburban in character as they grow into big "cities." Just as satellite cities reflected the dominant urban pattern of that earlier era, boomburbs may be the ultimate symbol of today's sprawling postwar metropolitan form.

Boomburbs are defined as places with more than 100,000 residents that are *not* the largest cities in their respective metropolitan areas and that have maintained double-digit rates of population growth in recent decades. The United States currently contains fifty-three boomburbs. Four of these have a population of more than 300,000, eight surpass 200,000, and forty-one exceed 100,000. The present study follows these important but seldom recognized places, which accounted for more than half of the past decade's growth in U.S. cities of 100,000 to 400,000 residents. Boomburbs now contain a quarter of all people who live in such places.

Boomburbs may be found throughout the nation, but they occur mostly in the Southwest, with almost half in California alone. Many boomburbs, especially those in the West, are products of master-planned-community development and of the need to form large water districts. Even a relatively

The authors thank William Frey and Frank Popper for invaluable comments on a draft of this chapter. They also thank Rebecca Sohmer for suggesting the term *boomburb*.

small metropolis such as Las Vegas, with its expansive master-planned communities and desert surroundings, contains two boomburbs. By contrast, no big region in the Northeast or Midwest, except Chicago, has a single boomburb. Even most large and rapidly growing Sun Belt metropolitan areas east of the Mississippi, such as Atlanta, lack boomburbs. Thus a region can boom and still wind up without boomburbs.

The South's suburbs are composed of mostly small, fragmented municipalities that capture tiny fractions of metropolitan population. This difference in municipal structure between the Sun Belt of the East and the Sun Belt of the West has important policy implications. The eastern Sun Belt's fragmented municipalities will likely produce more fragmented responses to regional problems. If, as many now argue, regional cooperation is becoming more essential for successfully addressing such problems as sprawl, then the South's lack of boomburbs may put that region at a disadvantage.

Because of their exceptionally fast growth rates, the boomburbs do face extreme degrees of development-related problems such as traffic congestion, sprawl, and stress on public services. But because of their large size and their potential to cooperate with other large municipalities, boomburbs may prove well positioned to participate in comprehensive regional solutions to these problems.

Boomburbs are fast-growing suburban cities.[1] They typically develop along the interstate beltways that ring large U.S. metropolitan areas. At highway exit ramps and major intersections there gather the commercial elements of the new suburban metropolis: the office parks, big-box retail, and (most characteristically) strip development. Beyond these strips of commercially developed land along the highways lie subdivisions dominated by large-lot, single-family homes.

Some may question whether boomburbs are merely updated satellite cities. Business, particularly manufacturing, has been decentralizing for many decades. In a 1915 publication entitled *Satellite Cities: A Case Study of Industrial Suburbs,* economist Graham Taylor described an emerging metropolitan pattern in which heavy industry was rapidly shifting to the suburbs in search of more space and lower costs. More than seventy-five years ago, sociologist Ernest Burgess noted that there was already business growth at Chicago's edge, which he characterized as being "centralized-decentralized" in structure.[2]

1. The emergence of these large suburban cities has recently come to the attention of the popular press. See Haya El Nasser and Paul Overberg, "Suburban Communities Spurt to Big-City Status," *USA Today*, November 19, 1997, p. A4.

2. Taylor (1975); Burgess (1925).

Early twentieth-century "satellite" and "centralized" suburbs mimicked big cities, at slightly lower density and scale. Satellites had all of the places that, according to James Borchert, defined a city: a main-street shopping area, high-density residential neighborhoods, and (by the late nineteenth century) factory districts.[3] In the 1920s it was even typical for larger satellite cities in the New York region, such as Newark, New Jersey, to have a signature art deco office tower, representing an already decentralizing service economy.

By contrast, boomburbs do not resemble traditional central cities—nor for that matter, older satellites. Boomburbs do possess most elements found in cities (such as housing, retailing, entertainment, and offices), but boomburbs are not typically patterned in a traditional urban form. Boomburbs almost always lack, for example, a dense business core. Boomburbs can thus be seen as distinct from traditional cities—not so much in their function as in their loosely configured, low-density spatial structure. Boomburbs are urban in fact but not in feel.

Except for missing a large downtown, boomburbs in regions of the Southwest such as Phoenix, Dallas, and Las Vegas are similar to their newer and less traditional central cities, with boomburb cities such as Mesa (near Phoenix) and Arlington (near Dallas) having density and urban form comparable to those of their respective core cities. Boomburbs in those metropolitan areas are an extension of the automobile-dependent city building that has dominated the spatial structure of many Sun Belt metropolitan areas.

The emergence of boomburbs that resemble their newer central cities shows that satellites still tend to follow the general urban form of their metropolitan area. In this sense, boomburbs that ring the newer, auto-based central cities are indeed updated satellite cities and true reflections of the new suburban-dominated metropolis.

Urban scholars such as William Sharpe and Leonard Wallock have been attempting for the past three decades to characterize the big suburban cities referred to here as boomburbs.[4]

In the early 1970s, as concern about the inner-city crisis waned and the decentralization of the metropolis reached new proportions, "the urbanization of the suburbs" suddenly became a topic of national interest. The ensuing flurry of articles and books introduced neologisms such as "outer city," "satellite sprawl," "new city," "suburban 'city,' " "urban fringe," and "neo city" to describe this phenomenon.

3. Borchert (1996).
4. Sharpe and Wallock (1994).

Despite years of effort to label the new suburban form, there has as yet emerged no single name for it. Instead, as Sharpe and Wallock note, observers use a whole array of inventive names to characterize the form—suggesting that planners, developers, journalists, and academics do not yet fully understand it. Part of the problem is that we are bound by a language that hierarchically ranks living space (urban, suburban, exurban, rural) when the old "ladder" image no longer applies. Properly naming the new suburban form is an important step in better understanding it. Pierce Lewis notes the following:

"Language is important. We cannot talk about a phenomenon unless we possess the vocabulary to describe it, and many observers still cannot agree on what to call this new amorphous form of urban geography."[5]

Boomburbs, as defined in the present analysis, correspond to what urban historian Robert Fishman refers to as "technoburbs"—that is, "a hopeless jumble of housing, industry, commerce, and even agricultural uses." In his view, today's sprawling suburban metropolitan areas can no longer be judged by the standards of the old metropolis, in part because the new suburban form "lacks any definable borders, a center or a periphery, or clear distinctions between residential, industrial, and commercial zones."[6]

Large parts—and in many cases the entirety—of boomburbs may fit what one of the present authors refers to as "edgeless cities," but several also contain what Joel Garreau has analyzed as "edge cities," which represent some of the few metropolitan focal points that exist outside the urban cores and older satellite suburbs.[7]

METHODS

The following methods were used in this study.

Selecting the Cities

Boomburbs were identified by a two-step process. The first step singled out cities with more than 100,000 people that are not the largest central cities in their respective metropolitan areas. The second step selected from among this group only the cities that have experienced double-digit (10 percent or more) population growth rates in the decades from 1950 onward as documented by the censuses in which the cities have appeared. The final list includes fifty-three boomburbs that had populations in the year 2000 rang-

5. Lewis (1995, p. 61).
6. Fishman (1987, p. 190; 1990, p. 25; 1994).
7. For "edgeless cities," see Lang (2000, forthcoming); Garreau (1991).

ing from slightly more than 100,000 (Westminster, Colorado) to nearly 400,000 (Mesa, Arizona). Altogether, boomburbs now contain 8,798,765 residents. (The complete list of boomburbs is shown in table 6-1 and discussed in the section on findings.)

Measuring Population Change

Population data for boomburbs are from the decennial censuses of 1950 to 2000. The percentage change and numerical change are calculated for each place. The comparison shows the extent to which boomburbs have grown during the past fifty years.

Many boomburbs did not exist in 1950, so the census following their date of origin was used as the basis for measuring their growth. Boomburb growth measurement starts from the first census in which they had reached the urban-place threshold of holding a population of at least 2,500.[8] By 1950, some thirty-one boomburbs had passed the urban threshold. By 1960, another twelve boomburbs had crossed this mark, followed by three in 1970, five in 1980, and two in 1990.

To facilitate comparisons of growth rates across boomburbs that did not appear in the same number of postwar censuses, an annual equivalent growth rate was calculated for each boomburb. This annual equivalent growth rate defines what would have been the constant annual percentage increase in the population of each new boomburb during the range of years for which census observations are available for it.

To illustrate, Gilbert, Arizona, first surpassed the 2,500 urban threshold in the 1980 census, with a population of 5,717. During the next two decades, Gilbert grew by 410 percent and 276 percent to reach a 2000 population of 109,697. Application of a constant annual equivalent growth rate of 16 percent to Gilbert's 1980 population for twenty years would have yielded that same 2000 population (109,697).

METHODS ISSUES

Not only are most boomburbs more populous than they were several decades ago but also they are physically larger now than then, because of land annexations. Data on land area of the forty-three boomburbs that existed in 1960 show that between 1960 and 1990, the average size of these

8. Because boomburbs have different dates of origin, a decision was made to standardize their starting point based on the first postwar census in which they crossed the urban-place threshold of 2,500 residents.

TABLE 6-1. The Boomburbs

Boomburb	State	Metro area	Year started	Starting population	2000 population	Change (percent)
Chandler	AZ	Phoenix	1950	3,799	176,581	4,548
Gilbert	AZ	Phoenix	1980	5,717	109,697	1,819
Glendale	AZ	Phoenix	1950	8,179	218,812	2,575
Mesa	AZ	Phoenix	1950	16,790	396,375	2,261
Peoria	AZ	Phoenix	1960	2,593	108,364	4,079
Scottsdale	AZ	Phoenix	1960	10,026	202,705	1,922
Tempe	AZ	Phoenix	1950	7,684	158,625	1,964
Anaheim	CA	Los Angeles	1950	14,556	328,014	2,153
Corona city	CA	Los Angeles	1950	10,223	124,966	1,122
Costa Mesa	CA	Los Angeles	1960	37,550	108,724	190
Fontana	CA	Los Angeles	1960	14,659	128,929	780
Fullerton city	CA	Los Angeles	1950	13,958	126,003	803
Irvine	CA	Los Angeles	1980	62,134	143,072	130
Lancaster	CA	Los Angeles	1950	3,594	118,718	3,203
Moreno Valley	CA	Los Angeles	1990	118,779	142,381	20
Ontario	CA	Los Angeles	1950	22,872	158,007	591
Orange	CA	Los Angeles	1950	10,027	128,821	1,185
Oxnard	CA	Los Angeles	1950	21,567	170,358	690
Rancho Cucamonga	CA	Los Angeles	1980	55,250	127,743	131
Riverside	CA	Los Angeles	1950	46,764	255,166	446
San Bernardino	CA	Los Angeles	1950	63,058	185,401	194
Santa Ana	CA	Los Angeles	1950	45,533	337,977	642
Santa Clarita	CA	Los Angeles	1990	110,642	151,088	37
Simi Valley	CA	Los Angeles	1970	56,676	111,351	96
Thousand Oaks	CA	Los Angeles	1960	2,934	117,005	3,888
Chula Vista	CA	San Diego	1950	15,927	173,556	990
Escondido	CA	San Diego	1950	6,544	133,559	1,941
Oceanside	CA	San Diego	1950	12,881	161,029	1,150
Daly City	CA	San Francisco	1950	15,191	103,621	582
Fremont	CA	San Francisco	1960	43,790	203,413	365
Santa Rosa	CA	San Francisco	1950	17,902	147,595	724
Sunnyvale	CA	San Francisco	1950	9,829	131,760	1,241
Aurora	CO	Denver	1950	11,421	276,393	2,320
Lakewood	CO	Denver	1960	19,338	144,126	645
Westminster	CO	Denver	1960	13,850	100,940	629
Coral Springs	FL	Miami	1980	37,349	117,549	215
Hialeah	FL	Miami	1950	19,676	226,419	1,051
Pembroke Pines	FL	Miami	1970	15,589	137,427	782
Clearwater	FL	Tampa	1950	15,581	108,787	598
Naperville	IL	Chicago	1950	7,013	128,358	1,730
Henderson	NV	Las Vegas	1950	3,643	175,381	4,714
North Las Vegas	NV	Las Vegas	1950	3,875	115,488	2,880
Salem	OR	Portland	1950	43,140	136,924	217
Arlington	TX	Dallas	1950	7,692	332,969	4,229
Carrollton	TX	Dallas	1960	4,242	109,576	2,483
Garland	TX	Dallas	1950	10,571	215,768	1,941
Grand Prairie	TX	Dallas	1950	14,594	127,427	773
Irving	TX	Dallas	1950	2,621	191,615	7,211
Mesquite	TX	Dallas	1960	27,526	124,523	352
Plano	TX	Dallas	1960	3,695	222,030	5,909
West Valley City	UT	Salt Lake City	1980	72,378	108,896	50
Chesapeake	VA	Norfolk	1970	89,580	199,184	122
Bellevue	WA	Seattle	1960	12,809	109,569	755

Source: Based on U.S. Bureau of the Census (2001).

cities increased from fifteen square miles to fifty square miles.[9] Comparisons across time can be somewhat tricky because the places annexed usually contained population.

The case of San Bernardino, California, illustrates how annexations added population to some of the boomburbs. San Bernardino annexed land in both the 1950s and 1960s. The 1950s annexations added 12,803 people to San Bernardino's 1960 population, and the 1960s annexations increased the city's 1970 population by 6,092 people. The factor that complicates comparisons across time is the fact that it cannot be determined how many of these people were already there at the time of annexation and how many moved into the annexed parts of San Bernardino after the land became part of the city.

Fortunately, this population measurement issue does not significantly affect most boomburbs because their current land area—even if considerably larger than the original town—was often substantially unoccupied in 1950. Therefore, most of the boomburbs' population growth has been through actual gains rather than through annexed households.

Some late-starting boomburbs were formed through combining existing towns or unincorporated places. Sometimes this resulted in a large initial population. For instance, Chesapeake, Virginia, was created in 1963 as the result of a merger between Norfolk County and the city of South Norfolk. The new city had an estimated population of 78,000 in 1963 and an enumerated population of 89,580 at the time of its first decennial census in 1970.

The present analysis does not track the pre-boomburb growth rates for areas that eventually became parts of boomburbs. Even so, it is safe to assume that most of these places had been experiencing fast growth rates, which in many cases precipitated their incorporation into an existing boomburb or their merger to form a new boomburb. Fremont, California, for example, was formed of several unincorporated towns that joined together in 1956 because the postwar boom was transforming them from small independent villages into one extended suburban city.

FINDINGS

Many interesting and even surprising findings emerge from the analysis. Let us examine some of the high points.

9. These are the types of municipalities that David Rusk refers to as "elastic" in that they can expand their boundaries to capture new growth. Rusk (1993).

Population Growth

Boomburbs' populations have grown swiftly during the past fifty years. All boomburbs grew quickly during the past several decades (table 6-1). Some places saw explosive growth. Of the boomburbs that had reached the 2,500 urban threshold by 1950, Dallas's suburb Irving grew by a spectacular 7,211 percent in the ensuing five decades. Henderson, Nevada, and Chandler, Arizona, also showed impressive gains in that same fifty-year period, growing by 4,714 percent and 4,548 percent, respectively. Plano, Texas, which crossed the urban threshold in 1960, exhibited even more spectacular growth, increasing in size by 5,909 percent in just four decades.

High Annualized Average Growth

Phoenix, Dallas, Las Vegas, and Denver boomburbs have registered very high annualized average growth rates (AGRs). At almost 9 percent, Phoenix's boomburbs had the fastest average AGR of all metropolitan areas in the Southwest. The Dallas and Las Vegas boomburbs also registered high average AGRs, exceeding 7 percent. The Denver boomburbs' average AGR followed at 5.6 percent. California boomburbs grew more slowly, with AGRs of 5.4 percent in San Diego, 4.5 percent in Los Angeles, and 4.4 percent in San Francisco. Salt Lake City lagged behind the rest of the region with a 2.1 percent boomburb AGR. Outside the Southwest, the four Florida boomburbs experienced a 5.6 percent average AGR.

The South and the West

Almost all boomburbs are located in the South and the West. According to boomburb metropolitan data (table 6-2), only one boomburb (located in the Chicago metropolitan area) exists outside the South and the West. Further, just nine, or 17 percent, of the U.S. boomburbs lie outside the Southwest itself, extending from Texas to California. In fact, Los Angeles, Dallas, and Phoenix alone contain thirty-two boomburbs, or 60 percent of the total. The Southeast, other than south Florida, contains few boomburbs. East of the Mississippi River there exists only one boomburb with a population greater than 200,000 (Hialeah, Florida). Clearly, boomburbs are mostly a western–Sun Belt phenomenon.

Los Angeles, with eighteen, has the highest number of boomburbs and the biggest cumulative boomburb population. Metropolitan Los Angeles is so large, however, that its boomburbs account for fewer than one in five residents. But at nearly 3 million, the total boomburb population approaches that of the central city of Los Angeles (3.7 million).

TABLE 6-2. Boomburb Metro Summary

Rank	State	Region	Number of boomburbs	Boomburg population	Metro population	Population in boomburb (percent)
1	AZ	Phoenix	7	1,371,159	3,251,876	42.2
2	CA	Los Angeles	18	2,963,724	16,373,645	18.1
3	CA	San Diego	3	468,144	2,813,833	16.6
4	CA	San Francisco	4	586,389	7,039,362	8.3
5	CO	Denver	3	521,459	2,582,506	20.2
6	FL	Miami	3	481,395	3,876,380	12.4
7	FL	Tampa	1	108,787	2,395,977	4.5
8	IL	Chicago	1	128,358	9,157,540	1.4
9	NV	Las Vegas	2	290,869	1,563,282	18.6
10	OR	Portland	1	136,924	2,265,223	6.0
11	TX	Dallas	7	1,323,908	5,221,801	25.4
12	UT	Salt Lake City	1	108,896	1,333,914	8.2
13	VA	Norfolk	1	199,184	1,569,541	12.7
14	WA	Seattle	1	109,569	3,554,760	3.1
Total			53	8,798,765	62,999,640	14.0

Source: See table 6-1.

At 42.2 percent, Phoenix has by far the highest percentage of its metropolitan population living in boomburbs. Phoenix and Dallas, with seven each, follow Los Angeles in the number of boomburbs. The Phoenix region also contains the second-highest number of residents living in boomburbs; the 1.37 million Phoenix boomburb population slightly exceeds that of the central city.

Boomburbs' Share of City Growth

Boomburbs have accounted for a large share of city growth in the 1990s. Boomburbs total 53 of the 199 U.S. cities that have population between 100,000 and 400,000. They also account for about one quarter (25.7 percent) of these cities' total population. But they captured fully *half* of the 1990 decade's population growth in these cities.[10] Cities in this size class gained 4.1 million new residents during the 1990s, some 2.1 million of whom live in the boomburbs.

Boomburbs are even more important to population growth among cities that have between 200,000 and 400,000 residents. As of 2000, boomburbs account for twelve of the forty-eight cities in this size class and for 24 percent of the total population living in these cities, and they grabbed a full 60 percent of such cities' total 1990s population growth.

10. Interestingly, in a recent study by Glaeser and Shapiro (2001) of the 1990 decade's growth rates of places having populations greater than 100,000, cities identified here as boomburbs actually accounted for three of the top five—and for eleven of the twenty-five fastest-growing municipalities.

Boomburbs' Share of State Growth

Boomburbs have also accounted for a large part of their states' growth during the past five decades and during the 1990s. By the 1990s, boomburbs also accounted for a significant share of their respective states' population growth. Among states with more than one boomburb, the 1990 shares ranged from 5.2 percent in Florida to 33.6 percent in Arizona. Boomburbs' share of their states' population growth during the 1990s also increased vis-à-vis the 1950s, jumping from 8.6 percent to 33.6 percent in Arizona and from 9.2 percent to 16.9 percent in California. In the other states with multiple boomburbs, boomburbs' share of state population growth increased by 4 percentage points or less from the 1950s to the 1990s.

Boomburbs' Population and Traditional Cities

Boomburbs' populations are larger than those of many traditional cities. Another way to grasp just how big many boomburbs have become is to compare their current populations with those of some better-known traditional cities. Mesa, Arizona—the most populous boomburb at 396,375 residents in 2000—is bigger than such traditional large cities as Minneapolis (382,618), Miami (362,470), and St. Louis (348,189). Arlington, Texas—the third biggest boomburb with 332,969 people—falls just behind Pittsburgh (334,536) and just ahead of Cincinnati (331,285). Even such smaller boomburbs as Chandler, Arizona, and Henderson, Nevada, with 176,581 and 175,381 residents respectively, now surpass older, mid-sized cities such as Knoxville (173,890), Providence (173, 618), and Worcester (172,648).

CONCLUSION

Some observers such as Carl Abbott have noted the role large suburban cities play in Sun Belt development, but most studies focus either on metropolitan areas as a whole or on their central cities. Many urban analysts such as Mark Gottdiener also assume that Sun Belt urban growth varies little between the East and the West. For instance, metropolitan areas such as Atlanta and Phoenix are described in one Brookings Institution study as sharing a similar growth pattern.[11] But recent research shows that Atlanta and Phoenix have widely divergent urban forms. The two metros also differ in the number of boomburbs—Atlanta has none, while Phoenix has seven. Atlanta boomed, but has no boomburbs; nor do other fast-growing metro areas in the Southeast such as Charlotte and Nashville.

11. Abbott (1993, 1995); Gottdiener (1994); Brookings Institution (2000).

Phoenix, Land of Boomburbs, Compared with Atlanta, the Fragmented Metropolis

Metropolitan Phoenix provides a good contrast with Atlanta and other major metropolitan areas of the South (table 6-3). During the 1990s, Phoenix and Atlanta registered the largest percentage gains among the nation's biggest metropolitan areas, growing 45.3 percent and 38.9 percent respectively.

TABLE 6-3. Comparing the Atlanta and Phoenix Metropolitan Areas

City or place	*Population (2000)*	*Land area (1990 square miles)*	*Density (1990, people per square mile)*
Atlanta metropolitan area			
Eight largest cities or places			
Atlanta	416,474	131.7	2,991
Roswell	79,334	32.6	1,472
Marietta	58,748	20.4	2,166
Smyrna	40,999	11.4	2,725
East Point	39,595	13.8	2,501
Alpharetta	34,854	19.0	684
Peachtree	31,580	23.3	816
Griffin	23,451	13.1	1,630
Metro area total	4,112,198		
Eight-city total	725,035	265.2	2,280
Eight-city share	17.6		
Seven-city total (minus largest city)	308,561	133.5	1,579
Seven-city share	7.5		
Seven-city average		19.1	
Phoenix metropolitan area			
Eight largest cities			
Phoenix	1,321,045	419.8	2,343
Mesa	396,375	108.6	2,654
Glendale	218,812	52.2	2,838
Scottsdale	202,705	184.3	706
Chandler	176,581	47.5	1,904
Tempe	158,625	39.5	3,591
Gilbert	109,697	27.1	1,075
Peoria	108,364	61.5	824
Metro area total	3,251,876		
Eight-city total	2,692,204	940.5	1,980
Eight-city share	82.8		
Seven-city total (minus largest city)	1,371,159	520.7	1,687
Seven-city share	42.2		
Seven-city average		74.4	

Source: See table 6-1.

Note: Density figures are based on 1990 population.

Phoenix, a metropolitan region with 3.25 million people, has seven boomburbs. The central city of Phoenix and its boomburbs combined have 2.69 million people and 83 percent of the region's population. To have just eight municipalities account for so large a share of their metropolitan population is very unusual, according to a Morrison Institute study.[12] Atlanta, by contrast, has just 18 percent of its population living in the eight largest surrounding cities. The combined populations of all of Atlanta's seven largest suburbs are much less than that of Mesa, Phoenix's most populous boomburb.

Atlanta's municipalities are physically smaller than those of Phoenix.[13] Roswell, Atlanta's most populous suburb, covers only 32.6 square miles. Meanwhile, Mesa spreads over 108 square miles. Gilbert, the physically smallest boomburb in the Phoenix metropolitan area, would rank second in land area and first in population if it were a suburb of Atlanta.

Interestingly, the seven big suburbs of Atlanta and the seven boomburbs of Phoenix have similar total densities, with 1,579 and 1,687 people per square mile respectively. It appears that the large physical size of Phoenix's boomburbs allows them to capture so much growth and account for a major share of the region's population.

Given that Phoenix metro's largest eight cities contain more than four-fifths of the metropolitan area's residents, regional action requires only that the leaders of these places work together. The mayors of Atlanta's big surrounding cities also could cooperate, but that cooperative effort would affect less than a fifth of total Atlanta metro residents. Thus the emergence of Phoenix's boomburbs gives that area a distinct advantage for regional solutions over Atlanta, where municipal fragmentation greatly complicates metropolitan-level action.

Why Are Boomburbs Most Common to the West?

Boomburbs do not happen randomly. Rather, they are mostly a product of a western–Sun Belt development that favors the establishment of physically large suburban municipalities. Two factors foster Western boomburb growth: large master-planned communities and water districting.

The West is home to enormous master-planned communities that are located within a single town. These communities gobble up unincorporated land as they grow. The land and its new residents are added to municipali-

12. Morrison Institute (2000).

13. All land area and population density statistics in this section and table 6-3 are based on 1990 census data. At the time this chapter was prepared, land area data from Census 2000 were not available.

ties, turning what were once small towns into boomburbs. Also, the public lands in the West that surround big metro areas are often transferred to developers in very large blocs, as described by Abbott.[14] By contrast, in the East master-planned-community builders must assemble their land from mostly smaller, privately held parcels.

Western water districts also play a role in promoting boomburbs. The West is mostly dry, and places seeking to grow must organize in order to access water. Bigger incorporated places are better positioned to grab a share of water supply—an incentive for fragmented suburbs to join together in a large incorporated city.

Homeowners Associations

The master-planned communities that dominate many boomburbs are organized into numerous homeowners associations. These associations act as small private governments that deliver a range of services to the boomburgs' residents (such as recreational facilities and trash collection), as described by Stephen E. Barton and Carol J. Silverman. David Gutterson asserts that homeowners associations may be so common and comprehensive in boomburbs that they to a large extent take the place of municipal government. The main political dynamic in boomburbs, according to Evan McKenzie, is often between city hall and the homeowners associations.[15] Homeowners associations press city hall to reduce the cost and reach of most municipal services, such as parks, that the master-planned communities are providing to residents as part of their association fee benefits.

Class and Race Diversity

In part because of their large size, boomburbs often contain a more diverse population than do smaller suburbs. Most boomburbs are affluent, but few are exclusive. Some lower-income neighborhoods exist within virtually all boomburbs. Boomburbs may also attract people of diverse racial and ethnic backgrounds.

California boomburbs in particular are increasing their minority population. In a recent study looking at racial change in the nation's largest cities based on the 2000 census, Alan Berube found that the two cities with the largest percentage loss in non-Hispanic whites were Anaheim and Riverside, California, which dropped 20.8 percent and 15.7 percent respectively.[16]

14. Abbott (1993, 1995).
15. Barton and Silverman (1994); Gutterson (1992); McKenzie (1994).
16. Berube (2001).

Boomburbs in southern California and south Florida may also contain a large share of foreign-born population. In 1990, according to George E. Hall and Deirdre A. Gaquin, Santa Ana and Anaheim in northern Orange County, California, had 50.9 percent and 28.4 percent foreign-born populations respectively. Hialeah, a suburb northwest of Miami, had a whopping 70.4 percent foreign-born population in the same year.[17]

The foreign-born figures in these three boomburbs correlate with (and perhaps cause) a high population density. In 1990 these three boomburbs maintained densities of 10,839 (Santa Ana), 9,792 (Hialeah), and 6,014 (Anaheim) people per square mile. The first two figures (for Santa Ana and Hialeah) approach the population density in large, older cities of the Northeast such as Philadelphia and Boston. Anaheim's density approaches that of such older cities of the Midwest as Cleveland and St. Louis.

Boomburbs Nearly "Built Out"

Many boomburbs have annexed ample land to expand their populations, but others are landlocked and near the point of "buildout." The simple fact is that most boomburbs are horizontal cities that grow outward rather than upward. Landlocked boomburbs—such as Tempe, Arizona—now have nowhere to go but up. Tempe's number of new housing permits has dropped to a few dozen, while its non-landlocked-boomburb neighbors of Chandler and Mesa are issuing permits by the thousands.

Landlocked boomburbs are at a crossroads. If they want to keep growing they must change their land use patterns to accommodate higher-density development. But their original competitive advantage has been their greenfield development opportunities.

The infill market remains untested in most boomburbs. Many now have the scale and the economic assets that technically make them central places, but their mostly centerless form does not offer the type of dense urban environments attractive to citiphile consumers of infill housing. The future of built-out boomburbs may depend on the success of urban-design movements, such as the New Urbanism, that introduce more traditional, citylike development into the suburbs.

REFERENCES

Abbott, Carl. 1993. *The Metropolitan Frontier: Cities in the Modern American West.* University of Arizona Press.

17. Hall and Gaquin (1997).

———. 1995. "'Beautiful Downtown Burbank': Changing Metropolitan Geography in the Modern West." *Journal of the West* (July): 8–18.

Barton, Stephen E., and Carol J. Silverman, eds. 1994. *Common Interest Communities: Private Governments and Public Interest.* University of California Press.

Berube, Alan. 2001. "Racial Change in the Nation's Largest Cities: Evidence from the 2000 Census." Census Series. Brookings Institution Center on Urban and Metropolitan Policy (April).

Borchert, James. 1996. "Residential City Suburbs: The Emergence of a New Suburban Type, 1880–1930." *Journal of Urban History* 22 (3): 283–307.

Brookings Institution. 2000. *Moving beyond Sprawl: The Challenge for Metropolitan Atlanta.* Brookings Institution Center on Urban and Metropolitan Policy.

Burgess, Ernest W. 1925. *Urban Community: Selected Papers from the Proceedings of the American Sociological Society.* University of Chicago Press.

Fishman, Robert. 1987. *Bourgeois Utopias: The Rise and Fall of Suburbia.* Basic Books.

———. 1990. "America's New City: Megalopolis Unbound." *Wilson Quarterly* 14 (1): 24–45.

———. 1994. "Space, Time, and Sprawl." *Architectural Digest* 64 (3-4): 45–47.

Garreau, Joel. 1991. *Edge City: Life on the New Frontier.* Doubleday.

Glaeser, Edward, and Jesse M. Shapiro. 2001. "City Growth and the 2000 Census: Which Places Grew and Why." Census Series. Brookings Institution Center on Urban and Metropolitan Policy (May).

Gottdiener, Mark. 1994. *The New Urban Sociology.* McGraw-Hill Inc.

Gutterson, David. 1992. "No Place like Home: On the Manicured Streets of a Master-Planned Community." *Harper's Magazine* (November): 55–64.

Hall, George E., and Deirdre A. Gaquin, eds. 1997. *County and City Extra: Annual Metro, City and County Data Book.* Bernan Press.

Lang, Robert E. 2000. "Office Sprawl: The Evolving Geography of Business." Survey Paper Series. Brookings Institution Center on Urban and Metropolitan Policy (October).

———. Forthcoming. *Edgeless Cities: Exploring the Elusive Metropolis.* Brookings.

Lewis, Pierce F. 1995. "The Urban Invasion of Rural America: The Emergence of the Galactic City." In Emery N. Castle, ed., *The Changing American Countryside: Rural People and Places.* University Press of Kansas.

McKenzie, Evan. 1994. *Privatopia: Homeowners Associations and the Rise of Residential Private Government.* Yale University Press.

Morrison Institute. 2000. *Hits and Misses: Fast Growth in Metropolitan Phoenix.* Arizona State University's Morrison Institute for Public Policy.

Rusk, David. 1993. *Cities without Suburbs.* Washington: Woodrow Wilson Center Press.

Sharpe, William, and Leonard Wallock. 1994. "Bold New City or Built-Up 'Burb'?" *American Quarterly* 46 (1):1–30.

Taylor, Graham R. 1915. *Satellite Cities: A Case Study of Industrial Suburbs.* Ayer Company.

U.S. Bureau of the Census. 2001. "Redistricting Data (P.L. 94-171). Summary File and 1990 Census." Department of Commerce (April 2).

7

Suburbs

Patterns of Growth and Decline

WILLIAM H. LUCY
DAVID L. PHILLIPS

Historically, the typical image of metropolitan growth and decline is simplistic: central cities lose population and suburbs continually gain, often at city expense. But this view is changing. According to figures from Census 2000, the median population growth rate for cities during the 1990s more than doubled vis-à-vis that of the 1980s, and nearly three-fourths of cities grew during the 1990s.[1] Meanwhile, contrary to popular perception, not all suburbs are growing: the 2000 census shows that more than one-third of the suburbs of thirty-five metropolitan areas are either stagnant in terms of population growth or are actually losing residents—some at a rather rapid rate. Suburbs are no longer monolithic communities free from the problems normally associated with struggling center cities. It may be common to talk about "the suburbs" as a group of homogeneous jurisdictions, but careful analysis reveals that suburbs are in fact highly diverse. Although many newly developing suburbs did experience rapid growth in people and jobs, many older suburbs in the Northeast and the Midwest, frequently inner-ring suburbs, experienced central-city-like challenges, including an aging infrastructure, inadequate housing stock, deteriorating schools and commercial corridors—and population decline.

The authors thank Steve Golden and Jeff Driscoll, graduate students at the University of Virginia School of Architecture, for their valuable research assistance.

1. This refers to cities with 1990 populations greater than 100,000. See Glaeser (2001).

METHODS

The present study examines the thirty-four most populous metropolitan areas in the United States in 2000, plus the Buffalo metropolitan area.[2] Individual suburbs within those metropolitan areas were chosen on the basis of their having had a population of 2,500 or more in 1980. The thirty-five metropolitan areas in the study had 2,586 suburban governments and census designated places (CDPs) in 1980. Military CDPs were usually not included, since their patterns of growth and decline generally do not reflect trends throughout a metropolitan area. The only criteria for suburb inclusion in this study were 1980 population size and consistent presence in U.S. censuses. Distance came into play only with the requirement that a place be within each metropolitan boundary. Thus inner and outer suburbs are included, as are pre– and post–World War II suburbs.

The census includes many CDPs as separate suburbs although they lack governmental responsibilities—this is especially common in the Baltimore and Washington metropolitan areas and in some fast-growing areas in the West.[3] The thirty-five metropolitan areas had thirty-eight main central cities: Minneapolis/St. Paul, San Francisco/Oakland, and Tampa/St. Petersburg all were treated as individual central cities. Another ten secondary central cities, which sometimes were smaller than more generally recognized suburbs, were included in the sample of 2,586 suburbs. Large suburbs sometimes referred to as "boomburbs" complicate the distinction between central cities and suburbs.[4] The largest of these boomburbs—Mesa, outside Phoenix—has more than 400,000 residents, making Mesa larger than the populations of such long-established central cities as St. Louis, Pittsburgh, and Buffalo.

Census designations for metropolitan statistical areas (MSAs), primary metropolitan statistical areas (PMSAs), and consolidated metropolitan statistical areas (CMSAs) were chosen depending on which category included most of the suburbs of a given central city without, if possible, including other major central cities with their own metropolitan areas. The spread of metropolitan areas into each other's territory makes some metropolitan boundary distinctions awkward and arguable. The choices made among

2. The Buffalo metropolitan area is included because in previous decades, it ranked among the top metropolitan areas in terms of population. By 2000, Buffalo had slipped to number 43.

3. See *www.people.virginia.edu/~dlp/ResearchSuburbs2000/lucyappendix.pdf* (June 2002) for a list of each studied suburb, along with an indication of its type of government or its CDP designation.

4. See Lang and Simmons (2001).

metropolitan designations did not significantly alter the percentages of suburban growth or decline found in those metropolitan areas. Population changes result from births, deaths, and net migration, but data about these components of population change are not yet available.

FINDINGS

The analysis shows several important findings regarding patterns of growth and decline in suburban population as based on recent census data. Let us examine several of the key results.

Uneven Growth

Suburban population as a whole grew during the 1990s, but growth was highly uneven from suburb to suburb. Census 2000 confirms that the decentralization of economic and residential life remains the prevailing trend in metropolitan America today but that this trend is by no means ubiquitous. The 2,586 studied suburbs in the thirty-five largest metropolitan areas did grow by an average of 14 percent during the decade, but only 63 percent of them actually grew while 37 percent of them in fact lost population or stayed the same.

Between 1990 and 2000, the overall population outside of central cities in these thirty-five metropolitan areas expanded by nearly 12.5 million, of which 7,417,836 corresponded to the analyzed suburbs (table 7-1) and 5,043,456 to unincorporated areas and new suburbs which did not have 2,500 or more residents in 1980 and therefore were not included in our sample. Some 27 percent (700) of the studied 2,586 suburbs in these metropolitan areas lost a total of 638,543 residents, an average decline rate of 6.1 percent per suburb during the decade. For more detail, a list of the thirty-five metropolitan areas and each of their overall and suburban population change in the last decade is presented in table 7-2.

Figure 7-1 categorizes the suburbs by pace of population change. Rather than strictly defining population change as an increase or decrease of one or more residents, it presents a category of "stagnant" suburbs that experienced very little population change (plus or minus 2.5 percent) during the decade. By this definition, 18 percent of all the suburbs in the study declined, 19 percent were stable, and 63 percent grew, as noted earlier. Thus 37 percent of all studied suburbs did not grow significantly during the 1990s—that is, their population declined or remained stable.

In metropolitan areas with a modest number of suburbs and a few very large population changes, a misleading picture of suburban transitions may

TABLE 7-1. Population Change, by Geographic Area, 1990–2000

Area	1990 population	2000 population	Change in population	Change in population (percent)
All 35 metropolitan areas	109,676,212	124,776,188	15,099,906	+13.8
All 38 central cities	34,060,549	36,698,911	2,638,362	+7.8
Outside central cities	75,615,915	88,077,207	12,461,292	+16.5
Suburbs in study	52,375,476	59,793,312	7,417,836	+14.2
Declining suburbs	11,087,890	10,449,347	–638,543	–5.8

Source: U.S. Bureau of the Census (1990; 2000).

arise. Many large changes are the result of new incorporations and boundary adjustments in unincorporated areas. And in a few cases, large changes are the result of unique circumstances (for instance, Wrightstown, New Jersey, a Philadelphia suburb, lost 80.5 percent of its 1990 population to mission changes at McGuire Air Force Base, and the St. Louis suburb of Kinloch City showed an enormous 83.4 percent decline in its population because of the St. Louis Airport Authority's buyout of 175 acres for noise mitigation purposes).

Suburbs in the Northeast and Midwest

Suburbs with declining populations were located predominately in slow-growing metropolitan areas in the Northeast and Midwest. Despite population changes' unevenness among suburbs, some clear patterns of suburban population change did emerge among metropolitan areas. The Pittsburgh metropolitan area had by far the greatest percentage and number of declining-population suburbs, with 108 (or 84.4 percent) of its 128 suburbs having lost population during the 1990s, at an average rate of 6.7 percent per suburb. Most suburbs in four other metropolitan areas also lost population during the decade—71.4 percent of the suburbs in the Buffalo metro area, 66.7 percent in Philadelphia, 57.3 percent in Detroit, and 54.0 percent in Cleveland.

Suburban population loss was heaviest in the Northeast, where 38.5 percent of metropolitan suburbs lost population, and in the Midwest, where population declines occurred in 31.8 percent of suburbs. By contrast, in the South only 13.6 percent of suburbs declined, along with just 10.5 percent in the West. The South and West also experienced by far the greatest percentages of overall metropolitan population growth—both at around 20 percent. Clearly, metropolitan areas in different parts of the country are growing in different ways.

TABLE 7-2. Metropolitan Areas and Their Declining Suburbs

	Metropolitan population			Suburbs		
Region and metropolitan area	2000	1990	Change (percent)	Number in study	Number declining	Declining (percent)
Northeast						
Boston, MA-NH	3,406,829	3,227,707	5.5	78	20	25.6
Buffalo-Niagara Falls, NY	1,170,111	1,189,288	−1.6	28	20	71.4
New York- NY-NJ-CT-PA	21,199,865	19,549,649	8.4	515	104	20.2
Philadelphia, PA-NJ	5,100,931	4,922,175	3.6	129	86	66.7
Pittsburgh, PA	2,358,695	2,394,811	−1.5	128	108	84.4
Northeast regional totals	33,236,431	31,283,630	6.2	878	338	38.5
Midwest						
Chicago, IL	8,272,768	7,410,858	11.6	213	28	13.2
Cincinnati—Hamilton, OH-KY-IN	1,979,202	1,817,571	8.9	67	27	40.3
Cleveland—Lorain-Elyria, OH	2,250,871	2,202,069	2.2	76	41	54.0
Columbus, OH	1,540,157	1,345,450	14.5	28	9	32.1
Detroit, MI	4,441,551	4,266,654	4.1	89	51	57.3
Indianapolis, IN	1,607,486	1,380,491	16.4	26	1	3.9
Kansas City, MO-KS	1,776,062	1,582,875	12.2	40	13	32.5
Milwaukee—Waukesha, WI	1,500,741	1,432,149	4.8	39	13	33.3
Minneapolis-St. Paul, MN-WI	2,968,806	2,538,834	16.9	96	16	16.7
St. Louis, MO-IL	2,603,607	2,492,525	4.5	106	49	46.2
Midwest regional totals	28,941,251	26,469,476	9.3	780	248	31.8
South						
Atlanta, GA	4,112,198	2,959,950	38.9	66	5	7.6
Baltimore, MD	2,552,994	2,382,172	7.2	67	12	17.9
Charlotte-Gastonia-Rock Hill, NC-SC	1,499,293	1,162,093	29.0	24	4	16.7
Dallas, TX	3,519,176	2,676,248	31.5	45	0	0.0
Houston, TX	4,177,646	3,322,025	25.8	43	4	9.3
Miami, FL	2,253,362	1,937,094	16.3	52	10	19.2
Norfolk-VA Beach-Newport News, VA-NC	1,569,541	1,443,244	8.8	10	1	10.0
Orlando, FL	1,644,561	1,224,852	34.3	37	5	13.5
San Antonio, TX	1,592,383	1,324,749	20.2	15	4	26.7
Tampa-St. Petersburg-Clearwater, FL	2,395,997	2,067,959	15.9	41	4	9.8
Washington, DC-MD-VA-WV	4,923,153	4,223,485	16.6	130	23	17.7
South regional totals	30,240,304	24,723,871	22.3	530	72	13.6
West						
Denver, CO	2,109,282	1,622,980	30.0	28	1	3.6
Las Vegas, NV-AZ	1,563,282	852,737	83.3	8	0	0.0
Los Angeles and Orange County, CA	12,366,637	11,270,720	9.6	138	21	15.2
Phoenix—Mesa, AZ	3,251,876	2,238,480	45.3	28	3	10.7
Portland—Vancouver, OR-WA	1,918,009	1,515,452	26.6	32	3	9.4
Sacramento-Yolo, CA	1,796,857	1,481,102	21.3	29	2	6.9
San Diego, CA	2,813,833	2,498,016	12.6	24	6	25.0
San Francisco and Oakland, CA	4,123,740	3,686,592	11.9	73	2	2.7
Seattle—Bellevue-Everett, WA	2,414,616	2,033,156	18.8	38	4	10.5
West regional totals	32,358,132	27,199,235	19.0	398	42	10.5
Total	124,776,118	109,676,212	13.8	2,586	700	27.1

Source: See table 7-1.

FIGURE 7-1. Pace of Population Change in Suburbs

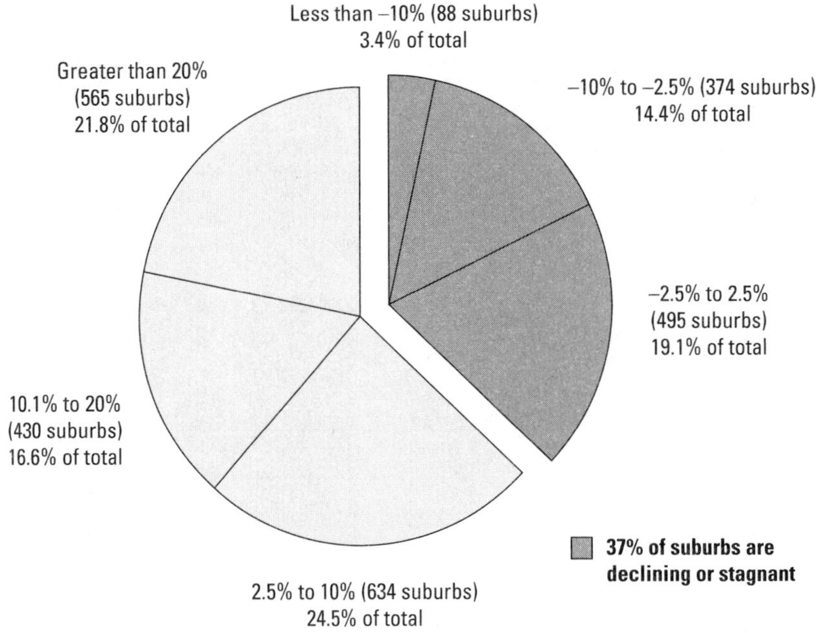

Source: U.S. Bureau of the Census (2000).

Suburban population growth and decline are apparently closely correlated with overall metropolitan-area condition (table 7-2). The "top" five declining or relatively stagnant metropolitan areas were also the top five in terms of the percentages of declining suburbs. By contrast, metropolitan areas that grew very quickly (by more than 30 percent) all had relatively low percentages of suburban population decline during the decade.

Table 7-3 divides metropolitan areas into three groups: metropolitan areas that grew by less than 10 percent, by 10 percent to 25 percent, and by 25 percent or more. Suburban population decline was much more frequent in the slow-growing metropolitan areas, where 37.6 percent of suburbs declined. The Buffalo and Pittsburgh metropolitan areas, which fell in population, had the highest frequency of population decline in their suburbs. Except for Baltimore and Norfolk, all slow-growing metropolitan areas were located in the Northeast and Midwest. In contrast, suburban population decline was least common in fast-growing metropolitan areas, where only 8 percent of the suburbs shrank in population. These fast-growing metropolitan areas were located exclusively in the South and West.

TABLE 7-3. Declining Suburbs by Rate of Metropolitan Area Growth

	Metropolitan population			*Suburbs*		
Growth rate	*Population 1990*	*Population 2000*	*Change 1990–2000 (percent)*	*Number*	*Number declining*	*Declining (percent)*
Less than 10% (13 metro areas)	58,590,734	62,501,575	6.7	1,470	553	37.6
10% to 25% (13 metro areas)	33,510,661	38,479,220	14.8	805	122	15.1
25% or more (9 metro areas)	17,574,817	23,795,323	35.4	311	25	8.0
Total	109,676,212	124,776,118	13.8	2,586	700	27.1

Source: See table 7-1.

Suburban population growth and decline were also correlated closely with the condition of a suburb's central city (table 7-4). The frequency of suburban population loss was much greater in the eleven metropolitan areas in which central cities lost population. Nearly half (49.6 percent) of the suburbs of depopulating central cities themselves lost population, compared with only 15.6 percent of suburbs of growing central cities.

In the twenty-four metropolitan areas in which central cities grew, only 269 suburbs declined in population, and more than 50 percent of these declining suburbs occurred in just four places—New York (104), Chicago (28), Los Angeles (21), and Boston (20). In six places with growing central cities, more than 20 percent of suburbs declined: New York (20.2 percent), San Diego (25.0 percent), Boston (25.6 percent), San Antonio (26.7 percent), Columbus (32.1 percent), and Kansas City (32.5 percent).

There were 124 suburbs of eight of the declining central cities that lost residents at a faster rate than did their central city. Philadelphia had the most suburbs that declined faster than the city (51 out of 129, or 39.5 percent); Pittsburgh was second with 18.0 percent of its suburbs declining faster than its central city; Detroit was third with 12.5 percent. Clearly, the forces leading to central city population loss seemed also to affect many of the suburbs of those central cities, sometimes to an even greater degree.

Declining Suburbs throughout the Metropolitan Area

Declining suburbs were not simply those immediately adjacent to or near the central city but were found throughout the metropolitan area. Suburban decline is often referred to as a phenomenon of the "inner suburbs," meaning those suburbs immediately adjacent to or near the central city. Sometimes that is indeed true: some inner suburbs did experience population

TABLE 7-4. Central Cities and Their Declining Suburbs

	Central city			Suburbs					
				All suburbs in study				Declining faster than city	
City	*Population 1990*	*Population 2000*	*Change 1990–2000 (percent)*	*Metro area total*	*Number declining*	*Suburbs declining (percent)*	*Average decline (percent)*	*Number*	*Average decline (percent)*
Atlanta	394,017	416,474	5.7	66	5	7.6	–27.6		
Baltimore	736,014	651,154	–11.5	67	12	17.9	–3.1	0	0.0
Boston	574,283	589,141	2.6	78	20	25.6	–2.0		
Buffalo	328,123	292,648	–10.8	28	20	71.4	–5.1	0	0.0
Charlotte	396,003	540,828	36.6	24	4	16.7	–4.7		
Chicago	2,783,726	2,896,016	4.0	213	28	13.2	–3.8		
Cincinnati	364,040	331,285	–9.0	67	27	40.3	–6.9	6	–12.3
Cleveland	505,616	478,403	–5.4	76	41	54.0	–3.8	8	–8.3
Columbus	632,958	711,470	12.4	28	9	32.1	–7.2		
Dallas	1,006,831	1,188,580	18.1	45	0	0.0	0.0		
Denver	467,610	554,636	18.6	28	1	3.6	–35.7		
Detroit	1,027,974	951,270	–7.5	89	51	57.3	–5.6	12	–10.0
Houston	1,630,672	1,953,631	19.8	43	4	9.3	–5.4		
Indianapolis	731,321	781,870	6.9	26	1	3.9	–1.6		
Kansas City	435,141	441,545	1.5	40	13	32.5	–4.4		
Las Vegas	258,295	478,434	85.2	8	0	0.0	0.0		
Los Angeles	3,485,398	3,694,820	6.0	138	21	15.2	–5.1		

Miami	358,548	362,470	1.1	52	10	19.2	–11.4		
Milwaukee	628,088	596,974	–5.0	39	13	33.3	–3.0	3	–5.6
Minneapolis	640,618	669,769	4.6	96	16	16.7	–2.7		
New York	7,322,564	8,008,278	9.4	515	104	20.2	–3.2		
Norfolk	261,229	234,403	–10.3	10	1	10.0	–3.2	0	0.0
Orlando	164,693	185,951	12.9	37	5	13.5	–13.3		
Philadelphia	1,585,577	1,517,550	–4.3	129	86	66.7	–6.4	51	–9.4
Phoenix	983,403	1,321,045	34.3	28	3	10.7	–2.8		
Pittsburgh	369,879	334,563	–9.5	128	108	84.4	–6.7	23	–13.3
Portland	437,398	529,121	21.0	32	3	9.4	–8.7		
Sacramento	369,365	407,018	10.2	29	2	6.9	–13.7		
San Antonio	935,927	1,144,646	22.3	15	4	26.7	–4.2		
San Diego	1,110,549	1,223,400	10.2	24	6	25.0	–29.8		
San Francisco	1,096,201	1,176,217	7.3	73	2	2.7	–3.1		
Seattle	516,259	563,374	9.1	38	4	10.5	–22.7		
St. Louis	396,685	348,189	–12.2	106	49	46.2	–10.1	12	–27.3
Tampa	518,644	551,679	6.37	41	4	9.8	–9.4		
Washington	606,900	572,059	–5.7	130	23	17.7	–8.7	9	–18.1
Total where cities are growing	27,250,424	30,390,413	11.5	1,717	269	15.6	–5.6		
Total where cities are declining	6,810,125	6,308,498	–7.4	869	431	49.6	–6.4	124	–12.5

Source: See table 7-1.

decline during the 1990s. But others grew and are quite healthy, such as two inner suburbs adjacent to Washington, D.C.—Alexandria and Arlington, Virginia—which grew by 15 percent and 11 percent respectively during the decade. Suburban decline was not uncommon around Washington, but it was heavily concentrated in the inner suburbs of Prince George's County, on the Maryland side.

In order to analyze the patterns of population decline more precisely, maps were created to pinpoint suburban decline geographically. For the maps to be properly illustrative, they focused on metropolitan areas in which a relatively large number of suburbs shrank in population. As noted earlier, this metropolitan-area population decline was found largely in the Midwest and the Northeast.

In metropolitan areas in the South and West, declining suburbs were less numerous and were generally spread throughout these regions. For instance, in the Atlanta metropolitan area only five suburban places declined, each one located in a different metropolitan county at varying distances from the city. Ten suburbs declined around Miami, almost all located ten to fifteen miles northwest and southwest of the city. The Los Angeles metropolitan area had the largest number of declining suburbs in the West, widely spread throughout the area, with only a slight concentration to the southeastern area near Long Beach. A quarter of San Diego's twenty-four suburban places declined, and again, these were widely scattered throughout the metropolitan area. Only one Denver metropolitan area suburb declined.

The maps illustrate different patterns of population growth and decline in the Chicago, Cincinnati, Cleveland, and Philadelphia metropolitan areas. Suburbs included in the present study are shaded. New post-1980 suburbs and suburbs lacking 2,500 residents in 1980 appear with an outline and no shading. The maps show that in these select metropolitan areas, suburban population decline was more common in the inner rings than in intermediate or outer locations. But a diverse range of patterns was found.

In the Cleveland metropolitan area (map 7-1), decline of inner suburbs is clearly prevalent. Nearly every suburb alongside Cleveland experienced some kind of population loss, as did the city itself. In the Cleveland metropolitan area, many intermediate suburbs and outer suburbs also declined, including the suburbs of Elyria and Lorain.[5]

5. Many large metropolitan areas have grown to encompass formerly independent cities like Elyria and Lorain, as well as other small municipalities. These suburban developments are different from those developments that have emerged entirely since World War II as bedroom suburbs. Classifying suburbs by development types and analyzing their potentially diverse decline propensities may yield additional perspective.

MAP 7-1. Cleveland-Lorain-Elyria, Ohio PMSA: Population Change in Suburban Places, 1990–2000

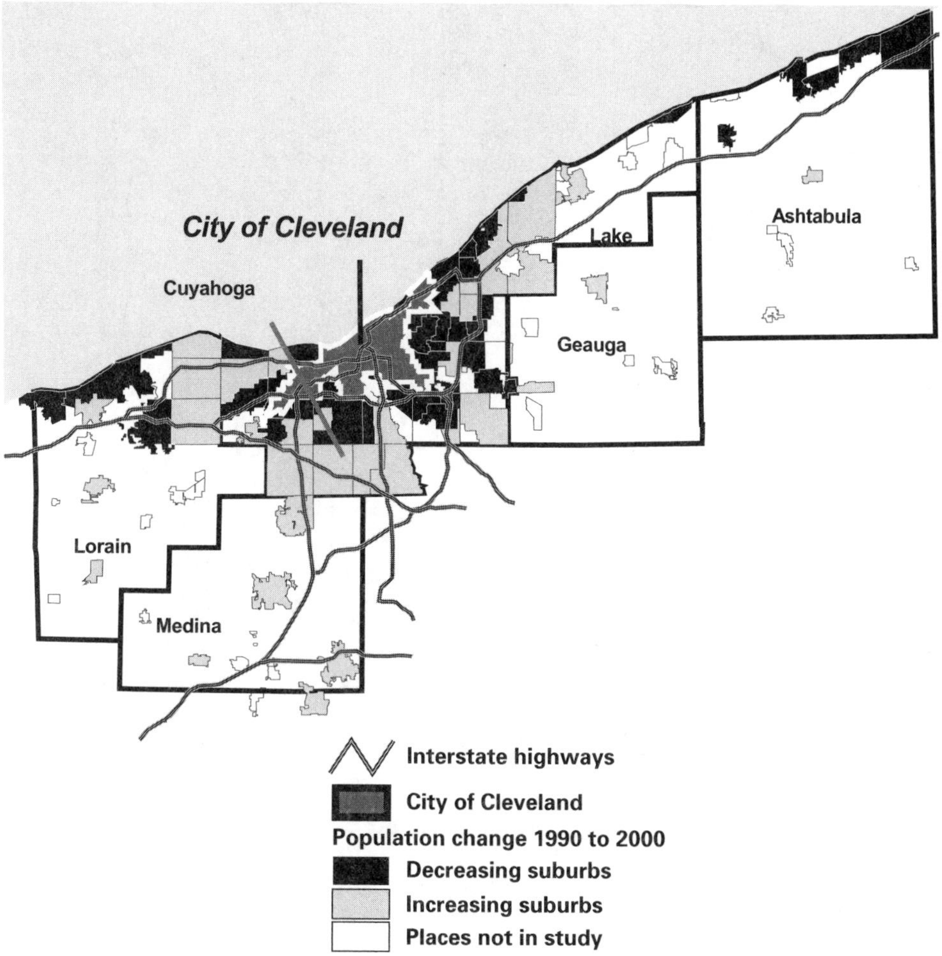

In the Chicago metropolitan area (map 7-2), suburban decline is not as spatially evident because of the overall health of the region and the large number (213) of total jurisdictions. Some inner suburbs did lose population, but most grew. Suburban decline was scattered, with more in a south-side sector than elsewhere. A small number of suburbs declined that were outside of the inner ring, but the vast majority of those still grew.

In the Philadelphia metropolitan area (map 7-3), population growth and decline were very uneven. As in Cleveland, most inner suburbs did lose population during the 1990s. To the southeast in New Jersey, a cluster of small

MAP 7-2. Chicago, IL PMSA: Population Change in Suburban Places, 1990–2000

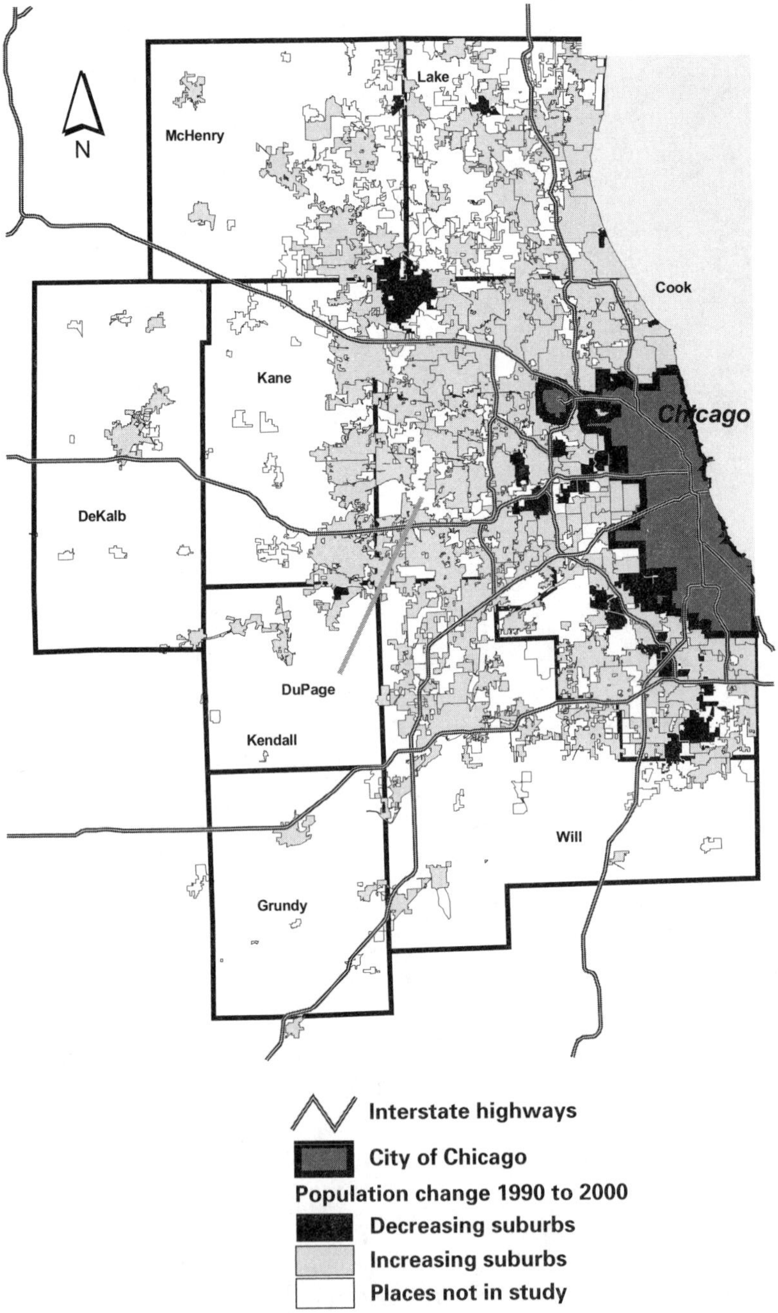

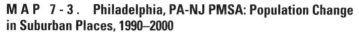

MAP 7-3. Philadelphia, PA-NJ PMSA: Population Change in Suburban Places, 1990–2000

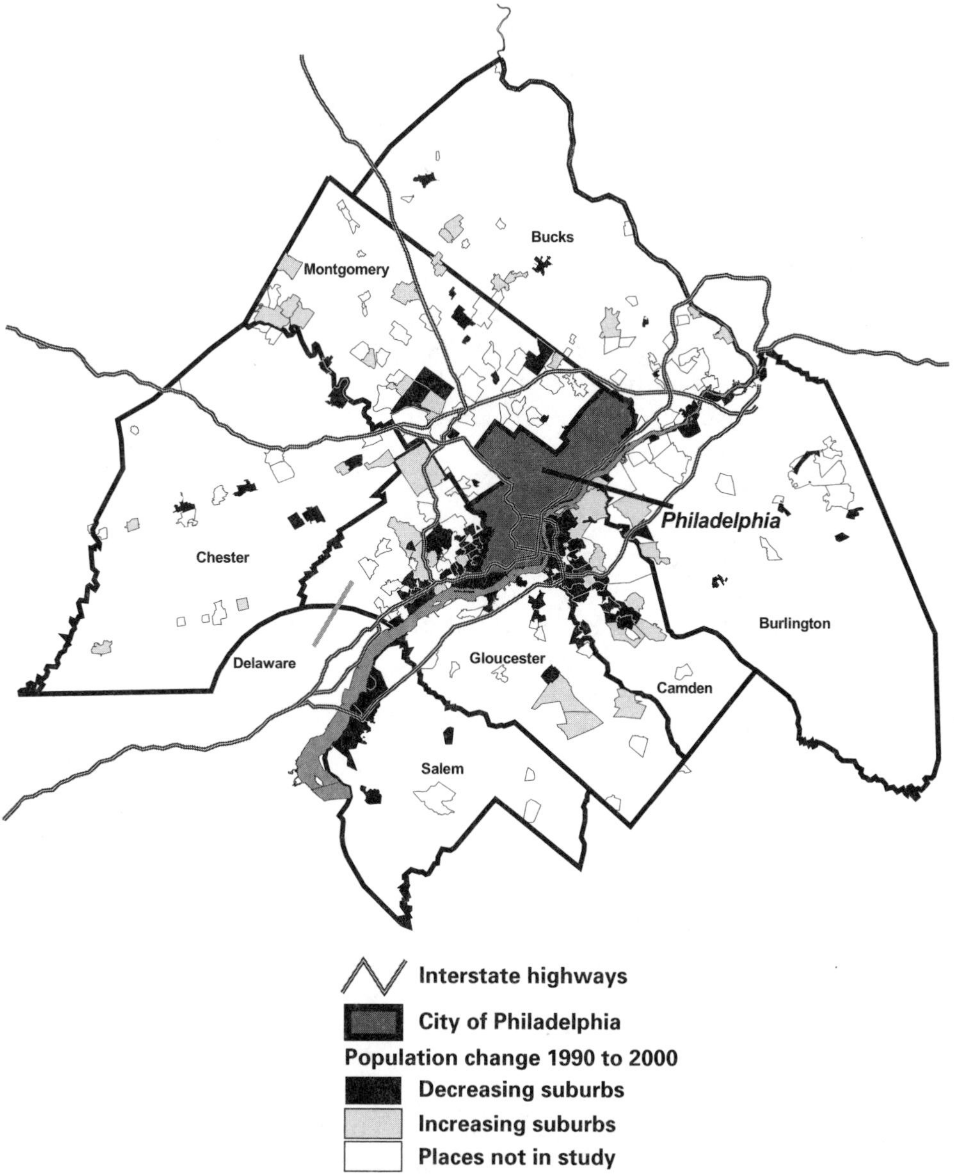

suburbs declined, including one separated from Philadelphia by nine other suburbs. A similar line stretched to the southwest in Pennsylvania, with decline occurring as far as the tenth suburb out from the city and in most, but not all, of those closer to the city. Some close-in suburbs on the New Jersey side saw an increase in their population, but beyond these, declining suburbs were dispersed ten and twenty miles from Philadelphia to the north, south, east, and west. Interspersed among these decliners were many growing suburbs.

Declining suburbs were common on Cincinnati's boundary (map 7-4), but growing suburbs touched the central city on each side. Across the Ohio River in Kentucky, growth close to the central city was clearly the dominant trend. Fingers of growth touched the city on its other sides, both in suburbs in the studied sample and in newer suburbs. Several declining suburbs as far as several miles from the city were located to the west, north, northeast, and southeast. As with Philadelphia and Cleveland, Cincinnati's central city population declined as well.

The foregoing examples reveal diverse patterns of suburban population decline. They show that suburban population loss is not limited to inner suburbs and that even in northeastern and midwestern metropolitan areas, many inner suburbs grew. They show also that suburban population decline cannot be explained as merely being central city population decline's contagion to associated suburbs.

Small Suburbs and Population Decline

Small suburbs are not buffered against the forces of population decline. Some observers believe that small suburban jurisdictions are preferable to larger ones, because public service and tax preferences of constituents may be relatively homogeneous, enabling local governments to be more responsive to existing or changing needs. On the other hand, small size and homogeneity make it more likely that there will be greater distinctions among jurisdictions and also make more apparent the existing distinctions in race and income. Indeed, some of this can be observed on the maps. Small jurisdictions are subject to rapid change from residential mobility, since an average of 45 to 50 percent of metropolitan residents move within five years.[6] In addition, substantial change can occur from residents' aging (and dying) in place, with fewer families with children being present as the years pass. Because of these implications of small size, the survey also examined population size in analyzing suburban decline.

6. U.S. Bureau of the Census (2000, 1990, 1980, 1970).

MAP 7-4. Cincinnati-Hamilton, Ohio, CMSA: Population Change in Suburban Places, 1990–2000

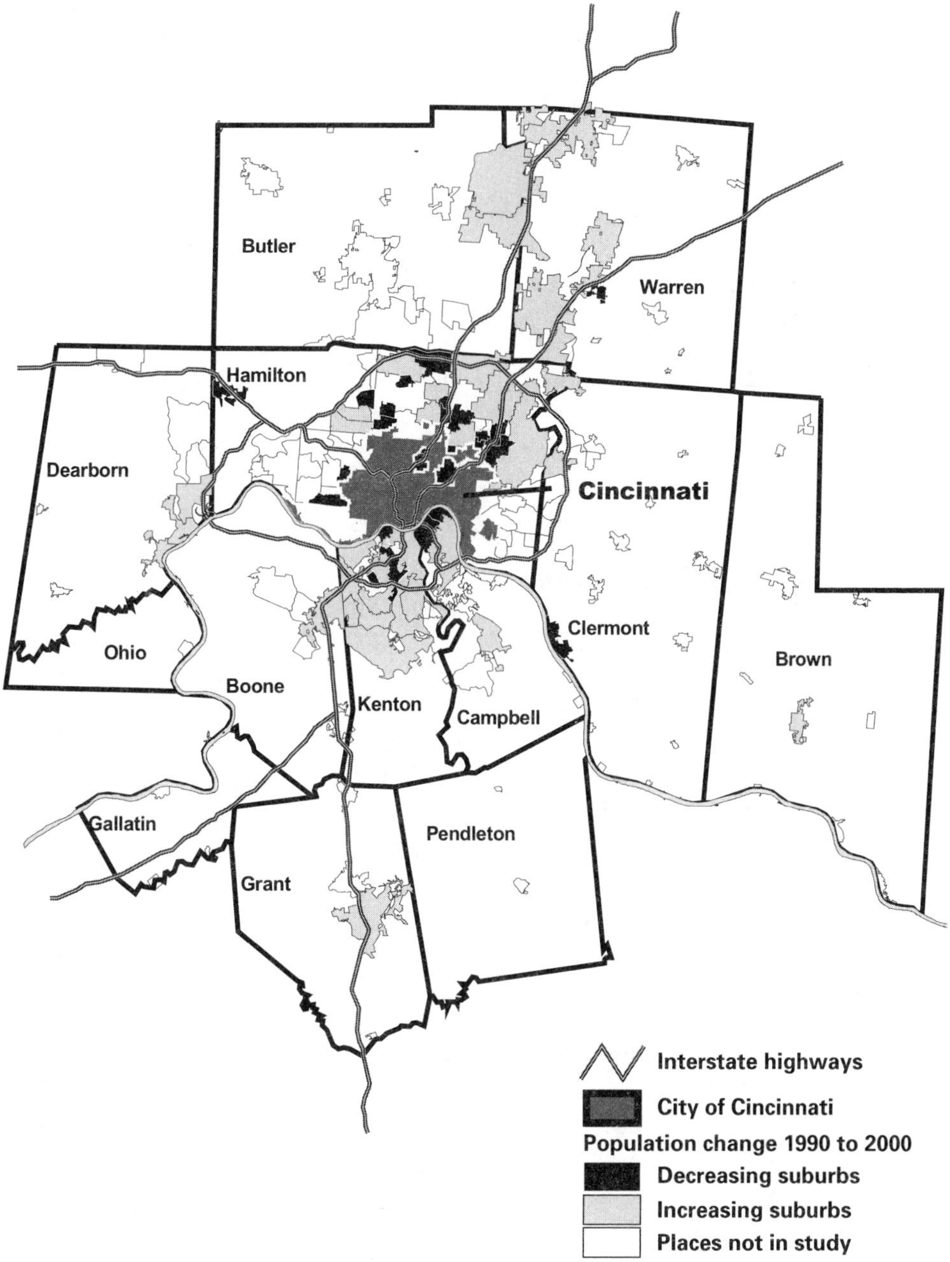

Table 7-5 separates suburbs into five population categories, according to size. Nearly one-third of the 1,223 small suburbs of fewer than 10,000 people lost population during the 1990s. Although it is true that any population change will be more apparent in small suburbs than in larger suburbs, what is clear is that small suburbs were not buffered against forces of decline.

What is more important is the fact that smaller suburbs are far more likely to be located in the Northeast and Midwest, which are the areas declining most rapidly in population. The Northeast and Midwest had more suburbs per metropolitan area (175.6 in the Northeast and 78.0 in the Midwest) than did the South (48.2) and West (44.6).[7] The Northeast and Midwest also had the largest number of small suburbs with fewer than 10,000 people (506 and 385, respectively). The West has by far the largest number of very large suburbs of more than 50,000 residents.

More than 32 percent of the suburbs smaller than 10,000 people declined in population. By contrast, only 18.4 percent of the large suburbs of more than 25,000 people declined. These differences are not overwhelming, but they do indicate that in terms of suburban growth and decline, small population size provides little inherent advantage.

Rapid Population Growth

Population growth in the 1990s was faster in unincorporated areas and in new suburbs than in existing suburbs. In one definition, "sprawling" development patterns result from metropolitan areas' increasing the amount of land consumed on the fringe but losing population in inner suburbs and central cities. Thus places like the Buffalo and Pittsburgh metropolitan areas, which lost population during the 1990s but continued to develop land on the fringe, can be said to be "sprawling" more than others because they are using their land more inefficiently.[8] Although the present study has emphasized suburban growth and decline, major population growth occurred well outside central cities in most of the studied thirty-five metropolitan areas. Growth outside of the central cities in the 1990s in these thirty-five metropolitan areas was 12,461,292 (16.5 percent).

Studied suburbs grew by 14.2 percent (7,417,836).[9] In areas outside the study area (new suburbs that did not have 2,500 or more residents in 1980,

7. Although the figure for the Northeast is clearly driven by the 515 suburbs in the New York metropolitan area, when New York is removed from the calculation the Northeast still averages 90.8 suburbs per metropolitan area.

8. See Fulton and others (2001).

9. That is, those with a population of 2,500 or more in 1980 and consistent presence in U.S. censuses since 1980.

TABLE 7-5. Decreasing and Increasing Population, by Size of Suburbs

	Total suburbs in survey		*Decreasing suburbs*			*Increasing suburbs*		
Population of suburbs	*Number of suburbs*	*Average change (percent)*	*Number of suburbs*	*Suburbs in size class (percent)*	*Average decrease (percent)*	*Number of suburbs*	*Suburbs in size class (percent)*	*Average increase (percent)*
Less than 5,000	529	11.2	207	39.1	–6.8	322	60.9	22.7
5,000 to 10,000	694	18.6	195	28.1	–5.6	499	71.9	28.1
10,000 to 25,000	777	14.2	190	24.4	–5.8	587	75.6	20.7
25,000 to 50,000	362	14.0	60	16.6	–7.0	302	83.4	18.2
More than 50,000	224	12.6	48	21.4	–5.7	176	78.6	17.6
Total suburbs	2,586	14.6	700	27.1	–6.1	1,886	72.9	22.3

Source: See table 7-1.

unincorporated areas, and those areas outside any CDP), population growth in the 1990s was 5,043,456, a rate of 21.7 percent (table 7-6). Growth was faster outside the study area in twenty-three of the thirty-five metropolitan areas (such as Atlanta, with 863,014 versus 266,777). Notable exceptions did occur. For instance, the Portland metropolitan area's studied suburbs increased by 54 percent, compared with only a 4.5 percent increase in other Portland suburban territory, and the Chicago and Seattle metropolitan areas also had much faster growth in studied suburbs than in their other suburban population, with 18 percent versus 6.2 percent (Chicago) and 32 percent versus 13 percent (Seattle).

CONCLUSION

This report has documented suburban population change based on census data. Growth and decline are uneven across the nation's metropolitan areas, but some interesting relationships are nonetheless apparent. A suburb's population growth and decline do bear some relationship to population growth and decline in that suburb's central city and metropolitan area. It is also clear that suburban decline is predominantly a phenomenon of the Northeast and Midwest in terms of overall numbers and of percentages of suburbs with declining populations.

Also interesting are the elements that are not necessarily key factors in suburban growth and decline. The size of suburbs does make some difference in terms of population change, and small suburbs are more likely to decline than larger ones, but this is not overwhelming. And although population decline is frequent in inner-ring suburbs close to the central city, the distribution does not conform to uniform patterns within, nor is it consistent among, metropolitan areas.

Several questions still persist, the most difficult of which is probably, "What difference do suburban population growth and decline make?" Many observers are not convinced that growth in itself conveys social benefits since it clearly involves certain environmental stresses. However, population decline intuitively appears to be undesirable. But if growth is not necessarily good, is decline necessarily bad? Suburban population growth and decline in themselves do not identify whether a suburb or central city is getting richer or poorer, either in terms of residents' income and other resources or in terms of the tax base that can be accessed by public agencies.

The present survey shows what has occurred and where it has taken place, but it says little about the "how" or "why" of the occurrence or about corresponding consequences. The "how" question is linked to components of

TABLE 7-6. Population Change Outside of the Study Area

	Total outside central city		*Suburbs in study*		*Other suburban population*	
Region and metropolitan area	*Population change*	*Change (percent)*	*Population change*	*Change (percent)*	*Population change*	*Change (percent)*
Northeast						
Boston, MA-NH	164,264	6.2	91,971	4.7	72,293	10.4
Buffalo-Niagara Falls, NY	16,298	1.9	–23,782	–5.0	40,080	10.4
New York- NY-NJ-CT-PA	964,502	7.9	561,895	6.4	402,607	11.6
Philadelphia, PA-NJ	246,783	7.4	–17,024	–1.6	263,807	11.9
Pittsburgh, PA	–800	0.0	–41,903	–4.0	41,108	4.2
Midwest						
Chicago, IL	749,620	16.2	705,588	18.0	44,032	6.2
Cincinnati-Hamilton, OH-KY-IN	194,386	13.4	51,011	8.5	143,375	16.7
Cleveland-Lorain-Elyria, OH	76,015	4.5	30,650	2.2	45,365	15.1
Columbus, OH	116,147	16.3	65,699	16.4	50,448	16.1
Detroit, MI	251,601	7.8	22,222	1.0	229,379	20.9
Indianapolis, IN	176,452	27.2	95,547	29.9	80,905	24.5
Kansas City, MO-KS	186,788	16.3	142,678	15.3	44,110	20.3
Milwaukee-Waukesha, WI	99,706	12.4	68,580	10.6	31,126	19.8
Minneapolis-St. Paul, MN-WI	400,821	21.1	326,031	20.4	74,790	25.2
St. Louis, MO-IL	159,578	7.6	91,774	7.5	67,804	7.8
South						
Atlanta, GA	1,129,791	44.0	266,777	30.7	863,014	50.9
Baltimore, MD	255,682	15.5	183,516	15.6	72,166	15.3
Charlotte-Gastonia-Rock Hill, NC-SC	192,306	25.1	86,963	30.2	105,343	22.0
Dallas, TX	661,225	39.6	585,016	40.4	76,209	34.3
Houston, TX	532,543	31.5	210,668	30.7	321,875	32.0
Miami, FL	312,346	19.8	126,112	10.1	186,234	55.5
Norfolk-VA Beach-Newport News, VA-NC	153,123	13.0	113,926	10.9	39,197	27.7
Orlando, FL	398,451	37.6	138,594	28.9	259,857	44.7
San Antonio, TX	58,921	15.2	25,801	18.7	33,120	13.2
Tampa-St. Petersburg-Clearwater, FL	295,003	19.0	165,099	23.6	129,904	15.3
Washington, DC-MD-VA-WV	734,509	20.3	327,355	13.1	407,154	35.9
West						
Denver, CO	399,276	34.6	214,375	22.3	184,901	96.3
Las Vegas, NV-AZ	490,406	82.5	331,280	81.7	159,126	84.3
Los Angeles and Orange County, CA	886,495	11.4	710,642	9.8	175,853	32.6
Phoenix-Mesa, AZ	675,754	53.8	610,550	56.5	65,204	37.3
Portland-Vancouver, OR-WA	310,755	28.8	285,817	54.1	24,938	4.5
Sacramento-Yolo, CA	278,102	25.0	176,803	22.2	101,299	32.1
San Diego, CA	202,966	14.6	111,374	9.5	91,592	42.4
San Francisco and Oakland, CA	357,132	13.8	342,849	14.4	14,283	6.71
Seattle-Bellevue-Everett, WA	334,345	22.0	233,387	31.6	100,958	13.0
Totals for 35 study metro areas	12,461,292	16.5	7,417,836	14.2	5,043,456	21.7

population change such as the number and size of individual households and the presence of children and the elderly. The question of "why" some suburbs have declined while others have grown is a bit more complicated, and like the question of consequences, it will require a deeper investigation into demographic, social, economic, and housing characteristics. Subsequent Brookings studies will address these questions.

REFERENCES

Fulton, William, Rolf Pendall, Mai Nguyen, and Alicia Harrison. 2001. "Who Sprawls Most? How Growth Patterns Differ across the United States." Brookings Institution Center on Urban and Metropolitan Policy.

Glaeser, Edward. 2001. "City Growth and the 2000 Census: Which Places Grew and Why." Brookings Institution Center on Urban and Metropolitan Policy.

Lang, Robert E., and Patrick A. Simmons. 2001. "Boomburbs: The Emergence of Large, Fast-Growing Suburban Cities in the United States." *Census Note* 06. Washington: Fannie Mae Foundation.

U.S. Bureau of the Census. 1970. *Census of Population 1970*. Government Printing Office.

———. 1980. *1980 Census of Population*. Department of Commerce.

———. 1990. *1990 Census of Population and Housing*. Summary Tape File 1. CD-ROM. Department of Commerce.

———. 2000. *2000 Census of Population and Housing*. Demographic Profile, FTP Files. *www.2.census.gov/census 2000/datasets/demographic profile/*, each state file: 2kh**.zip. Department of Commerce (May–June 2001).

8

Racial and Ethnic Change in the Nation's Largest Cities

ALAN BERUBE

Results from Census 2000 revealed growing racial and ethnic diversity nationally. In particular, the size of the Hispanic population edged out that of the black population, a milestone that the nation was not projected to reach until 2005. Nonwhite minorities—including Hispanics, blacks, Asians, American Indians, and Native Hawaiian/Pacific Islanders—were found to account for about 29 percent of the U.S. population, up from 24 percent in 1990. About four out of every five net new residents added to the United States in the 1990s were a minority.

The nation's largest cities were on the leading edge of the nation's growing diversity in the 1990s. Unlike what happened in the rest of the nation, however, population growth in the largest 100 U.S. cities did not occur among all racial and ethnic groups. The most consistent story of the decade in the top 100 cities was strong growth in Hispanic population and loss of white population.

This chapter examines changes during the 1990s in the racial and ethnic makeup of the 100 largest cities in the United States as of 1990, including regional patterns and the relationship between diversity and city population change. These changes may have significant implications for the mix of services cities will need to deliver, how cities will fund those services, and the face of local politics during the next ten years.

METHODS

The analysis uses data from the Census 2000 Redistricting Data Summary File and the 1990 Census Summary File-1 (short form) to describe changes during the 1990s in the racial/ethnic makeup of populations in the 100 largest cities in the United States as of 1990. In 1990 these cities had populations ranging from 171,000 (Newport News) to 7.3 million (New York).[1] The analysis focuses only on city populations and not on populations of the surrounding suburbs.[2]

Following conventional practice for analyzing trends in U.S. population diversity, the analysis separates the populations of the top 100 cities into both racial and ethnic categories. The Census Bureau considers race and Hispanic origin to be distinct concepts. On the Census 2000 short form, all respondents were asked whether or not they were Spanish/Hispanic/Latino. In the question following that one, all respondents were asked to report the race or races they considered themselves to be.[3] For the purposes of this present analysis, all individuals who identified themselves as Spanish/Hispanic/Latino are considered "Hispanic" regardless of the race they selected. Other race categories discussed in the analysis (white, black, Asian/Pacific Islander/Native Hawaiian, American Indian, and some other race) include only those individuals who did not identify themselves as Hispanic.[4]

Some argue that treating all self-identified Hispanics as a separate group, not categorizing them alongside their race counterparts, improperly conflates race and ethnicity. Results from Census 2000 suggest, though, that a substantial share of Hispanics do consider themselves to be of a race different from those options offered on the census form. Of the 35.3 million individuals who selected an Hispanic ethnicity in 2000, some 16.8 million (47 percent) identified themselves as "some other race" alone or in combination with another race. By contrast, less than 1 percent of the non-Hispanic population chose this option. Given that nearly half of Hispanics indicate that they do not fit into any of the available race categories and that the federal government, in implementing many of its programs, uses Hispanic-origin data in the same way as race data, the analysis

1. See chapter 2 in this volume for further discussion on the choice of these cities for this analysis.

2. For an analysis of changes in the racial/ethnic makeup of the suburbs of the 100 largest metropolitan areas, see Frey (2001a).

3. Choices printed on the form included the following: white, black/African-American, American Indian/Alaska Native, and a series of Asian and Pacific Islander races (such as Asian Indian, Chinese, Guamanian, Samoan). Individuals could also choose to fill in a different race.

4. Census 2000 separates Asian and Native Hawaiian/Pacific Islander race categories. In 1990 these were part of the same Asian/Pacific Islander category. This survey recombines the categories for ease of comparison with 1990 statistics and uses the label "Asians" to refer to the combined group.

follows conventional practice in considering Hispanics, regardless of race, as a separate population subgroup.[5]

Census 2000 gave respondents the opportunity for the first time to classify themselves as being of more than one race. This new option potentially complicates efforts to compare, at a city level, 1990 and 2000 population counts by race/ethnicity. In the analysis, the race categories represent individuals who classified themselves as that race only; individuals who classified themselves as being of more than one race are grouped in a "multiracial" category. Some unknown share of a given city's residents in 1990 could have reclassified themselves as multiracial in 2000; this may introduce a degree of error into the calculation of changes in the population of that city's other race/ethnicity groups. The census results, however, indicate that the degree of error is probably small. Only 1.2 million non-Hispanic individuals in the top 100 cities, or 2.2 percent of all residents, classified themselves as multiracial.

FINDINGS

The analysis produced several interesting insights as follows.

- Overall, population in the 100 largest cities in the United States shifted from majority white to "majority minority" between 1990 and 2000.
- The Hispanic population in the 100 largest cities grew by 3.8 million during the decade while white population shrank by more than 2 million.
- Despite regional differences, cities in every part of the country experienced rapid growth in minority populations, especially Hispanics and Asians.
- The fastest-growing large cities experienced increases in the size of all racial and ethnic populations during the 1990s, while slow-growing and declining cities lost white, and sometimes black, population.

Majority White to Majority Minority

The 1990s were a landmark decade in the demographic composition of America's largest cities. Between 1990 and 2000, the largest cities in the United States transitioned from majority white to "majority minority"—that is, whites went from representing more than half to less than half of the

5. For instance, federal statutes on civil rights, equal employment opportunity, community reinvestment, and public health all use data on Hispanic origin in much the same way as they use data on race. U.S. Bureau of the Census (1998).

overall population of these cities. The transformation was more than marginal: the combined white share of population in the 100 largest cities dropped dramatically, from 52 percent in 1990 to 44 percent in 2000.

The rapid racial and ethnic diversification of city populations represents a magnification of trends in the remainder of the country (figure 8-1). Overall, as white share of population in the 100 largest cities declined from 52 percent to 44 percent, its share in the rest of the country dropped by a somewhat smaller degree, from 82 percent to 75 percent. Hispanic share of population rose proportionately in both areas; in the largest cities nearly one in four individuals identified himself/herself as Hispanic, versus one in ten elsewhere. The largest racial/ethnic difference between the top 100 cities and the rest of the nation was in the black population; its share in cities remains almost three times as high as it is elsewhere.

The transformation to minority white population in the largest cities in the 1990s occurred in the aggregate and also in specific cities. In fact, 18 of the top 100 cities saw their white share of population drop from more than 50 percent to less than 50 percent during the decade (table 8-1). These cities were at the forefront of a diversifying nation and include many places in which changes in the racial and ethnic makeup of the population were most dramatic. Anaheim, for instance, experienced the largest decline in white share among the largest 100 cities, from 57 percent of the city's population in 1990 to 36 percent in 2000. Notably there are cities from every area of the country on this list of 18: cities in five states of the South, Milwaukee and St. Louis in the Midwest, Albuquerque and four California cities in the West, and Boston, Rochester, and Philadelphia in the Northeast. None of the 18 cities experienced less than a 7 percent drop in white share of population; even those cities near the bottom of the list still underwent a remarkable shift in a decade's time.

In total, of the largest 100 cities only 52 had majority white populations in 2000, down from 70 in 1990. Table 8-2 shows the cities with the ten highest and ten lowest minority population shares in 2000. The cities with the largest minority shares are quite diverse in and among themselves. Some are stagnating or declining cities with traditionally large minority populations, such as Detroit, Birmingham, Miami, and Newark; some are "on the rebound," adding diverse new residents to large existing minority bases, such as Oakland and Jersey City; and others, according to Robert Lang and Patrick A. Simmons, are fast-growing "boomburbs" in traditionally high-immigrant metros, such as Hialeah and Santa Ana.[6]

6. Lang and Simmons (2001).

FIGURE 8-1. Racial/Ethnic Makeup of 100 Largest Cities and Rest of Nation, 1990 and 2000

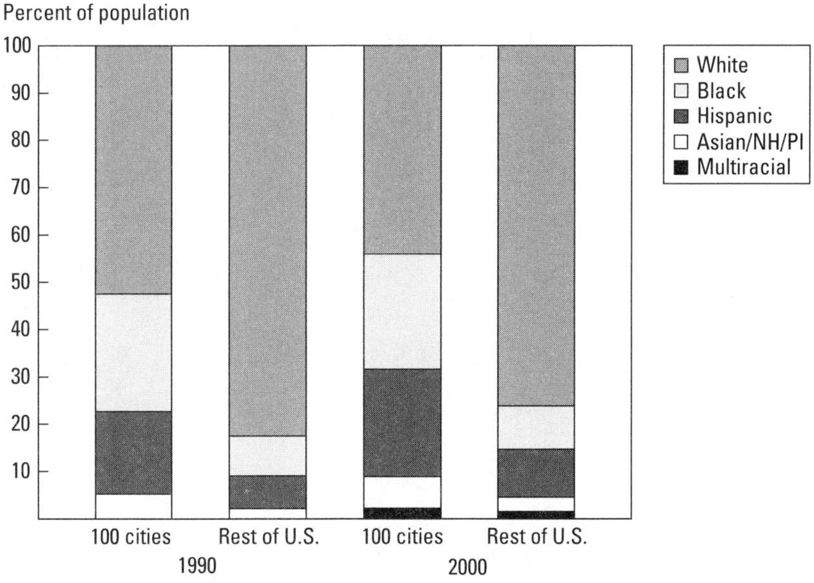

Source: Based on U.S. Bureau of the Census (2001).

On the other end of the spectrum, many of the majority-white cities were in the states of the West North Central and Mountain regions. Cities in the nation's agricultural belt, like Des Moines, Lincoln, and Omaha, continue to draw residents from their states' predominantly white populations. None received black residents to the degree that industrial cities of the Northeast and Rust Belt did in the early 1900s, and none today is a magnet for international immigration like New York, Houston, Atlanta, or most cities in California. Mountain state cities like Colorado Springs and Mesa are growing in large part by drawing white population from other parts of the United States.[7]

Hispanic Population Grows, White Population Shrinks

As in the rest of the nation, Hispanics were the fastest-growing major race/ethnic group in large cities in the 1990s. The boom in their population is owed both to increased immigration from Latin America during a decade

7. Many of these cities are in "Largely White Metro Areas—South and West" as described in Frey (2001a).

TABLE 8-1. Eighteen Large Cities That Went from Majority White to Majority Minority during the 1990s

Percent

City	White share[a] 1990	White share 2000	Decline
Anaheim, CA	56.6	35.9	20.8
Riverside, CA	61.3	45.6	15.7
Milwaukee, WI	60.8	45.4	15.4
Rochester, NY	58.3	44.3	14.0
Sacramento, CA	53.4	40.5	12.8
Fort Worth, TX	56.5	45.8	10.7
Augusta-Richmond, GA	54.0	43.7	10.3
Philadelphia, PA	52.1	42.5	9.6
Boston, MA	59.0	49.5	9.5
San Diego, CA	58.7	49.4	9.3
Mobile, AL	58.9	49.8	9.2
Montgomery, AL	56.1	47.1	9.0
Columbus, GA	57.3	48.6	9.0
Norfolk, VA	55.6	47.0	8.5
Albuquerque, NM	58.3	49.9	8.4
Baton Rouge, LA	52.9	44.7	8.1
Shreveport, LA	53.6	45.9	7.7
St. Louis, MO	50.2	42.9	7.3

Source: Based on U.S. Bureau of the Census (2001).

a. "White" refers to individuals who identified their race as white only and did not indicate Hispanic origin.

TABLE 8-2. Cities with Ten Highest and Ten Lowest Minority Population Shares, 2000

City	Minority share 2000 (percent)[a]
Cities with ten highest minority shares	
1 Hialeah, FL	91.9
2 Detroit, MI	89.5
3 Miami, FL	88.2
4 Santa Ana, CA	87.6
5 Newark, NJ	85.8
6 El Paso, TX	81.7
7 Honolulu, HI	81.3
8 Birmingham, AL	76.5
9 Oakland, CA	76.5
10 Jersey City, NJ	76.4
Cities with ten lowest minority shares	
1 Spokane, WA	12.1
2 Lincoln, NE	12.2
3 Madison, WI	18.0
4 Des Moines, IA	20.4
5 Lexington-Fayette, KY	20.9
6 Portland, OR	24.5
7 Omaha, NE	24.6
8 Colorado Springs, CO	24.7
9 Mesa, AZ	26.8
10 Fort Wayne, IN	26.9

Source: See table 8-1.

a. "Minority" refers to all individuals who classified themselves as Hispanic, a race other than white, or both.

of strong economic growth and enhanced job opportunity and to the higher fertility rates that accompany the younger age structure of first- and second-generation Hispanic families.[8] In the nation as a whole, nearly 40 percent of net new residents in the 1990s were Hispanic; the corresponding figure in the largest 100 cities was *more than 80 percent.*

Large increases during the 1990s in the numbers of Hispanics and Asians living in cities occurred alongside continuing declines in the number of white city residents. It was the combination of trends that resulted in the largest cities "tipping" from majority white to majority nonwhite in the 1990s (figure 8-2).

Size of White Population. The size of the overall decline in white population was not trivial. White population in the top 100 cities combined dropped by 2.3 million people during the decade, or 8.5 percent. Some 71 of these 100 cities experienced a decline in white population of at least 2 percent. As noted earlier, some of this population decline may be related to the introduction of the new multiple-race categories, but the "reclassification" effect is likely to be small.[9]

The phenomenon of white population decrease was widespread among the top 100 cities, but a few large cities dominated the overall decline. The five largest cities alone—New York, Los Angeles, Chicago, Houston, and Philadelphia—lost nearly 1 million white residents combined, or about 14 percent of their total 1990 white population.[10] As a result, no single racial/ethnic group predominated in those cities in 2000: whites made up one-third of all residents, Hispanics 30 percent, blacks 25 percent, and Asian/Pacific Islanders 8 percent.

A number of other large cities experienced much faster losses of white residents during the decade than did the five largest cities. In 20 cities white

8. Census 2000 indicates that nationally, 35 percent of Hispanic women are in their young child-bearing ages (15–34), compared with 27 percent of the population as a whole.

9. Less than 80 percent of all non-Hispanic multiracial residents of the 100 largest cities indicated "white" as one of their races on Census 2000. Many individuals that did indicate "white" as one of their races in 2000 likely identified with a racial minority group in Census 1990. A 1998 survey in Washington state found that while 13 percent of black individuals and 14 percent of "other race" individuals switched from a single race to a multirace category when the latter was made available, only 3 percent of white individuals did. Washington State Task Force on Race/Ethnicity Data (2000). Additionally, nearly one-fourth of all multiracial individuals in the 100 largest cities in 2000 were under the age of ten; these children thus represent additions to city multiracial populations, not reclassifications of residents existing in 1990.

10. Total population and population shares and growth rates by race/ethnicity for each of the 100 largest cities are available at *www.brook.edu/es/urban/citygrowthdata.xls.*

FIGURE 8-2. Absolute and Percent Population Change in 100 Largest Cities, by Race/Ethnicity Group, 1990–2000[a]

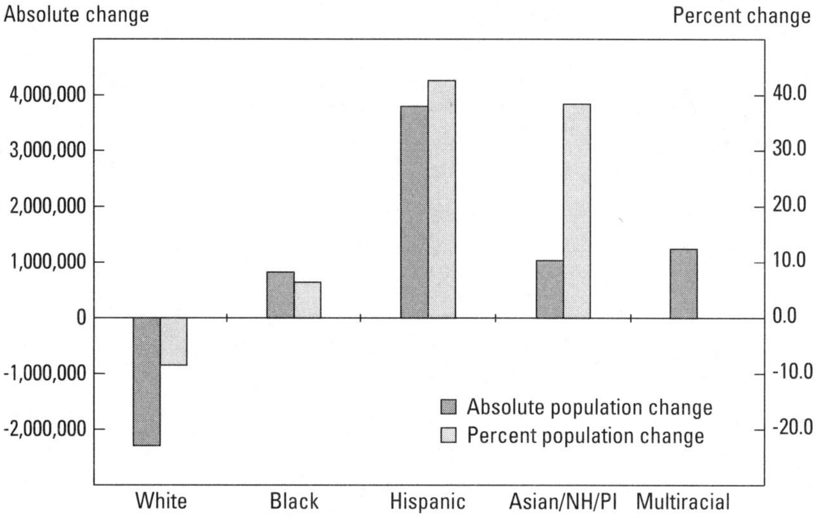

Source: See figure 8-1.

a. No percentage change is reflected for the multiracial population, as 2000 was the first census in which individuals could choose more than one race.

population loss exceeded 20 percent. Cities experiencing the largest declines included predominantly black cities like Detroit (53 percent) and Birmingham (40 percent), as well as cities with a large Hispanic presence like Long Beach (28 percent) and Jersey City (32 percent).

Size of Black Population. Across the 100 largest cities, black population grew at a modest 6.4 percent rate in the 1990s, slightly slower than overall population growth in these cities (9 percent). As a result, the black share of population in these cities shrank by a small amount. In 1990 blacks accounted for 24.7 percent of residents in the 100 largest cities; in 2000 they accounted for 24.1 percent.

Despite the overall gain, black population declined during the 1990s in 16 of the 100 largest cities. Of these 16 cities, 8 were in California alone, in high-priced markets such as San Francisco, San Diego, San Jose, and Los Angeles. Other high-cost cities like Atlanta and Washington also lost black residents during the decade, as did older industrial cities like St. Louis, Baltimore, Dayton, and Pittsburgh that experienced significant overall population loss.

Size of Hispanic Population. The 100 largest cities collectively added 3.8 million Hispanic residents in the 1990s, a dramatic 42.6 percent increase. The typical city witnessed an even larger gain—the median increase in Hispanic population across the 100 cities was 64.5 percent. Gains were widespread: 97 of the cities experienced an increase in Hispanic population, and Hispanic population in 32 cities more than doubled in size.

Ten Texas cities together gained 1 million Hispanics, more than one-fourth of the total gain across all 100 cities. Unlike some other U.S. regions in which Hispanic population increased largely as a result of immigration from Latin America, these Texas cities experienced significant natural increases in Hispanic population. Some 20 percent of Hispanics in the ten large Texas cities were under the age of 10 in 2000 versus 10 percent of non-Hispanic whites.

The rapid gains in Hispanic population that occurred in many cities shifted the ethnic makeup of their resident populations rather dramatically, particularly in cities in the Southwest and West. Hispanic share of population in the top 100 cities overall increased 5 percentage points in the 1990s, but 12 of the top 100 cities saw their Hispanic share of population increase by at least 10 percentage points. In Phoenix, for instance, where one in five residents was Hispanic in 1990, more than one in three was in 2000.

Size of Asian Population. Like the black population, Asians represented roughly the same proportion of overall population in the 100 largest cities at the end of the decade (6.6 percent) as they did at the beginning (5.2 percent). But the small change in share masked a significant increase in this population's growth in the 1990s in large cities—38.3 percent overall, a net increase of more than 1 million Asian residents.

As with Hispanic population, gains in Asian population were widespread: 95 of the top 100 cities experienced increases. But gains tended to be somewhat smaller than Hispanic gains: only 11 cities underwent a doubling (or more) of their Asian populations. Interestingly, growth centers for Asian population could be found outside of the traditional West Coast magnets for Asian immigration: Garland, Jersey City, New York, and St. Paul all saw their Asian population shares increase by at least 3 percentage points during the decade.

Comparison with Rest of the United States. The rapid rise in large-city Hispanic and Asian populations should not overshadow the fact that on the whole, their numbers actually grew faster during the 1990s in areas outside the 100 largest cities. The 100-city growth rates for Hispanics and Asians were 43 percent and 38 percent respectively; outside the 100 cities, their growth rates were 68 percent and 58 percent. Black population registered a 24 percent increase outside the largest cities, compared with only 6 percent within the cities. According to Alan Berube and William H. Frey, these differences reflect the overall trend of faster suburban than city growth in the 1990s and the fact that minority populations in increasing numbers are choosing smaller cities and suburbs.[11] Nevertheless, the rapid rise of minority populations in cities is of particular interest given that it occurred alongside white population loss and was the underlying reason for the shift to a "majority minority" population in the largest cities in 2000.

Minority Population Grows throughout Nation

Growth and decline in U.S. city populations in the 1990s was in some respects a regional story. Many of the large cities that experienced overall population declines were found in older Rust Belt cities in Ohio and in largely black-white cities in Alabama, Mississippi, and Louisiana. Fast-growing cities could be found in states throughout the Southeast, Southwest, and Rockies.

Growth in city minority populations, however, was a nationwide phenomenon. Fast-growing cities in the West and declining cities in the Midwest both experienced increases in their Hispanic and Asian populations. Interesting patterns by region emerged in the growth of racial/ethnic groups. Table 8-3 displays 1990–2000 growth rates and 2000 population shares for each major racial/ethnic group in the 100 largest cities by U.S. region.[12]

Northeast. Overall, growth rates for blacks and Hispanics in northeastern cities lagged behind those for cities in other regions in the country. Hispanic population across the 100 largest cities grew by 43 percent during the decade but by only 23 percent in cities of the Northeast. This reflects the large base population of Hispanics in New York City: that city's gain of 377,000 new Hispanic residents in the 1990s translated into only a 21 percent increase in its Hispanic population.

Asian population increases, however, were above average in the Northeast, with New York, Philadelphia, and Boston all showing strong

11. See chapter 2 in this volume; Frey (2001a, 2001b).

12. The subregions analyzed in this section are a slightly modified form of census divisions. Cities in the New England and Mid-Atlantic states are treated together as "Northeastern," and Baltimore is analyzed in the "Northeast" category rather than in the "South Atlantic" category. See chapter 2 in this volume for further details.

TABLE 8-3. Population Growth, 1990–2000, and Population Share, 2000, by Race/Ethnicity and U.S. Region

Percent

		Population growth, 1990–2000				Population share, 2000				
Region	*Cities*	*White*	*Black*	*Hispanic*	*Asian*	*White*	*Black*	*Hispanic*	*Asian*	*Multi-racial*
Northeast	10	–16	4	23	58	37	30	21	8	3
South Atlantic	16	–2	9	35	62	46	35	14	3	2
East North Central	13	–14	4	49	36	44	38	13	3	2
East South Central	8	–12	17	266	83	48	46	3	2	1
West North Central	8	–7	10	130	78	66	20	7	4	2
West South Central	16	–6	12	52	69	40	21	34	3	1
Mountain	8	9	29	92	77	58	6	29	3	2
Pacific	21	–9	–5	35	22	41	9	31	15	3
Total	100	–8	6	43	38	44	24	23	7	2

Source: See table 8-1.

gains. The Northeast's cities posted the largest absolute gain in Asian population during the decade of the eight regions studied. Overall, even though they had only half as many Asian residents as did the Pacific cities in 1990, northeastern cities gained 359,000 Asian residents in the 1990s versus 326,000 in the Pacific cities. At the same time, the northeastern cities experienced the largest percentage drop in white population: 16 percent. The decline was driven by large white population loss in New York City (362,000), Philadelphia (181,000), and Baltimore (83,000). Because these cities also saw substantial increases in their minority populations during the same period, the Northeast became the only region in which no single racial/ethnic group accounted for at least 40 percent of the population in 2000.

Southeast (South Atlantic and East South Central). Cities of the Southeast experienced stronger growth in racial/ethnic minority populations than did cities of the Northeast. In the case of Hispanic and Asian populations, many of these cities started from a small base and added minorities rapidly during the 1990s. For instance, the eight large cities in the Central Southeast states of Kentucky, Tennessee, Alabama, and Mississippi had the highest growth rates of any region for Hispanics and Asians. They were home to only 19,000 Hispanics in 1990 but added 50,000 new Hispanic residents during the decade. Their Asian populations grew by 83 percent, but the total net increase was less than 20,000, the smallest of all the regions. The South Atlantic cities also posted strong gains in these populations; their overall Hispanic growth rate was lower because of large base populations in Miami and Hialeah.

Black population also grew at above-average rates in southeastern cities, and blacks remain the dominant minority group in these places in 2000 (table 8-3). The cities of the Central Southeast posted some of the strongest black population gains. Even as total population in Jackson declined by 6 percent during the decade, black population grew by more than 18 percent. According to Frey, this city growth pattern reflects a broader trend in the 1990s of black families returning to the U.S. South.[13] Amid strong black population growth in cities like Charlotte (40 percent) and Virginia Beach (47 percent), however, some cities in the South Atlantic provided an exception to the trend. Black population in the city of Atlanta actually declined modestly (3 percent) in the 1990s; declines were even more dramatic in Washington, D.C., (14 percent) and Miami (18 percent).

Among the southeastern cities there were important differences in white population change in the 1990s. Many "black-white" cities in the Central Southeast lost significant portions of their white residents. Jackson and Birmingham, for instance, each experienced a 40 percent decline in white population during the decade. In the South Atlantic, overall white population loss was modest (2 percent) and was concentrated in Virginia cities (Richmond, Norfolk, Newport News, and Virginia Beach) and in the smaller Georgia cities (Augusta-Richmond and Columbus). Other cities in the South Atlantic like Atlanta, Charlotte, and Raleigh actually posted strong gains in white population during the 1990s.

Midwest (East North Central and West North Central). The Midwest's two halves—(1) older industrial cities in the East like Cleveland, Detroit, and Milwaukee and (2) cities in the West with smaller minority populations like Wichita, Lincoln, and Minneapolis—experienced very different growth patterns in the 1990s. About half of the eastern cities lost population, but seven out of eight western cities posted gains.

Amid these differing overall growth rates in the 1990s, most cities in the Midwest experienced significant increases in Hispanic and Asian populations. Many cities more than doubled their 1990 Hispanic populations during the decade: Columbus, Ohio, Indianapolis, Omaha, and Minneapolis all had large increases in Hispanic population in both absolute and percentage terms. Owing in large part to these Hispanic gains, cities in the eastern half of the Midwest had a racial/ethnic makeup quite similar to that of the cities of the South Atlantic in 2000 (table 8-3). In the western cities of the Midwest, Asian population gains were especially large. During the decade, the city of St. Paul nearly doubled its large existing Asian population: Asians

13. Frey (2001b).

accounted for one out of every eight St. Paul residents by 2000, the second-highest population share for that group outside of West Coast cities.

The defining difference between the cities of the eastern and western Midwest in the 1990s was in the degree of white population loss. A larger proportion of cities in the eastern half of the region lost white population, and those losses tended to be larger. Overall the western cities lost 7 percent of their white population in the 1990s, while the eastern cities lost 14 percent. The extreme example was Detroit, which lost more than half of its white residents. Chicago and Milwaukee also showed white population loss in excess of 100,000 residents. Chicago was notable in that it also lost a modest amount of black residents during the decade. By 2000 that city's population consisted of nearly equivalent shares of whites, blacks, and Hispanics and Asians combined.

Southwest (West South Central and Mountain). Hispanics made some of their most significant gains in representation in cities across the Southwest. In the cities of the Central Southwest, most of which are in Texas, Hispanic population grew by 52 percent in the 1990s. As a result Hispanics accounted for one-third of those cities' residents in 2000, up from one-fourth in 1990. Cities in the Mountain states were 29 percent Hispanic overall in 2000, up from 20 percent in 1990, thanks to a near doubling of Hispanic population in those cities during the decade. Two Arizona cities in the top 100 (Phoenix and Tucson) are now more than one-third Hispanic.

Where these two groups of southwestern cities diverge most is on white and black population shares. Mountain cities in general tend to have larger white shares, while cities of the Central Southwest have larger black shares. Blacks' share of population in these cities did not change much in the 1990s, even though cities in the Mountain states led the nation in overall black population growth (29 percent), and those in the Central Southwest showed strong gains as well (12 percent). White population share, by contrast, declined dramatically across the Southwest. Despite being the only region in which the large cities experienced an overall increase in white population, the Mountain states saw their white share of population drop from 70 percent in 1990 to 58 percent in 2000, largely as a result of booming Hispanic population. In the Central Southwest the decline in white share from 49 percent to 40 percent was owed to Hispanic growth and to absolute declines in white population: 13 out of 16 cities lost white residents in the 1990s.

Pacific. In California cities, strong Hispanic growth rates added to already sizable Hispanic base populations. In Anaheim and Los Angeles, Hispanics represented nearly one-half of all residents in 2000. In Orange County more than three-fourths of Santa Ana's residents are now Hispanic. Having long been magnets for international immigration from Mexico, California's cities are experiencing continued growth in Hispanic population owing increasingly to births in Hispanic families. Children under the age of ten made up 22 percent of Hispanic population in California's major cities in 2000 versus only 9 percent of the non-Hispanic white population.

The Pacific cities did, however, supply the one exception to the nationwide trend of growing minority population in the 1990s. Overall, these cities lost 5 percent of their combined black population during the decade. Of the seventeen cities nationwide in which black population decreased by at least 2 percentage points between 1990 and 2000, eight were in California. One of the largest declines occurred in San Francisco, which lost nearly a quarter (23 percent) of its black residents. Other major California cities—Los Angeles (12 percent), Oakland (12 percent), San Diego (6 percent) and San Jose (14 percent)—also showed declines in black population, as did Seattle (9 percent). This trend likely reflects a combination of factors, including decreased black migration to California and decreasing affordability of housing in West Coast cities during the late 1990s.

Minority Population Change in Fast-Growing versus Declining Cities

The "high-flier" cities offered a contrast with the racial and ethnic trends that prevailed in other categories of large cities during the 1990s. In these rapidly growing places, population grew across racial and ethnic lines. Cities that grew less fast and cities that stagnated or declined in population tended to lose white residents, and many lost black residents as well.

Among the largest 100 cities, 17 cities experienced population growth exceeding 20 percent during the 1990s. These cities were found largely in the Southeast (including Charlotte, Raleigh, and Greensboro), in the Mountain states (including Phoenix, Mesa, and Tucson), and in southern California. Overall, the population of these cities grew by 32 percent during the 1990s. Figure 8-3 shows that they constituted the only category of cities to exhibit an increase in white population (9 percent) in the aggregate. Other racial and ethnic populations grew by even faster rates in the high-flier cities. High fliers' overall black population, for instance, increased by 34 percent, and 16 of the 17 experienced double-digit growth rates in black population.

In contrast with the high fliers, eleven of the twenty-three studied cities that grew between 10 percent and 20 percent overall saw their white population shrink during the decade, and another five experienced no real change. Dallas, for instance, grew at an 18 percent clip overall but lost more

FIGURE 8-3. Change in Racial/Ethnic Population, by City Growth Category, 1990–2000

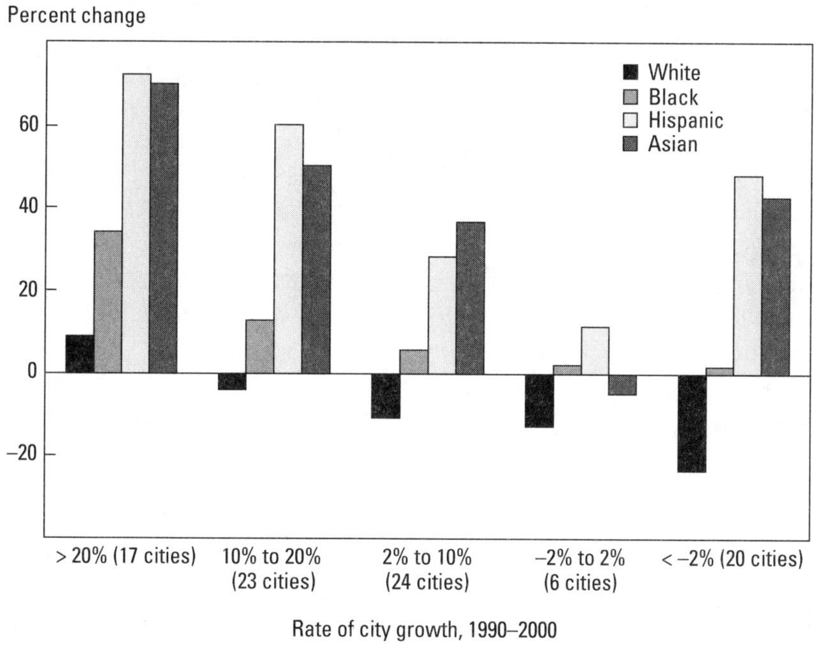

Source: See figure 8-1.

than 14 percent of its white population; the city's growth was driven largely by a doubling of its Hispanic population.

Among the modest growers (the twenty-four cities in which total population increased only between 2 percent and 10 percent), only Atlanta actually experienced a real increase in white population. In addition to Atlanta, a number of cities in that category also experienced a drop in black population, including many in California, as noted earlier.

The twenty shrinking cities in the study were characterized by large drops in white population, little overall change in black population, and strong gains in Hispanic and Asian population. In nearly every one of these cities, however, Hispanic and Asian population gains were large in percentage terms but small in absolute terms. Overall, Hispanic population in the twenty cities increased by 48 percent, but this translated into a total increase of only 151,000 Hispanic residents. For instance, Louisville's Hispanic and Asian populations grew by 171 percent and 95 percent respectively, but this represented an addition of only 4,800 total residents to the city; that city's 27,000-person decline in white population during the 1990s drove its overall 4.8 percent population loss. Overall, white population in the declining cities fell by more than 1 million during the decade (a 23 percent drop), and the percentage decrease in nearly every one of the cities was in the double digits. The only exception was Washington, D.C., where white population fell by just 7,000 (or 4 percent), but black population dropped by 55,000 (or 14 percent).

A strong link existed between change in a city's white population during the 1990s and change in its total population. The twenty cities with at least a 2 percent gain in white population grew by a combined 27 percent during the decade. The seventy-one cities that lost at least 2 percent white population grew by less than 6 percent overall. Nevertheless, although it served as an indicator of city growth, white population change did not *drive* city growth in the 1990s. Even the fastest-growing cities experienced the bulk of their population gains from increases in the presence of racial and ethnic minorities.[14]

CONCLUSION

This chapter demonstrates that large cities are on the front lines of a diversifying national population. Across all 100 cities considered for analysis, there appeared a consistent pattern of decreasing white population, rapidly growing Hispanic and Asian population, and modestly increasing black population.

The rapid diversification of city populations during the last decade has implications for the economic, social, and political climate of these places. Cities that grew the fastest were those that attracted new residents from all racial/ethnic populations. This finding suggests that cities hoping to achieve real growth need to provide a living environment attractive to families of varying race and ethnicity. A renewed focus on basic services like schools, safety, and infrastructure that benefit city residents in a broad way may be the approach most likely to appeal to households across the racial/ethnic spectrum.

In thinking about basic services such as these, cities will need to understand the unique characteristics of their resident populations and how the changing populations change specific services needs. In Aurora, Colorado, for instance, where one out of every fifteen residents in 1990 was Hispanic, now one out of every five is Hispanic. Large demographic shifts at the city level such as this are likely to affect the structure and delivery of services such

14. Of the 1.9 million net new residents in the cities that grew by at least 20 percent during the 1990s, only 18 percent were non-Hispanic whites.

as health care, public education, housing, and public transportation. These shifts may also affect cities' fiscal capacities and thus their ability to pay for these services. Understanding the context at the local level, through continued analysis of Census 2000 data, can help individual cities respond to change as well as anticipate future needs.

Despite increasing diversity at the city level, people of different races and ethnicities continue to live apart in many cities in the United States. In Washington, D.C., for instance, more than three-fourths of the black population lives in neighborhoods that are at least 80 percent black. No single racial/ethnic group makes up a majority of the population in Los Angeles, but the student population in the LA Unified School District is 71 percent Hispanic.[15] The social health of cities may rest in large part with how racial and ethnic diversity plays out at the neighborhood level. Researchers have begun to study this question with Census 2000 short-form data, and the socioeconomic data available from the long form will provide additional opportunities to examine diversity in all its aspects.

REFERENCES

Frey, William H. 2001a. "Melting Pot Suburbs: A Census 2000 Study of Suburban Diversity." Brookings Institution Center on Urban and Metropolitan Policy (June).

———. 2001b. "Census 2000 Shows Large Black Return to the South, Reinforcing the Region's 'White-Black' Demographic Profile." University of Michigan Population Studies Center.

Lang, Robert, and Patrick Simmons. 2001. "Boomburbs: The Emergence of Large, Fast-Growing Suburban Cities in the United States." *Census Note* 06. Washington: Fannie Mae Foundation (June).

U.S. Bureau of the Census. 1998. "Uses for Questions on Census 2000 Forms." *www.census.gov/dmd/www/content.htm* (April–May 2001). Department of Commerce.

———. 2001. Redistricting Data (P.L. 94-171). Summary File and 1990 Census. Department of Commerce.

Washington State Task Force on Race/Ethnicity Data. 2000. *www.ofm.wa.gov/race/racecategories.ppt* (April 2002). Office of Financial Management.

15. Gregory Rodríguez, "Where the Minorities Rule," *New York Times*, February 10, 2002, sec. 4, p. 6.

9

Melting Pot Suburbs
A Study of Suburban Diversity

WILLIAM H. FREY

Census 2000 data reveal that racial and ethnic diversity is rising substantially in America's suburbs. Among the nation's 102 largest metropolitan areas, with populations exceeding half a million, minorities constituted more than a quarter (27.3 percent) of the suburban populations in 2000, up from 19.3 percent in 1990.[1] Almost half (47 percent) of the minorities in the large metropolitan areas in the present study lived in the suburbs in 2000, compared with approximately 40 percent a decade ago.

Of course, these overall statistics mask variations across metropolitan areas and variations in residential patterns across different racial and ethnic groups. The 1990–2000 surge in minority suburbanization at the national level reflects disproportionate gains in the suburbs of thirty-five metropolitan areas identified in the present study as "Melting Pot" metros, which have experienced large, immigrant-driven Hispanic and Asian population growth in their cities and suburbs in recent decades. The national numbers also are influenced, although to a lesser extent, by metropolitan areas in the South and West that have seen increases in their black suburban populations. In metros located in the slow-growing North, the pace of minority suburbanization lags far behind that of the nation as a whole.

The author is grateful to senior project programmer Cathy Sun and other support staff at the University of Michigan Population Studies Center and the Milken Institute for assistance in preparing census data and to Alan Berube and Jennifer Bradley at the Brookings Center on Urban and Metropolitan Policy for their advice and editorial expertise.

1. Frey (2000, 2001a).

The study also outlines the differing minority suburbanization patterns of blacks, Hispanics, and Asians for 102 metropolitan areas and includes new findings on the residential patterns of people who identify themselves as belonging to more than one racial group, a new option in Census 2000.

METHODS

The methodology used in the analysis involved the definition or clarification of concepts relating to metropolitan areas, central cities, race categories, and measures of minority suburbanization.

Definitions of Metropolitan Area

The study evaluates 1990–2000 minority suburbanization patterns for the largest 102 metropolitan areas, with populations exceeding 500,000 as reported in Census 2000. The metropolitan areas are defined on the basis of metropolitan statistical areas (MSAs) and primary metropolitan statistical areas (PMSAs) and in the New England states on the basis of New England county metropolitan areas (NECMAs).

Definition of Central City

The definition of central cities and their suburbs ("suburbs" being the metropolitan-area component located outside of the metro's central cities) is based on Office of Management and Budget (OMB) standards in effect for Census 2000. These standards are consistently applied to both the 1990 and 2000 census data. OMB's roster of "central cities" often includes other places besides the one largest or best-known central city of the MSA. For instance, the central cities of the Detroit PMSA are defined by the OMB as being Detroit, Dearborn, Pontiac, and Port Huron. These central cities satisfy criteria associated with city size, density, and employment concentration that are uniformly applied across all metropolitan areas. Use of this broad OMB central city definition means that the present study's comparison of suburban populations consistently excludes not only the major central city but also the most urbanized municipalities in each area.

Application of Race Categories

The use of race categories in the study required a decision on how to apply the answers to the new question asked on Census 2000 forms in regard to respondents' race, since this new question is not strictly comparable to the race question asked in Census 1990. The change in the question allows respondents now to identify more than one racial category if they desire; it also decouples the 1990 race category Asian and Pacific Islander into two categories, Asian or Native Hawaiian and Other Pacific Islander.[2] Consistent with other studies in the Brookings Center on Urban and Metropolitan Policy Census 2000 series, the present study will consider whites and blacks to be those who identified themselves in Census 2000 as white only or black only. Similarly, the study classifies Asians as those who selected only one race in Census 2000. But in order to maintain comparability with the 1990 census, the study also considers as Asians those who defined themselves as Native Hawaiians and Other Pacific Islanders.

Those persons who selected more than one race in 2000 can be placed in a separate category of "two or more races." This category did not exist in 1990, which leads to a potential understatement of 2000 "single race" categories in comparison with their counterpart races in 1990. But the numbers of "two or more races" responses are relatively small. Among non-Hispanics only 3.8 percent of the population chose more than one race in 2000, and only 1.8 percent of whites did.

The study follows earlier research by combining the Hispanic-origin and race items into a single classification scheme, although the two are technically separate classifications.[3] All persons identifying themselves as Hispanic constitute one category, and all non-Hispanic persons are classified by their race (such as non-Hispanic whites or non-Hispanic blacks). For ease of exposition, the survey will use the terms "whites," "blacks," "Asians," and the like with the understanding that these categories pertain to non-Hispanic members of those race groups.

Measurement of Minority Suburbanization

The study employs several measures to assess minority suburbanization levels and the related changes that occurred during the past decade. The bulk of the study focuses on minority suburbanization at the metropolitan-area level. Assessing the minority share (for all minorities combined or for individual minority groups) of the total suburban population across different areas and assessing the 1990–2000 changes in this minority suburban population share, the analysis provides a comparison of metropolitan areas or groups of metropolitan areas with respect to minority representation within their suburbs in 2000 and with respect to the changes in such minority representation during the 1990s.

2. U.S. Bureau of the Census (2001).

3. Massey and Denton (1987); Denton and Massey (1991); Frey (1992); Frey and Fielding (1995); Frey and Farley (1996).

By using the city-suburb dissimilarity index, the study also examines the extent to which a minority group is disproportionately concentrated in the central city or the suburbs. Positive values of this index range from zero (indicating that the minority group is distributed between the central cities and suburbs exactly the same as whites) to 100 (indicating that all members of the minority group reside in the central city and all whites reside in the suburbs). The index value indicates the percentage of all minority group members that would have to relocate (in this case, to the suburbs) in order for that minority group to be distributed exactly the same as whites within that metro area. A negative value on the index indicates that the minority group is disproportionately concentrated in the suburbs in comparison with the white population. In this case, the index value indicates the percentage of the minority group's population that would have to relocate to the city in order for that minority population to be distributed within that metro area's suburbs and central cities in the same proportions as whites.[4]

The study also examines a minority group's contribution to 1990–2000 suburban population change, defined as the group's 1990–2000 suburban population change as a percentage of the total suburban population change. This measure is employed to show how current minority growth patterns have affected overall suburban population changes in the 1990s.

FINDINGS

The analysis of race and ethnicity changes in the 102 most populous metropolitan statistical areas, using Census 2000 data, indicates the following:

- Racial and ethnic diversity in suburban areas rose substantially in the last decade. Racial and ethnic minorities make up more than a quarter (27 percent) of suburban populations, up from 19 percent in 1990. "Melting Pot" metros such as Los Angeles, Chicago, Houston, New York, and Washington, D.C., have the highest minority suburban populations. By contrast, suburbs in slow-growing northern metropolitan areas have low minority populations.

4. The city-suburb dissimilarity index measures the dissimilarity between a minority group's city-suburb distribution and the white population's city-suburb distribution. Frey and Speare (1988, p. 260). It is calculated as the following: [(white suburb population/white metro area population)-(minority suburb population/minority metro area population)] × 100. A positive value, ranging from zero to 100, indicates an overrepresentation of the minority group in the city and denotes the percentage of the metro area's minority population that would have to relocate to the suburbs in order for that minority population to be distributed within the metro area like the white population. A negative value indicates an overrepresentation of the minority group in the suburbs.

- Minorities were responsible for the bulk of suburban population gains in a majority of the metro areas studied. Minority population gains were most pronounced in the thirty-five diverse Melting Pot metros and in areas in the South in which black and Hispanic populations increased. Many of the Melting Pot metros had drops in the white suburban population in the 1990s.
- Asians are more likely to live in major metropolitan suburbs than in cities. Almost half of the Hispanics and 39 percent of the blacks in the metropolitan areas surveyed live in the suburbs.
- People who identified themselves as belonging to "two or more races" show different suburbanization patterns from the suburbanization patterns of single-race identifiers. For instance, 56 percent of the white-and-black identifier group live in the suburbs. Interestingly, this number is centered squarely between the percentage of whites who live in the suburbs (73) and the percentage of blacks who live in the suburbs (39).

Suburban Diversity Varies across Metros

Levels of suburban diversity vary sharply across U.S. regions. "Melting Pot" metros such as Los Angeles, Chicago, Houston, New York, and Washington, D.C., have the most diverse suburban populations. For decades, discussions of race and space in urban America revolved around black migration to central cities and "white flight" to the suburbs. But recent migration patterns of several minority groups have created new patterns of minority suburbanization, which play out differently within different kinds of metropolitan areas:[5]

- Melting Pot metros. Some 35 of the 102 metropolitan areas in this survey are classified as Melting Pot metros because of their large proportion of Hispanics, Asians, American Indians/Native Alaskans, other races, and multiracial populations.[6] These metropolitan areas are also where the impact of rising Hispanic and Asian populations (composed of immigrants and their American-born descendants) is most

5. Frey and Geverdt (1998); Frey (2000).

6. "Melting Pot" metros denote metropolitan areas in which non-Hispanic whites compose no more than 69 percent of the 2000 population (the percentage of non-Hispanic whites nationwide is 69.1) and in which the combined population of Hispanics, non-Hispanic Asians, Hawaiians and other Pacific Islanders, Native Americans, Native Alaskans, persons of other races, and persons of two or more races exceeds 18 percent of the population (the sum of these groups is 18 percent of the national population). See note to appendix table 9A-1 for definitions of other categories in the metropolitan typology.

evident.[7] Melting Pot metros are found, not surprisingly, primarily in the high-immigration zones of the United States, including well-known immigrant magnets such as the New York, Los Angeles, San Francisco, Miami, and Chicago metropolitan areas as well as smaller places like El Paso and Bakersfield. (See appendix table 9A-1 for a list of metro areas by category.)

- Southern and western metropolitan areas: largely white-black metro areas: South. Most of the nineteen largely white-black metro areas in the South are destinations for increasing numbers of black domestic migrants.[8] These metro areas also attract whites and recently some Hispanics and Asians. Examples include Atlanta, Nashville, Baltimore, and Little Rock.
- Southern and western metropolitan areas: largely white metro areas: South and West. There are thirteen largely white metros in the South and West, including places like Seattle, Colorado Springs, and Tampa. Unlike Melting Pot metros, most of these areas are adding mostly white residents who are migrating from other communities in the United States, although many of these areas are also registering noticeable Hispanic gains.
- Northern metropolitan areas: largely white-black metro areas: North. This category includes six slow-growing metropolitan areas in the North (Northeast and Midwest Census Regions) with significant black populations, such as Philadelphia and Detroit. Most of these metropolitan areas were destinations for the black South-to-North migration of earlier decades but have experienced only modest increases in their minority populations in the 1990s.
- Northern metropolitan areas: largely white metro areas: North. There are twenty-nine largely white metros in the North, which register slow to modest overall population growth and suburban development. Boston, Minneapolis, and Cincinnati are among the metropolitan areas in this category.

Metro Differences in Suburban Minority Profiles

Census 2000 reveals sharp disparities in suburban minority representation across the categories just defined. The suburbs of the Melting Pot metros have significantly higher percentages of minorities than do suburbs in any other metro category (figure 9-1). In the Melting Pot metros overall, more

7. Frey (2001b).
8. Frey (2001a).

FIGURE 9-1. Minority Composition of Suburbs, by Metro Area Type, 1990, 2000[a]

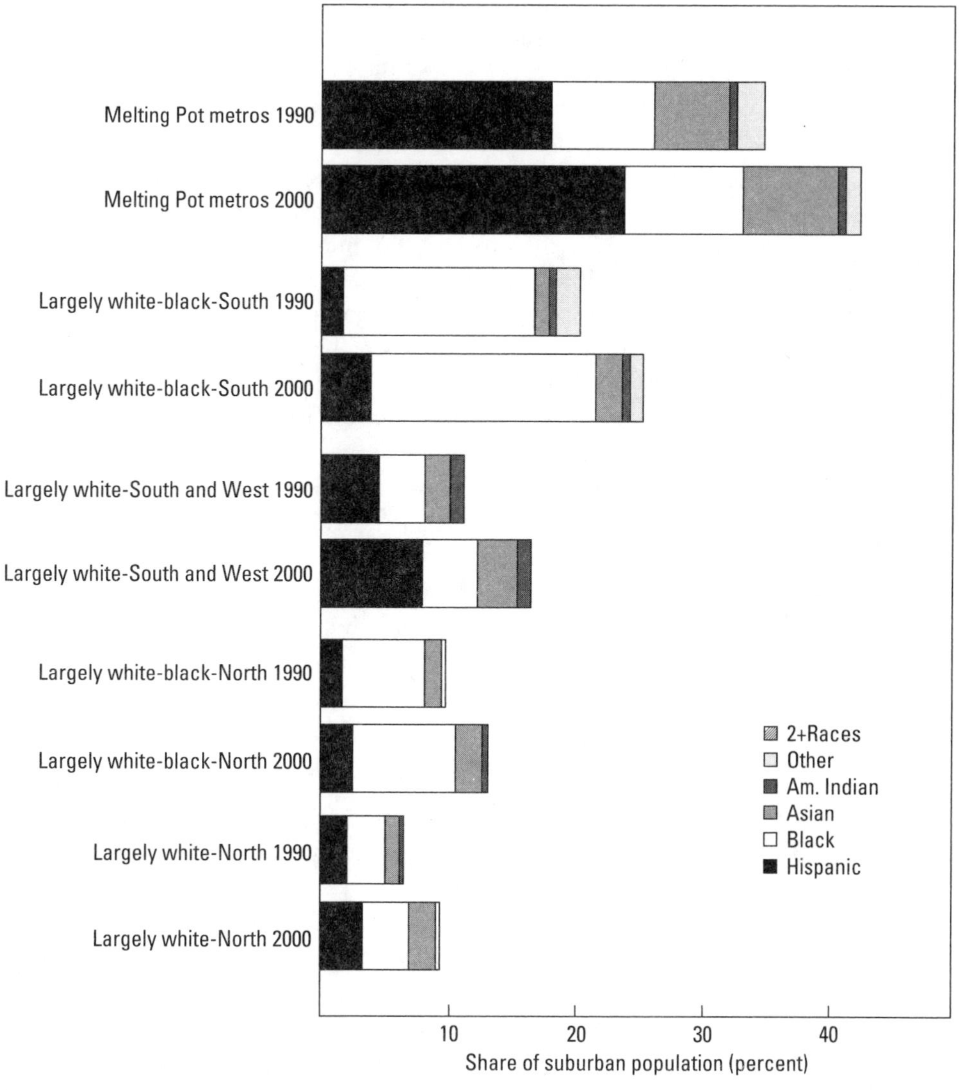

a. Population greater than 500,000.

than two out of every five (43.2 percent) suburban residents are members of minorities. In ten Melting Pot metros, minorities constitute more than half of the suburban population. Table 9-1 lists the twenty metro areas with the highest percentages of suburban minority residents—all of which are Melting Pot metros.

The southern and western metropolitan areas represent a second echelon of significant suburban minority representation. The minority suburban population share is 25.1 percent for the largely white-black metros in the South and 19.5 percent for largely white metros in the South and West. The areas with the lowest percentages of minority suburbanites are in the North—14.3 percent for largely white-black metros and 10.4 percent for largely white metros. Most of the metropolitan areas with small minority suburban populations have relatively small percentages of minority residents in the metropolitan area overall. For instance, Scranton-Wilkes Barre-Hazelton, with the lowest suburban minority share of 2.8 percent, is only 8 percent minority at the metropolitan level.

As figure 9-1 shows, metropolitan-area categories have different mixes of minority suburban residents. Hispanics are by far the largest minority in Melting Pot metro suburbs (at 23.7 percent), although both black and Asian populations there are sizable as well. Hispanics are also the largest minority (at 7.8 percent) in the suburbs of largely white metro areas in the South and West. In other types of metropolitan areas, blacks are the dominant suburban minority.

City-Suburb Dissimilarity Index

A high positive value on the city-suburb dissimilarity index indicates that compared with whites, minorities are disproportionately concentrated in the central city portions of a metropolitan area. A low positive value or zero indicates that minorities are distributed between the central cities and suburbs much as whites are. A negative value indicates an overrepresentation of minorities in the suburbs (table 9-2).

Most metro areas with high minority suburbanization levels also have low levels of city-suburb dissimilarity. The metropolitan areas with lowest city-suburb dissimilarity numbers are primarily Melting Pot metros and largely white metros in the South and West. Many of these western metropolises have low-density suburban-style development patterns and do not have sharp city-suburb differences in social class, housing attributes, and race.[9] The large metro areas of Los Angeles-Long Beach and Ft. Lauderdale

9. Frey and Speare (1988).

TABLE 9-1. Highest and Lowest Suburban Minority Shares, 2000

	Highest suburban minority, 2000		*Lowest suburban minority, 2000*	
Rank	*Metro area*[a]	*Percent*	*Metro area*[a]	*Percent*
1	McAllen-Edinburg-Mission, TX MSA	92.2	Scranton–Wilkes-Barre–Hazleton, PA MSA	2.8
2	El Paso, TX MSA	89.6	Fort Wayne, IN MSA	4.0
3	Honolulu, HI MSA	79.0	Knoxville, TN MSA	4.9
4	Miami, FL PMSA	78.5	Syracuse, NY MSA	5.2
5	Los Angeles-Long Beach, CA PMSA	68.8	Youngstown-Warren, OH MSA	5.5
6	Jersey City, NJ PMSA	62.5	Indianapolis, IN MSA	5.6
7	Albuquerque, NM MSA	55.9	Akron, OH PMSA	5.6
8	Fresno, CA MSA	54.7	Milwaukee-Waukesha, WI PMSA	6.0
9	Riverside-San Bernardino, CA PMSA	53.0	Buffalo-Niagara Falls, NY MSA	6.1
10	Bakersfield, CA MSA	51.5	Albany-Schenectady-Troy, NY MSA	6.1
11	Oakland, CA PMSA	47.6	Allentown-Bethlehem-Easton, PA MSA	6.4
12	Ventura, CA PMSA	45.0	Toledo, OH MSA	7.0
13	San Jose, CA PMSA	44.3	Pittsburgh, PA MSA	7.3
14	San Francisco, CA PMSA	42.7	Harrisburg-Lebanon-Carlisle, PA MSA	8.0
15	Stockton-Lodi, CA MSA	42.1	Rochester, NY MSA	8.3
16	Fort Lauderdale, FL PMSA	41.9	Columbus, OH MSA	8.3
17	San Antonio, TX MSA	41.6	Omaha, NE-IA MSA	8.4
18	Washington, DC-MD-VA-WV PMSA	40.5	Springfield, MA NECMA	8.5
19	Orange County, CA PMSA	40.2	Wichita, KS MSA	8.6
20	San Diego, CA MSA	40.2	Cincinnati, OH-KY-IN PMSA	8.6

Source: William H. Frey analysis of decennial census data.
a. Population greater than 500,000.

have zero dissimilarity values, indicating that minorities and whites are similarly distributed between city and suburbs.

Among the twenty metropolitan areas with the highest dissimilarity indexes, seventeen are located in the North (the others are Birmingham, Memphis, and Baltimore). These northern areas are typically slow-growing metros such as Detroit, Gary, and Buffalo, where blacks are the dominant minority and have historically been concentrated in the central cities.[10]

Minority Suburban Gains

During the 1990s minorities were responsible for the bulk of suburban (as well as central city) population gains for 65 of the nation's 102 large metro areas. This phenomenon is most pronounced in the Melting Pot areas.

Table 9-3 lists the twenty metropolitan areas with the greatest percentage gains in suburban minority populations. Fort Lauderdale, which increased its suburban minority percentage from 23.7 percent to 41.9 percent during the 1990s, tops the list. The list is composed of Melting Pot metros, with the exception of Atlanta. Twenty of the thirty-five Melting Pot metros increased their suburban minority shares by 10 percent or more during the 1990s.

10. Frey (1992).

TABLE 9-2. Highest and Lowest City-Suburb Dissimilarity Indexes for Minority versus White Populations, 2000

	Highest city-suburb dissimilarity, 2000		*Lowest city-suburb dissimilarity, 2000*	
Rank	*Metro area*[a]	*Index*[b]	*Metro area*[a]	*Index*[b]
1	Detroit, MI PMSA	61	McAllen-Edinburg-Mission, TX MSA	–18
2	Milwaukee-Waukesha, WI PMSA	58	El Paso, TX MSA	–8
3	Gary, IN PMSA	56	Ventura, CA PMSA	–6
4	Buffalo-Niagara Falls, NY MSA	56	Albuquerque, NM MSA	–5
5	Youngstown-Warren, OH MSA	54	Monmouth-Ocean, NJ PMSA	–3
6	Rochester, NY MSA	52	Bakersfield, CA MSA	–2
7	Birmingham, AL MSA	51	Riverside-San Bernardino, CA PMSA	–1
8	Syracuse, NY MSA	49	Los Angeles-Long Beach, CA PMSA	0
9	Fort Wayne, IN MSA	48	Fort Lauderdale, FL PMSA	0
10	Akron, OH PMSA	47	Colorado Springs, CO MSA	3
11	Bridgeport, CT NECMA	47	Honolulu, HI MSA	4
12	Cincinnati, OH-KY-IN PMSA	45	Miami, FL PMSA	4
13	Springfield, MA NECMA	44	West Palm Beach-Boca Raton, FL MSA	4
14	Philadelphia, PA-NJ PMSA	44	Jersey City, NJ PMSA	5
15	Cleveland-Lorain-Elyria, OH PMSA	44	Las Vegas, NV-AZ MSA	7
16	Memphis, TN-AR-MS MSA	44	Orlando, FL MSA	7
17	Allentown-Bethlehem-Easton, PA MSA	43	Phoenix-Mesa, AZ MSA	7
18	Kansas City, MO-KS MSA	43	Fresno, CA MSA	9
19	Indianapolis, IN MSA	42	San Diego, CA MSA	10
20	Baltimore, MD PMSA	41	Portland-Vancouver, OR-WA PMSA	11

Source: William H. Frey analysis of decennial census data.

a. Population greater than 500,000.

b. Index measures the percentage of a metropolitan area's minority population that would need to relocate to achieve a city-suburb distribution similar to whites. A negative score indicates a larger concentration of minorities in the suburbs than in the city.

Only two of the sixty-seven metros in other categories (Atlanta and Seattle) showed minority suburban increases of this magnitude.

In the 1990s, Melting Pot metros not only had strong gains in their suburban minority population shares but also depended on minorities for most of their suburban population growth. The suburbs of Melting Pot metros grew by 20.9 percent overall. Whites contributed only 5 percent of this growth, whereas Hispanics were responsible for more than half (52 percent). In fourteen Melting Pot metros, minorities contributed to more than half of the suburban population growth of the past decade. Some eighteen Melting Pot metro areas registered white suburban losses, meaning that minorities were responsible for all of the suburban population gains there.

Minorities contributed to more than half of the past decade's suburban population gains in thirty-three metropolitan areas in other categories. For instance, whites accounted for only 35 percent of the modest suburban growth in St. Louis while blacks accounted for most of the rest. In West Palm Beach-Boca Raton, whites accounted for 44 percent, Hispanics 29 percent, and blacks 13 percent of suburban growth.

TABLE 9-3. Largest Gains in Suburban Minority Share, 1990–2000

		Percent		
Rank	*Metro area*[a]	*2000*	*1990*	*Gain*
1	Fort Lauderdale, FL PMSA	41.9	23.7	18.2
2	Riverside-San Bernardino, CA PMSA	53.0	37.1	15.8
3	Oakland, CA PMSA	47.6	33.1	14.6
4	Las Vegas, NV-AZ MSA	34.7	20.2	14.4
5	Atlanta, GA MSA	36.9	22.8	14.2
6	Orlando, FL MSA	33.1	19.6	13.5
7	San Jose, CA PMSA	44.3	31.4	12.9
8	Bakersfield, CA MSA	51.5	38.8	12.7
9	Middlesex-Somerset-Hunterdon, NJ PMSA	31.8	19.2	12.6
10	Houston, TX PMSA	40.2	27.7	12.5
11	Orange County, CA PMSA	40.2	27.9	12.3
12	Honolulu, HI MSA	79.0	66.8	12.2
13	Miami, FL PMSA	78.5	66.5	12.0
14	Dallas, TX PMSA	31.0	19.4	11.6
15	Stockton-Lodi, CA MSA	42.1	30.9	11.2
16	Washington, DC-MD-VA-WV PMSA	40.5	29.4	11.0
17	Bergen-Passaic, NJ PMSA	35.1	24.4	10.7
18	San Diego, CA MSA	40.2	29.5	10.7
19	Jersey City, NJ PMSA	62.5	51.8	10.7
20	Los Angeles-Long Beach, CA PMSA	68.8	58.2	10.7

Source: William H. Frey analysis of decennial census data.

a. Population greater than 500,000. Percentages may not sum to 100 due to rounding.

White Suburban Loss

White suburban loss did not originate in the 1990s, but its magnitude and pervasiveness in that decade—especially in Melting Pot metros—are noteworthy.[11] The largest white suburban losses were in the Melting Pot metros. The suburbs of Los Angeles-Long Beach lost 381,000 whites during the 1990s, and the suburbs of Riverside-San Bernardino, Oakland, and Bergen-Passaic each lost more than 70,000 whites. In Honolulu, Los Angeles-Long Beach, San Francisco, Miami, Riverside-San Bernardino, and Bakersfield, the rate of white loss in the suburbs exceeded that in the central cities. To be sure, not all Melting Pot suburbs lost whites. Phoenix, Las Vegas, Austin, Tucson, and Dallas all had double-digit rates of white suburban population growth.

Table 9-4 lists twenty-four large metros that experienced white suburban losses in the 1990s. Some eighteen of these are Melting Pot metros, and one is adjacent to a Melting Pot metro. The remaining five areas that lost white suburbanites are largely white metros in the North that were less prosperous than other parts of the country in the 1990s.

11. Frey (1992).

TABLE 9-4. Suburban White Losses, 1990–2000, among Metro Areas, by Metro Area Type

Metro type	*White percent change 1990–2000*		*Minority percent change 1990–2000*		*White percent of total population*					
					Suburbs			*City*		
Metro area[a]	*Suburb*	*City*	*Suburb*	*City*	*2000*	*1990*	*Change*	*2000*	*1990*	*Change*
Melting pot metros										
Honolulu, HI MSA	–32.2	–25.3	26.7	11.0	21	33	–12	19	25	–7
Miami, FL PMSA	–22.2	–10.9	43.2	2.4	21	33	–12	18	20	–2
El Paso, TX MSA	–20.9	–24.0	70.4	21.3	10	20	–10	18	26	–8
Los Angeles-Long Beach, CA PMSA	–19.3	–16.9	28.1	21.7	31	42	–11	31	40	–9
San Jose, CA PMSA	–11.7	–15.8	53.5	48.4	56	69	–13	40	54	–14
Bakersfield, CA MSA	–10.9	9.5	49.4	102.7	48	61	–13	51	66	–15
Jersey City, NJ PMSA	–9.1	–26.1	40.7	30.5	38	48	–11	33	47	–14
Bergen-Passaic, NJ PMSA	–7.8	b	54.7	b	65	76	–11	b	b	b
Oakland, CA PMSA	–7.2	–12.3	71.1	14.7	52	67	–15	33	39	–6
San Francisco, CA PMSA	–6.8	0.5	39.2	13.2	57	67	–9	44	47	–3
Riverside-San Bernardino, CA PMSA	–5.6	–0.7	80.0	62.0	47	63	–16	49	61	–12
New York, NY PMSA	–5.2	–11.4	45.2	25.2	68	77	–8	35	43	–8
Newark, NJ PMSA	–4.6	–14.1	40.8	2.1	66	74	–8	14	16	–2
Middlesex-Somerset-Hunterdon, NJ PMSA	–3.2	b	90.2	b	68	81	–13	b	b	b
San Diego, CA MSA	–2.9	–7.8	55.8	39.2	60	70	–11	50	60	–10
Orange County, CA PMSA	–2.9	–19.7	68.7	53.4	60	72	–12	30	45	–15
Ventura, CA PMSA	–2.7	–4.2	41.4	54.2	55	64	–9	68	77	–9
Fresno, CA MSA	–0.2	–8.7	47.9	52.6	45	55	–10	36	49	–12
Largely white metros—North										
Nassau-Suffolk, NY PMSA	–4.1	b	56.4	b	76	84	–8	b	b	b
Hartford, CT NECMA	–2.9	–29.7	81.8	5.3	85	91	–6	33	43	–10
Pittsburgh, PA MSA	–2.1	–15.4	37.6	5.2	93	95	–2	67	72	–5
Scranton–Wilkes-Barre–Hazleton, PA MSA	–2.0	–11.7	72.6	101.8	97	98	–1	92	96	–4
Dayton-Springfield, OH MSA	–0.8	–13.4	46.9	5.9	89	92	–3	63	67	–5
Syracuse, NY MSA	–0.4	–21.6	65.0	28.1	95	97	–2	66	76	–10

Source: William H. Frey analysis of decennial census data.

a. Population greater than 500,000.

b. Metro areas with no central cities.

It might be tempting to use the term "white flight" to characterize the white population losses (suburban and overall) in these Melting Pot metros. Yet previous research on white domestic outmigration from high-immigration areas suggests that economic and amenity factors are more important than immigration and race in accounting for most of this movement.[12] White outflows from these areas contribute to the white gains registered for largely white-black metros and largely white metros in the South and West.

Comparing Minority Groups

Of the three large minority groups, only Asians are more likely to reside in the suburbs than in the central cities of the large metropolitan areas surveyed. More than half (54.6 percent) of Asians in these metro areas live in the suburbs. Nearly half (49.6 percent) of Hispanics in these metro areas reside in the suburbs, along with 38.8 percent of blacks. Blacks have shown the greatest increase in suburban living across these three broad racial groups; in 1990 not even one in three blacks lived in the suburbs of these metro areas.

These changes are also reflected in the groups' representation in the suburban population. Trends during the decade show Hispanics with the sharpest rise in suburbanization: they now constitute 12.1 percent of the suburban population of large metropolitan areas, up from 8.5 percent in 1990. Blacks are 8.4 percent of suburbanites, up from 7.1 percent in 1990, and the Asian share of the suburban population has risen to 4.4 percent from 3.2 percent in 1990. The combined Hispanic and Asian suburban population is more than double that of blacks, which reflects the greater tendency of Hispanics and Asians to locate in the suburbs and the fact that Hispanics and Asians posted larger 1990s population gains than did blacks.[13] The large-scale suburbanization of Hispanics and Asians is heavily skewed toward one subset of metros (figure 9-2).

The variation in minority suburban location patterns reflects a wide range of conditions across metropolitan areas, including the following: the city-suburb disparities in housing availability, costs, and discrimination; the relative mix and socioeconomic status of an area's minority groups; and the historic development of minority communities shaped by race-specific migration flows and residential patterns in the area.[14]

12. Frey and Liaw (1998).

13. Nationally the Hispanic population grew by 58 percent between 1990 and 2000, compared with 52 percent for Asians and 3.4 percent for blacks.

14. Frey and Speare (1988); Massey and Denton (1988); Alba and Logan (1991); Frey (1992).

FIGURE 9-2. Percent of Population Residing in Suburbs, by Race/Ethnicity, 1990, 2000[a]

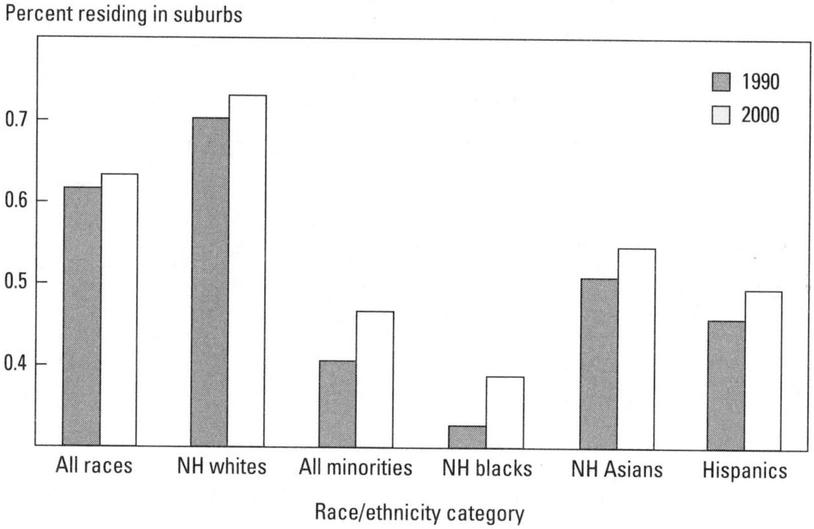

a. Population greater than 500,000.

Asians

Asians constitute a smaller percentage of the combined populations of large metropolitan areas (5.1 percent) than do either Hispanics (15.6 percent) or blacks (13.8 percent). Thus the share of suburban residents that are Asian is typically much smaller than the Hispanic or black share of suburbanites. But the proportion of the total Asian metropolitan population that lives in the suburbs is higher than of the other two groups. Asians tend to live in Melting Pot metros, as can be seen in table 9-5, which lists the metro areas with the largest suburban percentages of each main minority group.

After Honolulu, where almost half of the suburban population is Asian, the greatest suburban Asian representation occurs in San Jose, Oakland, San Francisco, Los Angeles-Long Beach, and Orange County. These, along with Middlesex-Somerset-Hunterdon in New Jersey, are the only metropolitan areas in which Asians make up more than 10 percent of suburbanites. Asian representation is at least 4 percent in the suburbs of 25 of the 102 large metros, including Seattle, Las Vegas, Chicago, New York, Dallas, Riverside-San Bernardino, Portland, and Washington, D.C. The metros in which the Asian suburban population grew the most (in percentage terms) during the 1990s were mostly Melting Pot metros.

TABLE 9-5. Highest Suburban Shares, 2000, and 1990–2000 Gains, by Race/Ethnicity

	Highest suburban percentage					
	Asians		*Hispanics*		*Blacks*	
Rank	*Metro area*[a]	*Percent*	*Metro area*[a]	*Percent*	*Metro area*[a]	*Percent*
1	Honolulu, HI MSA	47.7	McAllen-Edinburg-Mission, TX MSA	91.5	Columbia, SC MSA	28.0
2	San Jose, CA PMSA	23.3	El Paso, TX MSA	86.0	Charleston-North Charleston, SC MSA	25.9
3	Oakland, CA PMSA	17.0	Miami, FL PMSA	55.8	Atlanta, GA MSA	25.0
4	San Francisco, CA PMSA	16.9	Jersey City, NJ PMSA	53.1	Washington, DC-MD-VA-WV PMSA	22.0
5	Los Angeles-Long Beach, CA PMSA	13.7	Fresno, CA MSA	45.7	Baton Rouge, LA MSA	20.9
6	Orange County, CA PMSA	13.7	Los Angeles-Long Beach, CA PMSA	44.7	Richmond-Petersburg, VA MSA	20.8
7	Middlesex-Somerset-Hunterdon, NJ PMSA	11.2	Albuquerque, NM MSA	44.4	New Orleans, LA MSA	20.8
8	Bergen-Passaic, NJ PMSA	8.2	Bakersfield, CA MSA	41.9	Norfolk-Virginia Beach-Newport News, VA-NC MSA	20.6
9	Seattle-Bellevue-Everett, WA PMSA	8.1	Riverside-San Bernardino, CA PMSA	38.3	Miami, FL PMSA	19.5
10	Washington, DC-MD-VA-WV PMSA	7.3	Ventura, CA PMSA	34.8	Fort Lauderdale, FL PMSA	19.2

	Greatest gains in suburban percentage					
	Asians		*Hispanics*		*Blacks*	
Rank	*Metro area*	*Gain*	*Metro area*	*Gain*	*Metro area*	*Gain*
1	San Jose, CA PMSA	9.0	El Paso, TX MSA	12.7	Atlanta, GA MSA	6.3
2	Middlesex-Somerset-Hunterdon, NJ PMSA	5.8	Riverside-San Bernardino, CA PMSA	11.8	Fort Lauderdale, FL PMSA	6.0
3	Oakland, CA PMSA	5.4	Bakersfield, CA MSA	10.4	Baltimore, MD PMSA	3.9
4	Orange County, CA PMSA	3.9	Las Vegas, NV-AZ MSA	9.7	Wilmington-Newark, DE-MD PMSA	3.7
5	San Francisco, CA PMSA	3.8	Miami, FL PMSA	9.6	Washington, DC-MD-VA-WV PMSA	3.2
6	Seattle-Bellevue-Everett, WA PMSA	3.4	Fort Lauderdale, FL PMSA	8.7	New Orleans, LA MSA	3.1
7	Bergen-Passaic, NJ PMSA	3.1	Orlando, FL MSA	8.3	Richmond-Petersburg, VA MSA	2.9
8	Los Angeles-Long Beach, CA PMSA	2.7	Houston, TX PMSA	7.9	Gary, IN PMSA	2.6
9	Las Vegas, NV-AZ MSA	2.2	Ventura, CA PMSA	6.9	St. Louis, MO-IL MSA	2.5
10	Washington, DC-MD-VA-WV PMSA	2.0	San Diego, CA MSA	6.7	Orlando, FL MSA	2.3

Source: William H. Frey analysis of decennial census data.

a. Population greater than 500,000.

Metro areas with more-substantial and growing Asian populations tend to have low or negative levels of city-suburb dissimilarity (table 9-6). These areas include larger metros such as Los Angeles-Long Beach and Washington, D.C. Two-thirds (66) of the 102 large metro areas have Asian city-suburb dissimilarity indexes below 20. These include most of the Melting Pot and other West Coast metros in which the Asian presence is strong. One exception is San Francisco, home of one of the nation's oldest and largest Asian settlements, which has a higher-than-average Asian city-suburb dissimilarity index of 22. Metropolitan areas in which dissimilarity is highest tend to be either college towns (for example, Ann Arbor) or areas in which Asians have a small, new presence (such as Greensboro and Little Rock).

Hispanics

More than a third (36 percent) of the nation's 102 large metros have suburban populations that are more than 10 percent Hispanic. Hispanics make up more than 80 percent of the suburban population in two Texas border metros, 55.6 percent of suburbanites in the large immigrant magnet metro of Miami, and 44.7 percent of suburbanites in Los Angeles. Most of the areas in which Hispanics constitute more than 10 percent of suburbanites are Melting Pot metros. Denver (14.2 percent) and West Palm Beach-Boca Raton (12.3 percent) are exceptions.

Thirty metros increased their suburban Hispanic representation by at least 4 percent, with noticeable gains in Riverside-San Bernardino, Las Vegas, Miami, Fort Lauderdale, Orlando, Houston, and San Diego. These trends are especially significant in metros in which Hispanic representation is relatively new. In Atlanta the suburban Hispanic share increased from 2 percent to 6.8 percent, and in Salt Lake City it increased from 4 percent to 8.5 percent. Only one metropolitan area (Honolulu) registered a decline in the percentage of suburban residents who are Hispanic.

As table 9-6 shows, areas with highest Hispanic city-suburb dissimilarity are typically in the North, led by Allentown-Bethlehem-Easton at 55. Milwaukee, Cleveland, Buffalo, and Philadelphia are large northern metros with 40-plus dissimilarity indexes for Hispanics. Only 12 of the nation's 102 large metros have Hispanic dissimilarity indexes this high; 32 metros have indexes of less than 10. The latter are primarily Melting Pot metros and other southern or western metros with growing Hispanic populations. Larger metros such as San Francisco, Riverside-San Bernardino, and Ft. Lauderdale register negative city-suburb dissimilarity indexes, indicating a suburban concentration of Hispanics. The index for Los Angeles is

TABLE 9-6. Highest and Lowest City-Suburban Dissimilarity Indexes, by Race/Ethnicity

	Highest city-suburban dissimilarity indexes					
	Asians		Hispanics		Blacks	
Rank	Metro area[a]	Index	Metro area[a]	Index	Metro area[a]	Index
1	Ann Arbor, MI PMSA	45	Allentown-Bethlehem-Easton, PA MSA	55	Gary, IN PMSA	76
2	Baton Rouge, LA MSA	39	Milwaukee-Waukesha, WI PMSA	52	Detroit, MI PMSA	72
3	Greensboro–Winston-Salem–High Point, NC MSA	39	Cleveland-Lorain-Elyria, OH PMSA	52	Buffalo-Niagara Falls, NY MSA	67
4	Stockton-Lodi, CA MSA	37	Bridgeport, CT NECMA	51	Milwaukee-Waukesha, WI PMSA	66
5	Little Rock-North Little Rock, AR MSA	32	Springfield, MA NECMA	49	Rochester, NY MSA	65
6	Nashville, TN MSA	32	Buffalo-Niagara Falls, NY MSA	48	Syracuse, NY MSA	64
7	Charlotte-Gastonia-Rock Hill, NC-SC MSA	32	Rochester, NY MSA	48	Youngstown-Warren, OH MSA	64
8	Milwaukee-Waukesha, WI PMSA	31	Providence-Fall River-Warwick, RI-MA NECMA	45	Fort Wayne, IN MSA	60
9	Minneapolis-St. Paul, MN-WI MSA	31	Philadelphia, PA-NJ PMSA	44	Albany-Schenectady-Troy, NY MSA	58
10	Sacramento, CA PMSA	31	Harrisburg-Lebanon-Carlisle, PA MSA	43	Akron, OH PMSA	56
	Lowest city-suburban dissimilarity indexes					
	Asians		Hispanics		Blacks	
Rank	Metro area	Index	Metro area	Index	Metro area	Index
1	Ventura, CA PMSA	–9	McAllen-Edinburg-Mission, TX MSA	–19	McAllen-Edinburg-Mission, TX MSA	–10
2	Los Angeles-Long Beach, CA PMSA	–7	Jersey City, NJ PMSA	–14	Honolulu, HI MSA	–10
3	Miami, FL PMSA	–6	Honolulu, HI MSA	–12	Ventura, CA PMSA	–7
4	Fort Lauderdale, FL PMSA	–5	El Paso, TX MSA	–8	Monmouth-Ocean, NJ PMSA	–6
5	Washington, DC-MD-VA-WV PMSA	–2	Bakersfield, CA MSA	–7	El Paso, TX MSA	–5
6	Monmouth-Ocean, NJ PMSA	–1	Ventura, CA PMSA	–6	Miami, FL PMSA	1
7	Gary, IN PMSA	0	Albuquerque, NM MSA	–5	Colorado Springs, CO MSA	1
8	Dayton-Springfield, OH MSA	1	Fort Lauderdale, FL PMSA	–4	Riverside-San Bernardino, CA PMSA	2
9	Atlanta, GA MSA	1	Monmouth-Ocean, NJ PMSA	–2	Fort Lauderdale, FL PMSA	4
10	Richmond-Petersburg, VA MSA	1	Riverside-San Bernardino, CA PMSA	–2	West Palm Beach-Boca Raton, FL MSA	6

Source: William H. Frey analysis of decennial census data.

a. Population greater than 500,000.

zero, indicating that whites and Hispanics are distributed similarly between the city and suburbs.

Blacks

The highest suburban black shares tend to be in the largely white-black metros in the South, such as Columbia and Charleston in South Carolina, and Atlanta, where blacks constitute more than a quarter of suburban populations. Other large metros with large suburban black representation are the Melting Pot metros of Washington, D.C., Miami, and Ft. Lauderdale, where the suburban black percentage exceeds 19 percent. Overall, black suburban representation is not high. It exceeds 10 percent in only 24 of the 102 large metro areas.

During the 1990s, increases in the percentage of suburban residents who are black were not large. Atlanta and Ft. Lauderdale led all metros with a 6 percentage point increase in their suburban black shares. Black representation grew by 2 percent or more in the suburbs of only 13 metros in the 1990s. Moreover, the black share of the suburban population fell in 20 metros during the 1990s, because of greater levels of suburbanization by whites or by nonblack minority groups. This is the case for several largely white-black metro areas in the South, such as Memphis, Greensboro, Charleston, and Raleigh-Durham, which experienced high levels of white suburbanization along with black gains.

Many southern metros that are gaining blacks now exhibit black city-suburb dissimilarity indexes well below those of northern metros. Black city-suburb dissimilarity is highest for northern areas in this survey. Some thirty-two large metro areas, mostly in the North, show dissimilarity indexes above 40, and Gary, Detroit, Buffalo, Milwaukee, Rochester, and Syracuse have black dissimilarity indexes well above 60. By contrast, the index values for Atlanta, Washington, D.C., Houston, Norfolk, Columbia, Charleston, and Greenville are in the 14–19 range. At the lowest end of the spectrum is a mix of metros such as Miami, Ft. Lauderdale, and West Palm Beach, many of which have small but rising black populations.

Two or More Races

People who identified themselves as belonging to "two or more races" exhibit suburbanization patterns different from those of single-race identifiers. Also interesting are the suburban location patterns of people who are members of small race groups not included in the foregoing analysis and the suburban location patterns of non-Hispanic people who selected race group combinations for Census 2000. The "two or more races" combination category comprises fifty-seven different subcategories, most of which consist of very few people and are not easily incorporated into the metropolitan-area typology used in the foregoing analysis.

Whites, blacks, and Asians are considered racial groups, and thus it is possible to examine the suburban location rates for different combinations of these groups. As table 9-7 shows, persons identifying as either white and black or white and Asian have suburban location patterns that lie between the values of the individual groups. The percentage of white and black census respondents who live in the suburbs—55.9—lies almost squarely in between the rates for white (73.0) and black (38.8) single-race identifiers. A similar "average" value of 63.6 percent is also observed for the white and Asian group. (As noted earlier, 54.6 percent of Asians in major metropolitan areas live in the suburbs.) Of the 16,000 large-metro residents who identified themselves as white, black, and Asian, 57.7 percent live in the suburbs. This is also an "average" level, although it is slightly closer to the rate of the white and black group than to the white and Asian group.

It could well be that the same preferences and constraints associated with locating in the suburbs for whites, or blacks, or Asians work in combination for residents who identify (and are identified by others) with two or more

TABLE 9-7. Percent Residing in Suburbs for Selected Race-Group Combinations, Metro Areas, 2000[a]

Race-Hispanic group	*Population of group (thousands)*	*Percent residing in suburbs*
Selected single non-Hispanic race groups and all Hispanics		
White	112,256	73.0
Black	24,443	38.8
Asian[b]	9,183	54.6
Hispanic (any race)	27,783	49.6
Selected multiple non-Hispanic race groups		
White and black	473	55.9
White and Asian	693	63.6
White and black and Asian	16	57.7
2 or more races	3,283	56.4
2 or more races excluding black	2,206	59.4
2 or more races including black	1,077	50.2
Additional non-Hispanic groups		
American Indians/Native Alaskans	738	59.9
Hawaiians and Other Pacific Islanders	263	62.4
Other Races	374	48.4
Total	178,060	63.3

Source: William H. Frey analysis of decennial census data.

a. Population greater than 500,000.

b. Includes Asians and Hawaiians and Other Pacific Islanders.

of these racial groups. Thus, at least for studies of race-related residential location, it may well be advisable to examine multiracial groups separately rather than simply adding them to single-race groups.

Overall, of all individuals in large metropolitan areas who chose one of the sixty-three possible "two or more races" combinations, some 56.4 percent live in the suburbs, which is below the rate for the total population (63.3 percent) but above the rates for those identifying as blacks alone or Asians alone—again an "average" level.

If the "two or more races" group is divided into two subgroups—those in which blacks did not constitute one of the races and those that did include blacks—these two groups differ in predictable ways. Multiracial, nonblack combinations had a higher percentage of suburban residents (59.4 percent) than did the other multiracial combinations (50.2 percent). Thus it appears to make a difference for residential location if blacks are identified as one of the multiple races.

Suburban location percentages for three smaller race groups that were not explicitly included in the earlier analysis are as follows: American Indians/Alaska Natives, 59.9 percent; Hawaiians and Other Pacific Islanders, 62.4 percent; other races, 48.4 percent.

CONCLUSION

Minority suburbanization increased markedly during the 1990s, and minorities now constitute more than a quarter (27.3 percent) of suburban populations in the nation's largest metropolitan areas, up from 19.3 percent in 1990. Yet these national statistics belie the range of minority suburbanization patterns among the country's largest metropolitan areas and among different minority groups.

Melting Pot metro areas and the Hispanics locating within them are the major drivers of national minority suburbanization trends. The new suburban diversity patterns, particularly the fact that minorities are dominating suburban growth in more than half of the nation's largest metropolitan areas, raise many questions about "race and space" in America's metropolitan areas. Does the suburban experience for today's minorities represent the same upward-mobility transition that it did for whites in earlier decades? Are minorities resegregated into separate communities within the suburbs? Is the economic and social-status selectivity that is associated with suburban movers more diluted than in the past? We plan to address these questions in future Brookings studies.

TABLE 9A-1. Metro Areas, by Metro Typology and Other Characteristics

Metro type / Metro area	Metro size 2000 (thousands)	Percent in suburbs	Percent of city population					Percent of suburb population				
			Non-Hispanic white	All minorities[a]	Non-Hispanic black	Non-Hispanic Asian	Hispanic	Non-Hispanic white	All minorities[a]	Non-Hispanic black	Non-Hispanic Asian	Hispanic
Melting pot metros												
Los Angeles-Long Beach, CA PMSA	9,519	53.7	31.0	69.0	11.5	10.2	44.4	31.2	68.8	7.7	13.7	44.7
New York, NY PMSA	9,314	13.5	35.1	64.9	24.4	9.7	27.0	68.2	31.8	11.9	4.4	13.3
Chicago, IL PMSA	8,273	59.0	35.0	65.0	33.3	4.2	25.6	73.9	26.1	8.5	4.9	11.3
Washington, DC-MD-VA-WV PMSA	4,923	83.1	39.2	60.8	44.3	4.0	10.0	59.5	40.5	22.0	7.3	8.5
Houston, TX PMSA	4,178	50.8	31.9	68.1	24.3	5.1	37.2	59.8	40.2	10.4	5.3	22.8
Dallas, TX PMSA	3,519	58.5	38.3	61.7	22.7	3.5	33.9	69.0	31.0	9.4	4.4	15.3
Riverside-San Bernardino, CA PMSA	3,255	80.3	48.6	51.4	8.3	4.6	35.4	47.0	53.0	7.3	4.3	38.3
Phoenix-Mesa, AZ MSA	3,252	36.1	63.3	36.7	3.9	2.2	27.5	70.3	29.7	2.7	2.1	21.0
Orange County, CA PMSA	2,846	71.6	29.8	70.2	1.8	14.0	52.0	59.8	40.2	1.4	13.7	22.3
San Diego, CA MSA	2,814	50.9	50.1	49.9	7.0	12.8	26.4	59.8	40.2	4.0	5.6	27.0
Oakland, CA PMSA	2,393	76.0	32.8	67.2	27.5	17.1	18.1	52.4	47.6	7.7	17.0	18.6
Miami, FL PMSA	2,253	80.0	17.5	82.5	16.6	0.8	63.4	21.5	78.5	19.5	1.5	55.8
Newark, NJ PMSA	2,033	86.5	14.2	85.8	51.9	1.2	29.5	65.8	34.2	17.0	4.5	10.8
San Francisco, CA PMSA	1,731	55.1	43.6	56.4	7.6	31.1	14.1	57.3	42.7	3.2	16.9	19.1
Fort Worth-Arlington, TX PMSA	1,703	49.0	51.1	48.9	17.5	4.0	25.4	80.6	19.4	4.2	2.5	10.7
San Jose, CA PMSA	1,683	27.0	40.0	60.0	3.0	26.5	27.0	55.7	44.3	1.8	23.3	15.8
Orlando, FL MSA	1,645	88.7	50.8	49.2	26.1	2.7	17.5	66.9	33.1	11.7	2.7	16.4
Sacramento, CA PMSA	1,628	75.0	40.5	59.5	15.0	17.3	21.6	72.2	27.8	4.9	6.6	12.0
Fort Lauderdale, FL PMSA	1,623	90.6	57.5	42.5	28.5	1.0	9.5	58.1	41.9	19.2	2.4	17.5
San Antonio, TX MSA	1,592	25.8	32.8	67.2	6.4	1.5	57.9	58.4	41.6	6.3	1.4	32.1
Las Vegas, NV-AZ MSA	1,563	69.4	58.0	42.0	10.1	5.1	23.6	65.3	34.7	6.8	5.0	19.3
Bergen-Passaic, NJ PMSA[b]	1,373	100.0	...	...	...	...	...	64.9	35.1	7.6	8.2	17.3
Austin-San Marcos, TX MSA[b]	1,250	44.7	53.0	47.0	9.6	4.5	30.8	70.1	29.9	5.5	2.3	20.5
Middlesex-Somerset-Hunterdon, NJ PMSA	1,170	100.0	...	...	...	...	...	68.2	31.8	7.6	11.2	11.2
Fresno, CA MSA	923	49.0	36.2	63.8	7.6	10.2	42.4	45.3	54.7	2.0	3.8	45.7
Honolulu, HI MSA	876	57.6	18.7	81.3	1.5	62.0	4.4	21.0	79.0	2.8	47.7	8.4
Tucson, AZ MSA	844	42.3	54.2	45.8	4.1	2.5	35.7	71.4	28.6	1.2	1.5	20.6

(continued)

TABLE 9A-1. Metro Areas, by Metro Typology and Other Characteristics (*continued*)

Metro type / Metro area	Metro size 2000 (thousands)	Percent in suburbs	Percent of city population: Non-Hispanic white	All minorities[a]	Non-Hispanic black	Non-Hispanic Asian	Hispanic	Percent of suburb population: Non-Hispanic white	All minorities[a]	Non-Hispanic black	Non-Hispanic Asian	Hispanic
Ventura, CA PMSA	753	86.6	68.1	31.9	1.3	3.0	24.3	55.0	45.0	1.9	5.8	34.8
Albuquerque, NM MSA	713	37.1	49.9	50.1	2.8	2.2	39.9	44.1	55.9	1.3	0.7	44.4
El Paso, TX MSA	680	17.1	18.3	81.7	2.8	1.1	76.6	10.4	89.6	2.5	0.3	86.0
Bakersfield, CA MSA	662	62.7	51.1	48.9	8.9	4.2	32.5	48.5	51.5	3.8	2.8	41.9
Jersey City, NJ PMSA	609	50.4	33.1	66.9	22.4	13.7	26.2	37.5	62.5	2.1	5.0	53.1
McAllen-Edinburg-Mission, TX MSA	569	64.8	15.3	84.7	0.4	1.3	82.5	7.8	92.2	0.3	0.2	91.5
Stockton-Lodi, CA MSA	564	46.6	38.1	61.9	8.9	16.9	31.5	57.9	42.1	3.6	4.9	29.4
Vallejo-Fairfield-Napa, CA PMSA	519	45.0	46.3	53.7	14.6	14.5	19.7	63.5	36.5	7.5	6.3	18.4
Largely white-black metros—North												
Philadelphia, PA-NJ PMSA	5,101	68.7	40.7	59.3	42.9	4.4	10.0	83.7	16.3	9.2	2.9	2.8
Detroit, MI PMSA	4,442	74.2	20.3	79.7	70.3	1.1	5.2	86.9	13.1	6.2	2.8	2.1
St. Louis, MO-IL MSA	2,604	79.1	53.3	46.7	41.4	1.5	1.9	83.7	16.3	12.1	1.4	1.4
Cleveland-Lorain-Elyria, OH PMSA	2,251	73.2	45.2	54.8	43.1	1.2	8.4	86.5	13.5	9.3	1.4	1.5
Milwaukee-Waukesha, WI PMSA	1,501	55.9	49.4	50.6	33.4	2.9	11.7	94.0	6.0	1.3	1.5	2.1
Gary, IN PMSA	631	78.6	10.6	89.4	71.8	0.1	16.1	83.5	16.5	5.2	1.0	9.0
Largely white-black metros—South												
Atlanta, GA MSA	4,112	89.9	31.3	68.7	61.0	1.9	4.5	63.1	36.9	25.0	3.5	6.8
Baltimore, MD PMSA	2,553	73.1	32.4	67.6	62.3	1.6	1.9	78.8	21.2	14.3	3.1	2.0
Norfolk-Virginia Beach-Newport News, VA-NC MSA	1,570	26.7	56.5	43.5	34.2	3.1	3.6	73.9	26.1	20.6	1.8	1.9
Charlotte-Gastonia-Rock Hill, NC-SC MSA	1,499	50.0	58.8	41.2	30.0	2.8	6.8	83.6	16.4	10.7	1.0	3.4
New Orleans, LA MSA	1,338	61.8	29.3	70.7	64.0	2.2	3.0	70.3	29.7	20.8	2.1	5.2
Greensboro–Winston-Salem–High Point, NC MSA	1,252	56.8	54.7	45.3	35.0	2.2	6.4	85.7	14.3	8.6	0.7	3.9
Nashville, TN MSA	1,231	50.1	65.6	34.4	25.2	2.5	4.6	90.3	9.7	5.8	0.8	1.9
Raleigh-Durham-Chapel Hill, NC MSA	1,188	56.9	55.2	44.8	31.8	3.9	7.2	75.6	24.4	15.5	2.2	5.3
Memphis, TN-AR-MS MSA	1,136	40.3	33.6	66.4	61.0	1.4	2.9	78.9	21.1	16.9	1.4	1.7
Jacksonville, FL MSA	1,100	33.2	62.2	37.8	28.7	2.8	4.2	87.1	12.9	6.7	1.4	3.2

Richmond-Petersburg, VA MSA	997	76.8	34.8	65.2	60.0	1.2	2.4	72.8	27.2	20.8	2.3	2.3
Greenville-Spartanburg-Anderson, SC MSA	962	87.4	56.3	43.7	38.8	1.2	2.5	80.7	19.3	14.3	1.2	2.8
Birmingham, AL MSA	921	73.6	23.5	76.5	73.2	0.8	1.6	81.7	18.3	14.5	0.9	1.9
Baton Rouge, LA MSA	603	62.2	44.7	55.3	49.8	2.6	1.7	75.5	24.5	20.9	0.8	1.8
Wilmington-Newark, DE-MD PMSA	586	82.7	47.2	52.8	41.7	1.6	7.8	79.5	20.5	12.5	2.5	4.1
Little Rock-North Little Rock, AR MSA	584	45.8	60.6	39.4	33.7	1.4	2.6	88.7	11.3	7.7	0.5	1.5
Charleston-North Charleston, SC MSA	549	67.9	53.7	46.3	40.7	1.4	2.6	68.9	31.1	25.9	1.3	2.3
Mobile, AL MSA	540	63.2	49.8	50.2	46.1	1.5	1.4	79.6	20.4	16.3	0.9	1.3
Columbia, SC MSA	537	78.3	48.2	51.8	45.6	1.8	3.0	67.0	33.0	28.0	1.4	2.2
Largely white metros—North												
Boston, MA-NH NECMA	6,058	69.2	65.8	34.2	11.1	5.9	13.0	90.6	9.4	1.7	3.0	2.9
Minneapolis-St. Paul, MN-WI MSA	2,969	77.4	63.2	36.8	15.0	8.8	7.7	91.0	9.0	2.4	2.8	2.1
Nassau-Suffolk, NY PMSA[b]	2,754	100.0	...	...	...	...	...	76.4	23.6	8.1	3.5	10.3
Pittsburgh, PA MSA	2,359	85.8	66.9	33.1	27.0	2.8	1.3	92.7	7.3	4.9	0.8	0.6
Kansas City, MO-KS MSA	1,776	59.6	60.4	39.6	26.5	2.0	8.7	90.5	9.5	3.3	1.5	2.9
Bridgeport, CT NECMA	1,707	58.8	52.0	48.0	19.8	3.5	21.5	89.3	10.7	3.4	2.3	3.7
Cincinnati, OH-KY-IN PMSA	1,646	79.8	52.7	47.3	42.5	1.6	1.3	91.4	8.6	5.4	1.1	1.0
Indianapolis, IN MSA	1,607	47.6	68.4	31.6	24.6	1.4	3.8	94.4	5.6	2.0	1.1	1.5
Columbus, OH MSA	1,540	48.5	69.8	30.2	22.0	3.2	2.3	91.7	8.3	4.0	1.6	1.3
Buffalo-Niagara Falls, NY MSA	1,170	70.2	55.5	44.5	33.7	1.3	6.7	93.9	6.1	2.1	1.3	1.3
Hartford, CT NECMA	1,149	85.7	33.5	66.5	29.7	1.9	31.3	84.7	15.3	5.7	2.4	5.7
Monmouth-Ocean, NJ PMSA	1,126	92.0	90.4	9.6	1.7	2.5	4.5	84.3	15.7	5.9	2.8	5.8
Rochester, NY MSA	1,098	80.0	44.3	55.7	37.4	2.2	12.8	91.7	8.3	3.1	1.7	2.2
Grand Rapids-Muskegon-Holland, MI MSA	1,089	74.9	62.8	37.2	19.3	1.7	13.2	89.8	10.2	3.0	1.5	4.0
Providence-Fall River-Warwick, RI-MA NECMA	963	61.0	65.3	34.7	7.9	3.7	18.0	91.3	8.7	1.6	1.5	3.5
Dayton-Springfield, OH MSA	951	72.3	62.9	37.1	32.3	1.0	1.5	88.8	11.2	7.2	1.4	1.1
Albany-Schenectady-Troy, NY MSA	876	73.4	71.9	28.1	17.5	2.7	5.0	93.9	6.1	1.6	1.5	1.9
Syracuse, NY MSA	732	76.0	66.5	33.5	21.8	2.9	4.9	94.8	5.2	1.5	1.0	1.2
Omaha, NE-IA MSA	717	37.5	77.6	22.4	11.6	1.6	7.1	91.6	8.4	2.5	1.4	2.9
Akron, OH PMSA	695	64.7	68.8	31.2	26.1	1.6	1.2	94.4	5.6	2.7	1.1	0.7

(*continued*)

TABLE 9A-1. Metro Areas, by Metro Typology and Other Characteristics (*continued*)

Metro type / *Metro area*	*Metro size 2000 (thousands)*	*Percent in suburbs*	*Percent of city population* Non-Hispanic white	All minorities[a]	Non-Hispanic black	Non-Hispanic Asian	Hispanic	*Percent of suburb population* Non-Hispanic white	All minorities[a]	Non-Hispanic black	Non-Hispanic Asian	Hispanic
Allentown-Bethlehem-Easton, PA MSA	638	72.1	68.6	31.4	5.4	2.2	21.9	93.6	6.4	1.6	1.4	2.5
Harrisburg-Lebanon-Carlisle, PA MSA	629	85.5	53.7	46.3	30.8	2.1	11.0	92.0	8.0	3.7	1.5	1.8
Scranton–Wilkes-Barre–Hazleton, PA MSA	625	80.9	92.0	8.0	3.6	1.0	2.2	97.2	2.8	0.8	0.5	0.9
Toledo, OH MSA	618	44.5	69.8	30.2	21.5	1.1	5.3	93.0	7.0	1.5	1.2	3.3
Springfield, MA NECMA	608	57.1	60.6	39.4	12.2	1.7	23.5	91.5	8.5	1.5	1.9	3.8
Youngstown-Warren, OH MSA	595	78.3	57.1	42.9	36.6	0.4	3.7	94.5	5.5	2.8	0.4	1.3
Ann Arbor, MI PMSA	579	80.3	72.8	27.2	8.7	11.9	3.3	86.4	13.6	6.9	1.8	3.0
Wichita, KS MSA	545	36.9	71.7	28.3	11.3	4.0	9.6	91.4	8.6	1.7	1.0	3.6
Fort Wayne, IN MSA	502	59.0	73.1	26.9	17.2	1.6	5.8	96.0	4.0	0.7	0.7	1.6
Largely white metros—South and West												
Seattle-Bellevue-Everett, WA PMSA	2,415	68.3	69.7	30.3	6.8	13.3	5.5	79.3	20.7	3.1	8.1	5.1
Tampa-St. Petersburg-Clearwater, FL MSA	2,396	72.4	62.1	37.9	21.5	2.3	11.9	81.3	18.7	5.5	1.7	9.8
Denver, CO PMSA	2,109	73.7	51.9	48.1	10.8	2.8	31.7	77.0	23.0	3.4	3.1	14.2
Portland-Vancouver, OR-WA PMSA	1,918	64.9	76.9	23.1	5.6	6.3	6.7	84.1	15.9	1.0	4.0	7.8
Salt Lake City-Ogden, UT MSA	1,334	78.6	71.3	28.7	2.0	4.1	19.4	85.9	14.1	0.8	2.7	8.5
West Palm Beach-Boca Raton, FL MSA	1,131	86.1	64.2	35.8	18.3	1.7	13.6	71.6	28.4	12.7	1.5	12.3
Oklahoma City, OK MSA	1,083	41.8	67.5	32.5	13.0	3.4	8.9	80.4	19.6	6.8	1.4	3.8
Louisville, KY-IN MSA	1,026	71.3	65.4	34.6	29.5	1.3	1.8	88.6	11.4	7.5	1.0	1.5
Tulsa, OK MSA	803	51.1	67.1	32.9	15.3	1.8	7.2	80.4	19.6	2.4	0.7	2.5
Tacoma, WA PMSA	701	72.4	66.5	33.5	10.9	8.4	6.9	79.7	20.3	5.2	4.8	5.0
Knoxville, TN MSA	687	71.1	79.8	20.2	15.2	1.5	1.6	95.1	4.9	1.9	0.8	1.1
Sarasota-Bradenton, FL MSA	590	82.7	70.7	29.3	15.3	0.9	11.6	88.8	11.2	3.8	0.8	5.5
Colorado Springs, CO MSA	517	30.2	75.3	24.7	6.3	2.9	12.0	78.2	21.8	6.2	2.1	9.7

Source: William H. Frey analysis of decennial census data.

a. "All minorities" includes minority groups listed as well as Non-Hispanic: American Indians/Alaskan natives, Other races, and persons selecting more than one race. "Blacks" pertains to Non-Hispanic blacks; "Asian" pertains to Non-Hispanic Asians, Hawaiians, and Other Pacific Islanders; and "Hispanics" pertains to Hispanics of any race.

b. Metro area with no central city.

REFERENCES

Alba, Richard, and John R. Logan. 1991. "Variations on Two Themes: Racial and Ethnic Patterns in the Attainment of Suburban Residence." *Demography* 28 (3): 431–53.

Denton, Nancy, and Douglas S. Massey. 1991. "Patterns of Neighborhood Transition in a Multi-Ethnic World: U.S. Metropolitan Areas, 1970–1980." *Demography* 28 (1): 41–63.

Frey, William H. 1992. "Minority Population and Continued White Flight in U.S. Metropolitan Areas: Assessing Findings from the 1990 U.S. Census." *Research Report* 92-247. University of Michigan, Population Studies Center.

———. 2000. "Regional Shifts in America's Voting Age Population: What Do They Mean for National Politics?" *Research Report* 00-459. University of Michigan, Population Studies Center.

———. 2001a. "Census 2000 Shows Large Black Migration to the South, Reinforcing the Region's White-Black Demographic Profile." *Research Report* 01-473. University of Michigan, Population Studies Center.

———. 2001b. "Micro Melting Pots." *American Demographics* 25 (6): 20–23.

Frey, William H., and Reynolds Farley. 1996. "Latino, Asian, and Black Segregation in Multi-Ethnic Metro Areas: Are Multi-Ethnic Metros Different?" *Demography* 33 (1): 35–50.

Frey, William H., and Elaine L. Fielding. 1995. "Changing Urban Populations: Regional Restructuring, Racial Polarization, and Poverty Concentration." *Cityscape* 1 (2):1–66. U.S. Department of Housing and Urban Development, Office of Policy Development and Research.

Frey, William H., and Douglas Geverdt. 1998. "Changing Suburban Demographics: Beyond the 'Black-White, City-Suburb' Typology." *Research Report* 98-422. University of Michigan, Population Studies Center.

Frey, William H., and Kao-Lee Liaw. 1998. "The Impact of Recent Immigration on Population Redistribution within the United States." In *The Immigration Debate: Studies of the Economic, Demographic, and Fiscal Effects of Immigration*, edited by James P. Smith and Barry Edmonston, 338–48. Washington: National Academy Press.

Frey, William H., and Alden Speare Jr. 1988. *Regional and Metropolitan Growth and Decline in the United States.* Russell Sage Foundation.

Massey, Douglas, and Nancy Denton. 1988. "Suburbanization and Segregation in U.S. Metropolitan Areas." *American Journal of Sociology* 94 (November): 592–626.

———. 1987. "Trends in Residential Segregation of Blacks, Hispanics, and Asians: 1970–1980." *American Sociological Review* 52 (6): 802–25.

U.S. Bureau of the Census. 2001. "Overview of Race and Hispanic Origin, 2000." *Census 2000 Brief.* Department of Commerce.

10

Changing Patterns of Latino Growth in Metropolitan America

ROBERTO SURO
AUDREY SINGER

No shortage of analysis has described the fast and widespread growth of the Latino population in America. Numerous early commentators on Census 2000 remarked on the speed of the Latinos' dispersal across the country, noting that Hispanics had become the fastest growing U.S. minority group as they increased their numbers 58 percent—from 22.4 million to 35.3 million during the 1990s.[1] At the same time, analysts observed that Hispanic Americans had quickly become, at 12.5 percent of the population in 2000, the largest ethnic-racial group in the country, barely edging out African Americans at 12.3 percent.

Recent research on metropolitan areas has added detail to the story of the Hispanics' rise. An earlier study showed that growth in the Hispanic population in the 100 largest U.S. cities was swift and substantial in the 1990s, and that one-fifth of those cities' populations would have declined in the decade were it not for an influx of Latinos.[2] And another study of the nation's suburbs identified growing racial and ethnic diversity in suburban areas.[3] In particular, the suburbs of very diverse metropolitan areas saw substantial growth in their Latino population in the 1990s.

1. Asians also registered a high growth rate between 1990 and 2000 and even exceeded Latino population increases by one method of enumeration. However, using consistent racial definitions for 1990 and 2000 based on the number of respondents declaring a single race (as opposed to multiple ones), Hispanic population growth outpaced Asian growth as well as that of all other racial groups.
2. See Alan Berube, chapter 8, in this volume.
3. See William Frey, chapter 9, in this volume.

Still, important questions remain about how Latinos redistributed across and within metropolitan areas in the 1980s and 1990s. To be sure, the Hispanic population grew quickly in most of the nation's metropolitan areas between the 1980 Census and the 2000 count. In 2000, 69 percent of the U.S. population lived in the 100 largest metropolitan areas, whereas the share of the Latino population in the same metros was 78 percent. But even so, the magnitude and distribution of Hispanic population growth in the 100 largest U.S. metropolitan areas varied widely in absolute numbers and in key characteristics.

For example, the growth of the Hispanic population averaged 145 percent in the largest 100 metros between 1980 and 2000, but that average obscures a huge range of growth rates. The rate was 8 percent for Honolulu, HI; 105 percent for Los Angeles; and 1,180 percent for Raleigh, N.C. In addition, more than a quarter of the Latinos in the top 100 metro areas—some 9 million Hispanics—continued to reside in the great magnets of Los Angeles, New York, Chicago, and Miami in 2000. However, the booming economy of the 1990s, coupled with recent industrial restructuring in both urban and rural areas, redrew the map of Latino America during the decade.[4] In many instances, such developments attracted Latino workers to places where there had been little previous in-migration.

This chapter explores several geographic and temporal variations of Hispanic growth. First, we propose a typology that distinguishes among several different metropolitan growth patterns based on Census data covering 1980 to 2000. Then, we supplement this categorization by isolating and identifying two key Latino-growth subtrends in metropolitan areas during the 1990s—a period when the national Hispanic population more than doubled.

The findings that result show clearly that the Latino population is rapidly evolving and that its demographic impact on the nation is changing quickly. Significant concentrations of Hispanics are no longer confined to a few regions such as southern California or the Southwest, or only to a few cities like New York and Miami. Instead, in the coming years Hispanic population growth will most affect communities that had relatively few Latinos a decade ago.

In fact, a look at Hispanic demographic trends over the past twenty years reveals that Latinos have spread out faster than any previous immigrant or internal migration wave, such as that of the African Americans who migrated out of the deep South in the middle of the century.

4. See Kandel and Parrado (2002) for an analysis of nonmetropolitan Latino growth patterns.

The Latino population has, for example, grown in heartland cities beyond the immigrant gateways in much less time than it took for the European immigrants who arrived at the beginning of the twentieth century. Similarly, trends evident now could have a significant impact on cities like Atlanta or Washington, D.C., which had a sparse Hispanic presence only a couple of decades ago. What is more, change will occur even in the traditional settlement areas like Los Angeles and New York, where growth will likely continue, though at a slower rate. There, the Latinos have already begun to become a pervasive presence on the suburban fringes of the big cities.

In short, this chapter identifies the distinguishing characteristics of several distinct variations on the theme of Latino growth. Clearly, the growth of the Latino population is no longer limited to just a few regions.

METHODOLOGY

This study revolves around a categorization of Hispanic population growth rates—derived from census data as they were observed across a series of standard geographical locales consisting of the nation's 100 largest metropolitan areas as of 2000.[5]

Definition of Hispanic or Latino

The terms "Hispanic" and "Latino" are used interchangeably in this chapter and reflect popular use of the terms and the new Office of Management and Budget (OMB) terminology standards in effect for Census 2000. Although most Latinos in the United States share a common linguistic heritage—Spanish—the Hispanic population includes a diversity of birthplace, national origin, legal status, socioeconomic class, and settlement histories. Census 2000 asked separate questions on race and Hispanic or Latino ethnicity. Persons were asked to identify whether they were of "Spanish/Hispanic/Latino" origin. This question was independent of the race question, which asked people to identify whether they were white, black, Asian, American Indian, Native Hawaiian, or "some other race," and persons could mark as many categories as they identified. Therefore, persons of Hispanic

5. The Latino population counts used in all tables in this chapter are taken from two sources. The 1980 and 1990 counts came from the "GeoLytics CensusCD 40 Years" (long-form variables), while the 2000 data were obtained from the U.S. Bureau of the Census website (short-form variables).

or Latino origins may be of any race. This analysis includes Latinos who were born abroad as well as those born in the United States.[6]

Metropolitan Area Definitions

This study analyzes change in the Hispanic population during the 1980s and 1990s among the largest 100 metropolitan areas. The metropolitan areas analyzed are those defined by OMB as metropolitan statistical areas (MSAs) and primary metropolitan statistical areas (PMSAs). The 2000 metropolitan area definition was applied consistently to data from each decade.

Definitions of Central City and Suburbs

Central cities are defined in this study, largely in accordance with OMB standards, as the largest city in the metropolitan area in combination with any other city of over 100,000 (in 2000) that is part of the official MSA name.[7] The suburbs are the portion of the metropolitan area that is located outside the central city or cities.

Four Categories of Metropolitan Areas

Finally, for the purpose of this analysis we have classified the metropolitan areas into four categories according to whether their Hispanic base population exceeded or lagged the 8 percent national average in 1980 and whether their Latino population growth exceeded or lagged the 145 percent average growth between 1980 and 2000 for the 100 metros. Table 10-1 employs this typology to categorize the nation's metropolitan areas as distinct types of Latino-growth settings.

At several points the chapter also distinguishes areas that saw extraordinarily rapid growth, or "hypergrowth," defined as growth more than twice the national average rate for metropolitan areas, or more than 300 percent in the twenty-year period.

Finally, we use 1980 to 2000 data to construct our typology; however, the rest of the analysis examines primarily 1990 and 2000 data only.

6. The U.S. Latino population is composed of foreign-born and native-born persons from the Spanish-speaking countries of Latin America and the Caribbean as well as Puerto Rico, a U.S. territory. The largest source countries are Mexico, Cuba, Puerto Rico, Dominican Republic, El Salvador, Guatemala, Colombia, Ecuador, and Peru.

7. The Office of Management and Budget designates the city with the largest population in each metropolitan area a central city. Additional cities qualify for this designation if specified requirements are met for population size, commuting patterns, and employment-residence ratios.

TABLE 10-1. Latino Population and Share of Overall Population Growth for Four Metropolitan Area Types, 1980–2000

	1980			*1990*			*2000*			*Percent change in Latino population*			*Latinos as a percent of overall growth*
Metropolitan area	*Total*	*Latino*	*Latino (percent)*	*Total*	*Latino*	*Latino (percent)*	*Total*	*Latino*	*Latino (percent)*	*1980–90*	*1990–2000*	*1980–2000*	
Established Latino metros	35,161,592	7,180,206	20	39,098,721	10,286,158	26	43,957,950	14,119,006	32	43	37	97	79
New Latino destinations	54,800,178	1,309,221	2	62,620,505	2,333,640	4	73,078,851	5,282,035	7	78	126	303	22
Fast-growing Latino hubs	14,418,567	2,033,540	14	19,395,646	3,801,089	20	24,485,665	6,818,961	28	87	79	235	48
Small Latino places	30,666,478	666,145	2	30,719,535	811,802	3	31,946,791	1,203,339	4	22	48	81	42
Total	135,046,815	11,189,112	8	151,834,407	17,232,689	11	173,469,257	27,423,341	16	54	59	145	42

Source: See note 5 for all the tables in this chapter.

FINDINGS

An analysis of the U.S. Hispanic population across the 100 largest metropolitan areas finds that:

- The Hispanic population is growing in most metropolitan areas, but the rate and location of increase vary widely. Four distinct patterns of growth can be discerned. *Established Latino metros* such as New York, Los Angeles, Miami, and Chicago posted the largest absolute increases in Latinos between 1980 and 2000. However, *new Latino destinations* like Atlanta and Orlando charted the fastest growth rates, despite their historically smaller Hispanic bases. Metros with relatively larger Latino bases, such as Houston, Phoenix, and San Diego, meanwhile, became *fast-growing Latino hubs* during the past twenty years, with population growth averaging 235 percent. *Small Latino places*, such as Baton Rouge, posted much lower absolute and relative growth than the other locales.
- Fifty-four percent of all U.S. Latinos now reside in the suburbs; the Latino suburban population grew 71 percent in the 1990s. In 1990 the central city and suburban Hispanic populations in the 100 largest metros were nearly identical, but during the next decade suburban growth so outpaced central city growth that by 2000 the suburban Hispanic population exceeded the central city population by 18 percent. New Latino destinations saw the fastest growth of Latino suburbanites.
- Hispanic men outnumber Hispanic women by 17 percent in new Latino destination metros where the Latino population grew fastest. By contrast, in slower-growing metros with large and well-established Latino communities, more Hispanics live in family households, and gender ratios are more balanced.

Four Patterns of Latino Growth

The Latino population grew quickly in the nation's metropolitan areas between 1980 and 2000, yet not all places grew in the same way. To the contrary: wide variations in the rate and location of Latino growth are generating highly distinct local experiences in different types of metropolitan areas.

Four types of metropolitan settings for Latino growth can be discerned (table 10A-1 in the appendix to this chapter lists the 100 metros, grouped by type and rate of population increase).

Established Latino Metros (Large Base, Slow Growth): Sixteen Metros. Sixteen major metros constitute a kind of Hispanic heartland in America.

This category of metro contains all the major contemporary immigrant gateways such as New York, Los Angeles, Miami, and Chicago as well as a variety of western, southwestern, and border metros with large, long-standing Latino communities (table 10-2 lists the ten metros with the largest Hispanic populations in 2000).

Half of the U.S. Latino population across the 100 largest metros lived in these sixteen established Latino metropolises in 2000 (figure 10-1 shows the distribution of the population across metros). In absolute numbers, these major Latino centers started out with by far the largest stock of Hispanics in 1980 (7.2 million Latinos lived in them then), and experienced by far the greatest numerical growth in numbers, as they added 6.9 million Latinos to their populations by 2000. Moreover, just three cities—Los Angeles, New York, and Chicago—dominated this growth. Those three metros accounted for more than half of the growth among established Latino metros as they added 3.9 million Latinos. Notably, New York's rate of growth was virtually the same in the 1980s and 1990s. Chicago had greater growth in the 1990s than the 1980s, while the share for Los Angeles grew faster in the 1980s than in the 1990s.

The 97 percent rate of Hispanic growth in these metros over twenty years, meanwhile, lagged behind that in many other metros. But meanwhile, the rate of Latino population growth there was four times greater than the below average 25 percent growth in their overall populations. As a result, the 6.9 million Latinos added in this category between 1980 and 2000 represented 79 percent of the overall population growth in these areas (table 10-1). Consequently, the population growth that did occur in these metros is owed largely to the Latinos.

These established centers have the highest concentrations of Latinos among all metro types. Hispanics made up 20 percent of the population in these sixteen metros in 1980, but by 2000 the figure had hit 32 percent. Size and Latino concentration, meanwhile, seem to have had an inverse effect on the rate of Hispanic growth. Three of the eight cities where Latinos were 40 percent or more of the population in 2000 experienced markedly slower Hispanic growth in the 1990s than in the 1980s. In Los Angeles, for example, the Hispanic growth rate fell from 60 percent to 28 percent, and in Miami it decreased from 64 percent in the 1980s to 36 percent in the 1990s. These data suggest that Los Angeles and Miami in particular could be approaching a saturation point, where shortages of housing and jobs may put a brake on Hispanic population growth.

New Latino Destinations (Small Base, Fast Growth): Fifty-One Metros. Just over one-half of the largest 100 metropolitan areas in America posted

TABLE 10-2. Ten Metro Areas with the Largest Latino Populations, 2000

Metro	*Number of Latinos*	*Total population (percent)*	*Latino growth, 1980–2000 (percent)*
Los Angeles	4,242,213	45	105
New York	2,339,836	25	60
Chicago	1,416,584	17	143
Miami	1,291,737	57	123
Houston	1,248,586	30	211
Riverside-San Bernardino	1,228,962	38	324
Orange County	875,579	31	206
Phoenix	817,012	25	261
San Antonio	816,037	51	67
Dallas	810,499	23	324
Total	15,087,045	31	130

explosive growth of their initially small Latino communities between 1980 and 2000. This growth of these new Latino destinations reflects an astonishing and rapid entrance of the Hispanic population into new settlement areas.

From Wilmington to West Palm Beach, from Little Rock to Las Vegas, the new Latino destinations encompass a diverse collection of metropolitan areas scattered across thirty-five states in every region of the country. Within these fifty-one metros the Hispanic population grew at rates ranging from 147 percent (Knoxville) to 1,180 percent (Raleigh-Durham) over the twenty years. In 2000, 19 percent of all Hispanics among those in the largest 100 metros lived in these fifty-one metros.

The Hispanic growth rates for these metros must be understood in the context of rather modest absolute numbers. Their fast growth began from very small initial populations generally, and so even extraordinarily high growth rates usually did not involve large numbers of individuals. Across this category the initial 1980 Latino populations remained small. Sarasota, for example, registered an astounding 538 percent increase in its Hispanic population between 1980 and 2000, but it began this period with a mere 6,000 Latino residents. Even after twenty years of extraordinary growth Sarasota only had 38,682 Latinos, and that was in a state with a Hispanic population of 2.7 million.

Nevertheless, so much rapid growth spread out across so many metros emerges as a demographic phenomenon of consequence when it is viewed cumulatively. In 1980, 19 of these metros counted fewer than 10,000 Latinos, and only six had more than 50,000. But by 2000 only 2 remained

FIGURE 10-1. Latino Population for Four Metropolitan Area Types, 2000

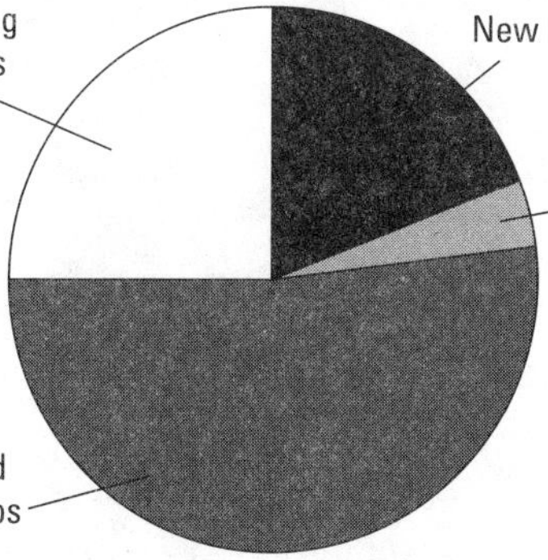

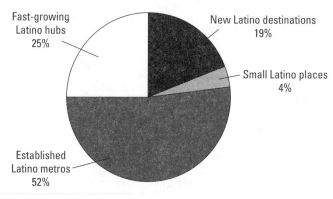

Source: See note 5.

below the 10,000 mark while 16 had more than 100,000. Add it up and the Latino population of all 51 of these metros in 2000 reaches 5.3 million—or 19 percent of the nation's total Latino population (figure 10-1). And the Latinization of the new destinations is becoming more consequential, even though the total for the entire category pales beside the huge absolute populations of the big metros with long-standing Latino populations. In fact, the total for these metros is just a bit smaller than the combined Latino populations of Los Angeles and Miami. Fully three-quarters of the Hispanics in these 51 metros (4 million people) were added to the population between 1980 and 2000. That accounts for about a quarter of the total Hispanic population growth measured in all the 100 top metros during that period.

The sheer pace of this mostly very recent growth is also noteworthy. In 1980 Latinos made up 2 percent of the population of these fifty-one metros, but by 2000 they were 7 percent of the population in this category. In all but eleven of these metros the rate of growth for the Hispanic population in the 1990s outstripped that in the 1980s, and in many cases it was substantially greater, at least doubling in twenty-eight metros from one decade to the next. None of the new Latino destinations experienced a Hispanic growth rate of less than 42 percent in the 1990s.

Another significant factor: this rapid Latino growth in new destinations usually accompanied rapid increases in the overall population. In these metropolitan areas, Latinos constituted only one factor in broader growth trends across metros that saw a 42 percent total growth over the twenty-year period as all but seven registered growth rates in the double digits. In this fashion, the new Hispanic residents in these places accounted for just 22 percent of the increased population. By comparison, in metros with established Latino communities, Hispanics composed by far the largest, and in some cases the only, factor in population growth, accounting for 79 percent of the overall population increase (table 10-1).

Eighteen of the new Latino destinations, finally, warrant discussion as sites of "hypergrowth." In each of these eighteen metros, the Hispanic population grew by more than 300 percent—or twice the national average—after 1980. Altogether, the combined Hispanic population of all these metros jumped 505 percent between 1980 and 2000 (table 10-3).

This collection of metros includes emerging immigrant gateways such as Washington, D.C., and Atlanta and several of the nation's fastest-growing metros such as Las Vegas and Orlando. Eleven of these metros lie in the Southeast, with three North Carolina cities—Charlotte, Greensboro, and Raleigh—epitomizing the "new economy" of the 1990s with rapid development in the finance, business services, and high-technology sectors. As a group, these Latino hypergrowth metros grew robustly from 1980 to 2000, posting overall population growth at a combined 54 percent rate over the two decades. All but five of the eighteen had faster overall growth in the 1990s than the 1980s, moreover. As a result, even the explosive new Latino growth in these cities remained a relatively modest portion of the overall population increase despite its incredible pace. In absolute terms, after all, the hypergrowth metros added a relatively modest 2.3 million Latinos between 1980 and 2000 at a time when their overall population increased by 11.2 million. Hispanics, in short, represented just 20 percent of the overall population increase.

But even so, the hypergrowth metros epitomized the sudden arrival of Latinos in new destinations. In thirteen of these hypergrowth metros in 1980 Hispanics represented 3 percent or less of their metro populations or one-quarter of a million Latinos, but by 2000 they numbered nearly 1.5 million and represented 6 percent of their collective overall populations. This underscores how, from a barely measurable minority, Latinos grew into a significant segment of the population in many places. Atlanta provides a case in point. There, the 24,550 Latinos counted in 1980 represented just 1 percent of the metro population. But after twenty years marked by a 995 percent growth rate, Atlanta's Latino population reached 268,851—or 7 percent of the total (table 10-3).

Fast-Growing Latino Hubs (Large Base, Fast Growth): Eleven Metros. Eleven metros—the fast-growing Latino hubs—grew at extraordinary rates

TABLE 10-3. "Hypergrowth" New Latino Destinations, 2000[a]

Metro	Number of Latinos	Total population (percent)	Latino growth, 1980–2000 (percent)
Raleigh-Durham	72,580	6	1,180
Atlanta	268,851	7	995
Greensboro	62,210	5	962
Charlotte	77,092	5	932
Orlando	271,627	17	859
Las Vegas	322,038	21	753
Nashville	40,139	3	630
Fort Lauderdale	271,652	17	578
Sarasota	38,682	7	538
Portland	142,444	7	437
Greenville	26,167	3	397
West Palm Beach	140,675	12	397
Washington, DC	432,003	9	346
Indianapolis	42,994	3	338
Minneapolis-St. Paul	99,121	3	331
Fort Worth	309,851	18	328
Providence	93,868	8	325
Tulsa	38,570	5	303
Total	2,750,564	9	505

a. Hypergrowth metros had Latino population growth greater than 300 percent between 1980 and 2000.

from very large base populations and now supplement the established Latino metros as major population centers on the map of Hispanic America.

Latinos made up a sizable 14 percent of the population in these metros in 1980, and over the next twenty years the Hispanic population grew by 235 percent to reach fully 25 percent of the 100 metros' overall population.

With the exception of Phoenix, the metros in this category lie in California or Texas. Two—Orange County and Riverside-San Bernardino—are suburban outliers of Los Angeles, and a third—Vallejo—is an exurb in the San Francisco Bay area. Three others—Bakersfield, Stockton, and Sacramento—lie in central California and reflect that state's growth away from the traditional coastal areas. All of the California metros grew at a faster rate in the 1980s than in the 1990s, while the opposite is true of the Texas and Arizona metros. Dallas and Houston, the two biggest metros in Texas, fit that pattern. So does Austin, one of several metros in this category that experienced exceptional economic growth in the high-technology sector. Dallas and Riverside-San Bernardino—even with their large initial Hispanic populations—met the standard for hypergrowth with increases of 358 percent and 324 percent, respectively, between 1980 and 2000. By 2000, some 6.8 million Hispanic people lived in one of these metros.

The fast-growing Latino hubs, meanwhile, assumed new functions in Hispanic America during the past two decades by moving beyond the status of secondary way stations. Aside from Houston and San Diego, none of these metropolitan areas have played a long-standing role as a major gateway for Latino immigrants. Bakersfield and Stockton were initially places where agricultural workers settled when they left the fields for the stability of city life. Orange County and Riverside-San Bernardino served as secondary stops for Hispanics who had already passed through Los Angeles. However, the rapid rates of Latino population growth since the 1980s suggest these metros have emerged as immigrant ports of entry even as they retained—and perhaps enlarged—their importance as secondary destinations.

Two other aspects of the growing hubs' emergence are these metros' initially lower Hispanic concentrations (compared with the established Latino metros), and their high overall growth rates.

Initially, the fast-growing hubs posted an average total population of 1.3 million and a Latino population share of 14 percent. By contrast, the more established Hispanic metros that grew more slowly over the next twenty years had a larger average total population of 2.2 million and a significantly higher 20 percent Hispanic population share. The faster-growing new hubs may have had more room to grow before approaching a potential saturation point.

At the same time, the overall population growth rates in the newer hubs far exceeded those in the established Latino metros with Latino populations of a million or more—Los Angeles, New York, Chicago, and Miami. In fact, the fast-growing Latino hubs exhibited the highest overall population growth of any of the four types of metropolitan areas. Altogether, the combined total population of these eleven metros grew by 70 percent between 1980 and 2000. In absolute numbers that represented an increase of 10 million people—4.8 million of whom were Latinos. By contrast, the established Hispanic metros posted a 25 percent overall twenty-year growth rate as they added just 8.8 million people and 6.9 million Latinos.

These figures suggest once again that Latino growth in the fast-growing Hispanic hubs remains just one element of a more generalized economic and population expansion. In these hubs, after all, Latino growth represented just 48 percent of the regions' overall twenty-year growth. By comparison, Hispanics accounted for 79 percent of the total growth in the more established metros. Such ratios underscore that the high overall growth rates in these big fast-growing metros stimulated and facilitated fast Latino growth much as it did in the smaller-scale new destinations such as Atlanta and Charlotte.

Small Latino Places (Small Base, Slow Growth): Twenty-Two Metros. About a quarter of the 100 metros in this survey, finally, remained largely on the periphery of major Hispanic growth trends. These cities were mostly located in the South and Midwest, though a number can be found in the northeastern Rust Belt. As a group, these cities harbored relatively few Latinos in 1980 and registered only slow to moderate growth in their Hispanic populations over the twenty-year period 1980 to 2000.

In absolute numbers, Hispanics made up only 4 percent of the population in these regions in 2000 compared with a 16 percent overall Hispanic population share in the 100 metros. In fact, fewer than 1.3 million Hispanics lived in these 22 metros in 2000. All told, only 4 percent of the Hispanic population of the 100 largest metros resided in the small Latino places in 2000 (figure 10-1).

Latino growth in these metro areas also lagged, reaching only 81 percent compared with the national 145 percent growth rate for the 100 metros. What is more, the relatively low Hispanic population growth in these places corresponded with the below-average total metro population growth (4 percent) between 1980 and 2000 in these metros. In this fashion, the small Latino places illustrate the extent to which Latino population growth remains a subset of growth trends for all groups. In these places, for example, it seems that the same factors discouraging population growth by other groups discouraged expansion of the Hispanic population to some degree.

Growing Number of Latinos in Suburbs

U.S. Hispanics traditionally have been urban dwellers, and many remain so now. Nevertheless, Census 2000 reveals that their distribution across the metropolitan landscape is changing dramatically. The Latinos, in short, are becoming suburbanites.

In 1990 the Latino population was almost evenly split between suburbs (8.7 million) and central cities (8.6 million) in the top 100 metropolitan areas. However, Hispanics flocked to the suburbs during the 1990s. During the decade their numbers there increased by 6.2 million to nearly 15 million compared with a 4 million increase to 12.6 million in the central cities. These changes implied a 71 percent increase in the number of Latinos living in the suburbs. All told, the suburbs accounted for 61 percent of the overall growth of the Hispanic population in these metros between 1990 and 2000 (table 10A-2 in the appendix to this chapter). By 2000, 54 percent of all Latinos resided in the suburbs.

Many Hispanics, by choosing the suburbs, are following the familiar path from city neighborhoods to the urban periphery. In addition, some suburban areas are serving as ports of entry for newly arriving immigrants. This holds both for metros with long-standing Hispanic populations and for those with newly acquired Latino communities, though suburban growth was disproportionately higher in the new Latino destinations. Moreover, some of the cities with the largest Hispanic populations—notably Los Angeles, New York, and Miami—also saw substantial increases in adjoining jurisdictions. From Long Island on the East Coast to southern California's Inland Empire, Latino populations grew at a rapid rate and in large numbers on the outer fringes of major metropolitan areas.

Disproportionate increases in the suburban Latino population are most evident in metros that experienced very rapid growth of their Latino populations overall and especially in those with a relatively small base population in 1990. Overall, 56 percent of the Hispanic growth in metros with established Latino communities occurred in the suburbs. For example, in Albuquerque, San Antonio, and San Jose—metros with large base populations and relatively slow growth—fewer Latinos were added to the suburban population than in central cities. Meanwhile, in new-destination metros, the suburbs registered 70 percent of the growth. In Washington, D.C., Atlanta, and Fort Lauderdale—metros that started with a small base population and experienced very rapid growth—more than 90 percent of the increase came in the suburbs. When Latino migrants ventured into new communities in the 1990s, the suburbs apparently held a powerful draw. In the future, as these migrant pioneers draw relatives from abroad, new, larger family units are likely to form in the suburbs.

Even when large, well-established Latino communities were available for settlement, much of the growth took place on the periphery of the metropolitan area. Indeed, in the metros with the largest Hispanic populations, which were also some of the nation's most populous metros, substantial growth took place beyond the central cities. In the Chicago metropolitan area, for example, 63 percent of the growth took place in the suburbs and in Miami growth was 96 percent.

Moreover, these big cities formed the core of regional clusters as the Hispanic population grew substantially in adjoining or nearby metros. The trend also prevailed in other regions. The Latino populations of Bergen-Passaic, N. J., and Nassau-Suffolk, N.Y., which adjoin New York to the east and west, together added some 218,000 Latinos between 1990 and 2000. Along the coast north of Miami, the population of the Fort Lauderdale and West Palm Beach metropolitan areas together increased by 242,000 Latinos.

In each case the outlying metros of the cluster grew faster than did the core metro, though not in absolute terms. In southern California, meanwhile, the peripheral growth actually outpaced more central growth by all measures. There, the Orange County, Ventura, and Riverside-San Bernardino metropolitan areas added 950,000 Latinos, which exceeded the growth in the Los Angeles-Long Beach metro in absolute numbers and the pace of growth.

These patterns suggest that even as Hispanic growth slows in the big metros with very large Latino communities, those areas serve as powerful magnets for a broader metropolitan region. Also, these patterns may reveal what other data indicate—namely, that while newly arrived immigrants still head for the more traditional ports of entry in large numbers, many better-established Latinos are moving away from those traditionally Hispanic communities to new areas within the same metropolitan cluster.

Hispanic Men Predominate in New Latino Destinations

Distinctive Latino local household structures are also emerging as demographic change affects different metropolitan areas. Most notably, the newest areas of Latino settlement exhibit gender ratios that favor men and gain more nonfamily households. By contrast, in places where the local Hispanic community has become larger and better established, family households develop and gender ratios balance out.

Prior research has shown how these dynamics work: the gender composition of migration to a particular place changes with the "maturity" of the flow to that area.[8] Historically, male immigrants from Latin America typically move toward opportunity first, without spouses or other nuclear family members. Subsequently, relatives and friends follow the immigrants, so that complete family units and eventually extended family and friendship networks form in the years and decades following initial settlement.

In this fashion, gender ratios suggest the newness of settlement. Gender ratios that favor men indicate growth owing to new migration flows and demarcate the newest areas of settlement. By contrast, metropolitan areas with older Latino communities typically show more balanced gender ratios since over time full families, and eventually a U.S.-born third-generation, join the male trailblazers. Nor does this dynamic apply only to the immigration of the foreign born. It also applies to the movement of immigrants from one area within the United States to another in what is called "secondary" migration. Even in metros where the Latino presence dates back

8. Durand and Massey (1992).

fifty or one hundred years or more, successive waves of immigrant newcomers continually refresh the Latino population, producing continuous demographic change and layering of the family structure and household composition.

Given these dynamics, Hispanic and non-Hispanic sex ratios (reflecting the number of men in a given population per 100 women) were calculated for all metropolitan areas, and the subtotals for metro types are shown in table 10-4. The patterns are clear. Overall, less mobile, non-Hispanic populations included greater numbers of working-age women in 2000, while the reverse was true for Hispanic populations. The non-Latino sex ratio rises to above 100 (indicating a tilt toward more men than women) in only a handful of metros, namely, those with military bases such as San Diego and El Paso, as well as San Francisco, where there is a substantial gay male population. By contrast, the working-age Hispanic population leans heavily toward men across most metros, and most metropolitan areas increased their Latino male populations relative to the female population between 1990 and 2000. This reflected a steady and widely dispersed settlement of newly arrived immigrants.

In general, the faster and newer a metropolitan area's Latino growth, the higher its sex ratio climbed in the 1990s. In metros with a small Latino presence the Latino gender balance edged upward from 100 to 108 between 1990 and 2000 (table 10-4). In metros that can be characterized as new Latino destinations, the Latino sex ratios surged from 107 in 1990 on average to 117 in 2000. Still more dramatically, the Latino sex ratio reached an average of 124 in the hypergrowth metros—meaning that Latinos outnumbered Latinas in these metropolitan areas by a full 24 percent. In this category, Raleigh-Durham's Latino population included an extraordinary 188 men for every 100 women, as large new flows of men arrived presumably without family members.

In keeping with these effects, where Latino residency is long-standing or Latino growth slower—as in many established Latino metros—sex ratios remained steady or declined as proportionally more Latino growth resulted from increases in families both from births and family reunification. For example, Chicago's gender ratio remained at 117 both in 1990 and 2000 as a steady gathering of families offset new immigrant arrivals. Sex ratios actually declined in maturing Hispanic communities such as Fresno, Los Angeles, and Ventura as the number of women there increased during the 1990s. In fact, in seven of the sixteen well-established Latino communities women outnumbered men, indicating the arrival of many more women and families, indicating more "mature" immigration.

TABLE 10-4. Sex Ratios for Non-Latino and Latino Working-Age Populations for Four Metropolitan Area Types, 2000[a]

	Non-Latino		Latino	
Metro area type	1990	2000	1990	2000
Established Latino metros	96	96	101	101
New Latino destinations	96	96	107	117
Fast-growing Latino hubs	100	99	114	113
Small Latino places	94	95	100	108
Total	96	96	104	107

a. Sex ratios are defined as the number of men in a given population per 100 women.

Household composition—which reflects whether unrelated individuals or families predominate in a community—also reveals the demographic change that accompanies various growth patterns. Similar to a tilt toward higher sex ratios, a proliferation of unrelated individuals can be an indicator of new migration; however in the small Latino places, it probably also indicates an aging population with elderly living alone. Conversely, a higher share of couple-headed households usually corresponds with longer-established communities. Examining household composition reveals that 22 percent of the households in new Latino destinations were nonfamily in 2000. Fast-growing Latino hubs and established Latino metros had the highest proportions of married couple households and posted the lowest proportions of nonfamily households across all metro types. Furthermore, half or more of the households in these two metro types contained children under 18, including both couple-headed and single-headed households. New Latino destinations, for their part, had shares of married-couple households and households with children comparable to the established Latino metros, suggesting some degree of secondary migration of family members (table 10-5).

In these ways, then, distinctive demographic variations across metropolitan areas confirm that Latino growth varies considerably from one locale to another. In newer settlement areas, where many workers reside without families, the share of nonfamily Latino households in 2000 far exceeds that in metros where Latinos have long been a major segment of the population. Meanwhile, some of the traditional Latino bastions are developing more stable Hispanic communities with a greater share of married couples with children. In this sense, Latino growth is an evolving process, and some cities are simply farther along in the process than others.

TABLE 10-5. Latino Households, by Household Type for Four Metropolitan Area Types, 2000

Percent

	Married couple families		Single householder (no spouse)		
Metro area type	*With children*	*Without children*	*With children*	*Without children*	*Nonfamily households*
Established Latino metros	34	19	16	12	20
New Latino destinations	34	18	16	10	22
Fast-growing Latino hubs	42	17	15	9	17
Small Latino places	28	18	18	10	26
Total	36	18	16	11	20

DISCUSSION

Taken together, these analyses of the nation's 100 largest metro areas reveal sharp differences in the pace and characteristics of Hispanic population growth across and within metropolitan areas. What is more, this assessment suggests that these variations result not only from demographic factors within Latino populations but from differences in the economic, social, and demographic trends influencing U.S. metropolitan areas. Accordingly, the list of metros that experienced the fastest Hispanic population growth in this analysis substantially overlaps with the list of those with the fastest total population growth. Conversely, the metros with the slowest overall growth recorded unusually slow Latino growth.

But this relationship should not be interpreted as simply a mechanical one in which Latino numbers rise merely as a function of overall growth. Las Vegas, for example, the fastest-growing metro in the nation between 1990 and 2000, grew by 200 percent during that period. However, the Hispanic population grew by 750 percent during those twenty years. That contrast—nearly a fourfold difference in growth rates—and similar spreads in many other metros suggests a complex relationship in which Hispanic growth can be spurred by overall growth even as it responds to its own dynamics.

For instance, in the past, a handful of central cities were the usual destination of immigrant newcomers from Latin America. The classic process entailed trailblazers leaving the ports of entry to seek opportunities in these frontier cities, largely in California, Texas, New York, and Illinois. Family, friends, and fellow countrymen followed initial migrants, and complete immigrant communities subsequently developed over time.[9] However, a

9. Saenz and Cready (1998); Massey and others (1993).

somewhat different process is now developing with the rapid growth of Hispanics in new Latino destinations. Those coming from abroad are now skirting traditional areas and settling directly in new places that promise economic and housing opportunities. In this fashion, the new frontier zone that has developed in the past twenty years now encompasses many metro areas of the Southeast.[10] And much of the Latino population growth is occurring outside of central cities directly in the suburbs.

Comparing the growth of the Latino population in central cities and suburbs within a metropolitan area also reveals distinctive patterns. Across the 100 metros, 61 percent of the increase in the Latino population occurred in the suburbs. As a result, the Census 2000 located 2.4 million more Latinos living in suburbs than in central cities. But again, not all the growth had the same quality. For example, the fastest suburban growth occurred in the new Latino destinations, while more established metros with larger bases and slower growth saw slower suburbanization. Yet again, some of the metros with the most established Latino communities saw rapid growth in adjoining jurisdictions, as occurred in the Long Island cities outside New York City.

Variations and contrasts like these, moreover, have clear public policy implications. Most generally, the findings presented here suggest public officials responsible for planning the allocation of services and resources need to tailor their decisionmaking to the growth variation in their service area. Housing demand, the need for classroom space, the demand for public transportation—all of these will vary greatly not only with the rate of growth in the Latino population but also with the type of growth. For example, Raleigh-Durham can probably expect to see its new Latino population mature in the next decade, gain married couples, and then produce more full families, which will produce a "spike" in its school-age population. Los Angeles, by contrast, may soon see the crest of the demographic wave that has so challenged its school system for the past two decades. Across the country, one-size-fits-all problem solving will not suffice.

A further policy implication involves the abruptness of growth in locales like Raleigh-Durham and the other new Latino destinations. Specifically, the need for policymakers to adapt quickly to vast change presents special challenges in metros that started with minuscule Latino populations and that experienced sudden, substantial growth. By contrast, the proximity of places like Orange County, CA, or Suffolk County, NY, to large and longtime urban concentrations of Hispanics has allowed for more gradual change and

10. Hernández-León and Zúñiga (2000).

more time to prepare for the growth of a population characterized by low-wage workers, large families, and substantial numbers of adults with little proficiency in English.

CONCLUSION

This survey reveals not only the vast and widespread growth of America's Hispanic population but also the emergence of new forms of growth and new areas of settlement across the nation's metropolitan landscape.

Variation is pervasive within the broad trend of Latino growth. Indeed, the variegated patterns of growth identified underscore the dynamism of the Hispanic population as it finds its place in American society. And yet, for all the flux and change on display in Census 2000, a look back to the 1990 and 1980 counts reveals distinct trends. These trends suggest, moreover, that the growth of the Latino population does seem to be following discernible pathways likely to carry into the future.

To begin with, the great Latino gateways—Los Angeles, New York, Miami, and Chicago—will continue to house massive concentrations of Hispanics. Yet even so, the growth rates that slowed in these vast metros in the 1990s are not likely to pick up and may slow even further. Of course, this in no way means the Latino population will necessarily stabilize in those cities. Rather, the great mainstays may be seeing a continued influx of new arrivals and a simultaneous outflow of Latinos leaving in search of better jobs, housing, and quality of life in other destinations.

Meanwhile, the move to the suburban fringes will surely continue as growth slows in already crowded central cities. Family composition and gender data as well as other indicators suggest that suburbs, particularly those on the periphery of these great gateways, are themselves becoming ports of entry where immigrants settle without ever having first stopped in the old urban barrios. Then, too, Latino families in search of the classic American suburban dream are also moving to the outskirts where housing is cheaper. Accordingly, more and more Latinos will be flocking to the suburbs in the coming decades.

In sum, the Latino population is on the move and spreading out as it grows. Most of the Hispanic population will remain concentrated in a handful of big metropolitan areas. And yet, much of the growth will take place elsewhere. On the periphery of big cities and in the suburbs of the nation's newest booming metros, the first wave of Latinos has already set up house and more are likely to come. In southern California, Texas, the New York City region, and South Florida, the Hispanic share of the population will continue to increase though more slowly than before. But at the same time, whenever and wherever conditions lend themselves to overall population growth and robust economic development, Latinos will be a big part of the mix.

TABLE 10A-1. Latino Population and Share of Total Population for Four Metropolitan Area Types, 1980–2000

	1980			1990			2000			Percent change in Latino population		
Metropolitan area[a]	Total	Latino	Latino (percent)	Total	Latino	Latino (percent)	Total	Latino	Latino (percent)	1980–90	1990–2000	1980–2000
Established Latino metros												
Albuquerque, NM MSA	515,614	191,068	37	589,131	217,340	37	712,738	296,373	42	14	36	55
Chicago, IL PMSA	7,246,032	583,265	8	7,410,858	819,676	11	8,272,768	1,416,584	17	41	73	143
Denver, CO PMSA	1,428,836	164,158	11	1,622,980	208,264	13	2,109,282	397,236	19	27	91	142
El Paso, TX MSA	479,899	297,196	62	591,610	411,248	70	679,622	531,654	78	38	29	79
Fresno, CA MSA	577,737	167,448	29	755,580	262,004	35	922,516	406,151	44	56	55	143
Jersey City, NJ PMSA	556,972	145,249	26	553,099	181,222	33	608,975	242,123	40	25	34	67
Los Angeles–Long Beach, CA PMSA	7,477,503	2,065,503	28	8,863,164	3,306,116	37	9,519,338	4,242,213	45	60	28	105
McAllen, TX MSA	283,229	230,287	81	383,545	326,923	85	569,463	503,100	88	42	54	118
Miami, FL PMSA	1,625,781	580,025	36	1,937,094	949,700	49	2,253,362	1,291,737	57	64	36	123
New York, NY PMSA	8,274,961	1,465,421	18	8,546,846	1,842,127	22	9,314,235	2,339,836	25	26	27	60
Oakland, CA PMSA	1,761,759	185,829	11	2,082,914	266,283	13	2,392,557	441,686	18	43	66	138
San Antonio, TX MSA	1,088,710	487,447	45	1,324,749	624,941	47	1,592,383	816,037	51	28	31	67
San Francisco, CA PMSA	1,488,871	166,360	11	1,603,678	226,734	14	1,731,183	291,563	17	36	29	75
San Jose, CA PMSA	1,295,071	226,388	17	1,497,577	307,113	21	1,682,585	403,401	24	36	31	78
Tucson, AZ MSA	531,443	111,378	21	666,880	161,053	24	843,746	247,578	29	45	54	122
Ventura, CA PMSA	529,174	113,184	21	669,016	175,414	26	753,197	251,734	33	55	44	122
	35,161,592	7,180,206	20	39,098,721	10,286,158	26	43,957,950	14,119,006	32	43	37	97
New Latino destinations												
Albany, NY MSA	824,729	8,351	1	861,424	14,440	2	875,583	23,798	3	73	65	185
Allentown, PA MSA	551,052	14,022	3	595,081	26,697	4	637,958	50,607	8	90	90	261
Atlanta, GA MSA[b]	2,233,324	24,550	1	2,959,950	55,045	2	4,112,198	268,851	7	124	388	995
Baltimore, MD PMSA	2,199,531	20,688	1	2,382,172	28,538	1	2,552,994	51,329	2	38	80	148
Bergen-Passaic, NJ PMSA	1,292,970	90,705	7	1,278,440	145,094	11	1,373,167	237,869	17	60	64	162
Birmingham, AL MSA	815,286	5,858	1	840,140	3,520	0	921,106	16,598	2	–40	372	183
Boston, MA–NH PMSA	3,148,490	72,698	2	3,227,633	130,896	4	3,406,829	202,513	6	91	47	181
Charlotte, NC–SC MSA[b]	971,391	7,469	1	1,162,093	9,817	1	1,499,293	77,092	5	31	685	932
Columbus, OH MSA	1,214,297	8,783	1	1,345,450	10,003	1	1,540,157	28,115	2	14	181	220
Fort Lauderdale, FL PMSA[b]	1,018,200	40,093	4	1,255,488	105,668	8	1,623,018	271,652	17	164	157	578

Fort Worth–Arlington, TX PMSA[b]	990,852	72,336	7	1,361,034	147,431	11	1,702,625	309,851	18	104	110	328
Grand Rapids, MI MSA	840,824	18,005	2	937,891	27,195	3	1,088,514	68,916	6	51	153	283
Greensboro–Winston Salem, NC MSA[b]	951,170	5,858	1	1,050,304	6,844	1	1,251,509	62,210	5	17	809	962
Greenville, SC MSA[b]	743,284	5,261	1	830,563	5,712	1	962,441	26,167	3	9	358	397
Harrisburg, PA MSA	555,158	5,998	1	587,986	9,336	2	629,401	19,557	3	56	109	226
Hartford, CT MSA	1,080,581	46,120	4	1,157,617	77,132	7	1,183,110	113,540	10	75	42	148
Indianapolis, IN MSA[b]	1,305,911	9,812	1	1,380,491	11,918	1	1,607,486	42,994	3	21	261	338
Jacksonville, FL MSA	722,252	14,150	2	906,727	22,206	2	1,100,491	42,122	4	57	90	198
Kansas City, MO–KS MSA	1,449,374	33,807	2	1,582,875	45,199	3	1,776,062	92,910	5	34	106	175
Knoxville, TN MSA	546,488	3,499	1	585,960	3,433	1	687,249	8,628	1	–2	151	147
Las Vegas, NV–AZ MSA[b]	528,000	37,767	7	852,737	86,570	10	1,563,282	322,038	21	129	272	753
Little Rock, AR MSA	474,484	4,118	1	513,117	4,741	1	583,845	12,337	2	15	160	200
Louisville, KY–IN MSA	953,850	5,631	1	948,829	5,040	1	1,025,598	16,479	2	–10	227	193
Memphis, TN–AR–MS MSA	938,777	8,754	1	1,007,306	7,546	1	1,135,614	27,520	2	–14	265	214
Middlesex–Somerset–Hunterdon, NJ PMSA	886,383	39,380	4	1,019,835	70,021	7	1,169,641	131,122	11	78	87	233
Milwaukee, WI PMSA	1,397,143	34,993	3	1,432,149	48,276	3	1,500,741	94,511	6	38	96	170
Minneapolis–St. Paul, MN–WI MSA[b]	2,198,190	22,985	1	2,538,834	34,334	1	2,968,806	99,121	3	49	189	331
Monmouth–Ocean, NJ PMSA	849,211	21,237	3	986,327	35,619	4	1,126,217	63,813	6	68	79	200
Nashville, TN MSA[b]	850,505	5,500	1	985,026	7,250	1	1,231,311	40,139	3	32	454	630
Nassau–Suffolk, NY PMSA	2,605,813	102,776	4	2,609,212	157,118	6	2,753,913	282,693	10	53	80	175
New Haven, CT PMSA	500,534	18,358	4	530,240	30,629	6	542,149	53,331	10	79	62	190
Norfolk–Virginia Beach–Newport News, VA–NC MSA	1,200,998	18,640	2	1,443,244	31,551	2	1,569,541	48,963	3	69	55	163
Oklahoma City, OK MSA	860,969	19,174	2	958,839	32,851	3	1,083,346	72,998	7	71	122	281
Omaha, NE–IA MSA	605,419	12,685	2	639,580	15,419	2	716,998	39,735	6	22	158	213
Orlando, FL MSA[b]	804,925	28,321	4	1,224,852	98,812	8	1,644,561	271,627	17	249	175	859
Portland–Vancouver, OR–WA PMSA[b]	1,333,572	26,544	2	1,515,452	49,344	3	1,918,009	142,444	7	86	189	437
Providence, RI–MA MSA[b]	1,076,557	21,526	2	1,134,365	45,893	4	1,188,613	93,868	8	114	98	325

(continued)

TABLE 10A-1. Latino Population and Share of Total Population for Four Metropolitan Area Types, 1980–2000 (*continued*)

	1980			1990			2000			Percent change in Latino population		
Metropolitan area[a]	*Total*	*Latino*	*Latino (percent)*	*Total*	*Latino*	*Latino (percent)*	*Total*	*Latino*	*Latino (percent)*	*1980–90*	*1990–2000*	*1980–2000*
Raleigh–Durham, NC MSA[b]	665,236	5,670	1	855,545	9,923	1	1,187,941	72,580	6	75	631	1180
Richmond, VA MSA	761,311	6,942	1	865,640	8,788	1	996,512	23,283	2	27	165	235
Salt Lake City, UT MSA	910,222	44,720	5	1,072,227	61,269	6	1,333,914	144,600	11	37	136	223
Sarasota, FL MSA[b]	350,693	6,064	2	489,483	15,186	3	589,959	38,682	7	150	155	538
Scranton, PA MSA	659,387	2,588	0	638,466	3,239	1	624,776	7,467	1	25	131	189
Seattle–Bellevue, WA PMSA	1,651,517	33,848	2	2,033,156	53,479	3	2,414,616	126,675	5	58	137	274
Springfield, MA MSA	569,774	24,708	4	588,043	48,024	8	591,932	74,227	13	98	53	203
Tacoma, WA PMSA	485,643	13,242	3	586,203	19,445	3	700,820	38,621	6	47	99	192
Tampa–St. Petersburg–Clearwater, FL MSA	1,613,603	80,433	5	2,067,959	136,027	7	2,395,997	248,642	10	69	83	209
Tulsa, OK MSA[b]	657,173	9,564	1	708,954	14,498	2	803,235	38,570	5	52	166	303
Washington, DC–MD–VA–WV PMSA[b]	3,477,873	96,767	3	4,223,485	221,458	5	4,923,153	432,003	9	129	95	346
West Palm Beach, FL MSA[b]	576,863	28,307	5	863,518	65,028	8	1,131,184	140,675	12	130	116	397
Wichita, KS MSA	441,844	12,651	3	485,270	18,437	4	545,220	40,353	7	46	119	219
Wilmington, DE–MD PMSA	458,545	7,265	2	513,293	11,701	2	586,216	27,599	5	61	136	280
	54,800,178	1,309,221	2	62,620,505	2,333,640	4	73,078,851	5,282,035	7	78	126	303
Fast-growing Latino hubs												
Austin, TX MSA	585,051	105,455	18	846,227	174,482	21	1,249,763	327,760	26	65	88	211
Bakersfield, CA MSA	403,089	87,119	22	543,477	150,558	28	661,645	254,036	38	73	69	192
Dallas, TX PMSA[b]	2,055,232	176,968	9	2,676,248	364,397	14	3,519,176	810,499	23	106	122	358
Houston, TX PMSA	2,754,304	401,602	15	3,322,025	697,208	21	4,177,646	1,248,586	30	74	79	211
Orange County, CA PMSA	1,932,709	285,722	15	2,410,556	556,957	23	2,846,289	875,579	31	95	57	206
Phoenix–Mesa, AZ MSA	1,599,970	226,194	14	2,238,480	374,275	17	3,251,876	817,012	25	65	118	261
Riverside–San Bernardino, CA PMSA[b]	1,558,182	289,803	19	2,588,793	675,918	26	3,254,821	1,228,962	38	133	82	324

Sacramento, CA PMSA	986,440	86,145	9	1,340,010	140,153	10	1,628,197	234,475	14	63	67	172
San Diego, CA MSA	1,861,846	274,530	15	2,498,016	498,578	20	2,813,833	750,965	27	82	51	174
Stockton, CA MSA	347,342	66,704	19	480,628	108,987	23	563,598	172,073	31	63	58	158
Vallejo, CA PMSA	334,402	33,298	10	451,186	59,576	13	518,821	99,014	19	79	66	197
	14,418,567	2,033,540	14	19,395,646	3,801,089	20	24,485,665	6,818,961	28	87	79	235
Small Latino places												
Akron, OH PMSA	660,328	3,000	0	657,575	3,844	1	694,960	5,874	1	28	53	96
Ann Arbor, MI PMSA	454,985	9,101	2	490,058	11,624	2	578,736	17,676	3	28	52	94
Baton Rouge, LA MSA	494,151	8,838	2	528,264	7,280	1	602,894	10,576	2	−18	45	20
Buffalo, NY MSA	1,242,826	15,700	1	1,189,288	23,521	2	1,170,111	33,967	3	50	44	116
Charleston, SC MSA	430,462	6,143	1	506,875	7,150	1	549,033	13,091	2	16	83	113
Cincinnati, OH–KY–IN PMSA	1,467,664	8,313	1	1,526,092	7,639	1	1,646,395	17,717	1	−8	132	113
Cleveland, OH PMSA	2,277,949	40,681	2	2,202,069	49,617	2	2,250,871	74,862	3	22	51	84
Columbia, SC MSA	410,088	5,370	1	453,331	5,740	1	536,691	12,859	2	7	124	139
Dayton, OH MSA	942,083	6,038	1	951,270	6,612	1	950,558	11,329	1	10	71	88
Detroit, MI PMSA	4,387,783	70,502	2	4,266,654	78,454	2	4,441,551	128,075	3	11	63	82
Gary, IN PMSA	642,781	46,449	7	604,526	47,116	8	631,362	66,207	10	1	41	43
Honolulu, HI MSA	762,565	54,619	7	836,231	54,680	7	876,156	58,729	7	0	7	8
Mobile, AL MSA	443,536	4,599	1	476,923	4,353	1	540,258	7,353	1	−5	69	60
New Orleans, LA MSA	1,303,800	51,203	4	1,285,270	52,563	4	1,337,726	58,545	4	3	11	14
Newark, NJ PMSA	1,963,388	131,805	7	1,915,928	183,986	10	2,032,989	270,557	13	40	47	105
Philadelphia, PA–NJ PMSA	4,781,494	118,624	2	4,922,175	165,844	3	5,100,931	258,606	5	40	56	118
Pittsburgh, PA MSA	2,571,223	12,910	1	2,394,811	11,881	0	2,358,695	17,100	1	−8	44	32
Rochester, NY MSA	1,030,630	19,383	2	1,062,470	29,712	3	1,098,201	47,559	4	53	60	145
St. Louis, MO–IL MSA	2,414,091	22,485	1	2,492,525	25,383	1	2,603,607	39,677	2	13	56	76
Syracuse, NY MSA	722,865	6,755	1	742,177	8,882	1	732,117	15,112	2	31	70	124
Toledo, OH MSA	616,864	16,656	3	614,128	18,675	3	618,203	27,125	4	12	45	63
Youngstown, OH MSA	644,922	6,971	1	600,895	7,246	1	594,746	10,743	2	4	48	54
	30,666,478	666,145	2	30,719,535	811,802	3	31,946,791	1,203,339	4	22	48	81
Total	135,046,815	11,189,112	8	151,834,407	17,232,689	11	173,469,257	27,423,341	16	54	59	145

a. One hundred largest metropolitan areas.

b. Hypergrowth metros that had Latino population growth greater than 300 percent between 1980 and 2000.

TABLE 10A-2. Growth in Latino Population, Central Cities and Suburbs, for Four Metropolitan Area Types, 1990–2000

	Metro area			Central city			Suburb		
Metropolitan area[a]	*1990*	*2000*	*Percent change*	*1990*	*2000*	*Percent change*	*1990*	*2000*	*Percent change*
Established Latino metros									
Albuquerque, NM MSA	217,340	296,373	36	131,465	179,075	36	85,875	117,298	37
Chicago, IL PMSA	819,676	1,416,584	73	535,315	753,644	41	284,361	662,940	133
Denver, CO PMSA	208,264	397,236	91	106,554	175,704	65	101,710	221,532	118
El Paso, TX MSA	411,248	531,654	29	355,260	431,875	22	55,988	99,779	78
Fresno, CA MSA	262,004	406,151	55	102,930	170,520	66	159,074	235,631	48
Jersey City, NJ PMSA	181,222	242,123	34	54,231	67,952	25	126,991	174,171	37
Los Angeles-Long Beach, CA PMSA	3,306,116	4,242,213	28	1,470,354	1,884,165	28	1,835,762	2,358,048	28
McAllen, TX MSA	326,923	503,100	54	64,572	85,427	32	262,351	417,673	59
Miami, FL PMSA	949,700	1,291,737	36	223,438	238,351	7	726,262	1,053,386	45
New York, NY PMSA	1,842,127	2,339,836	27	1,737,927	2,160,554	24	104,200	179,282	72
Oakland, CA PMSA	266,283	441,686	66	49,267	87,467	78	217,016	354,219	63
San Antonio, TX MSA	624,941	816,037	31	517,974	671,394	30	106,967	144,643	35
San Francisco, CA PMSA	226,734	291,563	29	96,640	109,504	13	130,094	182,059	40
San Jose, CA PMSA	307,113	403,401	31	204,012	269,989	32	103,101	133,412	29
Tucson, AZ MSA	161,053	247,578	54	117,267	173,868	48	43,786	73,710	68
Ventura, CA PMSA	175,414	251,734	44	15,935	24,573	54	159,479	227,161	42
	10,286,158	14,119,006	37	5,783,141	7,484,062	29	4,503,017	6,634,944	47
New Latino destinations									
Albany, NY MSA	14,440	23,798	65	3,225	5,349	66	11,215	18,449	65
Allentown, PA MSA	26,697	50,607	90	11,822	26,058	120	14,875	24,549	65
Atlanta, GA MSA[b]	55,045	268,851	388	7,640	18,720	145	47,405	250,131	428
Baltimore, MD PMSA	28,538	51,329	80	6,997	11,061	58	21,541	40,268	87
Bergen-Passaic, NJ PMSA	145,094	237,869	64	*	*	*	145,094	237,869	64
Birmingham, AL MSA	3,520	16,598	372	1,175	3,764	220	2,345	12,834	447
Boston, MA-NH PMSA	130,896	202,513	55	59,692	85,089	43	71,204	117,424	65
Charlotte, NC-SC MSA[b]	9,817	77,092	685	5,261	39,800	657	4,556	37,292	719
Columbus, OH MSA	10,003	28,115	181	5,968	17,471	193	4,035	10,644	164
Fort Lauderdale, FL PMSA[b]	105,668	271,652	157	10,574	14,406	36	95,094	257,246	171
Fort Worth-Arlington, TX PMSA[b]	147,431	309,851	110	107,987	220,185	104	39,444	89,666	127
Grand Rapids, MI MSA	27,195	68,916	153	8,447	25,818	206	18,748	43,098	130
Greensboro-Winston Salem, NC MSA[b]	6,844	62,210	809	2,415	25,785	968	4,429	36,425	722

Greenville, SC MSA[b]	5,712	26,167	358	567	1,927	240	5,145	24,240	371
Harrisburg, PA MSA	9,336	19,557	109	3,738	5,724	53	5,598	13,833	147
Hartford, CT MSA	77,132	113,540	47	43,372	49,260	14	33,760	64,280	90
Indianapolis, IN MSA[b]	11,918	42,994	261	7,463	30,636	311	4,455	12,358	177
Jacksonville, FL MSA	22,206	42,122	90	15,572	30,594	96	6,634	11,528	74
Kansas City, MO-KS MSA	45,199	92,910	106	27,154	55,243	103	28,380	37,667	33
Knoxville, TN MSA	3,433	8,628	151	986	2,751	179	2,447	5,877	140
Las Vegas, NV-AZ MSA[b]	86,570	322,038	272	31,249	112,962	261	55,321	209,076	278
Little Rock, AR MSA	4,741	12,337	160	1,427	4,889	243	3,314	7,448	125
Louisville, KY-IN MSA	5,040	16,479	227	1,490	4,755	219	3,550	11,724	230
Memphis, TN-AR-MS MSA	7,546	27,520	265	4,011	19,317	382	3,535	8,203	132
Middlesex-Somerset-Hunterdon, NJ PMSA	70,021	131,122	87	*	*	*	70,021	131,122	87
Milwaukee, WI PMSA	48,276	94,511	96	37,420	71,646	91	10,856	22,865	111
Minneapolis-St. Paul, MN-WI MSA[b]	34,334	99,121	189	17,627	51,890	194	16,707	47,231	183
Monmouth-Ocean, NJ PMSA	35,619	63,813	79	*	*	*	35,619	63,813	79
Nashville, TN MSA[b]	7,250	40,139	454	4,131	25,774	524	3,119	14,365	361
Nassau-Suffolk, NY PMSA	157,118	282,693	80	*	*	*	157,118	282,693	80
New Haven, CT PMSA	30,629	53,331	74	16,350	26,443	62	14,279	26,888	88
Norfolk-Virginia Beach-Newport News, VA-NC MSA	31,551	48,963	55	23,930	34,280	43	7,621	14,683	93
Oklahoma City, OK MSA	32,851	72,998	122	21,148	51,368	143	11,703	21,630	85
Omaha, NE-IA MSA	15,419	39,735	158	9,703	29,397	203	5,716	10,338	81
Orlando, FL MSA[b]	98,812	271,627	175	14,121	32,510	130	84,691	239,117	182
Portland-Vancouver, OR-WA PMSA[b]	49,344	142,444	189	14,693	45,093	207	34,651	97,351	181
Providence, RI-MA MSA[b]	45,893	93,868	105	23,744	52,146	120	22,149	41,722	88
Raleigh-Durham, NC MSA[b]	9,923	72,580	631	4,550	35,320	676	5,373	37,260	593
Richmond, VA MSA	8,788	23,283	165	1,744	5,074	191	7,044	18,209	159
Salt Lake City, UT MSA	61,269	144,600	136	15,220	34,254	125	46,049	110,346	140
Sarasota, FL MSA[b]	15,186	38,682	155	2,282	6,283	175	12,904	32,399	151
Scranton, PA MSA	3,239	7,467	131	520	1,999	284	2,719	5,468	101
Seattle-Bellevue, WA PMSA	53,479	126,675	137	19,097	35,546	86	34,382	91,129	165
Springfield, MA MSA	48,024	74,227	55	25,642	41,343	61	22,382	32,884	47
Tacoma, WA PMSA	19,445	38,621	99	6,270	13,262	112	13,175	25,359	92
Tampa-St. Petersburg-Clearwater, FL MSA	136,027	248,642	83	49,699	78,778	59	86,328	169,864	97
Tulsa, OK MSA[b]	14,498	38,570	166	9,340	28,111	201	5,158	10,459	103

(*continued*)

TABLE 10A-2. Growth in Latino Population, Central Cities and Suburbs, for Four Metropolitan Area Types, 1990–2000 (*continued*)

	Metro area			Central city			Suburb		
Metropolitan area[a]	*1990*	*2000*	*Percent change*	*1990*	*2000*	*Percent change*	*1990*	*2000*	*Percent change*
Washington, DC-MD-VA-WV PMSA[b]	221,458	432,003	95	31,358	44,953	43	190,100	387,050	104
West Palm Beach, FL MSA[b]	65,028	140,675	116	9,200	14,955	63	55,828	125,720	125
Wichita, KS MSA	18,437	40,353	119	14,314	33,112	131	4,123	7,241	76
Wilmington, DE-MD PMSA	11,701	27,599	136	4,809	7,148	49	6,892	20,451	197
	2,333,640	5,282,035	126	745,144	1,612,249	116	1,598,831	3,669,786	130
Fast-growing Latino hubs									
Austin, TX MSA	174,482	327,760	88	105,162	200,579	91	69,320	127,181	83
Bakersfield, CA MSA	150,558	254,036	69	35,033	80,170	129	115,525	173,866	51
Dallas, TX PMSA[b]	364,397	810,499	122	204,712	422,587	106	159,685	387,912	143
Houston, TX PMSA	697,208	1,248,586	79	442,943	730,865	65	254,265	517,721	104
Orange County, CA PMSA	556,957	875,579	57	279,238	421,010	51	277,719	454,569	64
Phoenix-Mesa, AZ MSA	374,275	817,012	118	224,667	528,253	135	149,608	288,759	93
Riverside-San Bernardino, CA PMSA[b]	675,918	1,228,962	82	114,154	185,337	62	561,764	1,043,625	86
Sacramento, CA PMSA	140,153	234,475	67	58,716	87,974	50	81,437	146,501	80
San Diego, CA MSA	498,578	750,965	51	223,616	310,752	39	274,962	440,213	60
Stockton, CA MSA	108,987	172,073	58	50,370	79,217	57	58,617	92,856	58
Vallejo, CA PMSA	59,576	99,014	66	11,201	18,591	66	48,375	80,423	66
	3,801,089	6,818,961	79	1,749,812	3,065,335	75	2,051,277	3,753,626	83

Small Latino places									
Akron, OH PMSA	3,844	5,874	53	1,503	2,513	67	2,341	3,361	44
Ann Arbor, MI PMSA	11,624	17,676	52	2,629	3,814	45	8,995	13,862	54
Baton Rouge, LA MSA	7,280	10,576	45	3,462	3,918	13	3,818	6,658	74
Buffalo, NY MSA	23,521	33,967	44	15,287	22,076	44	8,234	11,891	44
Charleston, SC MSA	7,150	13,091	83	504	1,462	190	6,646	11,629	75
Cincinnati, OH-KY-IN PMSA	7,639	17,717	132	2,319	4,230	82	5,320	13,487	154
Cleveland, OH PMSA	49,617	74,862	51	22,330	34,728	56	27,287	40,134	47
Columbia, SC MSA	5,740	12,859	124	2,033	3,520	73	3,707	9,339	152
Dayton, OH MSA	6,612	11,329	71	1,204	2,626	118	5,408	8,703	61
Detroit, MI PMSA	78,454	128,075	63	27,157	47,167	74	51,297	80,908	58
Gary, IN PMSA	47,116	66,207	41	6,282	5,065	−19	40,834	61,142	50
Honolulu, HI MSA	54,680	58,729	7	15,450	16,229	5	39,230	42,500	8
Mobile, AL MSA	4,353	7,353	69	2,152	2,828	31	2,201	4,525	106
New Orleans, LA MSA	52,563	58,545	11	15,900	14,826	−7	36,663	43,719	19
Newark, NJ PMSA	183,986	270,557	47	69,204	80,622	16	114,782	189,935	65
Philadelphia, PA-NJ PMSA	165,844	258,606	56	84,186	128,928	53	81,658	129,678	59
Pittsburgh, PA MSA	11,881	17,100	44	3,415	4,425	30	8,466	12,675	50
Rochester, NY MSA	29,712	47,559	60	18,936	28,032	48	10,776	19,527	81
St. Louis, MO-IL MSA	25,383	39,677	56	4,850	7,022	45	20,533	32,655	59
Syracuse, NY MSA	8,882	15,112	70	4,177	7,768	86	4,705	7,344	56
Toledo, OH MSA	18,675	27,125	45	11,958	17,141	43	6,717	9,984	49
Youngstown, OH MSA	7,246	10,743	48	3,596	4,282	19	3,650	6,461	77
	811,802	1,203,339	48	318,534	443,222	39	493,268	760,117	54
Total (all metro area types)	17,232,689	27,423,341	59	8,596,631	12,604,868	47	8,646,393	14,818,473	71

* Metros with no central city.

a. One hundred largest metropolitan areas.

b. Hypergrowth metros that had Latino population growth greater than 300 percent between 1980 and 2000.

REFERENCES

Castro, Max J., and Thomas D. Boswell. 2002. "The Dominican Diaspora Revisited: Dominicans and Dominican Americans in a New Century." *The North-South Agenda*, vol. 53. Dante B. Faschell North-South Center, University of Miami.

Durand, Jorge, and Douglas S. Massey. 1992. "Mexican Migration to the United States: A Critical Review." *Latin American Research Review* 27 (2): 3–42.

Hernández-León, Rubén, and Víctor Zúñiga. 2000. "Making Carpet by the Mile: The Emergence of a Mexican Immigrant Community in an Industrial Region of the U.S. Historic South." *Social Science Quarterly* 81 (1): 49–66.

Kandel, William, and Emilio Parrado. 2002. "Industrial Transformation and Hispanic Migration to the American South: The Case of the Poultry Industry." Paper presented at America's Changing Ethnic Landscapes, Athens, Ga. (April).

Massey, Douglas S., Rafael Alarcón, Jorge Durand, and Humberto González. 1987. *Return to Aztlan: The Social Process of International Migration from Western Mexico.* University of California Press.

Saenz, Rogelio, and Cynthia M. Cready. 1998. "The Role of Human and Social Capital in Geographic Mobility and Annual Earnings among Mexican Immigrants." Unpublished manuscript cited in Hernández-León and Zúñiga (2000).

11

Racial Segregation
Promising News

EDWARD L. GLAESER
JACOB L. VIGDOR

Census 2000 documents that for the third straight decade, segregation between blacks and nonblacks across American metropolitan areas has declined dramatically. During the 1990s the segregation levels of 272 metropolitan statistical areas (MSAs) declined, and only 19 MSAs experienced segregation increases.[1] Across metropolitan areas the average decline in segregation (without adjusting for population differences) was 5.5 percentage points.

The purpose of the present study is to examine the change in the levels of segregation across metropolitan areas during the 1990s and also over a longer period. Segregation does remain high in many large metropolitan areas, especially in the Midwest and Northeast, but it has generally decreased across the country and over time. The West and South are the fastest-growing and least segregated regions of the United States.

Regional differences may help to explain why previous authors have generally not focused on the declines in segregation across the country. In their seminal 1993 work on segregation in America, Douglas Massey and Nancy Denton focused primarily on larger cities in the Northeast and Midwest and therefore may have downplayed the importance of recent

1. Some larger urban agglomerations are referred to as consolidated metropolitan statistical areas (CMSAs), each of which is divided into two or more primary metropolitan statistical areas (PMSAs). In these areas, we calculate segregation indices for PMSAs in both 1990 and 2000. The largest MSA posting an increase in segregation was Baton Rouge. A complete list of metropolitan areas and their segregation levels and changes can be found in table 11A-1. See U.S. Bureau of the Census (1992, 2001).

overall segregation declines; although the continuing segregation of the "Rust Belt" cities is undoubtedly important, it is also important to document and understand the changes in segregation in the more vibrant and faster-developing areas of the country.[2]

METHODS

Two basic measures are generally used to capture the degree of residential segregation within an American city—the "dissimilarity" index and the "isolation" index:

- The "dissimilarity" index is a measure of the proportion of a racial group (in this case, blacks) that would have to move across census tracts in order for there to be a perfectly even proportion of members of that racial group (blacks) residing across the entire MSA.
- The "isolation" index indicates the percentage of black (or other race) residents in the census tract in which the average black (or other race) resident lives.[3]

In order to calculate these measures in the present analysis, four questions first had to be addressed. First, what is the appropriate geographical subarea to use as the basic study unit? Second, how do we define a city? Third, what is the appropriate definition of the black population? Fourth, what is the appropriate nonblack population to consider?

The Appropriate Geography

Various types of geographical subarea may be used for segregation measurement: wards, blocks, block groups, or census tracts. Academic work on segregation that looks at pre-1940 periods is forced to use political wards,

2. Massey and Denton (1993).

3. The dissimilarity index and isolation index are calculated in accordance with the following:

The dissimilarity index is calculated as:

$$\frac{1}{2}\sum_{\text{Sub-Areas}}\left|\frac{\text{Black Population in Sub-Area}}{\text{Black Population in MSA}}-\frac{\text{Non-Black Population in Sub-Area}}{\text{Non-Black Population in MSA}}\right|$$

This isolation index is:

$$(2)\quad \frac{\sum\limits_{\text{Sub-Areas}}\frac{\text{Black Population in Sub-Area}}{\text{Black Population in MSA}}*\frac{\text{Black Population in Sub-Area}}{\text{Total Population of Sub-Area}}-\frac{\text{Black Population in MSA}}{\text{Total Population in MSA}}}{1-\frac{\text{Black Population in MSA}}{\text{Total Population of MSA}}}$$

which are in a sense arbitrary and in any case exceedingly large (some contain tens of thousands of people). For analyzing the post-1940 period, there is the option of using blocks (equivalent to a city block in most urban areas), block groups (areas with roughly 1,000 inhabitants), or census tracts (which are larger units of roughly 4,000 people).

The advantage of blocks and block groups is that they are small and thus permit a better understanding of the microgeography of urban residence. The advantage of tracts is the relative ease of comparability over time: for most large cities, tract data are available beginning in 1940. Primarily for consistency with previous work, the present study uses the census tract as the relevant subarea.

The Relevant Definition of City

The question of city definition tends to come down to two choices. Segregation indices can be defined for different subunits of the metropolitan area, such as the central city, or alternatively, segregation indices can be defined for the metropolitan area as a whole. The present analysis will focus on segregation at the level of the metropolitan area as a whole. Although it is often quite interesting to know about segregation for central cities and for suburbs separately, an extremely high correlation does exist between segregation at the central city level and segregation at the metropolitan-area level, and if the analysis focused particularly on the central city level, the decline in segregation would tend to appear steeper.

The Appropriate Definition of "African American"

Another question that needs to be answered in order to implement these segregation measurements is exactly what it means to be African American. In previous censuses, "black" was an exclusive category, but Census 2000 allows respondents to identify themselves with multiple races, and therefore the measurement has become more complicated. On one hand, more than 95 percent of all respondents in the study sample who identified themselves as at least partly black identified themselves as only black. On the other hand, the remaining 5 percent are not distributed evenly across MSAs, and their presence could potentially skew segregation indices.

The segregation indices provided by the present analysis make use of two basic definitions, the more inclusive of which counts as African American anyone who checked "black" as one of his or her racial identities and the less inclusive of which counts as African Americans just those who checked only black and nothing else as their racial identity. In most cases, for the implementation of segregation indices this distinction actually appears to make little difference.[4]

The Relevant Nonblack Population

In choosing the relevant nonblack population, there are two basic options: all nonblacks together or just non-Hispanic whites. For ease of historical comparison, the study uses the first option, all nonblacks together. The essential difference between these two options lies in the treatment of Hispanics. (The Asian, Native American, and Pacific Islander populations are generally too small to influence segregation, and their residential patterns generally resemble those of non-Hispanic whites.)

Both options are actually quite reasonable, but it does need to be understood that when different definitions are used, different questions are answered. If just non-Hispanic whites are used as the comparison group, then the segregation measures will capture the extent to which blacks are segregated from this group. If all nonblacks are used, then segregation measures will capture the extent to which blacks are segregated from this broader group. This distinction matters because blacks are less segregated from Hispanics and thus from this broader group than they are from non-Hispanic whites—an interesting change from the early twentieth century, when blacks were more segregated from ethnic immigrants than they were from native whites.

The study also applies the usual segregation approach in a somewhat unorthodox way, looking at segregation for the entire country and for the four census regions and treating them as if they were cities, in order to ask about integration both within and across metropolitan areas. This is an important way to approach the changing level of integration for U.S. society as a whole, even though the analysis examines only particular tracts within the MSA and not the MSA as a whole.[5] Metropolitan areas are key because they now hold the vast majority of U.S. residents as well as the overwhelming majority of individuals living in close spatial proximity to their neighbors.

4. Dissimilarity indices calculated with these two different definitions (treating all nonblacks as the reference population, where nonblack is the group that is not considered black) are extremely similar to one another: the correlation coefficient is 0.995. The corresponding correlation between isolation indices is even higher, at 0.999.

5. More precisely, we shall focus on tracts in MSAs that had at least 1,000 black residents in 1990.

Interpreting the Measures

Both the dissimilarity index and the isolation index take on values from zero to one. The dissimilarity index can be interpreted as the proportion of black (or other race) people that would have to move across census tracts in order for there to be a perfectly even proportion of black (or other race) residents across the entire MSA. If a metropolitan area's dissimilarity index for blacks is 0.5, for example, it means that 50 percent of the black residents of that metropolitan area would have to move to another tract in order for there to exist a perfectly even representation of blacks across the entire MSA. If the index is 0.3, then 30 percent of the black residents would have to move for perfect representation. Generally, dissimilarity measures above 0.6 (or 60 percent having to move) are thought to represent hypersegregation. Definitionally, it is important to note that if the MSA as a whole is 10 percent black, then a component census tract's status as "integrated" (according to this measure) depends upon the studied census tract's itself correspondingly being 10 percent black.[6]

The isolation index captures the percentage of black residents in the census tract containing the average black resident, mathematically corrected for the fact that this number increases mechanically with the black share of the overall MSA population. A metropolitan-area isolation index of 0.5 indicates that the average black resident lives in a census tract in which the black share of the population exceeds the overall metropolitan average by roughly 50 percent. An index of 0.3 reveals that the average black resident lives in a census tract in which the black share of the population exceeds the overall metropolitan average by roughly 30 percent. The value of the isolation index can range from something close to zero (if each black person lives in an integrated census tract) to one (if all black metropolitan-area residents live together in completely segregated census tracts).

The two indices represent distinct although correlated dimensions of segregation. Dissimilarity captures the extent to which blacks are unevenly distributed relative to a baseline of perfect integration. For instance, if only 5 percent of the entire population of a particular MSA were black yet all black residents of the MSA lived in neighborhoods that were 20 percent black, then 75 percent of blacks would have to move to some other neighborhood (even though every black person may already live in a neighborhood with a large number of nonblacks) in order for there to be an even

6. This measure has the attractive feature that if the percentage of black residents in the city rises, there is no mechanical bias that causes the index to rise.

5 percent black distribution across all neighborhoods in the MSA. In other words, that MSA's dissimilarity index would equal 0.75—high enough for it to rank as the nation's eighth most segregated MSA in 2000 by that measure.

Isolation specifically captures the extent to which the average resident of a given race is surrounded primarily by other residents of that same race. In this example, the isolation index for blacks turns out to be 0.158, a more moderate value that would rank that MSA at 174 among 317 MSAs in 2000.

In actual practice, however, the two measures are highly correlated across cities, and the trends in the two variables match one another.[7] Cities that are highly segregated according to one measure tend to be highly segregated according to all measures. Thus the present analysis considers primarily only one of the two described measures—namely, the dissimilarity index.

FINDINGS

An analysis of racial segregation in roughly 300 metropolitan statistical areas using Census 2000 redistricting files indicates the following:

- Levels of segregation between blacks and nonblacks are currently at their lowest point since around 1920. Many metropolitan areas are still "hypersegregated," but overall, the 1990s continued a three-decade trend toward decreasing segregation throughout the United States.
- Out of 291 MSAs analyzed, all but 19 are more integrated than in 1990. The average decline in segregation was 5.5 percentage points.
- The decline in segregation comes about primarily from the integration of formerly entirely white census tracts. The number of overwhelmingly African American census tracts (80 percent or more African American) remained steady during the 1990s, but the number of African Americans living in those tracts dropped.
- The West is the most integrated region of the country, followed by the South. The Midwest and Northeast are still quite segregated.
- Segregation declined most sharply in places that were growing quickly, in places in which the percentage of blacks in the population was changing (growing or shrinking), and in places in which blacks constituted only a small portion of the population in 1990. Segregation remains extreme in the largest metropolitan areas.

7. $r^2 = 0.827$.

Decline of Segregation between Blacks and Nonblacks

Overall, in the 1990s the levels of segregation between blacks and nonblacks continued their thirty-year decline and are now at their lowest point since roughly 1920. During every decade between 1890 and 1970, segregation rose—and rose dramatically—across American cities. But starting in the 1970s, segregation began to fall. The sharpest decline in segregation occurred during the 1970s, when the average segregation level across metropolitan areas in the studied sample fell by almost 10 percentage points. Segregation also fell significantly during the 1980s and 1990s.

Figure 11-1 graphs the mean level of dissimilarity in U.S. metropolitan areas from 1890 to 2000, and figure 11-2 graphs the mean level of isolation for the same period.[8] These figures show that the 1990s decade continues a thirty-year trend of declining segregation within the United States. Black–nonblack segregation levels overall are currently at their lowest point since around 1920. During the 1990s the segregation level of blacks across all metropolitan-area census tracts shrank by 4.3 percentage points. In 1990 the average African American resident of a U.S. metropolitan area lived in a census tract that was 56 percent black, while in 2000 the average African American metropolitan resident lived in a census tract that is 51 percent black.

This is not to downplay the continuing existence of very segregated metropolitan areas. The large number of American metropolitan areas with extremely high levels of segregation remains quite striking. There exist 74 hypersegregated MSAs with measures of dissimilarity greater than 0.6 (approximately one-quarter of the MSAs). There exist also 160 partially segregated cities with segregation levels between 0.4 and 0.6 (half of the studied MSAs fit into this group). And there exist 83 "less segregated" MSAs, with segregation levels below 0.4.

Average Decline in Segregation

Segregation did decline in all but nineteen of the studied metropolitan areas, but in more than a third of the studied metropolitan areas this decline was slight (less than 5 percentage points). Table 11A-1 gives the

8. Indices before 1940 are based on ward data. Values in this figure have been corrected for the difference between ward-based and tract-based measures of segregation; see Cutler, Glaeser, and Vigdor (1999) for details. Indices before 1960 are based on cities; afterward they are based on metropolitan statistical areas (MSAs). Further details behind the figure are explained in the 1999 paper. A comprehensive data set on segregation from 1890 to today as assembled by these authors is posted at *www.nber.org* and at *www.pubpol.duke.edu/~jvigdor/segregation.*

FIGURE 11-1. Mean Dissimilarity, 1890–2000

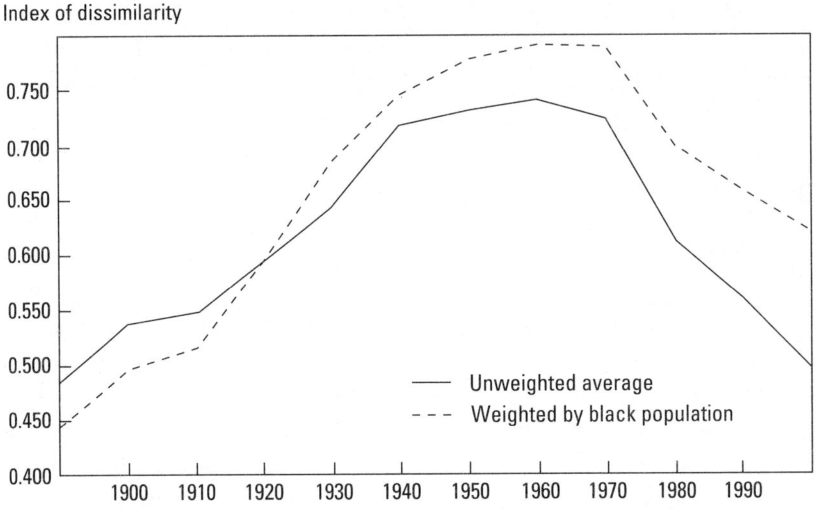

segregation changes for all metropolitan areas as of 2000. For those MSAs for which segregation indices were measured in 1990, the 1990 values and absolute changes between years are included as well. The table includes dissimilarity and isolation indexes using the restrictive single-race definition of black. The metropolitan areas in table 11A-1 have been categorized into five groups.

- First, there are those metropolitan areas with increasing segregation. This group includes only nineteen MSAs. The small size of this group suggests how ubiquitous the overall trend toward decreasing segregation actually is.
- Second, there are those metropolitan areas in which segregation has declined by less than 5 percentage points. This group represents 128 MSAs, or more than a third of the sample, suggesting that although segregation is almost universally falling, sometimes the declines are small indeed.
- The third group, which contains 100 MSAs, had dissimilarity index declines of 5 percentage points to 10 percentage points. These drops are large but not overwhelming.
- Fourth are the MSAs that have had dissimilarity drops of 10 percentage points or more—quite substantial changes. Of these forty-four metropolitan areas, twenty-six are located in the South or West, twelve are in the Midwest, and six are in the Northeast.

FIGURE 11-2. Mean Isolation, 1890–2000

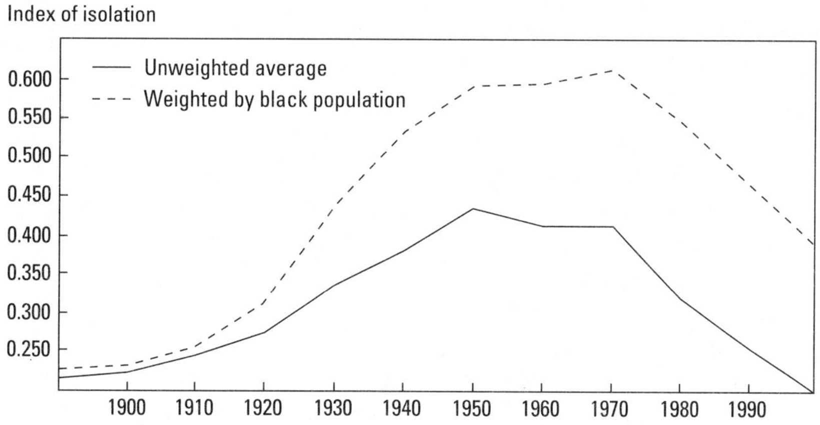

- Finally, the fifth group in table 11A-1 consists of those MSAs that were not included in the sample of metropolitan areas in 1990. Most of these twenty-six MSAs simply were not defined as of 1990; the others had black populations below 1,000 in 1990 and hence did not satisfy the selection criteria for the sample at that time.

In some cases these changes in segregation are associated with changing metropolitan-area definitions. The census redefines metropolitan areas to account for expanding cities, which may cause segregation measures to change. For instance, Ann Arbor—the metropolitan area with the greatest increase in dissimilarity between 1990 and 2000—expanded from one county to three during that period. The table indicates the metropolitan areas with land area increases of more than 50 percent between 1990 and 2000. Many of these MSAs absorbed other metropolitan areas.

Integration of Formerly All-White Census Tracts

The decline in segregation stems from the integration of formerly all-white census tracts rather than from the integration of overwhelmingly (80 percent or more) black census tracts. In 1960 some 61.8 percent of census tracts in the studied metropolitan areas were less than 1 percent black, and a striking 17.2 percent of metropolitan area census tracts had exactly zero black inhabitants. By contrast, in 2000 only 23.1 percent of census tracts were less than 1 percent black (table 11A-2). There has been a corresponding rise in the number of census tracts between 1 percent and 10 percent black. In 1960 only 18.3 percent of census tracts were moderately integrated, and roughly

6 percent of the metropolitan black population lived in these tracts. In 2000, by contrast, some 45 percent of census tracts have populations that are between 1 percent and 10 percent African American, and 13.6 percent of the metropolitan black population lives in these tracts. There has been a strong increase in the percentage of black metropolitan residents who live in a tract that is between 10 percent and 50 percent black. About half of the metropolitan black population now lives in a majority nonblack census tract. It is this shift—the disappearance of all-white tracts—that has really changed the segregation indices. It appears that the decline in segregation can be attributed primarily to African Americans' residence in areas that used to be completely white.

The decline in segregation does not in any sense represent an elimination of census tracts with very high percentages of African Americans. During the 1990s the number of census tracts with a black share of population exceeding 80 percent remained constant nationwide. No meaningful portion of the nationwide decline in segregation can be attributed to the movement of whites into highly black enclaves. The number of census tracts in which more than 80 percent of the residents are black has not decreased, but the number of African Americans residing in those census tracts has declined significantly. In 1960 such tracts were home to nearly half the metropolitan black population; in 1990 around 37 percent of blacks lived in such neighborhoods; and in 2000 less than 30 percent did so. To the extent that the remaining population in these tracts is drawn from the poorest segment of the black population, the concentration of urban poverty will continue to be a concern in the twenty-first century. A complete analysis of the economic profile of these neighborhoods must await more detailed information from the Census Bureau.

Regional Segregation Trends

There are regional segregation trends: the West and South are more integrated than the Midwest and Northeast, which remain highly segregated. To examine the importance of regional variation in segregation levels and changes, dissimilarity indices were calculated for the country as a whole and for each region in 1990 and 2000 (which means treating the country or each region as a huge city). Table 11A-3 shows the results. Over time, dissimilarity decreased in each region and in the United States as a whole. Segregation is declining in this country on a widespread basis: the overall national dissimilarity index was 0.695 in 1990 and 0.652 in 2000. Nevertheless, the 2000 index, although lower than the 1990 index, remains in the hypersegregated range.

Across regions, dissimilarity is consistently highest in the Midwest, followed by the Northeast, the South, and the West. In other words, the West is the most integrated region, followed by the South, the Northeast, and the Midwest—the latter two being still quite segregated. The regions with the lowest historical segregation levels have also experienced average or above-average declines in segregation during the past ten years. The largest regional reduction occurred in the South, with roughly equal changes in the Northeast, Midwest, and West.

These regional effects occur perhaps because the western and southern cities are newer (although a more thorough analysis of the socioeconomic determinants of segregation in 2000 must await the arrival of more detailed census figures). When blacks and whites settle new cities, they may be more likely to live near one another because the degree of racial animosity has declined over time or because the settlers of new cities tend to be of a relatively stable socioeconomic class. Especially in the West, newer cities might have a lower overall initial black population share, too low to lead to "tipping" in racially mixed neighborhoods. Whatever the reason, these regional variations existed in the past and persist today.

Segregation Decline and Economic and Demographic Change

Segregation decline seems linked to economic and demographic change: segregation has declined faster in places that were growing, in places that had either upwardly or downwardly changing black population levels, and in places that had only a small black population in 1990. But segregation has persisted at fairly high levels in the largest metropolitan areas.

Changes in segregation vary not only by region but also by several other key factors, including the following: overall population growth rate, change (either increase or decrease) in black population level, and the percentage of black residents in 1990. Also of interest is the relationship between segregation levels and the absolute size of the given metropolitan area's population.

Segregation Change and Population Growth Rate

The connection between U.S. region and reductions in segregation is partially explained by the connection between population growth and reductions in segregation. Metropolitan areas that are growing quickly have had sharper declines in segregation than metropolitan areas that are stagnant. Figure 11-3 shows that the faster-growing cities have had sharper declines in dissimilarity than the relatively stagnant cities. The fastest-growing MSAs (growth greater than 25 percent during the 1990s) had a dissimilarity decline

FIGURE 11-3. Changes in Dissimilarity, by MSA Growth Rate

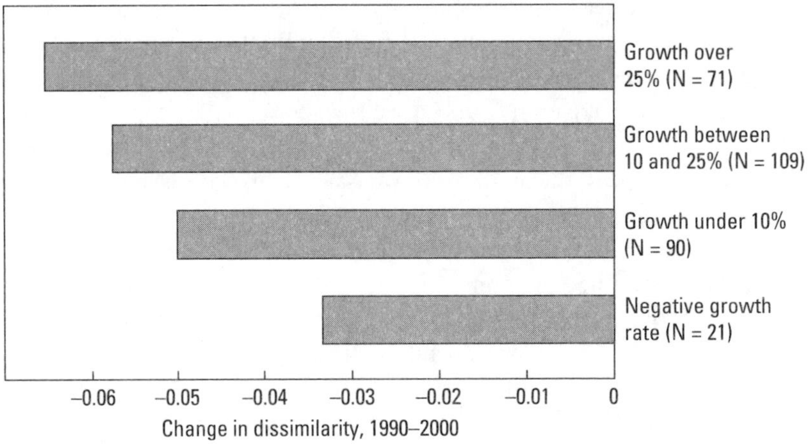

Note: N, Number of metropolitan areas in this category.

of 6.5 percentage points; modestly growing MSAs (between 10 and 25 percent) had a decline of 5.7 percentage points; in slow-growing MSAs dissimilarity declined by 5 percentage points; and in the shrinking MSAs dissimilarity fell by only 3.4 percentage points. This result may suggest that a city's population growth facilitates segregation changes. In the stagnant MSAs, neighborhood patterns most resemble those of the metropolitan area when it was first built and when the United States was much more segregated than today. Because quickly growing cities have no predetermined residential patterns, segregation patterns have adjusted to what appears to be a new norm of a more integrated America.

Segregation Change and Increase or Decrease in the Black Population

A clear and seemingly paradoxical connection exists between declining segregation levels and increasing and/or shrinking black population levels, as figure 11-4 demonstrates. Metropolitan areas with relatively steady black populations have segregation levels that are declining rather slowly (4.9 percentage points on average). But metropolitan areas with declining black populations have fairly rapidly falling levels of dissimilarity (7 percentage points on average), as do metropolitan areas with very fast-growing black populations (6.4 percentage points on average). A natural interpretation of this strange relationship is that changes in segregation occur with change in general. When blacks leave metropolitan areas, they often leave some of the

FIGURE 11-4. Changes in Dissimilarity, by Black Population Growth

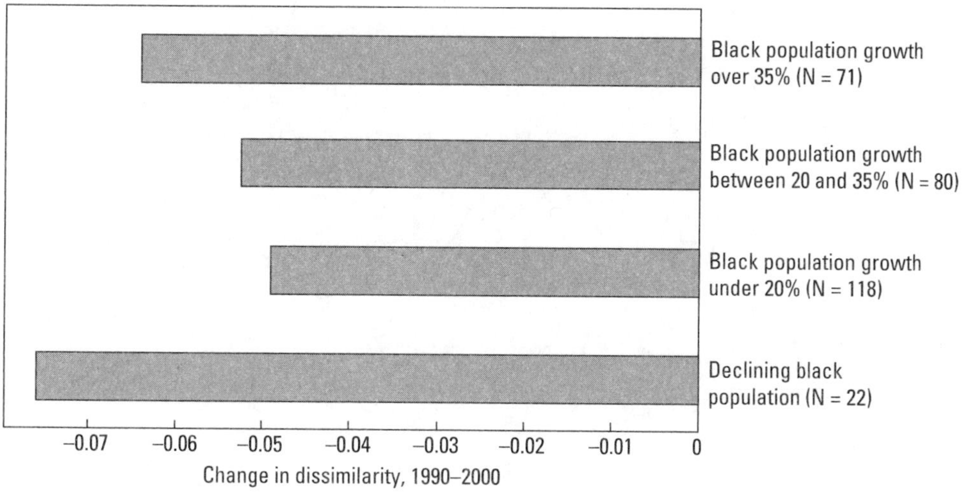

Note: N, Number of metropolitan areas in this category.

most segregated areas and end up reducing segregation. When they come to metropolitan areas, newer and more-integrated patterns of settlement occur, and segregation falls. It is particularly in those areas in which black populations are unchanged that segregation is also unchanged.

Segregation Change and Percentage of Black Metropolitan-Area Residents

Another variable that predicts changes in segregation is the initial share of the MSA's population that is African American. The MSAs with a large minority population in 1990 have seen a much lower reduction in segregation than have those with a small 1990 minority population (figure 11-5). The decline in segregation during the past decade has been largest (7.6 percentage points) for those MSAs in which black residents constituted less than 5 percent of the population in 1990; the MSAs with a 1990 population between 5 percent and 10 percent black experienced a 5.3 percentage point decline in segregation; the MSAs in which black residents constituted between 10 percent and 25 percent of the population in 1990 had only a 4.2 percentage point drop in segregation; and in MSAs that were more than 25 percent black in 1990, segregation declined the least, by 2.8 percentage points. One interpretation for this phenomenon is that the highly black

FIGURE 11-5. Changes in Dissimilarity, by Initial Percent Black

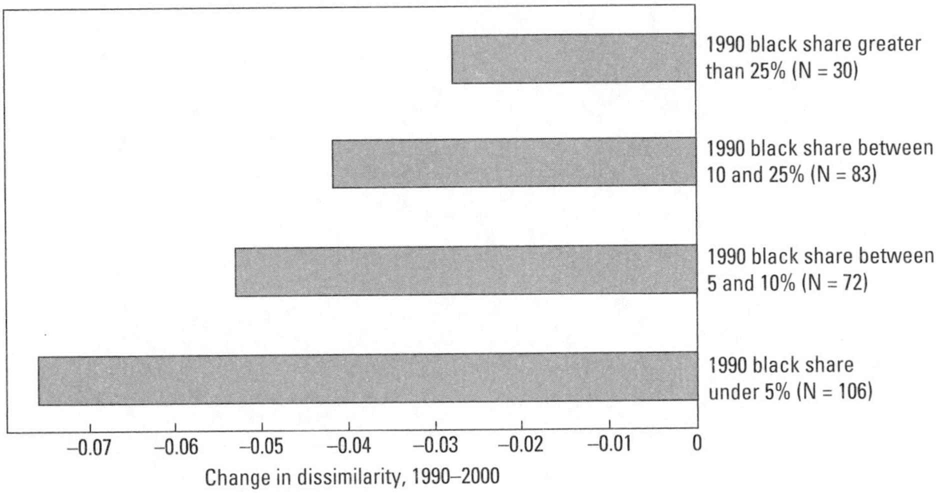

Note: N, Number of metropolitan areas in this category.

cities may be harder to integrate because the black populations are larger and existing color barriers are more extreme.

Segregation Level and Absolute Metropolitan-Area Population

Figure 11-6 shows the connection between 2000 segregation levels and an MSA's total 2000 population. Unlike the other measures, this one is not concerned with segregation changes over time but rather with the relationship between an MSA's segregation level at any one point and the MSA's overall population size. To perform the measurement, the MSAs were grouped together into four categories: most populous (more than 1,500,000 residents), highly populous (between 750,000 and 1,500,000), moderately populous (between 200,000 and 750,000), and less populous (fewer than 200,000). The result is that dissimilarity apparently increases with MSA size: the most populous areas are significantly more segregated than the unweighted national average, and the least populous areas are significantly less segregated than the unweighted national average. This relationship between segregation and city size has existed since before World War II. The greater density in larger MSAs might increase individuals' desire to be separate from members of other races. Larger metropolitan areas might also provide more opportunities for people to become sorted into homogeneous communities so as to realize shared preferences for

FIGURE 11-6. Dissimilarity, by MSA Size, 2000

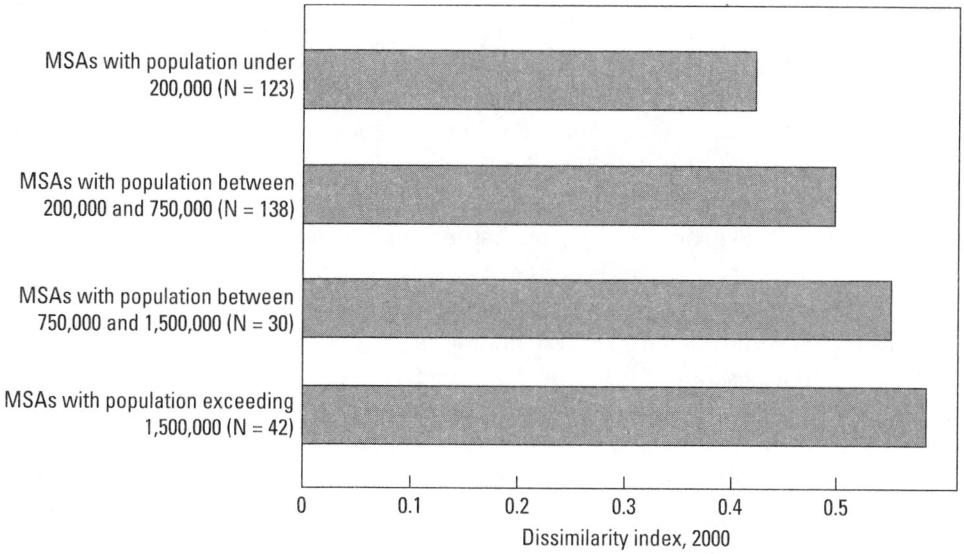

amenities or public services—preferences that may happen to vary by race. Alternatively, larger areas may simply on average be older and hence reflect the more segregated residential patterns of an earlier era.

CONCLUSION

Overall, segregation remains high in America, but there is promising news: a steady segregation decline has occurred during the past three decades. The highly segregated cities of the Midwest and the Northeast are becoming slightly less segregated. Detroit, the most segregated American city in 1990, continues to hold that dubious distinction, but dissimilarity in that city is at its lowest point since 1950, when the black population was a third of its current size. Milwaukee, the nation's second-most-segregated city, is more integrated than it has been since 1920, when the black population was a mere 2,229.[9] A similar story can be told of many of the nation's other most segregated metropolises.

Even more important, the regional shift southward and westward by the country's population is contributing strongly to recent declines in segrega-

9. Milwaukee's segregation in 1920 is measured at the ward level. If census tract data were available for Milwaukee before 1940, it would probably show that the city is more integrated now than it has ever been, according to the dissimilarity index.

tion, and the African American experience is turning out to be quite different in the Sun Belt from how it is in the Rust Belt. The newer, more rapidly growing cities of the West and the South are intrinsically less segregated than are many of the cities of the Midwest and the Northeast. And these cities of the West and the South are also becoming much less segregated over time. The nation's fastest-growing metropolitan areas, places such as Las Vegas, Phoenix, Austin, and Raleigh-Durham, feature remarkably low and declining segregation levels.

Two main policy-related lessons can be extracted from these data. First, a major change has occurred in segregation, probably as a result of the country's changing political environment. In the 1940s, discrimination by realtors and lenders was legal and was in fact effectively encouraged by federal policies on mortgage insurance underwriting. Restrictive covenants were legal, and groups of whites freely terrorized blacks who moved into white communities. By 1970 all of those conditions had changed. The contemporary decline in segregation shows the effectiveness of the civil rights revolution in this country between 1940 and 1970.

Second, some large metropolitan areas still register substantial amounts of segregation, and the past thirty years' changes seem to have affected many of those areas the least. Extreme segregation persists in this country, representing a significant challenge for America's going forward. The present study does indeed acknowledge the continuing hypersegregation of a significant number of American cities. But just as it would be wrong to deny the persistence of truly staggering levels of segregation in many cities, it would be wrong to deny the remarkable progress that has also been made. Across America, and especially in those cities that are newer and less bound by traditions of segregation, whites and blacks are now living closer to one another, reflecting rising black incomes and resolute government action against discrimination in housing (police action against mob violence by whites, the end of restrictive covenants, and the like). America must not forget its continuing obligation to its most isolated citizens, but it can also be justly proud of the changes that have occurred in segregation levels since 1970.

TABLE 11A-1. Black-Nonblack Dissimilarity and Isolation in U.S. Metropolitan Areas, 1990, 2000

Metropolitan area	*Dissimilarity 2000*	*Isolation 2000*	*Dissimilarity 1990*	*Isolation 1990*	*Change in dissimilarity*	*Change in isolation*
Group 1: Metropolitan areas with increases in dissimilarity						
Alexandria, LA	0.589	0.413	0.571	0.430	0.018	–0.018
Ann Arbor, MI[a]	0.615	0.235	0.499	0.205	0.115	0.031
Baton Rouge, LA	0.641	0.477	0.641	0.488	0.001	–0.010
Biloxi-Gulfport-Pascagoula, MS[a]	0.495	0.274	0.462	0.262	0.033	0.012
Brockton, MA[a]	0.574	0.116	0.490	0.096	0.084	0.019
Champaign-Urbana, IL	0.445	0.194	0.442	0.222	0.003	–0.028
Cumberland, MD-WV	0.512	0.114	0.474	0.029	0.038	0.085
Danville, VA	0.336	0.167	0.308	0.153	0.029	0.015
Erie, PA	0.641	0.228	0.636	0.244	0.005	–0.016
Gainesville, FL	0.414	0.247	0.387	0.220	0.027	0.028
Hickory-Morganton-Lenoir, NC	0.445	0.114	0.395	0.131	0.050	–0.017
Iowa City, IA	0.347	0.021	0.336	0.014	0.012	0.007
Jacksonville, NC	0.239	0.092	0.206	0.077	0.033	0.016
Lowell, MA-NH	0.441	0.023	0.420	0.015	0.021	0.008
New London-Norwich, CT-RI	0.539	0.092	0.496	0.092	0.042	0.000
Pine Bluff, AR	0.586	0.428	0.577	0.420	0.008	0.008
Terre Haute, IN	0.569	0.141	0.562	0.151	0.007	–0.010
Texarkana, TX-Texarkana, AR	0.419	0.221	0.404	0.240	0.015	–0.019
Tuscaloosa, AL	0.530	0.345	0.503	0.358	0.026	–0.013
Group 2: Metropolitan areas with small decreases in dissimilarity						
Abilene, TX	0.350	0.046	0.374	0.055	–0.024	–0.009
Akron, OH	0.651	0.391	0.693	0.439	–0.042	–0.048
Albany, GA	0.596	0.424	0.623	0.466	–0.026	–0.042
Albany-Schenectady-Troy, NY	0.609	0.264	0.620	0.266	–0.010	–0.002
Allentown-Bethlehem-Easton, PA	0.499	0.059	0.534	0.051	–0.035	0.008
Altoona, PA	0.492	0.023	0.522	0.026	–0.029	–0.002
Amarillo, TX	0.569	0.239	0.613	0.340	–0.044	–0.101
Anchorage, AK	0.330	0.037	0.333	0.044	–0.003	–0.006
Anniston, AL	0.486	0.301	0.501	0.306	–0.015	–0.005
Asheville, NC[a]	0.578	0.244	0.626	0.337	–0.047	–0.093
Athens, GA	0.432	0.225	0.456	0.219	–0.024	0.006
Augusta-Aiken, GA-SC	0.437	0.254	0.439	0.266	–0.002	–0.011
Baltimore, MD	0.666	0.529	0.709	0.593	–0.043	–0.064
Beaumont-Port Arthur, TX	0.641	0.446	0.687	0.516	–0.047	–0.071
Benton Harbor, MI	0.734	0.545	0.741	0.571	–0.008	–0.026
Binghamton, NY	0.494	0.050	0.516	0.036	–0.022	0.015
Birmingham, AL	0.696	0.563	0.719	0.583	–0.023	–0.020
Bloomington, IN	0.331	0.018	0.355	0.019	–0.024	–0.001
Bloomington-Normal, IL	0.340	0.043	0.386	0.037	–0.046	0.006
Boston, MA-NH	0.629	0.344	0.677	0.445	–0.048	–0.102
Bremerton, WA	0.414	0.036	0.457	0.045	–0.044	–0.009
Bridgeport, CT	0.636	0.256	0.675	0.311	–0.040	–0.056
Bryan-College Station, TX	0.408	0.132	0.438	0.175	–0.029	–0.042
Charleston-North Charleston, SC	0.434	0.238	0.480	0.294	–0.046	–0.056
Charleston, WV	0.558	0.172	0.596	0.193	–0.037	–0.021
Charlotte-Gastonia-Rock Hill, NC-SC	0.503	0.299	0.537	0.372	–0.033	–0.073

(*continued*)

TABLE 11A-1. Black-Nonblack Dissimilarity and Isolation in U.S. Metropolitan Areas, 1990, 2000 (*continued*)

Metropolitan area	*Dissimilarity 2000*	*Isolation 2000*	*Dissimilarity 1990*	*Isolation 1990*	*Change in dissimilarity*	*Change in isolation*
Charlottesville, VA	0.341	0.131	0.370	0.144	–0.028	–0.013
Chattanooga, TN-GA	0.683	0.461	0.724	0.511	–0.041	–0.050
Cheyenne, WY	0.295	0.018	0.345	0.030	–0.050	–0.012
Cincinnati, OH-KY-IN[a]	0.742	0.503	0.761	0.549	–0.019	–0.046
Clarksville-Hopkinsville, TN-KY	0.348	0.137	0.374	0.155	–0.026	–0.018
Colorado Springs, CO	0.378	0.057	0.425	0.074	–0.047	–0.017
Columbia, SC	0.498	0.336	0.531	0.375	–0.032	–0.039
Columbus, GA-AL	0.560	0.377	0.574	0.415	–0.014	–0.038
Danbury, CT	0.464	0.056	0.505	0.065	–0.041	–0.009
Dayton-Springfield, OH	0.710	0.515	0.751	0.561	–0.042	–0.045
Decatur, AL	0.567	0.272	0.616	0.356	–0.049	–0.085
Decatur, IL	0.536	0.249	0.584	0.285	–0.048	–0.036
Denver, CO	0.599	0.198	0.640	0.315	–0.041	–0.117
Detroit, MI	0.840	0.727	0.873	0.763	–0.033	–0.035
Dothan, AL	0.405	0.230	0.411	0.268	–0.006	–0.038
El Paso, TX	0.430	0.063	0.475	0.081	–0.045	–0.019
Elmira, NY	0.516	0.156	0.565	0.233	–0.049	–0.077
Evansville-Henderson, IN-KY	0.561	0.201	0.606	0.253	–0.045	–0.052
Fayetteville, NC	0.299	0.133	0.304	0.173	–0.006	–0.040
Flint, MI	0.765	0.616	0.809	0.664	–0.044	–0.049
Florence, AL	0.428	0.192	0.442	0.235	–0.014	–0.043
Florence, SC	0.416	0.269	0.464	0.332	–0.048	–0.063
Fort Wayne, IN[a]	0.710	0.400	0.742	0.441	–0.033	–0.041
Fresno, CA	0.425	0.088	0.469	0.181	–0.044	–0.093
Gadsden, AL	0.686	0.407	0.701	0.432	–0.014	–0.025
Greenville-Spartanburg-Anderson, SC[a]	0.436	0.224	0.485	0.282	–0.049	–0.058
Honolulu, HI	0.514	0.080	0.555	0.097	–0.040	–0.017
Houma, LA	0.453	0.177	0.478	0.191	–0.025	–0.014
Houston, TX	0.570	0.352	0.617	0.436	–0.048	–0.084
Huntsville, AL[a]	0.537	0.318	0.575	0.324	–0.038	–0.006
Indianapolis, IN	0.699	0.449	0.744	0.545	–0.044	–0.096
Jackson, MI	0.657	0.285	0.698	0.349	–0.041	–0.064
Jackson, TN[a]	0.554	0.362	0.589	0.421	–0.035	–0.059
Jamestown, NY	0.532	0.051	0.552	0.050	–0.019	0.000
Jersey City, NJ	0.586	0.353	0.631	0.437	–0.044	–0.085
Kalamazoo-Battle Creek, MI[a]	0.526	0.247	0.528	0.292	–0.002	–0.044
Kankakee, IL	0.687	0.476	0.717	0.557	–0.030	–0.082
Kansas City, MO-KS	0.683	0.466	0.721	0.548	–0.038	–0.082
Killeen-Temple, TX	0.348	0.105	0.378	0.122	–0.030	–0.018
Knoxville, TN	0.580	0.315	0.617	0.389	–0.037	–0.073
Lafayette, LA[a]	0.488	0.277	0.496	0.286	–0.009	–0.009
Lake Charles, LA	0.613	0.436	0.642	0.481	–0.029	–0.045
Lansing-East Lansing, MI	0.535	0.166	0.553	0.172	–0.018	–0.006
Lawrence, KS	0.261	0.017	0.266	0.020	–0.005	–0.003
Lawton, OK	0.295	0.092	0.329	0.139	–0.033	–0.047
Lima, OH	0.645	0.233	0.658	0.318	–0.013	–0.085
Little Rock-North Little Rock, AR	0.597	0.392	0.605	0.404	–0.008	–0.012
Longview-Marshall, TX	0.418	0.197	0.464	0.242	–0.047	–0.045
Lynchburg, VA[a]	0.379	0.186	0.403	0.233	–0.024	–0.048
Macon, GA	0.511	0.320	0.525	0.358	–0.014	–0.038

(*continued*)

TABLE 11A-1. Black-Nonblack Dissimilarity and Isolation in U.S. Metropolitan Areas, 1990, 2000 (*continued*)

Metropolitan area	*Dissimilarity 2000*	*Isolation 2000*	*Dissimilarity 1990*	*Isolation 1990*	*Change in dissimilarity*	*Change in isolation*
Madison, WI	0.442	0.068	0.489	0.070	–0.047	–0.002
Manchester, NH	0.399	0.014	0.447	0.010	–0.048	0.004
Mansfield, OH[a]	0.670	0.300	0.688	0.305	–0.018	–0.005
Melbourne-Titusville-Palm Bay, FL	0.476	0.171	0.523	0.227	–0.047	–0.057
Memphis, TN-AR-MS	0.660	0.520	0.691	0.573	–0.032	–0.052
Miami, FL	0.688	0.480	0.703	0.517	–0.016	–0.037
Milwaukee-Waukesha, WI	0.810	0.613	0.820	0.649	–0.011	–0.036
Mobile, AL	0.611	0.473	0.658	0.533	–0.047	–0.060
Monmouth-Ocean, NJ	0.610	0.278	0.658	0.332	–0.048	–0.054
Monroe, LA	0.687	0.576	0.711	0.597	–0.024	–0.021
Nashua, NH	0.324	0.010	0.354	0.008	–0.031	0.002
New Haven-Meriden, CT	0.631	0.324	0.666	0.366	–0.035	–0.042
New Orleans, LA	0.665	0.523	0.678	0.539	–0.013	–0.016
New York, NY	0.670	0.484	0.691	0.521	–0.021	–0.037
Newark, NJ	0.735	0.561	0.780	0.622	–0.045	–0.061
Norfolk-Virginia Beach-Newport News, VA	0.449	0.305	0.492	0.361	–0.043	–0.056
Ocala, FL	0.477	0.215	0.520	0.315	–0.043	–0.100
Odessa-Midland, TX[a]	0.412	0.134	0.421	0.142	–0.009	–0.008
Pensacola, FL	0.498	0.246	0.530	0.293	–0.033	–0.046
Peoria-Pekin, IL	0.698	0.333	0.701	0.338	–0.002	–0.006
Pittsburgh, PA	0.682	0.428	0.713	0.487	–0.032	–0.059
Richmond-Petersburg, VA	0.553	0.386	0.589	0.428	–0.036	–0.042
Riverside-San Bernardino, CA	0.370	0.065	0.390	0.080	–0.020	–0.015
Rochester, NY	0.646	0.363	0.663	0.392	–0.016	–0.029
Sacramento, CA	0.470	0.100	0.510	0.130	–0.040	–0.031
St. Joseph, MO[a]	0.430	0.051	0.440	0.062	–0.010	–0.012
St. Louis, MO-IL	0.731	0.567	0.770	0.626	–0.039	–0.059
San Francisco, CA	0.544	0.185	0.577	0.264	–0.033	–0.079
Santa Barbara-Santa Maria-Lompoc, CA	0.350	0.042	0.380	0.041	–0.030	0.001
Sharon, PA	0.660	0.297	0.667	0.298	–0.007	–0.001
Sherman-Denison, TX	0.447	0.082	0.495	0.137	–0.048	–0.054
Shreveport-Bossier City, LA	0.556	0.399	0.605	0.454	–0.049	–0.055
State College, PA	0.491	0.063	0.539	0.058	–0.048	0.005
Steubenville-Weirton, OH-WV	0.604	0.174	0.631	0.191	–0.027	–0.017
Syracuse, NY	0.689	0.358	0.732	0.410	–0.043	–0.052
Tacoma, WA	0.420	0.074	0.454	0.098	–0.035	–0.023
Toledo, OH	0.690	0.462	0.736	0.528	–0.046	–0.066
Tucson, AZ	0.322	0.023	0.368	0.036	–0.046	–0.014
Tyler, TX	0.455	0.251	0.496	0.334	–0.041	–0.083
Utica-Rome, NY	0.634	0.174	0.668	0.269	–0.034	–0.096
Vallejo-Fairfield-Napa, CA	0.419	0.112	0.437	0.129	–0.018	–0.017
Ventura County, CA	0.342	0.017	0.391	0.025	–0.049	–0.008
Victoria, TX	0.281	0.031	0.329	0.056	–0.048	–0.025
Vineland-Millville-Bridgeton, NJ	0.336	0.180	0.359	0.185	–0.024	–0.006
Waco, TX	0.451	0.220	0.496	0.309	–0.045	–0.089
Washington, DC-MD-VA-WV[a]	0.595	0.438	0.641	0.499	–0.046	–0.060
Wheeling, WV-OH	0.558	0.112	0.573	0.104	–0.015	0.007
Wilmington-Newark, DE-MD	0.511	0.308	0.545	0.347	–0.033	–0.039

(*continued*)

TABLE 11A-1. Black-Nonblack Dissimilarity and Isolation in U.S. Metropolitan Areas, 1990, 2000 (*continued*)

Metropolitan area	Dissimilarity 2000	Isolation 2000	Dissimilarity 1990	Isolation 1990	Change in dissimilarity	Change in isolation
Worcester, MA-CT	0.504	0.052	0.525	0.059	–0.020	–0.007
York, PA	0.678	0.194	0.710	0.233	–0.031	–0.039
Youngstown-Warren, OH[a]	0.720	0.439	0.749	0.484	–0.029	–0.044
Yuma, AZ[a]	0.334	0.021	0.350	0.034	–0.016	–0.013
Group 3: Metropolitan areas with 5–10 percent decreases in dissimilarity						
Albuquerque, NM	0.268	0.015	0.336	0.031	–0.068	–0.016
Atlanta, GA	0.615	0.461	0.673	0.532	–0.058	–0.071
Atlantic-Cape May, NJ	0.581	0.350	0.632	0.442	–0.051	–0.092
Austin-San Marcos, TX[a]	0.422	0.133	0.507	0.242	–0.085	–0.109
Bakersfield, CA	0.426	0.079	0.505	0.164	–0.079	–0.084
Bergen-Passaic, NJ	0.641	0.298	0.713	0.376	–0.072	–0.078
Buffalo-Niagara Falls, NY	0.756	0.549	0.807	0.624	–0.051	–0.076
Burlington, VT	0.313	0.007	0.386	0.013	–0.073	–0.006
Canton-Massillon, OH	0.580	0.231	0.636	0.285	–0.056	–0.054
Chicago, IL[a]	0.778	0.660	0.836	0.752	–0.058	–0.092
Cleveland-Lorain-Elyria, OH[a]	0.766	0.640	0.848	0.753	–0.082	–0.113
Columbia, MO	0.380	0.100	0.434	0.130	–0.055	–0.029
Columbus, OH	0.617	0.379	0.672	0.449	–0.056	–0.070
Dallas, TX	0.536	0.315	0.592	0.418	–0.056	–0.103
Davenport-Moline-Rock Island, IA-IL	0.521	0.172	0.585	0.225	–0.064	–0.053
Duluth-Superior, MN-WI	0.504	0.022	0.584	0.023	–0.080	–0.001
Dutchess County, NY	0.524	0.211	0.574	0.258	–0.051	–0.047
Elkhart-Goshen, IN	0.541	0.148	0.609	0.185	–0.068	–0.037
Eugene-Springfield, OR	0.297	0.004	0.395	0.008	–0.099	–0.003
Fitchburg-Leominster, MA	0.307	0.015	0.373	0.015	–0.067	0.000
Fort Smith, AR-OK	0.521	0.097	0.592	0.143	–0.071	–0.046
Fort Walton Beach, FL	0.285	0.051	0.382	0.091	–0.097	–0.040
Fort Worth-Arlington, TX	0.546	0.266	0.599	0.380	–0.054	–0.113
Galveston-Texas City, TX	0.533	0.282	0.597	0.364	–0.063	–0.082
Gary, IN	0.809	0.677	0.869	0.737	–0.060	–0.060
Glens Falls, NY	0.681	0.159	0.778	0.221	–0.097	–0.063
Grand Rapids-Muskegon-Holland, MI[a]	0.665	0.349	0.726	0.428	–0.061	–0.078
Greensboro–Winston-Salem–High Point, NC	0.545	0.344	0.611	0.446	–0.066	–0.103
Hagerstown, MD	0.612	0.387	0.677	0.399	–0.064	–0.012
Harrisburg-Lebanon-Carlisle, PA	0.700	0.350	0.759	0.416	–0.059	–0.066
Huntington-Ashland, WV-KY-OH	0.606	0.133	0.702	0.162	–0.096	–0.028
Jackson, MS	0.610	0.453	0.676	0.541	–0.067	–0.087
Jacksonville, FL	0.530	0.379	0.583	0.448	–0.053	–0.070
Janesville-Beloit, WI	0.598	0.159	0.693	0.210	–0.095	–0.051
Johnson City-Kingsport-Bristol, TN-VA	0.490	0.067	0.568	0.080	–0.077	–0.013
Johnstown, PA	0.686	0.135	0.747	0.158	–0.061	–0.022
Lafayette, IN[a]	0.330	0.014	0.390	0.019	–0.060	–0.005
Lakeland-Winter Haven, FL	0.501	0.269	0.568	0.333	–0.067	–0.064
Lancaster, PA	0.577	0.092	0.656	0.152	–0.080	–0.060
Las Cruces, NM	0.283	0.012	0.375	0.035	–0.092	–0.023
Lexington, KY	0.474	0.194	0.539	0.290	–0.065	–0.096
Lincoln, NE	0.372	0.029	0.444	0.053	–0.071	–0.024

(*continued*)

TABLE 11A-1. Black-Nonblack Dissimilarity and Isolation in U.S. Metropolitan Areas, 1990, 2000 (*continued*)

Metropolitan area	*Dissimilarity 2000*	*Isolation 2000*	*Dissimilarity 1990*	*Isolation 1990*	*Change in dissimilarity*	*Change in isolation*
Los Angeles-Long Beach, CA	0.570	0.270	0.641	0.365	–0.071	–0.095
Louisville, KY-IN	0.640	0.458	0.694	0.520	–0.054	–0.062
Lubbock, TX	0.453	0.244	0.544	0.314	–0.091	–0.071
Merced, CA	0.289	0.020	0.341	0.030	–0.052	–0.011
Middlesex-Somerset-Hunterdon, NJ	0.442	0.121	0.523	0.164	–0.081	–0.043
Minneapolis-St. Paul, MN-WI	0.561	0.179	0.612	0.226	–0.051	–0.047
Montgomery, AL	0.546	0.388	0.597	0.434	–0.050	–0.046
Muncie, IN	0.540	0.327	0.627	0.425	–0.087	–0.098
Naples, FL	0.548	0.150	0.599	0.305	–0.052	–0.155
Nashville, TN	0.554	0.352	0.604	0.433	–0.051	–0.082
Nassau-Suffolk, NY	0.691	0.353	0.743	0.431	–0.052	–0.078
Newburgh, NY-PA[a]	0.464	0.127	0.516	0.186	–0.052	–0.060
Oakland, CA	0.535	0.246	0.616	0.373	–0.081	–0.127
Oklahoma City, OK	0.526	0.294	0.595	0.366	–0.069	–0.071
Olympia, WA	0.355	0.018	0.435	0.023	–0.080	–0.005
Omaha, NE-IA	0.647	0.367	0.706	0.423	–0.058	–0.056
Orange County, CA	0.262	0.009	0.345	0.021	–0.083	–0.012
Orlando, FL	0.515	0.278	0.595	0.397	–0.080	–0.120
Owensboro, KY	0.494	0.091	0.580	0.125	–0.086	–0.034
Panama City, FL	0.476	0.210	0.547	0.286	–0.071	–0.076
Parkersburg-Marietta, WV-OH	0.364	0.010	0.427	0.014	–0.063	–0.005
Philadelphia, PA-NJ	0.687	0.528	0.751	0.608	–0.064	–0.080
Portland, ME	0.428	0.021	0.485	0.010	–0.057	0.011
Pueblo, CO	0.322	0.028	0.375	0.023	–0.053	0.005
Racine, WI	0.522	0.211	0.618	0.315	–0.096	–0.104
Raleigh-Durham-Chapel Hill, NC[a]	0.423	0.240	0.482	0.327	–0.059	–0.088
Reading, PA	0.534	0.083	0.610	0.117	–0.075	–0.034
Redding, CA	0.245	0.003	0.334	0.007	–0.089	–0.004
Reno, NV	0.277	0.012	0.370	0.025	–0.093	–0.013
Roanoke, VA	0.635	0.439	0.690	0.481	–0.055	–0.042
Saginaw-Bay City-Midland, MI	0.729	0.515	0.807	0.586	–0.079	–0.071
Salinas, CA	0.509	0.094	0.595	0.154	–0.086	–0.060
San Antonio, TX	0.462	0.139	0.512	0.203	–0.051	–0.064
San Diego, CA	0.438	0.095	0.503	0.141	–0.066	–0.046
San Jose, CA	0.251	0.012	0.322	0.021	–0.072	–0.010
Santa Rosa, CA	0.292	0.008	0.373	0.013	–0.080	–0.005
Savannah, GA	0.545	0.410	0.614	0.492	–0.069	–0.082
Scranton–Wilkes-Barre–Hazleton, PA	0.577	0.060	0.627	0.078	–0.050	–0.018
Seattle-Bellevue-Everett, WA	0.479	0.097	0.558	0.188	–0.079	–0.091
South Bend, IN	0.576	0.273	0.646	0.325	–0.070	–0.053
Spokane, WA	0.362	0.018	0.457	0.031	–0.095	–0.013
Springfield, IL	0.576	0.302	0.647	0.351	–0.071	–0.049
Springfield, MA	0.587	0.221	0.658	0.313	–0.072	–0.092
Stamford-Norwalk, CT[a]	0.578	0.187	0.635	0.264	–0.057	–0.078
Stockton-Lodi, CA	0.407	0.063	0.498	0.105	–0.092	–0.042
Tallahassee, FL	0.433	0.259	0.520	0.332	–0.087	–0.073
Tampa-St. Petersburg-Clearwater, FL	0.609	0.348	0.687	0.432	–0.078	–0.084
Topeka, KS	0.451	0.114	0.536	0.154	–0.085	–0.041

(*continued*)

TABLE 11A-1. Black-Nonblack Dissimilarity and Isolation in U.S. Metropolitan Areas, 1990, 2000 (*continued*)

Metropolitan area	Dissimilarity 2000	Isolation 2000	Dissimilarity 1990	Isolation 1990	Change in dissimilarity	Change in isolation
Trenton, NJ	0.596	0.394	0.660	0.464	–0.064	–0.069
Tulsa, OK	0.563	0.368	0.630	0.452	–0.067	–0.084
Visalia-Tulare-Porterville, CA	0.385	0.019	0.479	0.035	–0.094	–0.015
Waterbury, CT	0.539	0.158	0.609	0.229	–0.070	–0.071
Waterloo-Cedar Falls, IA	0.659	0.325	0.716	0.357	–0.056	–0.032
Wichita, KS	0.558	0.313	0.629	0.412	–0.071	–0.099
Wichita Falls, TX[a]	0.508	0.194	0.593	0.300	–0.085	–0.106
Williamsport, PA	0.614	0.123	0.685	0.106	–0.071	0.017
Yakima, WA	0.366	0.011	0.452	0.030	–0.086	–0.019
Yuba City, CA	0.301	0.019	0.397	0.040	–0.096	–0.021
Group 4: Metropolitan areas with greater than 10 percent decreases in dissimilarity						
Boise City, ID	0.237	0.002	0.357	0.006	–0.119	–0.004
Boulder-Longmont, CO	0.225	0.003	0.368	0.007	–0.142	–0.004
Brazoria, TX	0.355	0.072	0.464	0.124	–0.109	–0.052
Cedar Rapids, IA	0.414	0.046	0.527	0.062	–0.114	–0.016
Chico-Paradise, CA	0.357	0.014	0.466	0.042	–0.109	–0.028
Corpus Christi, TX	0.346	0.071	0.448	0.131	–0.102	–0.060
Daytona Beach, FL	0.538	0.307	0.691	0.452	–0.153	–0.145
Des Moines, IA	0.552	0.165	0.662	0.259	–0.110	–0.094
Enid, OK	0.283	0.015	0.396	0.040	–0.114	–0.025
Fayetteville-Springdale-Rogers, AR[a]	0.513	0.033	0.619	0.036	–0.106	–0.004
Fort Collins-Loveland, CO	0.292	0.004	0.489	0.009	–0.197	–0.005
Fort Lauderdale, FL	0.573	0.376	0.678	0.476	–0.106	–0.100
Fort Myers-Cape Coral, FL	0.656	0.384	0.766	0.531	–0.109	–0.148
Fort Pierce-Port St. Lucie, FL	0.569	0.378	0.712	0.540	–0.143	–0.162
Grand Forks, ND-MN[a]	0.411	0.029	0.558	0.054	–0.147	–0.025
Great Falls, MT	0.363	0.018	0.595	0.040	–0.233	–0.022
Green Bay, WI	0.423	0.086	0.539	0.152	–0.116	–0.066
Hamilton-Middletown, OH	0.474	0.186	0.601	0.293	–0.127	–0.106
Hartford, CT[a]	0.591	0.318	0.706	0.461	–0.115	–0.143
Joplin, MO	0.397	0.022	0.558	0.069	–0.161	–0.046
Kenosha, WI	0.466	0.088	0.598	0.128	–0.132	–0.040
Kokomo, IN	0.478	0.181	0.607	0.283	–0.128	–0.102
Las Vegas, NV-AZ[a]	0.362	0.119	0.468	0.271	–0.106	–0.152
Lawrence, MA-NH	0.448	0.022	0.558	0.046	–0.110	–0.024
McAllen-Edinburg-Mission, TX	0.393	0.023	0.500	0.005	–0.108	0.017
Modesto, CA	0.283	0.013	0.384	0.017	–0.101	–0.004
New Bedford, MA	0.425	0.033	0.528	0.052	–0.103	–0.019
Phoenix-Mesa, AZ[a]	0.343	0.051	0.444	0.109	–0.101	–0.058
Pittsfield, MA	0.451	0.041	0.555	0.062	–0.104	–0.021
Portland-Vancouver, OR-WA	0.493	0.131	0.673	0.275	–0.180	–0.144
Portsmouth-Rochester, NH-ME	0.330	0.007	0.520	0.041	–0.190	–0.035
Providence-Fall River-Warwick, RI-MA[a]	0.549	0.101	0.660	0.217	–0.112	–0.116
Rapid City, SD	0.279	0.005	0.407	0.031	–0.128	–0.026
Richland-Kennewick-Pasco, WA	0.313	0.010	0.424	0.029	–0.111	–0.018
Rockford, IL[a]	0.608	0.287	0.717	0.389	–0.109	–0.101
Salem, OR	0.337	0.015	0.443	0.034	–0.106	–0.019
Salt Lake City-Ogden, UT	0.343	0.014	0.490	0.031	–0.146	–0.018
San Angelo, TX	0.251	0.041	0.364	0.116	–0.113	–0.075

(*continued*)

TABLE 11A-1. Black-Nonblack Dissimilarity and Isolation in U.S. Metropolitan Areas, 1990, 2000 (*continued*)

Metropolitan area	*Dissimilarity 2000*	*Isolation 2000*	*Dissimilarity 1990*	*Isolation 1990*	*Change in dissimilarity*	*Change in isolation*
Santa Cruz-Watsonville, CA	0.221	0.003	0.428	0.013	–0.207	–0.010
Sarasota-Bradenton, FL[a]	0.641	0.284	0.742	0.459	–0.101	–0.175
Sioux City, IA-NE	0.434	0.025	0.546	0.044	–0.113	–0.019
Springfield, MO	0.470	0.054	0.581	0.077	–0.111	–0.024
West Palm Beach-Boca Raton, FL	0.609	0.380	0.734	0.529	–0.125	–0.149
Wilmington, NC[a]	0.461	0.256	0.582	0.416	–0.121	–0.160
Group 5: Metropolitan areas entering the sample in 2000						
Appleton-Oshkosh-Neenah, WI	0.477	0.042				
Auburn-Opelika, AL	0.376	0.202				
Barnstable-Yarmouth, MA	0.393	0.019				
Bellingham, WA	0.211	0.002				
Brownsville-Harlingen-San Benito, TX	0.283	0.002				
Dover, DE	0.318	0.103				
Fargo-Moorhead, ND-MN	0.358	0.007				
Flagstaff, AZ-UT	0.406	0.016				
Goldsboro, NC	0.399	0.218				
Greeley, CO	0.287	0.005				
Greenville, NC	0.319	0.162				
Hattiesburg, MS	0.528	0.343				
Jonesboro, AR	0.408	0.095				
La Crosse, WI-MN	0.391	0.012				
Myrtle Beach, SC	0.443	0.176				
Provo-Orem, UT	0.266	0.002				
Punta Gorda, FL	0.390	0.036				
Rochester, MN	0.460	0.036				
Rocky Mount, NC	0.399	0.219				
St. Cloud, MN	0.413	0.010				
San Luis Obispo-Atascadero-Paso Robles, CA	0.495	0.082				
Sheboygan, WI	0.546	0.084				
Sioux Falls, SD	0.384	0.013				
Sumter, SC	0.393	0.217				
Wausau, WI	0.389	0.005				
Yolo, CA	0.211	0.006				

Source: See text.

a. Denotes metropolitan areas where land area increased more than 50 percent between 1990 and 2000.

TABLE 11A-2. Distribution of Census Tracts by Percentage of Black Residents, 1990, 2000

Census tracts with	*Distribution of tracts*			*Distribution of the black population*		
Black share (percent)	*1960*	*1990*	*2000*	*1960*	*1990*	*2000*
Less than 1	61.8	31.2	23.1	0.9	0.8	0.9
1–5	12.8	27.6	32.4	2.7	5.9	6.4
5–10	5.5	11.1	12.5	3.4	6.4	7.2
10–50	11.1	18.2	20.8	22.8	30.4	35.6
50–80	3.9	4.9	5.1	23.1	19.2	20.4
Greater than 80	5.0	7.0	6.0	47.2	37.3	29.5
Number of tracts	22,706	43,847	50,847			
Black population				11,066,935	25,062,259	29,882,912

Source: See text.

TABLE 11A-3. Regional Variation in Segregation

	Dissimilarity		
Nation and region	*2000*	*1990*	*Change*
United States	0.652	0.695	–0.043
Northeast region	0.696	0.734	–0.038
Midwest region	0.745	0.779	–0.034
South region	0.591	0.636	–0.045
West region	0.547	0.581	–0.034

Source: See text.
Note: Sample consists of census tracts in sample MSAs.

REFERENCES

Cutler, D. M., E. L. Glaeser, and J. L. Vigdor. 1999. "The Rise and Decline of the American Ghetto." *Journal of Political Economy* 107 (3): 455–506.

Massey, Douglas, and Nancy Denton. 1993. *American Apartheid.* Harvard University Press.

U.S. Bureau of the Census. 1992. Census of Population and Housing, 1990. Summary of Tape File 3A. Department of Commerce.

———. 2001. Census of Population and Housing, 2000: Public Law 94-171 Data Files. Department of Commerce.

12

Ethnic Diversity Grows, Neighborhood Integration Lags

JOHN R. LOGAN

Census 2000 was awaited with much anticipation for the news it would bring regarding trends in residential segregation. Would black-white segregation continue the slow decline that had begun by 1970, or had there been a breakthrough in civil rights and in white attitudes that would cause the drop to accelerate in the 1990s? How would continued rapid growth of the Hispanic and Asian populations affect their residential patterns?

Based on a series of studies using data largely from the 1970–80 decade, Douglas Massey and Nancy Denton concluded that African Americans faced a near-apartheid situation of persistent high segregation that was barely responsive to improvements in black socioeconomic standing.[1] Unlike Hispanic and Asian minorities, who experienced substantially lower levels of residential separation from whites than did blacks, the country's African Americans remained highly segregated from whites even in regions in which blacks registered relatively high levels of income and education. Reductions in black-white segregation were found primarily in metropolitan regions with small black populations.[2]

Studying the subsequent decade (1980–90), Reynolds Farley and William H. Frey found evidence for more widespread declines in segregation of African Americans, although the larger declines were still found in metro-

The author thanks Brian Stults, Vadivel Kumari, Jacob Stowell, Deirdre Oakley, and other staff members at the Mumford Center for their participation in the project.

1. Massey and Denton (1993).
2. Gross and Massey (1991).

politan regions with few blacks.[3] Farley and Frey predicted that future black population gains in areas of the West and New South—where segregation is less entrenched—would ameliorate overall levels of segregation in the next ten years.

Less has been written about trends in the Hispanic and Asian experience after 1980. The very rapid growth of these two groups makes it imperative to look beyond the black-white color line in any investigation of the dynamics of segregation. Indeed, in several major metropolitan regions of the West (such as Los Angeles, Portland, and Seattle) African Americans are now the smallest of the three minorities.

The present chapter evaluates what has been learned from the initial full-count results of Census 2000 in regard to residential segregation of each of these three minority groups from whites, tracing the trends that have occurred during a full twenty-year period and drawing on census results from 1980, 1990, and 2000.[4]

METHODS

Using Census 2000 boundary definitions, the present analysis uses Census 2000, Census 1990, and Census 1980 data on 331 metropolitan areas. Most metropolises consist of one or two large central cities and a surrounding hinterland that is primarily suburban. The boundaries of metropolitan areas may have shifted (in some cases substantially) during the 1980–2000 period. Within metropolises, the census tract is the geographic unit used in the calculation of segregation measures; in Census 2000 census tracts contained an average of 4,200 residents.

Segregation is typically measured in two ways. The first is the dissimilarity index (D), which captures the degree to which two groups are evenly spread among census tracts in a given city. Evenness is defined with respect to the racial composition of the city as a whole. The dissimilarity index ranges from 0 to 100, giving the percentage of one group that would have to move to achieve an even residential pattern in which every tract replicates the group composition of the city. A value of 60 or more is considered very high. For example, a D score of 60 for black-white segregation means that 60 percent of either group must move to a different tract for the two groups to become equally distributed. Values of 40 to 50 are usually considered moderate levels of segregation, while values of 30 or less are considered low.

3. Farley and Frey (1994).
4. U.S. Bureau of the Census (1981, 1991, 2001) for Census data in this chapter.

Demographers typically interpret change either up or down in the following way:

- Change of 10 points and more in one decade equals a very significant change;
- Change of 5 to 10 points in one decade equals moderate change;
- Change of less than 5 points in one decade equals small change or no real change at all.

Change can be cumulative, and small changes in a single decade—if they are repeated for two or three decades—can constitute a significant trend.

The second widely used measure of segregation is a class of exposure index (P*) referring to the racial/ethnic composition of the tract in which the average member of a given group lives. Exposure of a group to itself is called the isolation index, and exposure of one group to other groups is called the exposure index. Both range from 0 to 100. For instance, an isolation index score of 80.2 for whites means that the average white lives in a neighborhood that is 80.2 percent white. An exposure index score of 6.7 for white-black exposure indicates that the average white lives in a neighborhood that is 6.7 percent black. Even if segregation (as measured by the dissimilarity index) remains the same over time, growth in a minority population will tend to make that minority population more isolated, through group members' continuing residence in neighborhoods in which they are becoming a larger share of the population.

FINDINGS

Several interesting findings have emerged from the analysis, including the following:

- In general, black-white segregation in metropolitan areas has declined in the past two decades, while the segregation of Hispanics and Asians from whites has remained about the same.
- In the 1990s, whites still live in primarily all-white neighborhoods, while blacks, Hispanics, and Asians live in more integrated places with higher minority representation.
- Black-white segregation (as measured by the dissimilarity index) and isolation remain high, especially in older Rust Belt metro areas, but both have dropped in medium-sized metro areas in the South.
- Hispanic-white segregation and isolation are high in metro areas with the largest Hispanic populations; in fact, Hispanic isolation has increased as the Hispanic population has grown.

- Asian-white segregation and isolation are moderate in metro areas with large Asian populations, but while Asian segregation has remained unchanged in the past two decades, isolation has increased.
- Minority segregation and isolation have increased in the suburbs during the 1990s as suburbs have become more diverse.

Black-White Segregation Decline; Hispanic-White Segregation Unchanged

In general, black-white segregation in metropolitan areas has declined in the past two decades, while the segregation of Hispanics and Asians from whites has remained about the same. Table 12-1 lists the national averages for levels of minority-white segregation for 1980, 1990, and 2000, weighted by the number of minority group members in the metropolitan region. Throughout the analysis, the categories used are non-Hispanic whites, non-Hispanic blacks, Hispanics (of all races), and Asians (including Hispanic Asians).

Black-white segregation declined by 5 points during the 1980s (very close to the 4-point drop reported at the block group level for 232 metro areas by Farley and Frey).[5] The change continued at a slower rate in the 1990s (a decline of just under 4 points). The good news is that these small changes are cumulating over time. The source of concern is that at this pace it may take forty more years for black-white segregation to come down even to the current level of Hispanic-white segregation.

The segregation of Hispanics and Asians from whites has remained almost the same during these twenty years, edging slightly upward. In 136 metropolises the segregation of Asians from whites increased during the twenty-year span, and in 189 metropolises Hispanic-white segregation increased. As a result, the disparity between them and African Americans has diminished substantially. Despite these changes, blacks remain much more segregated from whites than are Hispanics or Asians.

In the 1990s whites still live in primarily all-white neighborhoods, while blacks, Hispanics, and Asians live in more integrated places with higher minority representation. Census 2000 shows that growing ethnic diversity in the nation is accompanied by a high degree of residential separation. The average non-Hispanic white person continues to live in a neighborhood that looks very different from those neighborhoods in which the average black, Hispanic, and Asian lives. Based on national metropolitan averages, figure 12-1 illustrates typical neighborhood diversity as experienced by the different groups. Stark contrasts are readily apparent between the typical

5. Farley and Frey (1994).

TABLE 12-1. Segregation of Minorities from Whites: National Averages, 1980–2000

Index of dissimilarity	*1980*	*1990*	*2000*
Blacks from whites	73.8	68.8	65.0
Hispanics from whites	50.7	50.6	51.5
Asians from whites	41.2	42.0	42.1

Source: State University of New York, Albany, Lewis Mumford Center (*www.albany.edu/mumford/census* [June 2002]).

experience of whites versus that of each minority group. The typical white lives in a neighborhood that is 80.2 percent white, 6.7 percent black, 7.9 percent Hispanic, and 3.9 percent Asian.

The experience of minorities is very different. For instance, the typical black lives in a neighborhood that is 51.4 percent black, 33.0 percent white, 11.4 percent Hispanic, and 3.3 percent Asian. The typical Hispanic lives in

FIGURE 12-1. Diversity Experienced in Each Group's Typical Neighborhood, National Metropolitan Average, 2000

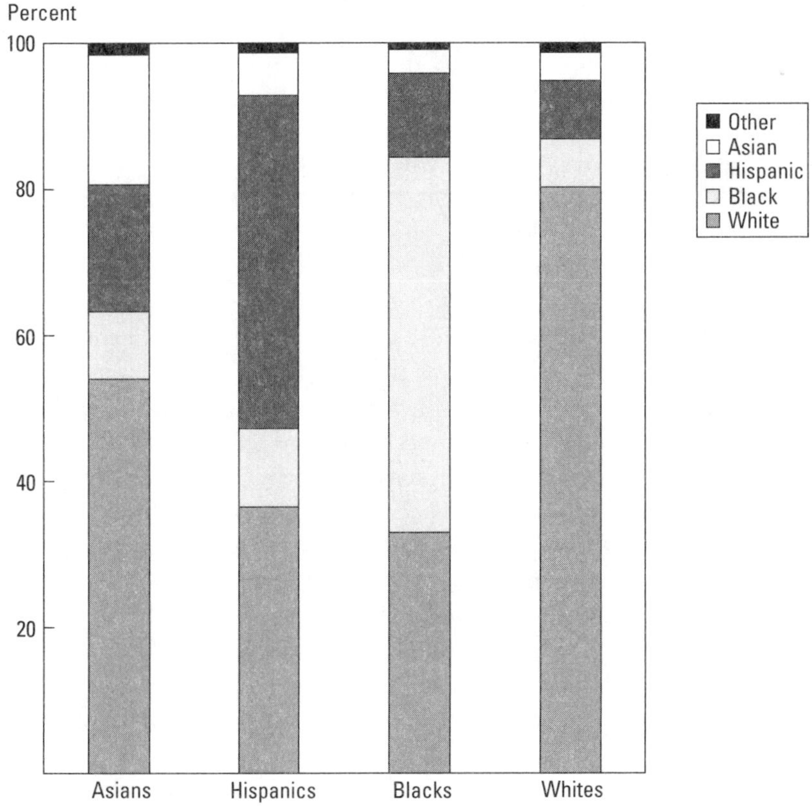

a neighborhood that is 45.5 percent Hispanic, 36.5 percent white, 10.8 percent black, and 5.9 percent Asian. The typical Asian lives in a neighborhood that is 17.9 percent Asian, 54.0 percent white, 9.2 percent black, and 17.4 percent Hispanic.

The basic message here is that whites live in neighborhoods with low minority representation while minorities live in neighborhoods with high minority representation and limited white representation. Blacks, Hispanics, and Asians live in more integrated neighborhoods than do whites.

Black-White Segregation in Rust Belt High but Dropping in the South

Black-white segregation (as measured by the dissimilarity index) and isolation remain high, especially in older Rust Belt metro areas, but both have dropped in medium-sized metro areas in the South. Black-white segregation remains very high except in the metropolitan areas with the smallest black populations. As shown in figure 12-2, over the past twenty years segregation declined by more than 12 points in metro areas with less than 5 percent black population and by nearly 10 points in areas that are 10 percent to 20 percent black. But in those areas with 20 percent or more blacks, the decline was only half that (about 6 points). The total black population of this latter set of metro areas (20 percent or more black) is nearly 15 million, about half the national total. This means that the African American population in the United States is about equally divided between regions in which moderate progress has been made since 1980 and regions in which progress is very slender.

Tables 12-2 and 12-3 list the fifty U.S. metropolitan regions with the largest black populations in 2000. Of these the ten metros with the highest levels of segregation are Detroit, Milwaukee, New York, Chicago, Newark, Cleveland, Cincinnati, Nassau-Suffolk (New York), St. Louis, and Miami. These mainly Rust Belt metro areas represent the regions of the country in which black-white segregation has been most resistant to change. Declines have occurred in these metros, but six of the ten registered a segregation decline of only 4 points or less during the past twenty years.

At the other extreme, segregation has now fallen into what social scientists consider the moderate range (under 50) in several metros appearing on this same list of the fifty U.S. metropolitan regions with the largest black populations in 2000. These include several midsized metropolitan regions in the South: Charleston, Greenville (South Carolina), Norfolk, Raleigh-Durham, and Augusta. Riverside-San Bernardino (California) also falls in

FIGURE 12-2. Black-White Segregation: Percent of Blacks in Metro Area, 1980–2000

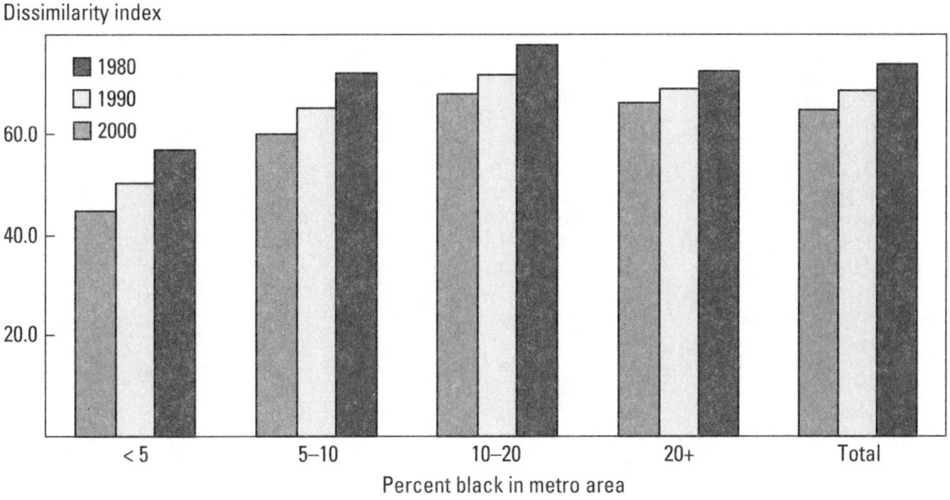

this category. In most of these, segregation has declined by 5 or 10 points, or even more, since 1980.

Despite these signs of progress in the South, there are also examples of persistent segregation in large southern cities. For instance, in New Orleans metrowide segregation dropped by only 2 points during the twenty years and remains above the national average (at 69.3). In Atlanta the news is mixed: metro level segregation has declined by 12 points, mainly because of a shift of African Americans to the suburbs, but it is still slightly above the national average (at 65.6), and segregation in the city of Atlanta has actually risen in the past twenty years (from 79.5 to 81.6) and is much higher than the national average for cities.

Another way to assess segregation is by level of isolation (the percentage minority composition of the neighborhood in which the average minority group member lives). The Detroit metropolis, highest in the dissimilarity index, is also highest in the isolation index. The average black in the Detroit metro area lives in a tract that is 79 percent black, the same as in 1980. Some other Rust Belt metro areas are also among the top ten in isolation (Chicago, Cleveland, Milwaukee, Newark). Southern metro areas tend to rank high in isolation despite their moderate segregation levels because their black populations are often very large. Hence Memphis, Birmingham, Jackson, and New Orleans are all in the top ten in isolation.

TABLE 12-2. Dissimilarity Index: Black-White Segregation, Top Fifty Metro Areas

2000 rank	Area name	2000 black population	Black suburban (percent)	2000 segregation	1990 segregation	1980 segregation
1	Detroit, MI	1,037,674	21.0	85	88	88
2	Milwaukee-Waukesha, WI	240,859	5.4	82	83	84
3	New York, NY	2,217,680	7.1	82	82	82
4	Chicago, IL	1,575,173	27.3	81	84	88
5	Newark, NJ	457,825	68.4	80	83	83
6	Cleveland-Lorain-Elyria, OH	425,722	37.6	77	83	86
7	Cincinnati, OH-KY-IN	220,034	34.1	75	77	79
8	Nassau-Suffolk, NY	238,293	100.0	74	77	78
9	St. Louis, MO-IL	486,602	53.0	74	78	83
10	Miami, FL	448,173	82.1	74	73	81
11	Birmingham, AL	278,254	35.7	73	74	76
12	Philadelphia, PA-NJ	1,040,144	32.7	72	77	78
13	Indianapolis, IN	230,843	7.4	71	75	80
14	New Orleans, LA	503,720	34.6	69	69	72
15	Kansas City, MO-KS	235,277	16.5	69	73	78
16	Memphis, TN-AR-MS	494,641	15.9	69	69	70
17	Baltimore, MD	712,002	39.1	68	72	75
18	Los Angeles-Long Beach, CA	950,765	43.9	68	73	81
19	Houston, TX	734,732	30.8	68	67	76
20	Pittsburgh, PA	200,229	53.5	67	71	73
21	Baton Rouge, LA	193,449	40.9	67	67	71
22	West Palm Beach-Boca Raton, FL	163,774	81.4	67	76	84
23	Boston, MA-NH	247,675	28.6	66	70	77
24	Atlanta, GA	1,202,260	78.7	66	69	77
25	Tampa-St. Petersburg-Clearwater, FL	147,162	39.5	65	71	79
26	Louisville, KY-IN	248,058	40.8	65	71	74
27	Mobile, AL	148,754	37.9	64	68	70
28	Columbus, OH	1,312,419	71.3	63	68	73

(continued)

What is most striking about these figures is that with very few exceptions the isolation index is above 40 in the largest metro regions: African Americans live in neighborhoods in which they are an absolute majority, or a near majority, in almost all of these very large metros.

Hispanic Isolation Increases

Hispanic-white segregation and isolation are high in metro areas with the largest Hispanic populations. In fact, Hispanic isolation has increased as the Hispanic population has grown. No net change has occurred in segregation since 1980. As shown in figure 12-3, Hispanic-white segregation remains high in the metropolitan areas with the biggest Hispanic populations. In

TABLE 12-2. Dissimilarity Index: Black-White Segregation, Top Fifty Metro Areas (*continued*)

2000 rank	Area name	2000 black population	Black suburban (percent)	2000 segregation	1990 segregation	1980 segregation
29	Washington, DC-MD-VA-WV	218,565	15.2	63	66	70
30	Oakland, CA	319,836	47.8	63	68	74
31	Fort Lauderdale, FL	349,610	86.5	62	71	84
32	Jackson, MS	201,470	35.3	62	70	71
33	Fort Worth-Arlington, TX	194,002	19.3	60	63	78
34	Dallas, TX	537,789	37.2	59	63	78
35	Greensboro–Winston-Salem–High Point, NC	255,112	24.6	59	62	67
36	Minneapolis-St. Paul, MN-WI	180,006	36.8	58	62	68
37	Shreveport-Bossier City, LA	147,387	21.9	57	62	65
38	Orlando, FL	196,127	19.0	57	61	74
39	Nashville, TN	232,243	78.2	57	61	66
40	Richmond-Petersburg, VA	303,953	53.7	57	61	65
41	Charlotte-Gastonia-Rock Hill, NC-SC	310,821	26.4	55	56	62
42	San Diego, CA	174,418	38.0	54	58	64
43	Jacksonville, FL	241,161	10.6	54	59	69
44	Columbia, SC	173,380	69.0	52	56	59
45	Charleston-North Charleston, SC	170,564	57.3	47	51	57
46	Greenville-Spartanburg-Anderson, SC	170,249	72.0	46	50	54
47	Riverside-San Bernardino, CA	263,591	78.1	46	45	55
48	Norfolk-Virginia Beach-Newport News, VA-NC	493,863	17.9	46	49	60
49	Raleigh-Durham-Chapel Hill, NC	273,724	39.3	46	49	52
50	Augusta-Aiken, GA-SC	165,512	35.4	46	46	49

Source: See table 12-1.

areas with a smaller Hispanic presence, segregation from whites is lower but rising.

As is the case for blacks, the metro areas with the largest Hispanic populations are also the most highly segregated. Tables 12-4 and 12-5 list the fifty metropolitan regions with the most Hispanic residents. Of these the most segregated are New York, Newark, Los Angeles, Chicago, Philadelphia, Salinas (California), Boston, Bergen-Passaic, Ventura, and California's Orange County. Since 1980 Hispanic segregation increased in six of these ten (and in twenty-eight of the fifty).

Laredo has the lowest level of segregation but is an outlier in another way because its population is predominantly Hispanic (nearly 95 percent).

TABLE 12-3. Isolation Index: Percentage of Blacks in the Neighborhood of the Average Black Resident, Top Fifty Metro Areas

2000 rank	Area name	2000 black (percent)	1990 black (percent)	1980 black (percent)	2000 value	1990 value	1980 value
1	Detroit, MI	23.4	22.0	20.2	79	81	79
2	Memphis, TN-AR-MS	43.6	40.6	39.8	73	74	74
3	Chicago, IL	19.0	19.0	19.8	73	78	83
4	Birmingham, AL	30.2	28.7	28.6	72	73	74
5	Jackson, MS	45.7	42.3	40.9	71	75	75
6	Cleveland-Lorain-Elyria, OH	37.7	34.5	31.8	71	76	77
7	New Orleans, LA	18.9	17.1	16.1	71	69	70
8	Milwaukee-Waukesha, WI	16.0	13.6	10.7	67	69	69
9	Newark, NJ	22.5	21.4	20.5	67	69	70
10	Baltimore, MD	27.9	25.7	25.4	66	70	73
11	Baton Rouge, LA	32.1	29.5	27.6	66	67	66
12	St. Louis, MO-IL	18.7	17.0	17.0	65	70	75
13	Shreveport-Bossier City, LA	37.6	34.4	32.6	64	65	68
14	Mobile, AL	27.5	27.3	28.3	63	67	70
15	Atlanta, GA	29.2	25.1	24.1	63	65	72
16	Philadelphia, PA-NJ	20.4	18.7	18.5	62	67	69
17	Miami, FL	19.9	19.1	16.6	62	63	67
18	New York, NY	23.8	23.2	21.9	60	62	63
19	Washington, DC-MD-VA-WV	26.7	25.1	26.3	59	62	67
20	Richmond-Petersburg, VA	30.5	29.0	28.8	58	60	64
21	Cincinnati, OH-KY-IN	13.4	12.4	12.3	58	61	64
22	Columbia, SC	32.3	30.2	28.5	56	57	59
23	Louisville, KY-IN	14.3	12.8	12.9	54	60	65
24	Kansas City, MO-KS	13.2	12.6	12.8	53	60	68
25	Fort Lauderdale, FL	21.5	14.9	10.9	53	56	71
26	Indianapolis, IN	14.4	13.1	12.7	53	59	65
27	Augusta-Aiken, GA-SC	34.7	31.7	30.2	52	50	52
28	Norfolk-Virginia Beach-Newport News, VA-NC	31.5	28.1	28.0	52	53	60

(continued)

Hispanic isolation reflects mostly the size of the Hispanic population and is by far the highest (above 80) in four Texas border regions that are largely Mexican (Laredo, McAllen, Brownsville, and El Paso). Corpus Christi and San Antonio are among the top ten in isolation.

Isolation increased in virtually all of the fifty regions on the list, reflecting Hispanic population growth. Hispanic isolation is nonetheless very low at the bottom of the list, in some cases because the underlying level of segregation is also low (Portland and Sacramento) and in other cases because although segregation is moderate to high, the Hispanic population is small (Atlanta, Washington, Boston).

TABLE 12-3. Isolation Index: Percentage of Blacks in the Neighborhood of the Average Black Resident, Top Fifty Metro Areas (*continued*)

2000 rank	*Area name*	*2000 black (percent)*	*1990 black (percent)*	*1980 black (percent)*	*2000 value*	*1990 value*	*1980 value*
29	Jacksonville, FL	21.9	19.8	21.4	51	56	65
30	West Palm Beach-Boca Raton, FL	14.5	12.0	13.2	50	59	69
31	Charleston-North Charleston, SC	31.1	30.1	30.6	50	53	57
32	Greensboro–Winston-Salem–High Point, NC	20.4	19.3	19.1	49	55	60
33	Columbus, OH	14.2	12.1	11.2	48	53	57
34	Houston, TX	17.6	18.1	18.7	47	54	67
35	Pittsburgh, PA	8.5	7.5	7.3	47	51	54
36	Nashville, TN	15.9	15.3	16.0	46	52	56
37	Charlotte-Gastonia-Rock Hill, NC-SC	20.7	19.8	20.3	45	51	56
38	Raleigh-Durham-Chapel Hill, NC	23.0	24.1	24.5	43	48	53
39	Tampa-St. Petersburg-Clearwater, FL	10.4	8.8	9.1	43	49	58
40	Dallas, TX	15.3	15.5	16.0	42	50	68
41	Nassau-Suffolk, NY	8.7	7.0	6.1	41	46	49
42	Orlando, FL	14.1	11.7	12.7	41	47	61
43	Boston, MA-NH	7.3	6.2	5.1	39	45	53
44	Greenville-Spartanburg-Anderson, SC	17.7	17.4	17.0	38	41	43
45	Fort Worth-Arlington, TX	11.4	10.4	10.4	35	44	63
46	Oakland, CA	13.4	14.2	14.8	35	46	56
47	Los Angeles-Long Beach, CA	10.0	10.5	12.4	34	42	60
48	Minneapolis-St. Paul, MN-WI	6.1	3.5	2.3	23	25	30
49	San Diego, CA	6.2	6.0	5.5	15	19	27
50	Riverside-San Bernardino, CA	8.1	6.5	4.9	15	14	20

Source: See table 12-1.

Asian-White Segregation

Asian-white segregation and isolation are moderate in metro areas with large Asian populations, but while Asian segregation has remained unchanged in the past two decades, isolation has increased. Asian-white segregation is in the moderate range and has remained virtually unchanged since 1980. As illustrated in figure 12-4, very slight segregation increases have occurred in areas with few Asians, as well as in areas with large Asian populations.

Tables 12-6 and 12-7 list the forty metro regions with the most Asians. Of these the ten most highly Asian-white segregated metro areas have large

FIGURE 12-3. Hispanic-White Segregation: Percent of Hispanics in Metro Area, 1980–2000

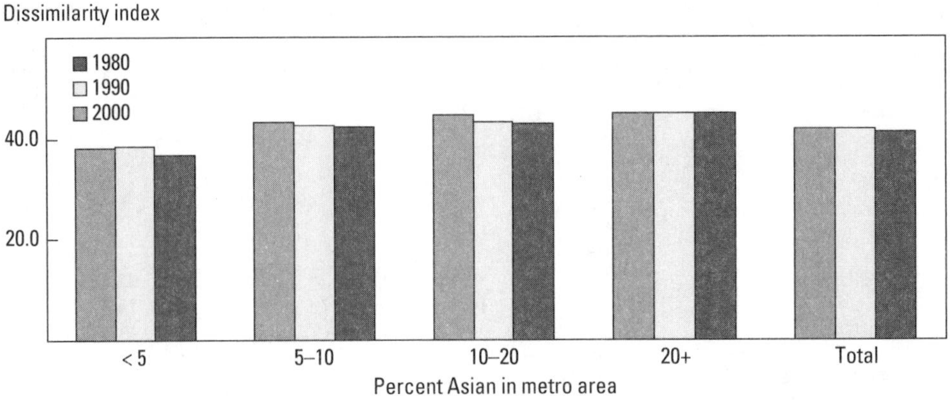

Asian populations: New York, Stockton-Lodi (California), Houston, Sacramento, San Francisco, Los Angeles, Vallejo-Fairfield-Napa, San Diego, Detroit, and Atlanta. Segregation has been increasing in nine of these ten, although in some cases by only a point or two. Much lower levels of Asian-white segregation are found in places like Phoenix and Las Vegas, where Asians range below 6 percent of the total population.

Asian isolation, like that of Hispanics, is closely related to the group's population size. In several metros Asians live in tracts that are on average more than 25 percent Asian: San Francisco (40 percent), San Jose (38 percent), Oakland, Los Angeles, New York, and Orange County. The Asian isolation increase in some of these places during the past twenty years has been dramatic: from 11 percent to 38 percent for San Jose, from 13 percent to 29 percent for Oakland, and from 7 percent to 26 percent for Orange County. Despite only moderate levels of segregation (most often, the dissimilarity index values are less than 50), Asian isolation is rising because Asian population growth is resulting in the rapid formation of Asian residential enclaves in these regions.

Minority Segregation Increases in Suburbs

Minority segregation and isolation have increased in the suburbs during the 1990s as suburbs have become more diverse. National averages indicate slow and continuing declines of black-white segregation and no change in Hispanic-white and Asian-white segregation. Although segregation and isolation remain higher in the central cities, segregation and isolation patterns persist in the suburbs as well.

TABLE 12-4. Dissimilarity Index: Hispanic-White Segregation, Top Fifty Metro Areas

2000 rank	Area name	2000 Hispanic population	Hispanic suburban (percent)	2000 segregation	1990 segregation	1980 segregation
1	New York, NY	2,339,836	7.1	67	66	65
2	Newark, NJ	270,557	70.2	65	67	67
3	Los Angeles-Long Beach, CA	4,242,213	53.9	63	61	57
4	Chicago, IL	1,416,584	38.8	62	63	64
5	Philadelphia, PA-NJ	258,606	38.2	60	63	63
6	Salinas, CA	187,969	46.7	60	57	55
7	Boston, MA-NH	202,510	43.5	59	55	55
8	Bergen-Passaic, NJ	237,869	100.0	58	59	61
9	Ventura, CA	251,734	90.2	56	53	54
10	Orange County, CA	875,579	51.9	56	50	43
11	Houston, TX	1,248,586	38.7	56	50	50
12	Dallas, TX	810,499	38.9	54	50	49
13	Bakersfield, CA	254,036	68.4	54	56	55
14	San Francisco, CA	291,563	62.4	54	50	46
15	Phoenix-Mesa, AZ	817,012	30.1	53	49	53
16	Atlanta, GA	268,851	93.0	53	36	31
17	Middlesex-Somerset-Hunterdon, NJ	131,122	100.0	52	50	53
18	San Jose, CA	403,401	17.8	52	48	46
19	San Antonio, TX	816,037	16.2	51	54	58
20	San Diego, CA	750,965	51.4	51	46	42
21	Denver, CO	397,236	55.8	50	47	49
22	Tucson, AZ	247,578	29.8	50	50	54
23	Fort Worth-Arlington, TX	432,003	80.6	48	45	48
24	Washington, DC-MD-VA-WV	309,851	28.9	48	43	32
25	Fresno, CA	406,151	50.8	48	48	47
26	Oakland, CA	441,686	76.4	47	39	37
27	Nassau-Suffolk, NY	282,693	100.0	47	43	38
28	Brownsville-Harlingen-San Benito, TX	327,760	34.9	47	44	39
29	Austin-San Marcos, TX	282,736	32.9	47	43	47
30	Corpus Christi, TX	208,132	27.6	46	48	53
31	El Paso, TX	531,654	18.8	46	51	54
32	Santa Barbara-Santa Maria-Lompoc, CA	136,668	31.3	46	42	39
33	Detroit, MI	128,075	53.2	46	40	41
34	Tampa-St. Petersburg-Clearwater, FL	248,642	68.3	45	46	51
35	Jersey City, NJ	242,123	67.4	45	43	49
36	McAllen-Edinburg-Mission, TX	503,100	67.2	45	41	45
37	Miami, FL	1,291,737	77.9	44	51	53
38	West Palm Beach-Boca Raton, FL	140,675	84.8	43	43	45
39	Riverside-San Bernardino, CA	1,228,962	81.5	43	37	39
40	Visalia-Tulare-Porterville, CA	322,038	64.9	43	42	39

(*continued*)

TABLE 12-4. Dissimilarity Index: Hispanic-White Segregation, Top Fifty Metro Areas (*continued*)

2000 rank	Area name	2000 Hispanic population	Hispanic suburban (percent)	2000 segregation	1990 segregation	1980 segregation
41	Las Vegas, NV-AZ	186,846	61.3	43	30	23
42	Salt Lake City-Ogden, UT	144,600	61.8	43	33	35
43	Albuquerque, NM	296,373	39.6	41	42	46
44	Orlando, FL	271,627	88.0	41	31	31
45	Sacramento, CA	234,475	62.5	40	36	35
46	Stockton-Lodi, CA	172,073	45.0	37	36	38
47	Modesto, CA	141,871	54.4	36	34	37
48	Portland-Vancouver, OR-WA	142,444	68.3	35	27	22
49	Fort Lauderdale, FL	271,652	94.7	32	27	28
50	Laredo, TX	182,070	8.7	29	34	42

Source: See table 12-1.

America's suburbs have always had considerable diversity behind their white, middle-class image. Now they are being radically transformed.[6] The total suburban population was 18 percent minority in 1990, but that figure has risen to 27 percent minority as of 2000.[7] The total suburban white population scarcely changed in the decade (up 5 percent), but the number of black suburbanites grew rapidly (up 38 percent), and the number of Hispanics and Asians in U.S. suburbs exploded (up 72 percent and 84 percent, respectively). Although the suburbs of Salt Lake City, Portland, Milwaukee, and California's Orange County still have very small black populations (all below 2 percent), blacks now constitute more than 20 percent of the suburban population in other metros such as Atlanta, Richmond, New Orleans, Fort Lauderdale, Miami, and Washington, D.C.

Hispanics are more than 25 percent of the suburban population in Miami (55.8 percent), Los Angeles (44.7 percent), Riverside (38.3 percent), and San Diego (27.0 percent). At the other extreme, they are less than 2 percent of suburban residents of Pittsburgh, Cincinnati, Buffalo, St. Louis, Indianapolis, and Cleveland.

The Asian population is generally smaller but nevertheless accounts for 10 percent of the suburban residents of San Francisco, Oakland, Los Angeles, Orange County, and the Middlesex-Somerset-Hunterdon suburban area of northern New Jersey. Still, Asians constitute only 1.5 percent of the suburban population in Pittsburgh, Charlotte, Cincinnati, Indianapolis, and Greenville.

6. Alba and others (1999).

7. See Frey, chapter 9, in this volume.

TABLE 12-5. Isolation Index: Percentage of Hispanics in the Neighborhood of the Average Hispanic Resident, Top Fifty Metro Areas

2000 rank	Area name	2000 Hispanic (percent)	1990 Hispanic (percent)	1980 Hispanic (percent)	2000 value	1990 value	1980 value
1	Laredo, TX	94.3	93.9	91.5	95	94	92
2	McAllen-Edinburg-Mission, TX	88.3	85.2	81.3	90	87	85
3	Brownsville-Harlingen-San Benito, TX	84.3	81.9	77.1	88	86	81
4	El Paso, TX	78.2	69.6	61.9	83	78	74
5	Miami, FL	57.3	49.2	35.7	71	68	59
6	Salinas, CA	46.8	33.9	25.3	68	59	49
7	Corpus Christi, TX	54.7	52.0	48.5	66	65	65
8	San Antonio, TX	51.2	47.4	44.9	66	65	66
9	Los Angeles-Long Beach, CA	44.6	37.8	27.6	63	58	50
10	Visalia-Tulare-Porterville, CA	50.8	38.6	29.8	61	51	42
11	Fresno, CA	44.0	35.4	29.0	58	51	46
12	Bakersfield, CA	38.4	28.0	21.6	57	49	42
13	Ventura, CA	33.4	26.4	21.4	56	48	43
14	Jersey City, NJ	39.8	33.3	26.2	55	50	47
15	Orange County, CA	30.8	23.4	14.8	54	46	33
16	Albuquerque, NM	41.6	37.1	36.2	54	50	52
17	Santa Barbara-Santa Maria-Lompoc, CA	34.2	26.6	18.5	50	41	31
18	Riverside-San Bernardino, CA	37.8	26.5	18.6	50	38	33
19	Houston, TX	29.9	21.3	14.6	49	41	36
20	Tucson, AZ	29.3	24.5	21.0	49	45	45
21	Chicago, IL	17.1	11.4	8.1	48	43	38
22	New York, NY	25.1	22.1	17.7	46	44	41
23	Phoenix-Mesa, AZ	25.1	17.0	14.1	46	36	34
24	Dallas, TX	23.0	14.0	9.0	45	32	24
25	San Diego, CA	26.7	20.4	14.8	44	35	28
26	San Jose, CA	31.7	21.8	14.9	41	36	33
27	Modesto, CA	24.0	21.0	17.5	41	30	24
28	Austin-San Marcos, TX	26.2	21.0	17.7	40	34	36
29	Bergen-Passaic, NJ	17.3	11.6	7.0	39	34	28
30	Stockton-Lodi, CA	30.5	23.4	19.2	38	32	29
31	Denver, CO	18.8	13.0	11.4	38	30	29
32	Fort Worth-Arlington, TX	18.2	11.1	7.3	37	29	26
33	Newark, NJ	13.3	10.0	6.7	36	33	27
34	Middlesex-Somerset-Hunterdon, NJ	11.2	7.0	4.4	34	27	24
35	San Francisco, CA	16.8	14.5	11.1	34	29	22
36	Las Vegas, NV-AZ	20.6	10.4	7.6	34	16	10
37	Oakland, CA	18.5	13.1	10.5	30	21	18
38	Orlando, FL	16.5	8.2	3.5	27	14	6
39	Philadelphia, PA-NJ	5.1	3.6	2.5	27	27	21
40	Fort Lauderdale, FL	16.7	8.6	4.0	23	12	6
41	West Palm Beach-Boca Raton, FL	12.4	7.7	4.9	23	16	13
42	Nassau-Suffolk, NY	10.3	6.3	3.9	23	15	10

(continued)

TABLE 12-5. Isolation Index: Percentage of Hispanics in the Neighborhood of the Average Hispanic Resident, Top Fifty Metro Areas (*continued*)

2000 rank	Area name	2000 Hispanic (percent)	1990 Hispanic (percent)	1980 Hispanic (percent)	2000 value	1990 value	1980 value
43	Tampa-St. Petersburg-Clearwater, FL	10.4	6.7	5.1	23	19	19
44	Salt Lake City-Ogden, UT	10.8	5.8	4.9	22	11	10
45	Sacramento, CA	14.4	10.8	8.8	21	16	14
46	Boston, MA-NH	5.9	4.3	2.3	21	16	12
47	Washington, DC-MD-VA-WV	8.8	5.4	2.9	20	13	5
48	Atlanta, GA	6.5	2.0	1.1	20	5	2
49	Detroit, MI	2.9	2.0	1.7	19	10	8
50	Portland-Vancouver, OR-WA	7.4	3.3	2.0	15	6	3

Source: See table 12-1.

As suburbs become more diverse racially and ethnically, are minorities becoming likelier to live in the same neighborhoods as whites? The answer is that there occurred an approximately 5-point drop in black-white segregation in U.S. suburbs in the 1980s, but that during the 1990s there has occurred virtually no change. As new minority residents have entered suburbia, they have become separated from whites to the same degree as ten years before.

As is true in the metropolis as a whole, the group most segregated from whites in the suburbs is African Americans, although with substantial

FIGURE 12-4. Asian-White Segregation, 1980–2000

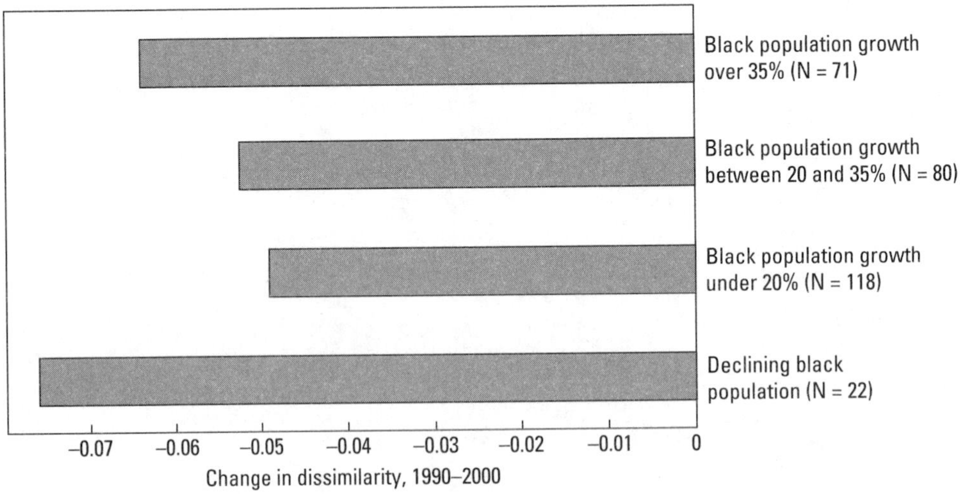

TABLE 12-6. Dissimilarity Index: Asian-White Segregation, Top Forty Metro Areas

2000 rank	*Area name*	*2000 Asian population*	*Asian suburban (percent)*	*2000 segregation*	*1990 segregation*	*1980 segregation*
1	New York, NY	913,199	6.7	51	48	49
2	Stockton-Lodi, CA	72,934	22.1	50	56	43
3	Houston, TX	235,970	52.3	49	47	44
4	Sacramento, CA	173,952	55.1	49	49	48
5	San Francisco, CA	430,146	41.2	49	50	51
6	Los Angeles-Long Beach, CA	1,232,085	60.6	48	46	47
7	Vallejo-Fairfield-Napa, CA	65,361	28.2	47	46	43
8	San Diego, CA	294,966	33.3	47	48	46
9	Detroit, MI	118,464	86.8	46	43	41
10	Atlanta, GA	149,252	94.1	45	43	36
11	Dallas, TX	155,492	64.3	45	42	39
12	Boston, MA-NH	181,984	60.7	45	44	48
13	Jersey City, NJ	61,068	27.1	45	42	47
14	Chicago, IL	415,244	62.5	44	46	47
15	Philadelphia, PA-NJ	188,414	60.3	44	44	41
16	Middlesex-Somerset-Hunterdon, NJ	137,936	100.0	43	37	35
17	Minneapolis-St. Paul, MN-WI	138,066	53.2	43	42	30
18	Fort Worth-Arlington, TX	62,074	38.8	42	41	37
19	San Jose, CA	459,401	24.6	42	39	32
20	Oakland, CA	449,146	76.4	42	40	38
21	Austin-San Marcos, TX	49,599	29.6	41	40	35
22	Orange County, CA	424,828	71.4	40	34	28
23	Baltimore, MD	77,932	84.5	39	39	38
24	Fresno, CA	73,129	27.3	39	46	29
25	Washington, DC-MD-VA-WV	366,991	89.7	39	36	32
26	Riverside-San Bernardino, CA	165,511	79.2	38	34	31
27	Bergen-Passaic, NJ	119,021	100.0	36	35	34
28	Orlando, FL	52,466	88.7	36	32	33
29	Nassau-Suffolk, NY	108,249	100.0	36	33	31
30	Newark, NJ	89,171	95.6	35	31	31
31	Seattle-Bellevue-Everett, WA	270,728	58.0	35	37	40
32	Tacoma, WA	52,598	62.4	34	38	35
33	Tampa-St. Petersburg-Clearwater, FL	53,724	67.0	34	35	34
34	Norfolk-Virginia Beach-Newport News, VA-NC	52,321	17.5	34	36	38
35	Portland-Vancouver, OR-WA	111,732	55.6	32	32	29
36	Salt Lake City-Ogden, UT	49,957	72.0	30	32	25
37	Denver, CO	75,021	75.8	30	30	27
38	Ventura, CA	48,117	91.8	30	32	38
39	Las Vegas, NV-AZ	95,096	69.0	30	29	23
40	Phoenix-Mesa, AZ	84,126	35.0	28	28	28

Source: See table 12-1.

TABLE 12-7. Isolation Index: Percentage of Asians in the Neighborhood of the Average Asian Resident, Top Forty Metro Areas

2000 rank	Area name	2000 Asian (percent)	1990 Asian (percent)	1980 Asian (percent)	2000 value	1990 value	1980 value
1	San Francisco, CA	24.8	20.6	14.1	40	36	30
2	San Jose, CA	27.3	17.4	7.7	38	25	11
3	Oakland, CA	18.8	12.9	6.6	29	21	13
4	Los Angeles-Long Beach, CA	12.9	10.8	5.8	29	23	15
5	New York, NY	9.8	6.5	3.0	27	20	16
6	Orange County, CA	14.9	10.3	4.5	26	17	7
7	Vallejo-Fairfield-Napa, CA	12.6	10.4	5.8	24	22	13
8	Middlesex-Somerset-Hunterdon, NJ	11.8	5.5	1.8	23	12	4
9	Stockton-Lodi, CA	12.9	12.4	5.7	23	26	11
10	San Diego, CA	10.5	7.9	4.8	22	18	11
11	Jersey City, NJ	10.0	6.7	2.8	20	15	8
12	Sacramento, CA	10.7	7.7	4.2	20	16	13
13	Seattle-Bellevue-Everett, WA	11.2	6.8	4.0	19	15	12
14	Bergen-Passaic, NJ	8.7	5.2	1.9	16	10	4
15	Chicago, IL	5.0	3.4	2.0	15	12	9
16	Houston, TX	5.6	3.8	1.8	15	10	5
17	Washington, DC-MD-VA-WV	7.5	4.8	2.5	14	9	5
18	Fresno, CA	7.9	7.7	2.7	14	17	4
19	Boston, MA-NH	5.3	3.0	1.2	13	10	11
20	Minneapolis-St. Paul, MN-WI	4.7	2.6	0.9	12	11	2
21	Tacoma, WA	7.5	4.9	3.0	12	11	5
22	Dallas, TX	4.4	2.5	0.9	11	6	2
23	Riverside-San Bernardino, CA	5.1	3.9	1.5	11	7	3
24	Philadelphia, PA-NJ	3.7	2.1	1.0	10	7	4
25	Ventura, CA	6.4	5.2	3.0	10	9	7
26	Portland-Vancouver, OR-WA	5.8	3.5	1.9	9	6	3
27	Newark, NJ	4.4	2.8	1.3	9	5	2
28	Austin-San Marcos, TX	4.0	2.3	0.9	9	6	2
29	Las Vegas, NV-AZ	6.1	3.1	2.0	9	4	3
30	Atlanta, GA	3.6	1.8	0.6	8	5	1
31	Nassau-Suffolk, NY	3.6	2.2	0.7	8	5	2
32	Fort Worth-Arlington, TX	3.9	2.4	1.0	8	7	2
33	Detroit, MI	2.7	1.3	0.8	8	4	2
34	Baltimore, MD	3.1	1.8	1.0	7	4	2
35	Norfolk-Virginia Beach-Newport News, VA-NC	3.3	2.4	1.6	6	5	4
36	Salt Lake City-Ogden, UT	3.7	2.4	1.2	6	5	2
37	Denver, CO	3.2	1.7	0.7	5	4	2
38	Orlando, FL	3.6	2.3	1.3	5	3	1
39	Phoenix-Mesa, AZ	2.6	1.6	0.8	4	3	1
40	Tampa-St. Petersburg-Clearwater, FL	2.2	1.1	0.5	4	2	1

Source: See table 12-1.

differences across regions. Portland suburbs have the lowest level of black-white segregation (31.4), but seven of the fifty largest suburban regions have black-white segregation scores above 70, even after a drop of 1 to 5 points during the past decade—namely, the suburban portion of Newark (77.1), Cleveland (74.9), Nassau-Suffolk (74.4), Chicago (73.4), Bergen-Passaic (73.2), Miami (72.4), and St. Louis (71.7).

Hispanics overall have become slightly more segregated from whites, but only by 4 points (42.7 to 46.5). Again, the more interesting pattern is the difference between areas in which Hispanics remain a small suburban minority and those in which they are present in larger numbers. In the former (areas less than 3 percent Hispanic), segregation was lower to begin with and declined substantially. In the latter (areas more than 10 percent Hispanic), segregation was higher to begin with and rose from 46.8 to 48.4. Segregation of suburban Hispanics is highest in Los Angeles (62.0), Newark (59.7), Bergen-Passaic (57.8), San Francisco (54.3), and Chicago (54.0). It is below 25.0 in the Pittsburgh and Detroit suburbs.

Asian-white segregation in U.S. suburbs increased by 3 points in the past twenty years (37.5 to 40.5). This stability was fairly uniform across regions and was about the same in suburban areas with few Asians as in those with many. But the absolute levels of segregation vary considerably, from the three most highly segregated regions, with their suburban Asian-white segregation scores above 50.0 (Houston, San Francisco, and Los Angeles) to several regions having scores below 30.0.

The persistence of residential segregation for minority groups means that newly suburban group members tended to move into the same array of neighborhoods in which co-ethnics were already living in 1990. Given the rapid growth of each group, this implies that suburban racial and ethnic enclaves may have emerged or grown substantially in many metro areas, especially in those areas in which the group is well represented.

Isolation indexes among suburban minorities show a similar trend. In metro areas in which Hispanics make up more than 10 percent of the suburban population, the average Hispanic in 1990 lived in a neighborhood that was 44 percent Hispanic, a figure that has risen to 49 percent in 2000. In metro areas in which Asians are more than 4 percent of the suburban population, the average Asian now lives in a neighborhood that is 16 percent Asian, up from 12 percent in 1990. For African Americans there occurred no net change in metro areas in which more than 10 percent of the suburban population is black: already in 1990, the average black person in these suburbs lived in a neighborhood that was nearly half black (46 percent), and the same is true today.

CONCLUSION

These demographic trends raise political questions in two ways: whose voice will be heard in the public arena? What new issues will have to be addressed? In terms of representation, the rising share of black and Hispanic residents has already altered the political balance in many cities. As minorities now continue to move to suburbs, demographic change may presage shifts in the traditionally conservative approach to public policy supported by suburban politicians. Indeed, the old divide between urban and suburban public officials may diminish. But at the same time, new divisions are arising within suburbia (between municipalities, school districts, and other jurisdictional lines). Segregation reinforces political cleavages between white and minority neighborhoods in both cities and suburbs.

Other research has shown that minority neighborhoods tend to be poorer, less safe, and less capable of supporting high-quality public services.[8] Hence an enduring issue of public policy is whether the increasing diversity of the United States is accentuating divisions between successful and unsuccessful neighborhoods. This may take the form of familiar disparities associated with the city-suburb boundary, or it may involve new inequalities among communities at the fringe of the metropolis. Most important, in the absence of strong policies in favor of racial balance, residential segregation is likely to be reproduced in school segregation. One result is that black and Hispanic children now attend schools with double the poverty rate of schools attended by white children.

Residential segregation is not a priority concern on the public agenda. Americans by and large presume that this particular battle for civil rights was won decades ago. Census 2000 reveals that the progress in reducing black-white segregation is very slow and that the process has advanced less in the 1990s than in the 1980s, less in the suburbs than in the central cities, and less in places with a larger black population. Since the end of large-scale migration of blacks from the South, some contraction of urban ghettos has occurred, as well as some dispersion to the outer city and inner suburbs. But because black-white segregation had reached such a high level by 1970 or 1980, it will take decades at the current rate for progress to be very visible in people's lives. In some of the most important metropolitan centers of the North—places like New York, Newark, Cincinnati, Milwaukee, and Detroit—the process of change has barely begun.

Hispanics and Asians, the faster-growing minority groups, are just as segregated from whites today as twenty years ago. Where these minorities are

8. Logan and others (1996); Logan and Stults (1999).

present in the smallest proportions, they are also least segregated residentially and least likely to develop residential enclaves—as is true also with African Americans. The census results suggest that minorities are being successfully incorporated into such communities. But a different set of dynamics seems to come into play for places in which the most minority group members live and where consequently they make up a more substantial share of the population. In these places, segregation is higher and more unyielding over time, and minority population growth is more likely to be associated with the creation or intensification of ethnic enclaves. Even in some suburban regions there are new and growing neighborhoods that are largely black, Hispanic, or Asian.

Rather than disappearing, residential segregation is extending beyond the city limits and adding new colors, and it promises to persist as an American dilemma well into the twenty-first century.

REFERENCES

Alba, Richard D., John R. Logan, Brian Stults, Gilbert Marzan, and Wenquan Zhang. 1999. "Immigrant Groups and Suburbs: A Reexamination of Suburbanization and Spatial Assimilation." *American Sociological Review* 64 (June): 446–60.

Farley, Reynolds, and William H. Frey. 1994. "Changes in the Segregation of Whites from Blacks during the 1980s: Small Steps toward a More Integrated Society." *American Sociological Review* 59 (February): 23–45.

Gross, Andrew, and Douglas Massey. 1991. "Spatial Assimilation Models: A Micro-Macro Comparison." *Social Science Quarterly* 72 (June): 347–60.

Logan, John R., Richard D. Alba, Tom McNulty, and Brian Fisher. 1996. "Making a Place in the Metropolis: Locational Attainment in Cities and Suburbs." *Demography* 33 (November): 443–53.

———, and Brian Stults. 1999. "Racial Differences in Exposure to Crime: The City and Suburbs of Cleveland in 1990." *Criminology* 37 (May): 251–76.

Massey, Douglas, and Nancy Denton. 1993. *American Apartheid*. Harvard University Press.

U.S. Bureau of the Census. 1981. *1980 Census of Population and Housing*. Summary Tape File 1A. Department of Commerce.

———. 1991. *1990 Census of Population and Housing*. Summary Tape File 1A. Department of Commerce.

———. 2001. Census 2000 Redistricting Data Summary File. Department of Commerce.

13

City Families and Suburban Singles

An Emerging Household Story

WILLIAM H. FREY
ALAN BERUBE

Changes in population during the 1990s have been the focus of much of the debate thus far around the meaning of Census 2000 with regard to cities and metropolitan areas. It was a decade of population gains for most large cities, including some that had stagnated or declined in previous decades, like New York and Chicago. Meanwhile, suburban population growth continued to outpace that of the cities. Regional distinctions were also important: cities and suburbs both grew fastest in the South and West, while several cities in the Northeast and Midwest continued to experience population declines.[1]

Analysis of population change in itself, however, offers only a partial picture of metropolitan growth dynamics in the 1990s. Change in the number and composition of *households* may be a better indicator of changes in metropolitan housing demand, tax base, and services needs than population change. For instance, in the 1990s the city of Washington, D.C., lost 6 percent of its population, but the number of households remained relatively stable (1 percent loss). This implies that on net the city lost larger families with children but gained and retained smaller, childless households. Looking at household change and not just at population change helps to explain the continued high demand for housing in that city. Washington's

The authors are grateful to senior project programmer Cathy Sun and other support staff at the University of Michigan Population Studies Center, to the Milken Institute for assistance in preparing census data, and to Amy Liu and Audrey Singer at the Brookings Center on Urban and Metropolitan Policy for advice and editorial expertise.

1. See Alan Berube, chapter 2, in this volume.

experience, however, is different from that of other cities such as New York, Detroit, Phoenix, and Los Angeles. Recent household change dynamics differ sharply across metropolitan areas, reflecting shifting household types and location preferences that are shaping cities and suburbs in new ways.

The present study interprets the results of Census 2000 to reveal important differences between household growth and population growth in U.S. metropolitan areas and their component central cities and suburbs during the 1990s. Additionally, the study shows that the types of households that fueled city and suburban population growth (or that served to stem city population loss) differed widely across U.S. regions.

METHODS

The methodology employed in the present analysis involved defining or fine-tuning a number of key concepts related to the measurement of household growth by types in different areas and regions of the United States.

Definitions of Metropolitan Area

The study evaluates population and household changes during the 1990s for the country's 102 largest metropolitan areas—namely, those metros with 500,000 or more inhabitants as reported in Census 2000. The metropolitan areas analyzed are those defined by the Office of Management and Budget (OMB) as metropolitan statistical areas (MSAs) and primary metropolitan statistical areas (PMSAs) and those defined in the New England states as New England county metropolitan areas (NECMAs).

Definition of Central City and Suburbs

The present analysis defines central cities and their suburbs (the portion of the metropolitan area located outside of the central city) largely in accordance with OMB definitions in effect for Census 2000. These definitions are applied consistently to both 1990 and 2000 census data. OMB standards sometimes combine multiple cities to form the official "central city" for a given metropolitan area.[2] These standards were modified slightly for purposes of our analysis, in that the largest or best-known city/cities in most large metropolitan areas have been designated as the "central city." The

2. OMB designates the city with the largest population in each metropolitan area as a central city. Additional cities qualify for this designation if specified requirements are met concerning population size, commuting patterns, and employment/residence ratios. These standards, implemented after Census 1990, can be viewed at *census.gov/population/www/estimates/mastand.html.*

study generally treats as central cities the place or places listed in the official OMB metropolitan-area name. In the Detroit PMSA, for example, OMB recognizes the cities of Detroit, Dearborn, Pontiac, and Port Huron as the combined "central city." Our analysis includes only Detroit as the "central city," and the remainder of the Detroit PMSA is treated as suburbs. We have in this manner modified the official definition of "central city" for 56 of the 102 metropolitan areas in the study.[3] Central cities are designated for only 97 of the 102 metropolitan areas in our study, so the populations of the remaining metro areas are classified as suburban.

Typology of Metropolitan Areas

Portions of the analysis employ a metropolitan-area typology introduced in a previous Brookings Census 2000 series survey.[4] The typology distinguishes among metropolitan areas on the basis of their regional locations and dominant racial-ethnic structures. This typology is useful in the present study because the nature of household growth in the 1990s is reflective of both of these factors. The 102 metropolitan areas are classified as follows:

- "Melting Pot" metros (35 metro areas);
- North, largely white-black metros (6 metro areas);
- North, largely white metros (29 metro areas);
- South, largely white-black metros (19 metro areas); and
- South and West, largely white metros (13 metro areas).

Melting Pot metros such as New York, Los Angeles, El Paso, and Bakersfield have large proportions of Hispanic, Asian, American Indian/ Native Alaskan, multiracial, and "other race" populations and are located primarily in high-immigration zones of the United States.

The two metro categories in the North include primarily slow-growing metropolitan areas in the census Northeast and Midwest regions. "North, largely white-black" areas such as Philadelphia and Detroit have significant African American populations, and "North, largely white" areas such as Boston and Minneapolis have smaller minority populations.

3. For the present study, we have excluded some officially designated central cities (in metros with multiple central cities) to include only central cities that are named in the metropolitan area name (thus omitting officially designated smaller cities that were not named); include only one central city in the following multiple-central-city metropolitan areas: Austin, Buffalo, Charlotte, Cleveland, Milwaukee, Richmond, Wilmington, and Seattle; and designate only two central cities in the following metropolitan areas: Raleigh-Durham, Allentown-Bethlehem, and Scranton-Hazleton. In other cases the officially defined single- or multiple-central-cities designation was utilized.

4. Frey (2001).

Metropolitan areas in the South and West categories are located in those faster-growing census regions. "South, largely white-black" metros include areas like Atlanta, Baltimore, and Little Rock that have significant African American populations; "South and West, largely white" areas include areas with a smaller minority presence, such as Seattle, Colorado Springs, and Tampa.[5] Appendix table 13A-1 contains a complete listing of the 102 metro areas arranged by their classifications.

Household Type Definitions

The study distinguishes among five different household types in accordance with definitions established by the decennial census. Table 13-1 presents these categories and the shares of all U.S. households represented by each type in 1990 and 2000. A "family" is defined by the presence of two or more people in the household who are related by birth, marriage, or adoption, and "children" refers to a parent's own children under the age of 18. A great deal of demographic diversity exists not only among but also within these household types. Each of the five major household types comprises a spectrum of households with a wide range of service needs and with varying abilities to contribute to the local tax base—differences dictated in large part by household size and by the age of household members. The five household types are as follows:

- Married with children. As the children of baby boomers age and leave home, the traditional "nuclear family" household type accounts for a shrinking portion of all U.S. households. In 2000 less than 25 percent of all households nationwide were of this type, compared with 40.3 percent in 1970.
- Married without children. The 28 percent of households consisting of married couples without children includes young, often two-earner couples that have not yet had children, older "empty nester" couples whose children may recently have left home, and elderly couples who may have grandchildren of their own.

5. "Melting Pot" metro denotes a metro area in which non-Hispanic whites constitute no more than 69 percent of the 2000 population and in which the combined populations of Hispanics, non-Hispanic Asians, Hawaiians and other Pacific Islanders, Native Americans and Native Alaskans, and those of another race or of two or more races exceed 18 percent of the population. "Largely white-black" metros are the remaining areas, in their respective regions, in which blacks constitute at least 16 percent of the population; "largely white" metro denotes the residual areas in each region. "South and West" pertains to metros located in the South and West census regions; "North" pertains to metros located in the Northeast and Midwest census regions.

TABLE 13-1. Share of All U.S. Households by Household Type, 1990, 2000

Percent

Type of household	1990	2000
Family households	70.2	68.1
Married couple	55.1	51.7
With own children under 18	26.7	23.5
No own children under 18	28.4	28.1
Other family	15.0	16.4
With own children under 18	9.3	9.2
No own children under 18	5.7	7.1
Nonfamily households	29.8	31.9
Persons living alone	24.6	25.8

Source: William H. Frey analysis of decennial census data.

- Other families with children. These households are usually single-parent family households, and females head four out of five of them. Disadvantaged single mothers who gave birth at a young age make up a significant portion of these households, and the category also includes most divorced and separated parents with children, never-married mothers who chose to have children at a later age, and unmarried partners with children.
- Other families without children. These households include single adults with parents living with them, single parents with a child (or children) older than eighteen living in their home, and adult relatives (such as brothers and sisters) living in the same household.
- Nonfamilies. More than 80 percent of nonfamily households consist of single persons living alone; more than one-third of these are sixty-five and older. Other nonfamily households consist of nonrelatives living together, including unmarried partners with no children.

Household growth and decline can occur in a more dynamic and more varied fashion than does population change. Changes in the number of households result not only from in-migration or outmigration but also from household formation and dissolution. New households form largely when "coming of age" late teens and young adults leave their parents' homes to form their own. Changes in other existing households can also affect household growth: for instance, two nonfamily single households may combine to form a married-couple household; likewise, a divorce may create two households from one. Life transitions can also lead to changes in household type, as when a household consisting of a married couple without children experiences the birth of a child (thus creating a "married-couple-with-children" household) or the death of a spouse (thus creating a nonfamily household).

FINDINGS

Several interesting results emerged from the present analysis, some of them perhaps unexpected. The primary findings include the following:

- In the 1990s, central city population growth was at a three-decade high, but household growth was at a three-decade low.
- Fast-growing cities in the South and West experienced significant increases in married couples with children, while slow-growing cities in the Northeast and Midwest experienced declines in such families.
- Suburbs now contain more nonfamily households (largely young singles and elderly people living alone) than married couples with children.
- Cities in high-immigration metros are becoming more "suburban" in their household composition, while suburbs in slow-growing northern metros are becoming more "urban" in theirs.

Central City Population and Household Growth

Metropolitan household and population changes in the last decade occurred within the context of larger U.S. demographic forces, with the 1990s representing a dramatic shift in household and population dynamics from just two decades prior. In the 1970s U.S. population growth was slower than in the 1950s and 1960s, as the baby boomers entering adulthood during that decade had children at lower rates than did their earlier counterparts. At the same time, however, households grew at a record pace in the United States during the 1970s. As boomers entered traditional household formation ages, not only were they more numerous than previous generations at those ages but also they waited longer than their parents to "double up" and form couples to start families, thus creating more households per capita.

With the boomers dominating the American demographic landscape, the number of U.S. households in the 1970s in fact grew at more than twice the rate of the U.S. population (27 percent versus 11.4 percent) (figure 13-1). This growth differential narrowed somewhat during the 1980s, but the household gains generated by the late boomers during that decade still exceeded population gains by more than half. In the 1990s, however, the gap between U.S. population growth and household growth narrowed considerably. Household growth was at a three-decade low and population growth at a three-decade high.

Following the national trend, central cities in all metropolitan areas experienced faster population growth and slower household growth in the 1990s than in the 1970s or 1980s. As figure 13-2 shows, central city population

FIGURE 13-1. U.S. Household and Population Growth by Decade, 1970–2000

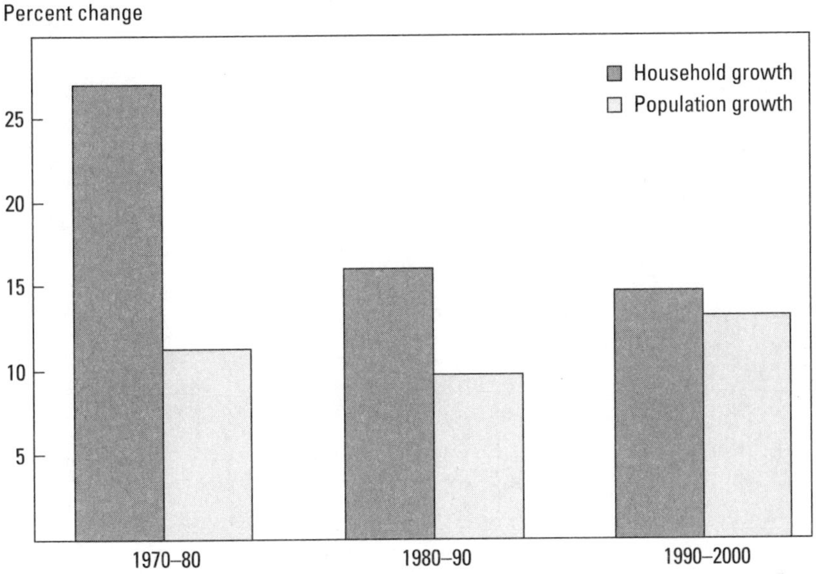

growth during the 1970s was barely positive (0.1 percent), becoming much stronger in the 1980s (7.0 percent) and continuing this upward trend during the 1990s (9.8 percent). During the same period, cities experienced declines in the household growth rate similar to, though less steep than, the household growth rate decline experienced by the nation as a whole—from 14.6 percent in the 1970s to 9.9 percent in the 1990s.

This shift in the direction of household-versus-population growth is based on separate demographic forces. The recent declines in household growth are attributable to the smaller postboomer generation's entering its household formation years in the 1990s. The recent increases in population growth can be attributed in large part to waves of immigrants whose first, second, and third generations are living in cities and have younger age structures and often higher birth rates. In addition, the households these newcomers form are different from those formed in the 1970s by "coming of age" baby boomers. Immigrants and children of immigrants are more likely to marry earlier and to form larger "married-couple-with-children" households. As we explore later in greater detail, the character of city households, especially in fast-growing cities, is quite different today from what it was twenty to thirty years ago.

FIGURE 13-2. Central City Household and Population Growth, by Decade, 1970–2000[a]

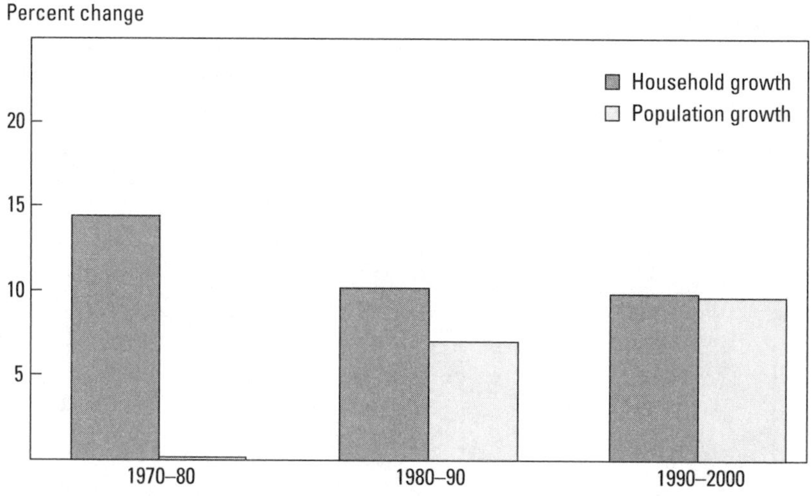

a. Central cities of all U.S. metropolitan areas.

One implication of these trends is that the household growth "cushion" that central cities enjoyed during earlier decades no longer exists. In the 1970s, cities with declining or only modestly growing populations could nevertheless count on continued demand for housing among new boomer households. With population growth and household growth virtually at parity during the 1990s, however, cities in general seemed able to enjoy sustained housing demand and growing tax bases only if their populations were increasing.

These dominant city trends of reduced household formation and increased population growth, especially the growth of families with children among immigrant groups, did not hold across all central cities. Among the cities in the study, population growth in the 1990s ranged from a decline of 13 percent (Hartford) to a gain of 85 percent (Las Vegas). But overall, three-fourths of central cities did show population gains. Table 13-2 displays the fifteen central cities in this study with the highest population growth during the 1990s and the fifteen cities with the largest population declines. Notably, the cities showing the greatest population growth were all located in the South and West census regions; those with the greatest population declines were overwhelmingly in the North and Midwest.[6] (See appendix table

6. Glaeser and Shapiro (2001).

TABLE 13-2. Population and Household Growth Rates, 1990–2000, Central Cities with Greatest Population Growth and Decline in Metro Areas with Population over 500,000

Percent

Area	Central city growth rates: Population	Central city growth rates: Household	Difference
Metro areas with greatest central city population growth			
1 Las Vegas, NV-AZ MSA	85	77	–8
2 Bakersfield, CA MSA	41	34	–8
3 Austin, TX MSA	41	38	–3
4 McAllen-Edinburg-Mission, TX MSA	40	47	6
5 Portland-Vancouver, OR-WA PMSA	39	35	–4
6 Charlotte, NC-SC MSA	37	36	–1
7 Phoenix-Mesa, AZ MSA	35	28	–7
8 Raleigh-Durham, NC MSA	34	32	–2
9 Colorado Springs, CO MSA	28	28	–1
10 Greensboro–Winston-Salem–High Point, NC MSA	25	25	0
11 Fort Worth-Arlington, TX PMSA	22	19	–3
12 San Antonio, TX MSA	22	24	2
13 West Palm Beach-Boca Raton, FL MSA	21	21	–1
14 Fresno, CA MSA	21	15	–6
15 Orange County, CA PMSA	21	11	–10
Metro areas with greatest central city population decline			
1 Hartford, CT NECMA	–13	–13	0
2 St. Louis, MO-IL MSA	–12	–11	1
3 Youngstown-Warren, OH MSA	–12	–10	2
4 Gary, IN PMSA	–12	–7	5
5 Baltimore, MD PMSA	–12	–7	5
6 Buffalo, NY MSA	–11	–10	1
7 Syracuse, NY MSA	–10	–8	2
8 Pittsburgh, PA MSA	–10	–6	3
9 Cincinnati, OH-KY-IN PMSA	–9	–4	5
10 Birmingham, AL MSA	–9	–6	2
11 Dayton-Springfield, OH MSA	–8	–6	2
12 Detroit, MI PMSA	–7	–10	–3
13 Albany-Schenectady-Troy, NY MSA	–6	–4	2
14 Scranton-Hazleton, PA MSA	–6	–4	3
15 Toledo, OH MSA	–6	–1	4

Source: William H. Frey analysis of decennial census data.

Note: Pertains to MSAs, PMSAs, and (in New England) NECMAs, as defined in June 2000 by the Office of Management and Budget with modifications for central cities. See text.

13A-2 for a complete listing of population and household growth rates in the 102 metropolitan areas).

Almost uniformly, the rapidly growing cities experienced faster population growth than household growth. The most notable example was Las Vegas. Its population growth rate during the decade was 85 percent, and its household growth rate was only 77 percent. This implies that average household size in Las Vegas was on the rise in the 1990s. A number of likely reasons underlie this trend, including an inflow of larger households, births to families already living in the city in 1990, and "doubling up" by two or more families into one housing unit. Some other cities in which the population growth rate was much higher than the household growth rate during the 1990s are Phoenix, Bakersfield, Fresno, and the central cities of California's Orange County (Santa Ana, Anaheim, and Irvine). The housing pressures accompanying the large population increases in these cities were eased in part by their slower increases in numbers of households.

Conversely, cities with falling populations lost households also, but at slower rates than they lost population. Baltimore, Gary, and Cincinnati all experienced much more rapid declines in population than in households. In effect, the household "cushion" still existed for these cities, although it was much smaller than in previous decades. The problems accompanying their population losses were perhaps muted to some extent by their slower declines in households. This pattern of faster population decline than household decline indicates that these cities lost, on net, larger families at higher rates than they did smaller families and single-person households. The relatively large number of elderly residents in these cities also suggests that the latter's faster population decreases may have occurred in part as a result of deaths in existing family households.[7]

Gains and Losses in Married-with-Children Households

Closer examination of changes in the types of households that lived in cities in the 1990s shows important differences between fast-growing and slow-growing/ declining cities. Overall, "married with children" families form a significantly smaller percentage of all U.S. households than in previous decades.[8] Yet fast-growing cities in the U.S. South and West experienced

7. The median age in 2000 in the fifteen cities with the largest population gains in the 1990s was 31.5; among the fifteen cities with the largest population declines, the median age was 33.7.

8. Census 2000 indicates that less than one-fourth (23.5 percent) of all households are "married couples with children." U.S. Bureau of the Census (2001). Such households constituted 40.3 percent of all households in 1970, 30.4 percent in 1980, and 26.3 percent in 1990.

large increases in numbers of family households, especially married couples with children.[9] Meanwhile, in slow-growing cities of the Northeast and Midwest in the 1990s, married-couple family households, particularly those with children, declined at much faster rates than did nonfamilies and other families. (See appendix table 13A-1).

Fast-growing cities in the 1990s are characterized by the considerable presence of married couples, including those with children, among their resident and new-arrival populations (upper panel of table 13-3). In thirteen of the fifteen fastest-growing central cities, married-couple households (with and without children) account for more than 40 percent of all households, and they account for 50 percent or more of central-city households in metro areas such as Las Vegas, Bakersfield, McAllen (Texas), and California's Orange County. (For purposes of comparison, married couples account for 39 percent of the combined city households for all metro areas in the study.). In eight of these fifteen metros, the central city's "married-with-children" household share equals or exceeds the national average of 23.5 percent. In part, the large percentages of married-couple households in these fast-growing central cities in the South and West reflect the fairly expansive borders of these cities, which are not as "hemmed in" as most cities of the Northeast and Midwest and are thus able to incorporate a more "suburban" population within their boundaries.

Married-couple households were not the only types driving population growth in the fast-growing cities of the 1990s. Most of these cities experienced significant growth in all types of households (upper right panel of table 13-3). Nearly all of the central cities in these metros saw their nonfamily households increase by more than one-third, and their growth rates for families not headed by a married couple often exceeded those for married-couple households. But the growth of married-couple households reinforced the latter's already sizable base population in these fast-growing cities. As table 13-4 indicates, eight of the fifteen fastest-growing metro area central cities were also among the fifteen central cities with the highest share of "married with children" families in 2000. In most of the nation's fastest-growing central cites in major metropolitan areas, distinctive residential growth dynamics arise from the large immigrant and migrant populations and from the inflow of young married couples and married couples with children.

Cities that experienced population declines in the 1990s offered a stark contrast to the "married-with-children" phenomenon in growing cities. In declining cities in the 1990s, population tended to drop at a faster rate than

9. Frey (2002).

TABLE 13-3. 2000 Household Type Shares and 1990–2000 Rates of Household Type Growth, Central Cities with Greatest Population Growth and Decline in Metro Areas with Population Greater than 500,000

Percent

	Central city household type shares						*1990–2000 rates of household growth*				
	Married couples		*Other families*				*Married couples*		*Other families*		
Central cities of metro areas	*No child*	*W/child*	*No child*	*W/child*	*Non-families*	*Total*	*No child*	*W/child*	*No child*	*W/child*	*Non-families*
Metro areas with greatest central city population growth											
1 Las Vegas, NV-AZ MSA	27	22	8	10	34	100	76	79	85	70	97
2 Bakersfield, CA MSA	24	29	7	14	27	100	27	35	50	25	57
3 Austin, TX MSA	20	19	7	8	47	100	31	31	55	42	39
4 McAllen-Edinburg-Mission, TX MSA	27	33	9	11	20	100	50	36	65	55	43
5 Portland-Vancouver, OR-WA PMSA	23	17	6	9	45	100	28	38	33	37	45
6 Charlotte, NC-SC MSA	23	21	8	10	39	100	20	30	29	48	49
7 Phoenix-Mesa, AZ MSA	24	24	7	11	34	100	15	25	48	30	55
8 Raleigh-Durham, NC MSA	21	18	7	10	44	100	22	30	31	36	49
9 Colorado Springs, CO MSA	27	25	5	9	34	100	24	18	50	33	37
10 Greensboro–Winston-Salem–High Point, NC MSA	24	17	8	11	39	100	14	20	21	30	44
11 Fort Worth-Arlington, TX PMSA	23	25	8	11	34	100	7	17	30	19	49
12 San Antonio, TX MSA	24	24	9	12	31	100	19	14	36	30	36
13 West Palm Beach-Boca Raton, FL MSA	28	16	7	8	43	100	9	19	13	29	43
14 Fresno, CA MSA	21	25	9	15	30	100	4	17	33	11	30
15 Orange County, CA PMSA	22	35	9	10	24	100	0	25	9	–1	32
Metro areas with greater central city population decline											
1 Hartford, CT NECMA	14	12	12	23	40	100	–23	–15	–7	–6	–13
2 St. Louis, MO-IL MSA	15	11	12	15	48	100	–27	–19	–9	–1	–5
3 Youngstown-Warren, OH MSA	22	13	11	15	38	100	–24	–31	–4	4	4
4 Gary, IN PMSA	19	11	17	20	33	100	–14	–36	12	–8	7
5 Baltimore, MD PMSA	17	10	15	16	43	100	–23	–27	–5	–2	7
6 Buffalo, NY MSA	16	12	10	17	45	100	–26	–24	–8	7	–4
7 Syracuse, NY MSA	16	12	8	16	49	100	–24	–23	–10	14	–3
8 Pittsburgh, PA MSA	20	11	10	10	48	100	–19	–20	–18	2	5
9 Cincinnati, OH-KY-IN PMSA	16	11	8	14	51	100	–17	–25	–7	5	6
10 Birmingham, AL MSA	19	13	14	15	40	100	–23	–25	3	11	3
11 Dayton-Springfield, OH MSA	20	14	10	14	43	100	–18	–23	–4	2	4
12 Detroit, MI PMSA	14	13	17	21	35	100	–23	–13	2	–9	–9
13 Albany-Schenectady-Troy, NY MSA	17	12	8	13	50	100	–19	–22	–14	27	3
14 Scranton-Hazleton, PA MSA	24	16	9	9	42	100	–15	–18	–12	23	9
15 Toledo, OH MSA	22	16	8	13	40	100	–13	–21	–1	20	11

Source: William H. Frey analysis of decennial census data.

TABLE 13-4. Major Metro Central Cities with Greatest Shares of Married Couples with Children, 2000

Metro area central cities		Married couples with children (percent)[a]
1	Santa Ana-Anaheim-Irvine, CA	34.7
2	McAllen-Edinburg-Mission, TX	33.2
3	San Jose, CA	29.9
4	El Paso, TX	29.7
5	Bakersfield, CA	28.6
6	Riverside-San Bernardino, CA	27.1
7	Vallejo-Fairfield-Napa, CA	26.2
8	Stockton-Lodi, CA	25.9
9	Fresno, CA	25.4
10	Fort Worth-Arlington, TX	25.2
11	Colorado Springs, CO	24.7
12	Phoenix-Mesa, AZ	24.2
13	San Antonio, TX	24.1
14	Norfolk-Virginia Beach-Newport News, VA	23.6
	National Average	*23.5*
15	Ventura, CA	22.7

Source: William H. Frey analysis of decennial census data.
a. Married couples with children as percent of total central city households.

did households, and the number of larger married-couple households—especially those with children—*decreased* faster than did other household types. As the bottom right panel of table 13-3 indicates, central cities in five of these fifteen metro areas lost at least a quarter of their total "married-with-children" households (Youngstown-Warren, Gary, Baltimore, Cincinnati, and Birmingham). Married couples with children made up at least 20 percent of households in most of the fastest-growing central cities in 2000 but far less than 20 percent of households in each of the fifteen declining central cities (bottom left panel of table 13-3).

Yet only the "top" two declining cities, Hartford and St. Louis, experienced net losses in all five household types. Many of the declining cities in fact continued to experience growth in nonfamily households in the 1990s. In most of these cities, this nonfamily household type, largely representing younger singles and elderly persons living alone, constituted at least 40 percent of all households in 2000. The bottom right panel of table 9-3 shows that ten of these fifteen central cities experienced modest growth in their nonfamily household population. A rise in nonfamily households in the declining cities does not necessarily imply that such cities continued to attract coming-of-age singles in the 1990s. As indicated earlier, this nonfamily growth could be attributable in part to the death of spouses in elderly married-couple families, as could some of the decreases in "married-without-children" households that these cities witnessed during the decade.

Families with children and not headed by a married couple were also on the rise in most of the declining cities in the 1990s. Ten of the fifteen fastest-declining central cities saw growth in this household type, which most often represents single parents with children, and in some cases cohabiting partners with children. Three of these ten cities—Albany, Scranton, and Toledo—experienced greater than 20 percent growth in this household type and a nearly equivalent *decline* in the number of married families with children. In twelve of the fifteen fastest-declining cities, "other families with children" now account for a greater share of households than do "married-with-children" households (bottom left panel of table 13-3). In theory, the "other-families-with-children" household type could have grown as the result of increased divorce, spousal deaths, or families of this type moving to the declining cities. In all likelihood, however, this growth reflects a number of other trends in these cities, including continued births to younger unwed mothers and increasing rates of cohabitation among unwed parents.

The selective outmigration of larger married-couple family households is characteristic of older, declining central cities. Most such cities are located in regions of the country where neither central cities nor suburbs are gaining residents from other parts of the United States. Additionally, none of these central cities is benefiting appreciably from the recent immigration waves that have fueled growth in many of the fast-growing cities. In earlier decades these older, declining central cities could count on baby boomer "coming of age" households, including married-couple households, to locate there prior to moving to the suburbs. Their prospects for growth from this source are no longer so strong.

In between the fast-growing and the declining cities lies a small group of cities that staged a population "comeback" in the 1990s after losing population in the 1980s.[10] Household statistics indicate that different types of households accounted for the turnaround in each of these cities—Atlanta, Chicago, Denver, and Memphis. Denver experienced increases in married couples with and without children, but Atlanta and Memphis saw declines in this household type. Single-parent families with children were on the decline in Atlanta and Chicago but increased by 28 percent in Memphis, where they now represent 17 percent of all households. In all of the "comeback" cities, singles "coming of age" represented a renewed source of household growth: across all four cities, nonfamily households increased in number by 16 percent, and those headed by persons twenty-five to thirty-four years old increased by 21 percent.

10. Berube (2002).

More Nonfamily than Married-with-Children Households in Suburbs

Despite a three-decade high in central city population growth in the 1990s, suburban growth continued to dominate the metropolitan landscape. The household source of that suburban population growth, however, was quite different from the household source traditionally associated with the suburban life-style.

Overall, the population in central cities of the top 102 metropolitan areas grew by 9 percent during the decade, and the number of suburban residents in these metros grew by nearly 17 percent. The suburbs maintained an even more significant edge over cities in terms of household growth, with an increase of 18 percent in the 1990s, versus 8.6 percent in cities.[11] Faster suburban household growth was not limited to certain types of households. Across four of the five major household types, suburban growth rates were roughly double central city growth rates (figure 13-3). And while central cities experienced a net loss of 2 percent of their "married-without-children" households, such households actually increased by 10 percent in the suburbs.

Notably, the suburbs of major metropolitan areas are home to growing numbers of household types traditionally associated with cities. Overall, nonfamilies and single-parent families were the fastest-growing household types in major metropolitan suburbs in the 1990s. The profile of these household types in suburbs may differ somewhat from their profile in cities; for instance, a greater share of "other families with children" households in the suburbs than in the cities may be the product of divorce, separation, or cohabitation.

As a result of this rise in smaller nonfamily and single-parent family household types in the suburbs, household growth maintained an edge over population growth in the suburbs in the 1990s. This implies that average suburban household size decreased during the decade. In contrast, in the central cities, household and population growth were nearly equivalent and average household size was stable. One implication of the decrease in average household size in the suburbs in the 1990s may be higher per capita housing demand. The type of housing that these smaller households seek may be somewhat different from that demanded by the larger household types that have traditionally predominated in the suburbs.

11. These figures, which are for central cities in the 102 metropolitan areas discussed in the study, differ slightly from those in figure 13-2, which are for central cities in all OMB-defined metropolitan areas.

FIGURE 13-3. Suburb and Central City Household Change, by Household Type, 1990–2000[a]

a. Metro areas with population of more than 500,000.

This trend has changed the household makeup of suburbs rather significantly. Figure 13-4 shows the share of all households that each major household type represented in the suburbs in 2000. Nonfamilies now represent a larger share of total suburban households than do traditional "married with children" households (appendix table 13A-2). As they did in 1990, households with children under eighteen still make up about one-third (35 percent) of all suburban households. Now, however, nearly one in every four (24 percent) suburban households with children is not headed by a married couple, as compared with fewer than one in five a decade ago.

High-Immigration Cities "Suburbanizing"; Northern Suburbs "Urbanizing"

For much of the post–World War II era, a suburban residence was generally associated with child raising. City households relocated to suburban communities chosen on the basis of their mix of available housing, community services, and quality of school systems. As a consequence, the share of "married with children" central city households began to shrink over time.[12]

12. Frey and Kobrin (1982).

FIGURE 13-4. Household Type Shares in Suburbs, 2000[a]

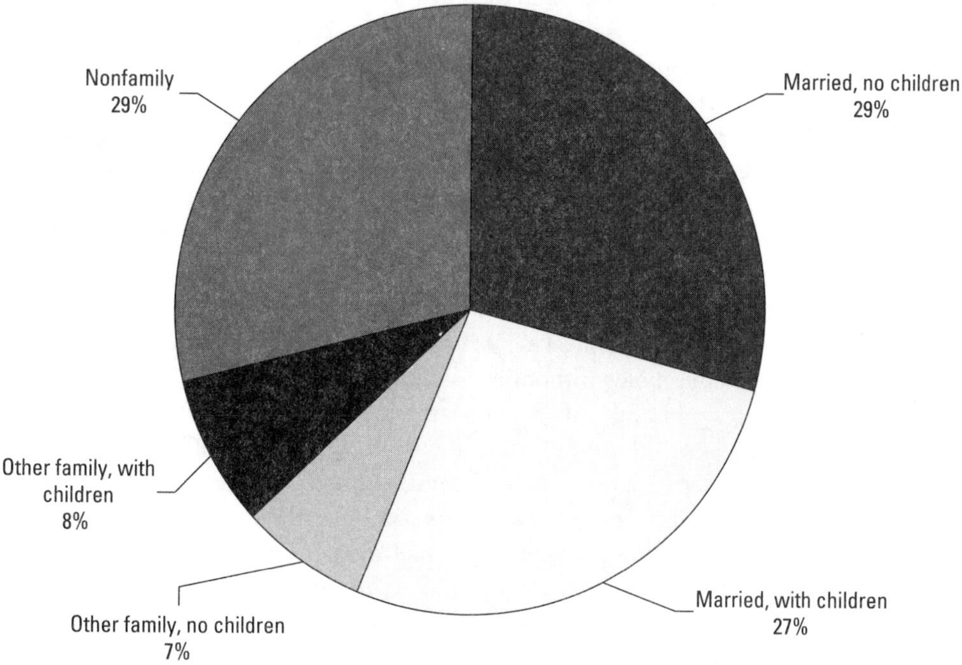

a. Metro areas with population greater than 500,000.

Conversely, cities were associated with "coming-of-age" singles and childless married couples, as well as with traditionally more disadvantaged groups like single-parent families and elderly homeowners. To a large extent, these residential patterns still hold in much of metropolitan America. But important regional trends emerged in the 1990s that blur some of the long-established demographic distinctions between cities and suburbs. In general, cities in high-immigration metros and in fast-growing metros in the South and West experienced increases in "married with children" families, while in the suburbs of slower-growing northern metros the numbers of single-parent family and small nonfamily households were on the rise.

City Patterns by Metro Type. The image of "suburbs only" as favored locales for two-parent families is changing as new waves of immigrants make their homes in central cities, especially in selected Melting Pot metropolitan areas. Among new immigrant minorities, Hispanics in particular, birth rates are higher and married-couple families with children are more prevalent than among the general population. Census 2000 shows that among

Hispanics, 45 percent of all families are married couples with children and 35 percent of females are in their prime child-bearing ages (fifteen to thirty-four), in comparison with 35 percent and 27 percent respectively for the total U.S. population. Comparable numbers for Asians in 2000 are 46 percent married couples with children and 33 percent of women in their younger child-bearing ages.

The right-hand panel of table 13-5 reveals that the highest rates of central city household growth were in Melting Pot metro areas and in New Sun Belt metro areas located in the South and West.[13] Melting Pot central cities and cities in the largely white metros of the South and West experienced significant increases in "married with children" households. Cities in other metro types experienced net losses of such households, as well as of married-couple households without children (appendix table 13A-2).

In part because of the increases in these families during the 1990s, Melting Pot metros led other metro categories in the "married couples with children" share of their city households (20 percent). In fact, thirteen of the top fifteen metro areas for central city "married with children" household shares are Melting Pot metros with significant Hispanic and/or Asian populations (table 13-4). For instance, more than one-third of Orange County's central city households are married-couple families with children. The combined population of Orange County's central cities (Santa Ana, Anaheim, and Irvine) is 52 percent Hispanic, 14 percent Asian, and 30 percent non-Hispanic white. In contrast, Orange County's suburbs are 60 percent non-Hispanic white, and the married-couple share of Orange County's suburban households (27 percent) is lower than that of its central cities.

Central cities located in the largely white metro areas of the South and West also exhibit relatively high shares of married-couple families both with (17 percent) and without (23 percent) children, as well as significant growth (9 percent) in "married-with-children" households. Most of these areas experienced significant domestic in-migration over the 1990s, including an influx of married-couple populations.[14]

The other New Sun Belt category of metros, the largely white-black metros of the South, included a few cities with growing married-couple populations such as Charlotte, Greensboro, and Raleigh. But the majority of cities in the largely white-black metros of the South actually lost married-couple households both with and without children. These include a few cities with declining populations (Baltimore, Birmingham, Greenville

13. Frey (2002).
14. Frey (2002).

TABLE 13-5. 2000 Shares and 1990–2000 Rates of Growth for Household Types, by Type of Metro Area

Percent

		Household type shares, 2000						*1990–2000 rates of household growth*					
		Married couples		*Other families*				*Married couples*		*Other families*			
Metro area[a]	*Number*	*No child*	*W/child*	*No child*	*W/child*	*Non-families*	*Total*	*No child*	*W/child*	*No child*	*W/child*	*Non-families*	*Total HHs*
Central cities													
Melting Pots	33	21	20	10	11	38	100	2	13	14	21	12	11
North—largely white-black	6	17	13	13	17	40	100	−20	−17	−1	5	1	−5
North—largely white	26	20	16	8	12	44	100	−9	−8	1	17	11	3
South—largely white-black	19	21	16	10	13	40	100	−1	−3	12	22	21	11
South and West—largely white	13	23	17	7	9	44	100	2	9	16	24	20	13
Central city total	97	21	18	10	12	40	100	−2	6	10	19	13	9
Suburbs													
Melting Pots	35	28	28	7	9	28	100	11	18	26	43	22	19
North—largely white-black	6	30	25	7	8	31	100	4	2	10	31	27	12
North—largely white	29	30	26	6	7	30	100	5	4	6	34	25	12
South—largely white-black	19	30	27	7	9	28	100	21	15	32	55	40	27
South and West—largely white	13	31	25	6	8	30	100	18	15	36	45	36	25
Suburbs total	102	29	27	7	8	29	100	10	12	20	41	27	18

a. Central cities and suburbs of metro areas with population greater than 500,000.

[South Carolina], New Orleans, and Richmond), as well as modestly growing central cities such as Atlanta. The cities in this group experienced substantial losses of white families in previous decades and now contain slightly above-average shares of nonfamily households and single-parent households.

Northern metro areas, in general, were the most likely to experience slow growth or decrease in their central city populations and households during the 1990s. All six of the North's largely white-black metro central cities declined in both population and households. These areas with significant inner-city black populations continued to lose white families during the 1990s as they had in previous decades. Consequently, the cities there have smaller "married with children" shares than cities in other metro types, and they experienced larger 1990–2000 declines in these shares. Somewhat similar household and population dynamics characterize the North's largely white metros. Central cities in fourteen of these twenty-six metro areas lost population in the 1990s, and a number of them appear among the declining central cities listed in tables 13-2 and 13-3. Because of selective suburbanization over many decades, most cities in this category now house somewhat smaller shares of married couples than do cities in other types of metros. Overall, central cities in the North's largely white metros lost married-couple families during the 1990s.

The importance of married-couple family households to city growth in the 1990s is most apparent in a comparison of household growth rates in Melting Pot cities versus the largely white cities of the North. Differences are rather small between them in terms of the growth of their nonfamily and single-parent family households, which together represent roughly half of all households in these cities. But the loss of married-couple families in the northern cities stands in stark contrast with the Melting Pot cities' significant gains in "married with children" households and with their increases, however modest, in childless married-couple households. As a result, overall household growth in Melting Pot cities significantly outpaced household growth in the largely white cities of the North.

Suburban Patterns by Metro Type. In general, suburbs of the New Sun Belt experienced faster growth in all types of households than did the northern suburbs, especially in the case of larger "married with children" households. Across the suburbs of all types of metro areas, the number of single-parent and nonfamily households increased by double-digit rates. In Melting Pot metros and New Sun Belt metros, these single-parent and nonfamily household increases were accompanied by considerable growth in married-couple families (table 13-5). But in northern suburbs (for both largely white-black metros and largely white metros), growth in nonfamily and single-parent family households virtually dwarfed married-couple family growth. Married-couple families grew between 2 percent and 5 percent overall in these northern suburbs, but single-parent and nonfamily households grew at rates exceeding 25 percent. By 2000 nonfamily suburban household share exceeded "married-with-children" suburban household share by significant amounts in both metro types of the North.

In the North's metros, the differences were stark not only between different suburban household types but also between the suburbs and the central cities. Because of past migration patterns, married-couple families still constitute more than 50 percent of total households in the suburbs of each of these metropolitan areas—much higher than married-couple families' 30 percent share in the cities; in several of these metros, however, that gap narrowed in the 1990s. In the 1990s the suburbs of the North's largely white-black metros saw their nonfamily households grow by 27 percent, while nonfamily households grew by only 1 percent in the respective cities; the city of Detroit, for instance, lost 9 percent of its nonfamily households in the 1990s, while Detroit's suburbs saw this household type grow by nearly a third (appendix table 13A-2). Similarly, single-parent families also grew much faster in the suburbs of the North's largely white-black metros (31 percent) than in the cities (5 percent). Three of those six metro areas actually showed absolute declines in their suburban "married with children" households during the decade. Thus several household types traditionally associated with the city (singles "coming of age," single parents, and elderly people living alone) are becoming increasingly common in slow-growing northern suburbs.

The majority of household growth in suburbs of the North's metros came in the form of single-parent families and smaller nonfamilies, while other metro types' suburbs experienced significant growth in all types of households. The largest increases occurred in the New Sun Belt suburbs of the South and West, where the total number of households jumped by more than 25 percent during the decade. In general, the New Sun Belt suburbs experienced growth in all types of households at faster rates than did the suburbs of the North; the differential was greatest in the case of larger "married with children" households, which in New Sun Belt suburbs increased at roughly five times the rate (15 percent) of such households' increase in suburbs of the North (3 percent). The large married-couple household increases in some suburbs of the South's largely white-black metros were coincident with declines in the central city in this household type. In the Nashville metro area, for instance, the number of married-couple households in the city declined while the number in the suburbs grew by more than 30 percent.

Melting Pot suburbs experienced patterns of household change most similar to those occurring in their cities. As was the case in the cities, the growth of nonfamily households in Melting Pot suburbs during the decade (22 percent) was comparable to the growth of "married with children" households (18 percent). Single-parent families were the fastest-growing household type in suburbs (43 percent) and cities (21 percent) alike. In part because of these similar growth patterns, cities and suburbs in Melting Pot metros looked more like one another in 2000 than did cities and suburbs in other metro area types, echoing earlier findings on the similarities in racial/ethnic makeup between cities and suburbs in Melting Pot metros.[15]

CONCLUSION

The 1990–2000 decade ushered in a new context for population and household dynamics in the nation's metropolitan areas. Conventional residential patterns in the nation's cities and suburbs were challenged by large demographic trends, including the aging of baby boomers, increased inflows and high fertility of immigrant families, and migration to New Sun Belt areas in the U.S. South and West.

The growth of child-centered city populations in America's Melting Pot and New Sun Belt metropolitan areas presents several challenges. It may create new needs for public services like child care and infant health care, it may further test the adequacy of urban school systems, and it may put new stresses on the fiscal positions of these cities. But at the same time, household patterns in the fastest-growing cities suggest that burgeoning family populations create opportunities for viable neighborhoods and continued growth that may not exist in other central cities.

Meanwhile, in northern suburbs the growth of smaller households is presenting challenges and opportunities of its own. With increasing numbers of nonfamily and single-parent family households calling these suburbs home, the need for affordable multifamily housing in these jurisdictions is on the rise. There may also be an increase in the demand for services like transportation and home health care for elderly homeowners who are

15. Frey (2001).

"aging in place" in the suburbs. Further analysis will illuminate whether the inner suburban communities in these northern metros are being transformed into functional extensions of their central cities with respect to household structures, housing, and socioeconomic characteristics.

The changing household makeup of cities and suburbs and the continued decline of many northern cities are occurring within a nationwide context of decentralizing households and population. The trend of faster growth in the suburbs than in the cities is not confined to certain types of metro areas nor to certain types of households. It pervades fast-growing and slow-growing metros alike and is true of married-couple households, single-parent households, and singles. The actual degree of growth disparity between cities and suburbs may differ across different regions of the United States, but the consistent overall ascendancy of the suburbs in this respect raises significant questions about how cities are poised to compete in their metropolitan economies for jobs and residents during the next ten years. It remains to be seen whether the increasing demographic similarity between cities and suburbs across the United States will bolster efforts to enhance regional cooperation.

TABLE 13A-1. Central City and Suburb Household Type Shares, 2000, and Household Type Changes, by Type of Metro Area, 1990–2000

Percent

	Central city household types (shares sum to 100)					Central city household growth rates				
	Married couples		Other families			Married couples		Other families		
Metro area[a]	*No child*	*W/ child*	*No child*	*W/ child*	*Non-families*	*No child*	*W/ child*	*No child*	*W/ child*	*Non-families*
Melting Pot metros										
Albuquerque, NM MSA	24	19	7	11	39	10	4	25	36	30
Austin, TX MSA	20	19	7	8	47	31	31	55	39	42
Bakersfield, CA MSA	24	29	7	14	27	27	35	50	57	25
Bergen-Passaic, NJ PMSA	...	...	...	...	...	...	...	...	...	...
Chicago, IL PMSA	18	17	12	12	40	–6	4	5	–1	9
Dallas, TX PMSA	19	19	9	11	41	–2	17	24	31	11
El Paso, TX MSA	25	30	10	13	23	10	1	38	24	21
Fort Lauderdale, FL PMSA	21	11	7	9	52	–10	–1	0	12	10
Fort Worth-Arlington, TX PMSA	23	25	8	11	34	7	17	30	49	19
Fresno, CA MSA	21	25	9	15	30	4	17	33	30	11
Honolulu, HI MSA	28	18	11	6	38	–4	–4	13	18	11
Houston, TX PMSA	21	22	10	11	36	10	20	25	24	14
Jersey City, NJ PMSA	19	18	13	13	37	–1	4	5	10	15
Las Vegas, NV-AZ MSA	27	22	8	10	34	76	79	85	97	70
Los Angeles-Long Beach, CA PMSA	19	23	10	11	38	–7	12	2	21	3
McAllen-Edinburg-Mission, TX MSA	27	33	9	11	20	50	36	65	43	55
Miami, FL PMSA	22	15	14	12	38	–6	4	5	–2	10
Middlesex-Somerset-Hunterdon, NJ PMSA[b]	...	...	...	...	...	...	...	...	...	...
New York, NY PMSA	20	18	12	12	39	–5	11	10	19	8
Newark, NJ PMSA	16	15	17	20	32	–7	–7	8	2	2
Oakland, CA PMSA	18	16	11	12	43	–3	10	9	–2	6
Orange County, CA PMSA	22	35	9	10	24	0	25	9	32	–1
Orlando, FL MSA	19	13	8	12	48	2	8	30	43	34
Phoenix-Mesa, AZ MSA	24	24	7	11	34	15	25	48	55	30
Riverside-San Bernardino, CA PMSA	21	27	9	15	28	–7	5	22	32	4
Sacramento, CA PMSA	20	18	9	12	41	–6	3	20	18	11
San Antonio, TX MSA	24	24	9	12	31	19	14	36	36	30
San Diego, CA MSA	23	22	7	8	40	2	13	12	16	15
San Francisco, CA PMSA	19	12	8	4	56	5	2	3	–9	13
San Jose, CA PMSA	26	30	9	8	26	9	12	15	7	10
Stockton-Lodi, CA MSA	23	26	8	14	29	5	11	21	36	11
Tucson, AZ MSA	22	18	8	11	42	8	8	36	38	22
Vallejo-Fairfield-Napa, CA PMSA	26	26	8	11	28	7	2	38	31	16
Ventura, CA PMSA	26	23	7	9	34	–1	7	15	28	13
Washington, DC-MD-VA-WV PMSA	14	8	12	11	54	–12	–7	–9	5	5

Suburb household types (shares sum to 100)					Suburb household growth rates				
Married couples		Other families			Married couples		Other families		
No child	W/ child	No child	W/ child	Non-families	No child	W/ child	No child	W/ child	Non-families
30	27	8	11	24	37	10	57	52	60
29	32	5	8	25	55	50	68	72	50
27	29	7	13	24	–4	0	25	28	8
29	26	9	7	28	–6	12	5	29	13
29	30	7	7	28	6	14	18	41	24
28	31	6	9	26	34	31	56	61	43
21	49	7	12	10	61	39	123	110	64
27	21	8	9	35	3	41	40	85	29
31	30	6	8	25	25	17	46	53	39
29	31	8	11	21	9	16	35	30	17
32	31	10	8	19	13	–9	50	32	36
28	35	6	9	22	33	21	52	49	26
23	19	11	9	38	–4	9	10	30	23
29	21	7	10	33	66	74	99	113	81
24	29	10	11	27	–4	8	13	26	1
26	42	8	11	12	58	48	80	63	53
26	24	11	11	28	4	17	34	39	8
30	29	7	6	28	1	20	10	43	22
29	28	8	7	28	–6	12	1	33	13
28	27	9	8	28	–5	11	5	32	13
27	27	7	8	31	4	18	22	22	12
28	27	7	7	30	4	21	17	33	13
30	24	7	9	30	24	28	54	77	44
33	23	6	8	31	54	52	68	73	61
27	30	7	11	24	11	18	47	54	21
28	25	6	10	30	17	20	43	41	31
33	30	6	9	23	19	0	39	41	31
28	27	7	10	28	3	13	27	30	16
28	24	7	6	35	–1	11	7	13	5
28	26	7	6	34	1	22	4	8	3
29	32	7	10	22	7	19	25	41	18
37	22	5	7	29	41	23	56	57	51
30	28	6	10	26	10	4	44	37	24
29	33	7	9	23	6	11	20	32	15
27	27	7	8	31	14	17	20	49	27

(continued)

TABLE 13A-1. Central City and Suburb Household Type Shares, 2000, and Household Type Changes, by Type of Metro Area, 1990–2000 (*continued*)

Percent

Metro area[a]	Central city household types (shares sum to 100): Married couples, No child	Married couples, W/ child	Other families, No child	Other families, W/ child	Non-families	Central city household growth rates: Married couples, No child	Married couples, W/ child	Other families, No child	Other families, W/ child	Non-families
North—largely white-black metros										
Cleveland, OH PMSA	16	12	13	18	41	–21	–20	–3	13	2
Detroit, MI PMSA	14	13	17	21	35	–23	–13	2	–9	–9
Gary, IN PMSA	19	11	17	20	33	–14	–36	12	–8	7
Milwaukee, WI PMSA	18	14	10	16	42	–20	–18	5	7	7
Philadelphia, PA-NJ PMSA	19	14	14	14	40	–18	–14	–3	21	6
St. Louis, MO-IL MSA	15	11	12	15	48	–27	–19	–9	–1	–5
North—largely white metros										
Akron, OH PMSA	22	15	9	13	40	–11	–14	2	17	9
Albany-Schenectady-Troy, NY MSA	17	12	8	13	50	–19	–22	–14	27	3
Allentown-Bethlehem, PA MSA	25	16	8	11	40	–14	–11	0	35	9
Ann Arbor, MI PMSA	20	18	4	5	52	1	2	5	6	17
Boston, MA-NH NECMA	16	12	10	11	52	–6	0	–6	12	11
Buffalo, NY MSA	16	12	10	17	45	–26	–24	–8	7	–4
Cincinnati, OH-KY-IN PMSA	16	11	8	14	51	–17	–25	–7	5	6
Columbus, OH MSA	20	17	7	12	45	3	3	14	34	28
Dayton-Springfield, OH MSA	20	14	10	14	43	–18	–23	–4	2	4
Fort Wayne, IN MSA	23	19	7	12	39	9	9	21	39	27
Grand Rapids-Muskegon-Holland, MI MSA	21	19	8	13	39	–8	–7	17	10	20
Harrisburg-Lebanon-Carlisle, PA MSA	18	12	9	15	45	–12	–17	–4	12	3
Hartford, CT NECMA	14	12	12	23	40	–23	–15	–7	–6	–13
Indianapolis, IN MSA	23	18	8	12	40	–3	–7	15	30	22
Kansas City, MO-KS MSA	22	17	9	12	40	–9	–10	8	16	10
Minneapolis–St. Paul, MN-WI MSA	17	15	7	10	51	–14	–3	2	12	7
Monmouth-Ocean, NJ PMSA[b]	...	...	...	...	...	...	...	...	...	...
Nassau-Suffolk, NY PMSA[b]	...	...	...	...	...	...	...	...	...	...
Bridgeport, CT NECMA	18	17	13	17	35	–21	–9	7	19	–3
Omaha, NE-IA MSA	24	20	7	10	39	7	12	18	25	25
Pittsburgh, PA MSA	20	11	10	10	48	–19	–20	–18	2	5
Providence-Fall River-Warwick, RI-MA NECMA	21	17	8	13	40	–11	–6	1	39	13
Rochester, NY MSA	14	11	9	19	47	–23	–23	–2	15	0
Scranton-Hazleton, PA MSA	24	16	9	9	42	–15	–18	–12	23	9
Springfield, MA NECMA	**	**	**	**	**	**	**	**	**	**
Syracuse, NY MSA	16	12	8	16	49	–24	–23	–10	14	–3
Toledo, OH MSA	22	16	8	13	40	–13	–21	–1	20	11
Wichita, KS MSA	25	22	6	10	37	4	8	24	27	18
Youngstown-Warren, OH MSA	22	13	11	15	38	–24	–31	–4	4	4

Suburb household types (shares sum to 100)					Suburb household growth rates				
Married couples		Other families			Married couples		Other families		
No child	W/ child	No child	W/ child	Non-families	No child	W/ child	No child	W/ child	Non-families
31	23	7	7	32	2	–3	8	28	24
29	25	7	7	32	4	3	8	24	31
30	25	7	9	29	8	–3	23	30	30
32	27	5	6	31	13	6	10	43	42
30	26	7	7	29	2	5	7	32	22
29	25	7	9	30	5	–2	16	38	25
33	25	6	7	29	10	4	12	36	32
30	24	6	8	32	4	–4	1	41	25
34	25	6	6	28	7	2	9	49	31
31	28	5	7	29	26	18	27	37	41
28	25	7	8	33	2	6	0	26	20
31	23	7	7	32	–3	–4	2	30	24
30	27	6	8	28	13	5	14	40	37
32	28	5	8	27	16	9	16	42	36
33	23	6	8	30	3	–10	10	37	27
34	30	4	7	25	10	–6	11	38	28
31	30	5	8	27	18	12	26	49	40
34	24	5	7	31	10	–2	10	46	25
30	24	6	7	33	–3	1	–2	44	20
32	29	5	8	26	24	22	26	55	42
31	28	5	8	29	17	10	33	44	33
29	29	5	8	29	21	14	26	41	40
31	26	7	6	30	7	12	13	38	28
32	30	9	6	23	–4	7	7	30	22
29	25	7	8	31	–5	8	–1	30	15
31	31	5	8	25	14	–4	23	29	26
32	22	7	7	32	–3	–7	–2	24	18
30	23	7	8	32	1	–1	5	44	24
31	26	5	8	30	3	–3	4	38	25
31	21	8	7	34	–1	–10	–7	29	19
26	20	7	11	35	–4	–7	0	21	19
30	25	6	9	31	2	–8	3	37	24
32	27	5	7	30	14	–2	14	38	30
33	32	4	8	23	9	3	27	37	26
34	23	7	7	29	4	–11	13	26	26

(continued)

TABLE 13A-1. Central City and Suburb Household Type Shares, 2000, and Household Type Changes, by Type of Metro Area, 1990–2000 (*continued*)

Percent

	Central city household types (shares sum to 100)					*Central city household growth rates*				
	Married couples		*Other families*			*Married couples*		*Other families*		
Metro area[a]	*No child*	*W/ child*	*No child*	*W/ child*	*Non-families*	*No child*	*W/ child*	*No child*	*W/ child*	*Non-families*
South—largely white-black metros										
Atlanta, GA MSA	15	9	12	13	51	–4	–10	2	–5	23
Baltimore, MD PMSA	17	10	15	16	43	–23	–27	–5	–2	7
Baton Rouge, LA MSA	21	15	10	13	41	–7	–10	16	18	18
Birmingham, AL MSA	19	13	14	15	40	–23	–25	3	11	3
Charleston–North Charleston, SC MSA	21	15	9	13	42	18	–4	40	47	49
Charlotte, NC-SC MSA	23	21	8	10	39	20	30	29	49	48
Columbia, SC MSA	18	13	9	12	48	7	9	19	45	35
Greensboro–Winston-Salem–High Point, NC MSA	24	17	8	11	39	14	20	21	44	30
Greenville-Spartanburg-Anderson, SC MSA	21	13	10	12	44	–13	–19	–3	8	13
Jacksonville, FL MSA	25	22	8	12	33	10	3	25	51	24
Little Rock-North Little Rock, AR MSA	24	17	8	12	39	–4	–11	14	26	14
Memphis, TN-AR-MS MSA	19	15	13	17	37	–11	–7	16	28	21
Mobile, AL MSA	24	18	10	13	35	–4	–12	9	20	13
Nashville, TN MSA	23	16	8	10	42	1	–4	19	22	30
New Orleans, LA MSA	18	13	13	16	40	–10	–12	8	0	7
Norfolk–Virginia Beach–Newport News, VA-NC MSA	24	24	7	12	33	–1	–11	16	41	21
Raleigh-Durham, NC MSA	21	18	7	10	44	22	30	31	49	36
Richmond, VA MSA	17	10	11	13	48	–17	–13	–1	11	6
Wilmington, DE-MD PMSA	16	11	13	16	45	–14	–13	–4	24	4
South and West—largely white metros										
Colorado Springs, CO MSA	27	25	5	9	34	24	18	50	37	33
Denver, CO PMSA	20	15	7	8	50	20	15	7	8	50
Knoxville, TN MSA	22	13	8	10	48	22	13	8	10	48
Louisville, KY-IN MSA	19	12	10	13	45	19	12	10	13	45
Oklahoma City, OK MSA	26	20	7	11	37	26	20	7	11	37
Portland-Vancouver, OR-WA PMSA	23	17	6	9	45	23	17	6	9	45
Salt Lake City-Ogden, UT MSA	22	21	7	9	41	22	21	7	9	41
Sarasota-Bradenton, FL MSA	27	12	7	9	45	27	12	7	9	45
Seattle, WA PMSA	20	13	6	5	56	20	13	6	5	56
Tacoma, WA PMSA	23	19	7	12	40	23	19	7	12	40
Tampa–St. Petersburg–Clearwater, FL MSA	23	15	8	10	43	23	15	8	10	43
Tulsa, OK MSA	25	18	7	10	40	25	18	7	10	40
West Palm Beach–Boca Raton, FL MSA	28	16	7	8	43	28	16	7	8	43

Source: William H. Frey analysis of decennial census data.

a. Population greater than 500,000.

b. Metro areas with no central cities.

Suburb household types (shares sum to 100)					Suburb household growth rates				
Married couples		Other families			Married couples		Other families		
No child	W/ child	No child	W/ child	Non-families	No child	W/ child	No child	W/ child	Non-families
27	28	7	10	28	31	32	58	76	48
30	26	7	8	29	8	9	16	55	34
29	30	7	11	24	32	5	46	50	45
32	26	7	7	27	17	9	25	47	40
30	26	8	10	27	14	–13	17	36	32
32	27	7	8	26	21	19	25	53	41
29	25	7	10	29	22	8	22	45	41
34	25	6	8	26	12	8	16	46	30
32	24	7	9	28	18	8	25	55	41
33	25	6	8	28	40	23	40	58	46
33	27	6	9	26	31	7	47	57	54
32	31	6	9	22	34	13	38	46	35
33	26	7	9	24	31	9	34	37	50
32	30	6	8	24	38	26	49	70	65
28	25	9	10	28	12	–6	27	30	24
30	25	8	11	27	18	8	21	41	30
30	29	5	7	29	34	41	27	60	50
29	26	7	10	28	17	12	24	52	34
29	25	7	9	30	10	8	24	55	33
32	36	4	9	20	41	29	64	55	55
28	28	5	9	30	28	28	5	9	30
35	25	6	7	27	35	25	6	7	27
31	25	6	9	29	31	25	6	9	29
30	25	6	9	30	30	25	6	9	30
30	28	5	8	29	30	28	5	8	29
28	37	6	8	21	28	37	6	8	21
41	14	5	6	34	41	14	5	6	34
28	27	5	8	31	28	27	5	8	31
30	28	5	10	27	30	28	5	10	27
34	18	6	8	34	34	18	6	8	34
34	30	5	9	22	34	30	5	9	22
34	18	6	7	35	34	18	6	7	35

TABLE 13A-2. Population and Household Growth Rates for Central Cities and Suburbs, by Type of Metro Area, 1990–2000

Percent

	Central city growth			*Suburb growth*		
Metro areas[a]	*Population*	*Households*	*Difference*[b]	*Population*	*Households*	*Difference*[b]
Melting Pot metros						
Albuquerque, NM MSA	17	19	3	29	35	6
Austin, TX MSA	41	38	–3	56	54	–2
Bakersfield, CA MSA	41	34	–8	12	5	–7
Bergen-Passaic, NJ PMSA[b]	...	...	...	7	7	–1
Chicago, IL PMSA	4	4	0	16	16	0
Dallas, TX PMSA	18	12	–6	40	38	–1
El Paso, TX MSA	9	13	4	52	57	5
Fort Lauderdale, FL PMSA	2	3	1	33	27	–6
Fort Worth-Arlington, TX PMSA	22	19	–3	28	29	0
Fresno, CA MSA	21	15	–6	23	17	–6
Honolulu, HI MSA	2	4	3	7	12	5
Houston, TX PMSA	20	16	–3	31	29	–2
Jersey City, NJ PMSA	5	8	3	14	12	–1
Las Vegas, NV-AZ MSA	85	77	–8	82	78	–4
Los Angeles-Long Beach, CA PMSA	6	5	–2	8	5	–3
McAllen-Edinburg-Mission, TX MSA	40	47	6	53	55	2
Miami, FL PMSA	1	3	2	20	14	–5
Middlesex-Somerset-Hunterdon, NJ PMSA	...	...	...	15	15	0
New York, NY PMSA	9	7	–2	7	7	0
Newark, NJ PMSA	–1	0	0	7	7	0
Oakland, CA PMSA	7	4	–3	17	13	–4
Orange County, CA PMSA	21	11	–10	17	14	–3
Orlando, FL MSA	13	23	10	38	36	–1
Phoenix-Mesa, AZ MSA	35	28	–7	59	58	–1
Riverside-San Bernardino, CA PMSA	13	6	–6	28	22	–6
Sacramento, CA PMSA	10	7	–3	26	25	–1
San Antonio, TX MSA	22	24	2	15	17	2
San Diego, CA MSA	10	11	1	15	13	–2
San Francisco, CA PMSA	7	8	1	8	5	–3
San Jose, CA PMSA	14	11	–4	10	7	–3
Stockton-Lodi, CA MSA	14	13	–1	21	17	–4
Tucson, AZ MSA	20	19	–1	37	41	4
Vallejo-Fairfield-Napa, CA PMSA	15	12	–3	15	15	0
Ventura, CA PMSA	9	9	0	13	13	–1
Washington, DC-MD-VA-WV PMSA	–6	–1	5	20	22	1
North—largely white-black metros						
Cleveland, OH PMSA	–5	–5	1	4	9	4
Detroit, MI PMSA	–7	–10	–3	8	13	5
Gary, IN PMSA	–12	–7	5	8	13	5
Milwaukee, WI PMSA	–5	–3	1	12	20	7
Philadelphia, PA-NJ PMSA	–4	–2	2	7	11	3
St. Louis, MO-IL MSA	–12	–11	1	8	11	4
North—largely white metros						
Akron, OH PMSA	–3	0	3	10	16	6
Albany-Schenectady-Troy, NY MSA	–6	–4	2	4	10	5

(*continued*)

TABLE 13A-2. Population and Household Growth Rates for Central Cities and Suburbs, by Type of Metro Area, 1990–2000 (*continued*)

Percent

Metro areas[a]	Central city growth: Population	Central city growth: Households	Central city growth: Difference[b]	Suburb growth: Population	Suburb growth: Households	Suburb growth: Difference[b]
Allentown-Bethlehem, PA MSA	1	0	–1	10	14	4
Ann Arbor, MI PMSA	4	10	6	22	28	6
Boston, MA-NH NECMA	3	5	2	7	10	3
Buffalo, NY MSA	–11	–10	1	2	6	4
Cincinnati, OH-KY-IN PMSA	–9	–4	5	13	18	5
Columbus, OH MSA	12	17	5	16	21	4
Dayton-Springfield, OH MSA	–8	–6	2	3	8	5
Fort Wayne, IN MSA	19	20	1	5	10	5
Grand Rapids-Muskegon-Holland, MI MSA	5	6	1	20	24	3
Harrisburg-Lebanon-Carlisle, PA MSA	–4	–3	2	9	13	3
Hartford, CT NECMA	–13	–13	0	4	8	3
Indianapolis, IN MSA	7	10	3	27	30	3
Kansas City, MO-KS MSA	1	2	1	19	22	3
Minneapolis-St. Paul, MN-WI MSA	5	1	–3	21	25	4
Monmouth-Ocean, NJ PMSA	...	...	...	14	16	2
Nassau-Suffolk, NY PMSA	...	...	...	6	7	2
Bridgeport, CT NECMA	–2	–4	–2	5	6	1
Omaha, NE-IA MSA	16	17	1	8	12	4
Pittsburgh, PA MSA	–10	–6	3	0	4	4
Providence-Fall River-Warwick, RI-MA NECMA	4	5	1	6	10	4
Rochester, NY MSA	–5	–5	0	6	9	4
Scranton-Hazleton, PA MSA	–6	–4	3	–1	4	5
Springfield, MA NECMA	...	...	...	1	5	4
Syracuse, NY MSA	–10	–8	2	1	7	6
Toledo, OH MSA	–6	–1	4	8	15	6
Wichita, KS MSA	13	13	0	11	13	2
Youngstown-Warren, OH MSA	–12	–10	2	3	7	5
South—largely white-black metros						
Atlanta, GA MSA	6	8	2	44	41	–3
Baltimore, MD PMSA	–12	–7	5	16	19	3
Baton Rouge, LA MSA	4	7	3	21	28	6
Birmingham, AL MSA	–9	–6	2	18	22	4
Charleston-North Charleston, SC MSA	17	30	13	5	11	7
Charlotte, NC-SC MSA	37	36	–1	25	28	3
Columbia, SC MSA	19	25	6	18	25	6
Greensboro–Winston-Salem–High Point, NC MSA	25	25	0	16	17	2
Greenville-Spartanburg-Anderson, SC MSA	–5	–1	5	20	24	4
Jacksonville, FL MSA	16	18	2	34	38	4
Little Rock-North Little Rock, AR MSA	3	5	3	23	31	7
Memphis, TN-AR-MS MSA	7	9	3	22	28	6
Mobile, AL MSA	1	4	3	22	29	7
Nashville, TN MSA	12	15	3	38	42	4
New Orleans, LA MSA	–2	0	2	8	13	4

(*continued*)

TABLE 13A-2. Population and Household Growth Rates for Central Cities and Suburbs, by Type of Metro Area, 1990–2000 (*continued*)

Percent

	Central city growth			*Suburb growth*		
Metro areas[a]	*Population*	*Households*	*Difference*[b]	*Population*	*Households*	*Difference*[b]
Norfolk-Virginia Beach-Newport News, VA-NC MSA	2	7	6	18	20	2
Raleigh-Durham, NC MSA	34	32	–2	42	42	0
Richmond, VA MSA	–3	–1	2	21	23	2
Wilmington, DE-MD PMSA	2	0	–1	16	19	3
South and West—largely white metros						
Colorado Springs, CO MSA	28	28	–1	35	41	6
Denver, CO PMSA	19	13	–5	35	34	–1
Knoxville, TN MSA	5	10	4	22	27	5
Louisville, KY-IN MSA	–5	–1	3	13	19	6
Oklahoma City, OK MSA	14	14	1	12	17	4
Portland-Vancouver, OR-WA PMSA	39	35	–4	21	21	0
Salt Lake City-Ogden, UT MSA	16	9	–7	27	30	3
Sarasota-Bradenton, FL MSA	8	7	0	24	24	1
Seattle, WA PMSA	9	9	0	22	23	1
Tacoma, WA PMSA	10	9	–1	24	28	4
Tampa-St. Petersburg-Clearwater, FL MSA	7	7	0	20	20	0
Tulsa, OK MSA	7	7	0	20	23	3
West Palm Beach-Boca Raton, FL MSA	21	21	–1	33	31	–1

Source: William H. Frey analysis of decennial census data.

Note: Pertains to MSAs, PMSAs, and (in New England) PMSAs, as defined in June 2000 by the Office of Management and Budget, with modifications for central cities as discussed in text and footnote 3.

a. Population more than 500,000.

b. Household growth rate minus population growth rate.

REFERENCES

Frey, William H. 2001. "Melting Pot Suburbs: A Census 2000 Study of Suburban Diversity." Census 2000 Series. Brookings Institution Center on Urban and Metropolitan Policy.

———. 2002. "Metro Magnets for Minorities and Whites: Melting Pots, the New Sunbelt, and the Heartland." *Research Report.* University of Michigan Population Studies Center.

Frey, William H., and Elaine L. Fielding. 1995. "Changing Urban Populations: Regional Restructuring, Racial Polarization, and Poverty Concentration." In *Cityscape* 1 (2):166. U.S. Department of Housing and Urban Development, Office of Policy Development and Research.

Frey, William H., and Douglas Geverdt. 1998. "Changing Suburban Demographics: Beyond the 'Black-White, City-Suburb' Typology." Research Report 98-422. University of Michigan's Population Studies Center.

Frey, William H., and Frances E. Kobrin. 1982. "Changing Families and Changing Mobility: Their Impact on the Central City." *Demography* 19 (3): 261–77.

Frey, William H., and Alden Speare Jr. 1988. *Regional and Metropolitan Growth and Decline in the United States.* Russell Sage Foundation.

Glaeser, Edward L., and Jesse M. Shapiro. 2000. "City Growth and the 2000 Census: Which Places Grew, and Why." Census 2000 Series. Brookings Institution Center on Urban and Metropolitan Policy.

Lucy, William H., and David L. Phillips. 2001. "Suburbs and the Census: Patterns of Growth and Decline." Census 2000 Series. Brookings Institution Center on Urban and Metropolitan Policy.

Orfield, Myron W. 1997. "Metropolitics: A Regional Agenda for Community and Stability." Brookings Institution and Lincoln Institute of Land Policy.

Singer, Audrey, Samantha Friedman, Ivan Cheung, and Marie Price. 2001. "The World in a Zip Code: Greater Washington, D.C., as a New Region of Immigration." Brookings Institution Center on Urban and Metropolitan Policy.

Speare, Alden, Jr. 1993. "Changes in Urban Growth Patterns, 1980–90." Working Paper. Cambridge, Mass: Lincoln Institute of Land Policy.

U.S. Bureau of the Census. 2001. "Households and Families: 2000." *Census 2000 Brief.* Department of Commerce.

Contributors

Alan Berube
Brookings Institution

Benjamin Forman
Massachusetts Institute of Technology

William H. Frey
University of Michigan
Milken Institute

Edward L. Glaeser
Harvard University

Bruce Katz
Brookings Institution

Robert E. Lang
Metropolitan Institute, Virginia Tech
Fannie Mae Foundation

John R. Logan
University at Albany,
State University of New York

William H. Lucy
University of Virginia

David L. Phillips
University of Virginia

Jesse M. Shapiro
Harvard University

Patrick A. Simmons
Fannie Mae Foundation

Audrey Singer
Brookings Institution

Rebecca R. Sohmer
Fannie Mae Foundation

Roberto Suro
Pew Hispanic Center

Jacob L. Vigdor
Duke University

Index

THE BROOKINGS INSTITUTION

The Brookings Institution is an independent organization devoted to nonpartisan research, education, and publication in economics, governance, foreign policy, and the social sciences generally. Its principal purposes are to aid in the development of sound public policies and to promote public understanding of issues of national importance. The Institution was founded on December 8, 1927, to merge the activities of the Institute for Government Research, founded in 1916, the Institute of Economics, founded in 1922, and the Robert Brookings Graduate School of Economics and Government, founded in 1924. The Institution maintains a position of neutrality on issues of public policy. Interpretations or conclusions in Brookings publications should be understood to be solely those of the authors.